Bernhard Limberger

MELISSA MÜLLER is the author of numerous books on the history of the Third Reich, including *Lost Lives, Lost Art,* and editor of *Until the Final Hour: Hitler's Last Secretary*. Her biography of Anne Frank has been translated into eighteen languages to date. Müller lives in Munich with her family.

Additional Praise for *Anne Frank: The Biography*

"Flawlessly researched and compellingly written . . . In her comprehensive and nuanced portrait of Anne and her collapsing world, Müller has given us Anne Frank for adults."

—*The Christian Science Monitor*

"Müller offers an especially impressive portrait of Anne's father, Otto, as well as a chilling, convincing theory about the Dutch informant who likely led the Gestapo to the secret annex."

—Carolyn Alessio, *Chicago Tribune* (Editor's Choice)

"A thoughtful book, honorable and fluent . . . humane."

—Robert Skloot, *The Nation*

"Müller succeeds in rounding out the picture of the sensitive and talented Jewish schoolgirl through interviews with friends and family, letters, and previously unavailable documents."

—*Minneapolis Star Tribune*

"In this updated edition of her superb 1998 biography, Müller adds immeasurably to a well-known story. . . . An invaluable complement to an immortal testimony."

—*Kirkus Reviews* (starred review)

"The author's literary gifts and exhaustive research distinguish *Anne Frank: The Biography* as both an absorbing and definitive text."

—Deborah Hornblow, *Hartford Courant*

ANNE FRANK

THE BIOGRAPHY

UPDATED AND EXPANDED WITH NEW MATERIAL

MELISSA MÜLLER

Translated by Rita and Robert Kimber

PICADOR A METROPOLITAN BOOK HENRY HOLT AND COMPANY NEW YORK

www.picadorusa.com
www.twitter.com/picadorusa • www.facebook.com/picadorusa
picadorbookroom.tumblr.com

Picador® is a U.S. registered trademark and is used by Henry Holt and Company
under license from Pan Books Limited.

For book club information, please visit www.facebook.com/picadorbookclub
or e-mail marketing@picadorusa.com.

Designed by Kelly S. Too

The Library of Congress has cataloged the Henry Holt hardcover edition as follows:

Müller, Melissa, 1967–
[Mädchen Anne Frank. English]
Anne Frank : the biography / Melissa Müller ; translated by Rita and Robert
Kimber.—Second U.S. edition.
pages cm
"Updated and expanded with new material."
"Originally published in Germany in 1998 under the title *Das Mädchen Anne Frank*
by Paul List Verlag, Munich; first published in the United States in 1998 by Metropolitan Books;
second edition published in Germany in 2013 by S. Fischer Verlag, Frankfurt"—
Title page verso.
Includes index.
ISBN 978-0-8050-8731-4 (hardcover)
ISBN 978-0-8050-9626-2 (e-book)
1. Frank, Anne, 1929–1945. 2. Jews—Netherlands—Amsterdam—Biography.
3. Jewish children in the Holocaust—Biography. 4. Holocaust, Jewish (1939–1945)—
Netherlands—Amsterdam—Biography. 5. Amsterdam (Netherlands)—Biography.
I. Title.
DS135.N6F7349713 2013
940.53'18092—dc23
[B] 2013000297

Picador Paperback ISBN 978-1-250-05015-1

Picador books may be purchased for educational, business, or promotional use. For information
on bulk purchases, please contact Macmillan Corporate and Premium Sales Department
at 1-800-221-7945, extension 5442, or write specialmarkets@macmillan.com.

Originally published in Germany in 1998 under the title
Das Mädchen Anne Frank by Paul List Verlag, Munich

First U.S. hardcover edition published in 1998 by Metropolitan Books,
an imprint of Henry Holt and Company

First U.S. paperback edition published in 1999 by Picador

Second edition published in Germany in 2013 by S. Fischer Verlag, Frankfurt

Second U.S. hardcover edition published in 2013 by Metropolitan Books,
an imprint of Henry Holt and Company

Second Picador Edition: June 2014

D 10 9 8 7 6 5 4

This book belongs to the survivors.

CONTENTS

FOREWORD TO THE NEW EDITION

Anne Frank's diary, written between 1942 and 1944 in hiding in Amsterdam, is the most widely read document about the Nazi crimes, and it has made Anne Frank one of the best-known figures of our time. She was four when she left her native Germany, thirteen when she went into hiding, and not yet sixteen when she died in a concentration camp, one of the six million Jewish victims of Hitler's racial madness.

Over the past sixty years, Anne Frank has become a universal symbol of the oppressed in a world of violence and tyranny. Her name invokes humanity, tolerance, human rights, and democracy; her image is the epitome of optimism and the will to live. Millions of young people in search of their own identity regard her as their spokesperson, indeed, as their heroine. She is seen as "Hitler's most famous victim." Her diary has been interpreted as an eternal testament of courage and hope, relevant to all, and often, though only secondarily, as a document of the Holocaust. Some of the things she wrote have acquired near proverbial status, and—frequently taken out of context—they have been used as slogans for any number of points of view. If there were Jewish saints, someone would probably have long since proposed her beatification.

I was thirteen when I read the diary for the first time. I identified with Anne's struggle for self-realization, a struggle most adolescents wage, but she entered hers armed with unusual clarity about her goals and an acute awareness of her gifts. In so many of the things she wrote, she spoke for me. The resentment she felt toward her mother was something I felt, too. And I was deeply affected by the knowledge that the diary had been written by a victim of persecution, by a girl hunted in a reign of terror, who had died about eight months after writing her last diary entry. My youthful, naïve "Why?"—why did this happen?—met only with excuses or, more often, with silence.

In my midtwenties, I read Anne's diary again, this time in the so-called definitive edition, which contains several entries, some of them very personal, omitted from the original version of the diary edited by Otto Frank. When I finished, I was beset by more questions than I had started with: I wondered what Anne's relatives on either side of her family experienced during this period when the moral principles of millions of people dissolved and concern for others became an alien concept. What was the environment in which she began to mature? Who were her friends? What were the turning points in her childhood? Her diary, after all, deals with just one-seventh of her life. Once again I was left with no satisfactory answers.

And so my search began—initially in the 1990s—a search for the person behind the legend, a search for the incidents and events that shaped the life and personality of Annelies Marie Frank. I wanted to explore the family background and the social milieu in which her life was rooted. Hers was a strong character, but it was still impressionable, still developing. This biography, therefore, is not an attempt to probe the psychology and define the contours of a life lived to completion. It is instead an effort to follow Anne attentively on a personal and intellectual journey that was broken off abruptly and prematurely. My goal was to gather as many fragments of the mosaic as possible and create as authentic a picture of Anne's brief life as I could, illuminating the familial and social circumstances that provided the foundation of her life and left their mark on it.

In its honesty and clarity, Anne's diary speaks for itself. This biography is of course intended not to replace her diary but to supplement it. The world revealed in Anne's account—both her immediate world and the larger one beyond the secret annex—is necessarily fragmentary, and, as the critical edition of the diary has shown, Otto Frank's editorial work made her outlook appear even more limited. (The critical edition of the diary labels the version that Otto Frank published in 1947 as version C, with Anne's original text known as version A, and the revisions that Anne herself made in the spring of 1944 as version B; quotes from Anne's diary in this book follow the same terminology.) I have tried to provide a broader, more objective view, to answer questions my reading of the diary raised, to follow leads as far as I could, to refuse to be content with half answers and further mere idealization of Anne. This broader view has let me fill in the details that made up her life and the lives of the people about whom she wrote: her immediate relatives, her closest friends, and her acquaintances. At the same time, any record of the life of Anne Frank inevitably documents the sufferings of the Jews under the Nazi regime, the progression from hate propaganda to isolation, humiliation, deprivation of civil rights, and, finally, organized mass murder.

I could never have written this book without the help of the last generation that had personal experience of the Holocaust and without the trust—won step by step over time—of those who knew Anne Frank personally and who now live scattered all over the world. Without their willingness to revisit their memories and reveal details of their lives they had kept silent about for more than fifty years—either because no one had inquired before or because they had not been ready to speak—many of the facts that have found their way into this book would have been lost forever. During my research, I located upward of twenty contemporaries of Anne Frank's. I met many more who knew her father, Otto Frank, after the war. In the course of numerous interviews, some of these people became close friends. After months of making cautious overtures, I was able to win Miep Gies's trust. She not only provided much important information that has gone into this book but, to my great pleasure, also agreed to write a concluding note for it.

The people I interviewed shared with me the stories that link them to Anne Frank and her family. They showed me photographs, letters, handwritten notes, and revealing documents—many of them unpublished—and so helped me draw a multifaceted picture of Anne's life. They also helped me home in on questions that millions of other readers have asked: Who betrayed the Franks? What suffering did Anne experience in her last eight months of life? What were her plans for her diary? What kind of person was Anne's mother, Edith Holländer Frank, whom Anne judged so severely but who had a formative influence on her? Anne's father, Otto Frank, was the only member of the family left after the war to pass judgment on his daughter's diary. Through the selection of the diary entries he released for publication, he determined the picture the world has gotten of him and his family. As late as the 1990s, however, we knew next to nothing about Anne's mother, not even the kind of education she received. For more than fifty years, she and the rest of the Holländers have remained in the shadows. It was one of my further aims in this book to flesh out our knowledge of Edith Frank and to assess her influence on who her daughter became. I could not have achieved this without the help of Holländer family members living all over the world. A great many offices in Germany assisted, too, defying bureaucratic tradition by opening their archives to me, the first author to be granted such access.

I also owe a debt of particular gratitude to Cor Suijk. This close friend of Otto Frank's for many years agreed to let me be the first to see, and make use of, two diary entries that had been kept secret until then: one dated February 8, 1944, the other the last "introduction" to the diary Anne had written.

When my book was published in the late summer of 1998, its revelation of the existence of those long-hidden pages caused a stir in the international press for weeks on end and even rated a front-page story in the *New York Times*. Interest focused primarily on the content of those pages, but behind the scenes a struggle was going on over who would retain ownership of the actual pages. How that struggle was resolved is now history (and is summarized in the epilogue of this edition).

Since the first edition of this book appeared, my interest in Anne Frank and her world has continued unabated. I have followed up on new clues, reexamined conscious and unconscious assumptions that have been voiced for decades, reconsidered some of my insights, and corrected errors. In the first edition of this book, I revisited the long-unanswered question of who could have betrayed the Franks and their fellow residents in the secret annex. The Amsterdam criminal police conducted two investigations of the main suspect, Willem van Maaren, without reaching a firm conclusion. Miep Gies had assured me repeatedly that she did not think him the culprit, and, adept as she was at keeping her own counsel, she otherwise remained silent concerning the betrayal.

So it seemed to me all the more important back then to offer some new suppositions and thereby stimulate further discussion. I focused on a seemingly innocuous cleaning woman whose loose talk a few weeks before the arrest had frightened the helpers, and four years after my book appeared, theories about the by no means innocuous Tonny Ahlers created a considerable stir but again led to no conclusive proof.

Today we know that Lena Hartog and Tonny Ahlers represented two among many dangers. More and more people kept an eye on the annex, drew their own conclusions, possibly passed them on, and thus—whether inadvertently or knowingly—put the annex residents in danger of their lives. I have followed up on all the leads my research uncovered, and in chapter 9 of this revised edition I have portrayed this network of people who might well have had their suspicions about the annex and could possibly have betrayed its secret.

It is a privilege and a challenge for an author to be able to rewrite a book. We make high demands of ourselves and assume our readers will have equally high expectations. We biographers know, of course, that the definitive biography is as far beyond our reach as ultimate historical truth, and therefore we examine each stone of the mosaic carefully.

Time has worked both for me and against me in this enterprise. Against me because many of my contemporary witnesses have died in the last several years—most recently Miep Gies in 2010—and because their memories are fading. Time has also worked for me, however, as important new sources and research possibilities have become available since the first appearance of this book. In some cases, I gained access to material that was unavailable to scholars in the 1990s. The Internet allowed me to consult digitalized archives all over the world, to make new contacts, and to uncover connections that previously remained hidden to me. All this helped me in turn to evaluate the subjective memories of contemporary witnesses and to come closer to solving many a riddle. Without the intensive exchange I have enjoyed with Gerlof Langerijs in Amsterdam over many years, this book would not have the depth of factual detail it now has. Gerlof knows the Amsterdam municipal archives and many other Dutch archives, both online and off, intimately. He shares my penchant for accuracy, he helped me solve numerous linguistic problems, and he located several descendants of key figures in this book, with whose help we were able to answer many questions.

"History is that certainty produced at the point where the imperfections of memory meet the inadequacies of documentation," says a character in Julian Barnes's *The Sense of an Ending*. He could be describing the daily struggle the interpretation of sources demands. New sources bring new questions, new contradictions, and occasionally even new answers. Reality often lies far from what has been handed down. That holds true, too, for the various hypotheses about the betrayal.

The historian Yehuda Bauer has said that a historian should not only analyze history but also tell true stories. I have tried to tell the story of Anne Frank, her family, and her friends in such a way that people will listen. My listeners, I hope, will reflect on the Nazis' crimes, on the historical facts and the social conditions that provided the background for the Nazis' murderous campaign against the Jews. Once we recognize that the world cannot be portrayed in black and white alone, not even the world of National Socialism, and once we recognize that the presumably good and the presumably evil often blur together—even in this book sometimes—we cannot shift all responsibility away from ourselves. "Until all mankind, without exception, undergoes a great change," Anne wrote in her diary on May 3, 1944, a month before her fifteenth birthday, "wars will be waged, everything that has been built up, cultivated and grown will be cut down and disfigured, to begin all over again after that!" History does not repeat itself, but man does. We human beings drift with the tide, losing sight of our ideals. Then—captives of our prejudices—we begin all over again. Yet we persist in setting our hopes on the human capacity to learn, so we cannot stop telling stories, stories like Anne Frank's, that will not let us forget.

January 2013, Melissa Müller

FRANK

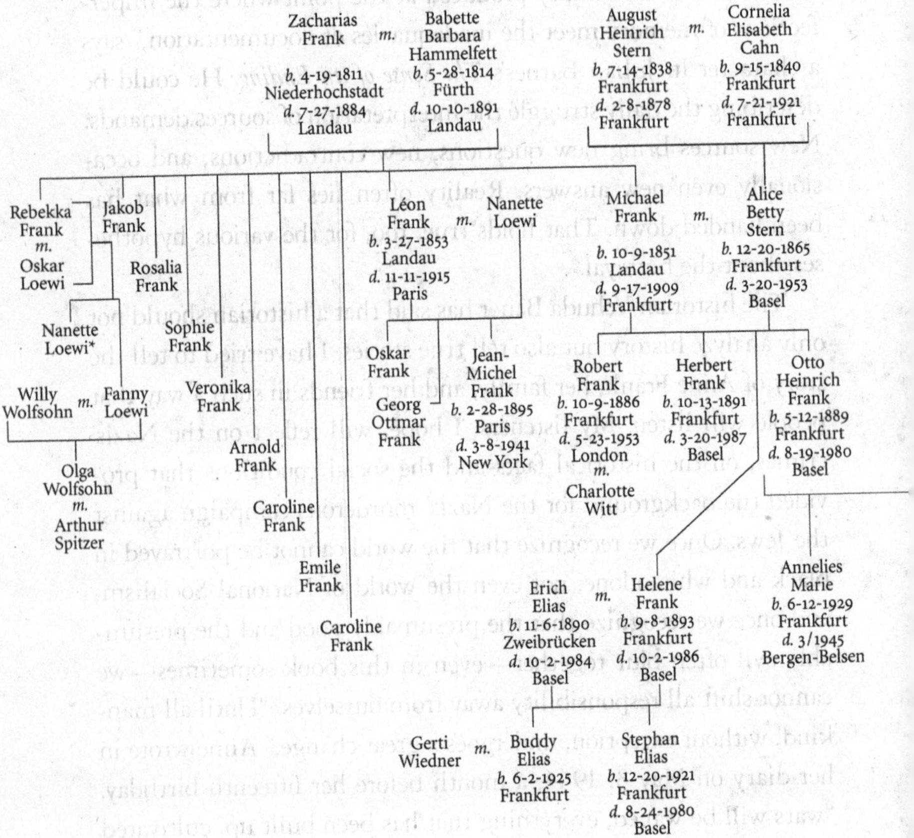
Zacharias Frank m. Babette Barbara Hammelfett
b. 4-19-1811 Niederhochstadt d. 7-27-1884 Landau
b. 5-28-1814 Fürth d. 10-10-1891 Landau
August Heinrich Stern m. Cornelia Elisabeth Cahn
b. 7-14-1838 Frankfurt d. 2-8-1878 Frankfurt
b. 9-15-1840 Frankfurt d. 7-21-1921 Frankfurt
Rebekka Frank m. Oskar Loewi
Jakob Frank
Rosalia Frank
Sophie Frank
Veronika Frank
Arnold Frank
Caroline Frank
Emile Frank
Caroline Frank
Léon Frank m. Nanette Loewi
b. 3-27-1853 Landau d. 11-11-1915 Paris
Michael Frank m. Alice Betty Stern
b. 10-9-1851 Landau d. 9-17-1909 Frankfurt
b. 12-20-1865 Frankfurt d. 3-20-1953 Basel
Nanette Loewi*
Willy Wolfsohn m. Fanny Loewi
Olga Wolfsohn m. Arthur Spitzer
Oskar Frank
Georg Ottmar Frank
Jean-Michel Frank b. 2-28-1895 Paris d. 3-8-1941 New York
Robert Frank b. 10-9-1886 Frankfurt d. 5-23-1953 London m. Charlotte Witt
Herbert Frank b. 10-13-1891 Frankfurt d. 3-20-1987 Basel
Otto Heinrich Frank b. 5-12-1889 Frankfurt d. 8-19-1980 Basel
Erich Elias m. Helene Frank
b. 11-6-1890 Zweibrücken d. 10-2-1984 Basel
b. 9-8-1893 Frankfurt d. 10-2-1986 Basel
Annelies Marie b. 6-12-1929 Frankfurt d. 3/1945 Bergen-Belsen
Gerti Wiedner m. Buddy Elias
b. 6-2-1925 Frankfurt
Stephan Elias b. 12-20-1921 Frankfurt d. 8-24-1980 Basel

* = Wife of Léon Frank

(Courtesy of Buddy Elias)

HOLLÄNDER

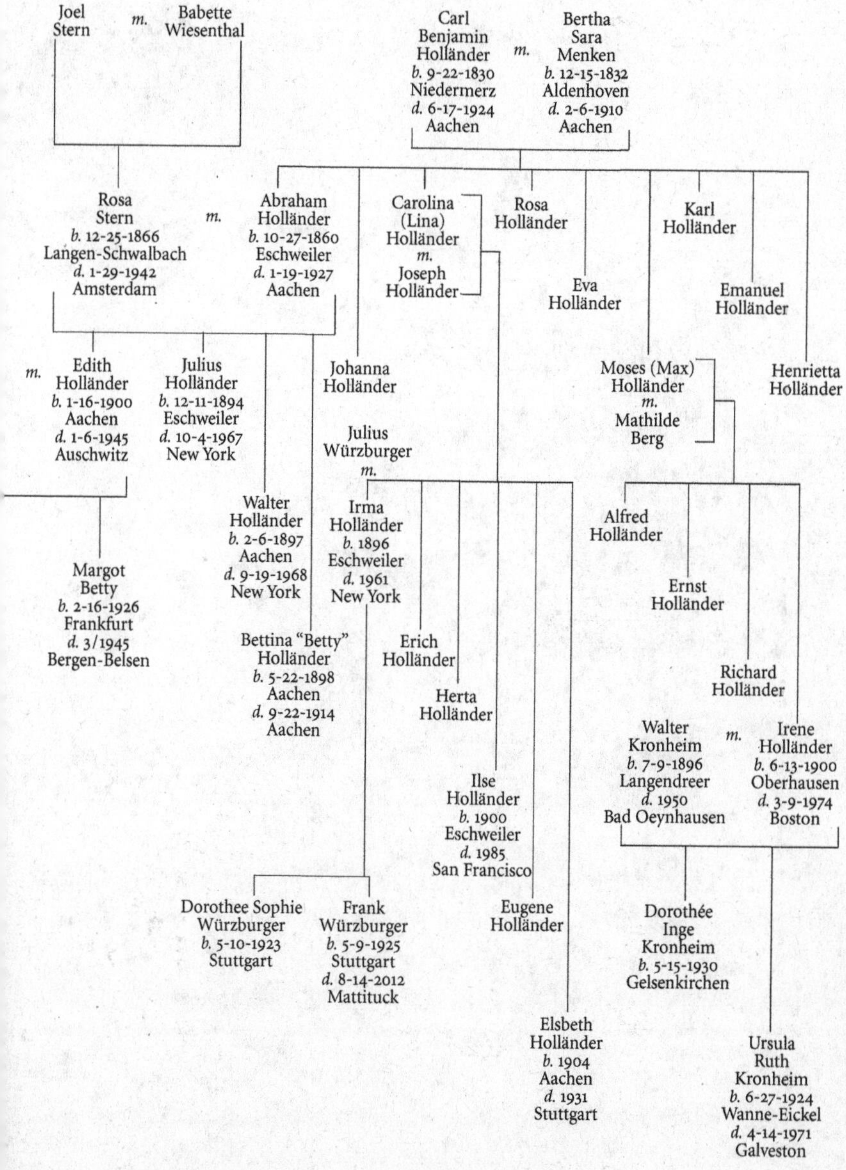

(Courtesy of Betty Wallerstein and Eduardo Mauricio Fraifeld)

1

THE ARREST

Hush. Be quiet. Whisper. Walk softly . . . take off your shoes. Who's still in the bathroom? The water's running. For God's sake, don't flush the toilet! After two years you should know better than to be so careless. Empty the chamber pots. Shove the beds back out of the way. The church bells are already ringing the half hour. When the workers arrive at 8:30, there has to be dead silence.

The usual morning ritual in the secret annex. At 6:45 the alarm clock goes off in Hermann and Auguste van Pels's room, so loud and shrill that it wakes the Franks and Fritz Pfeffer, who sleep one floor below. A well-aimed blow from Mrs. van Pels silences the alarm. The floor creaks, softly at first, then louder. Mr. van Pels gets up, creeps down the steep stairs, and, the first in the bathroom, hurries to finish.

Anne waits in bed until she hears the bathroom door creak again. Her roommate, Fritz Pfeffer, is next. Anne sighs, relieved, enjoying these few precious moments of solitude. With eyes closed, she listens to the birdsong in the backyard and stretches in her bed. *Bed* is hardly the word for the narrow sofa she has lengthened by putting a chair at one end. But Anne thinks it's luxurious. Miep

Gies, who brings the Franks their groceries, has told her that others in hiding are sleeping on the floor in tiny windowless sheds or in damp cellars. Dutifully, Anne gets up and opens the blackout curtains. Discipline rules their lives here. She glances at the world outside. The foggy Friday morning promises to turn into a gloriously warm summer day. If she could just, only for a few minutes . . . But she must be patient. It won't be much longer now. The attempt to assassinate Hitler two weeks ago has revived everyone's hopes . . . Perhaps she can go back to school in the fall. Her father and Mr. van Pels are sure that everything will be over in October, that they will be free . . . It is already August. August 4, 1944.

An hour and forty-five minutes is all they have to prepare for another day. An hour and forty-five minutes passes quickly when eight people have to wash up, store their bedding, push the beds aside, and put tables and chairs back where they belong. After work begins at 8:30 in the warehouse below, they can't make a sound. It would be easy to give themselves away. The warehouse foreman, Willem van Maaren, is suspicious enough as it is.

Before a light breakfast at nine, they occupy themselves as quietly as possible, reading or studying, sewing or knitting. And they wait. They must be especially careful during this next half hour. Anyone who absolutely has to get up tiptoes across the room like a thief, in stocking feet or soft slippers, and they have to whisper. If someone laughs or pricks a finger and says "ouch!" everyone glares. But once the office staff has arrived and the rattling typewriters, the ringing telephone, and the voices of Miep Gies, Bep Voskuijl, and Johannes Kleiman—all friends and helpers of the residents in the secret annex—form a backdrop of sound, the danger is diminished somewhat. Eventually Miep will come to pick up the "shopping list." In fact, Miep will have to settle for whatever she can get them, and every day she gets a little less. But she knows how eagerly the inhabitants of the secret annex await her. Anne barrages Miep with questions, as she does every morning. And Miep, as she does every morning, puts Anne off until later. Only after Miep has sworn to return for a longer visit in the afternoon will Anne let her go back to her office. Otto Frank retires with Peter van Pels to Peter's tiny room on the top floor. A dictation in English is the lesson plan for today. Peter is having trouble with this irritating language, so Otto spends his mornings helping him. It's a way to pass time. On the floor below, Anne and her sister, Margot, lose themselves in their books. Patience. Patience is a virtue the mercurial Anne has had to learn these last two years.

In the warehouse, on the ground floor, the spice mill is running with its familiar monotonous clatter. Van Maaren has the door onto Prinsengracht wide open to let in the light and warmth of this soft summer day.

Ten-thirty. The foreman and his two assistants have a lot of work to do before the noon break. Suddenly several men appear in the shop—the German security service, the Sicherheitsdienst, or SD. No one in the shop noticed their arrival. The men—one of them in the uniform of the "Green Police," the others in civilian clothes—are armed. They claim to be executing a search warrant. A few words are exchanged, then van Maaren—totally astonished—points toward the stairs with his thumb. His coworker, Lammert Hartog, stands nervously to one side. The visitors hurry up the stairs to the offices on the second floor. One stays behind for a while to keep an eye on the staff.

Without knocking, one of the men, tall and thin, enters the office shared by Miep, Bep, and Mr. Kleiman. Miep doesn't even look up at first; people often walk into the office unannounced. Only when she hears his harsh command, "Sit still and not a word out of you!" does she raise her head and find herself staring into the barrel of a pistol. "Don't move from your seat," the man orders, then disappears.

Gruff voices can be heard through the double folding doors.

The officer and his Dutch henchmen, all of them agents of the Amsterdam city police and experienced bounty hunters, all of them members of the Nationalsozialistische Bewegung der Niederlande (NSB)—the National Socialist Movement of the Netherlands—all of them family men of advanced age, have surprised Victor Kugler at his desk in the next room; they keep their pistols trained on him.

"Who owns this building?" the uniformed man bellows at him in German. Kugler, who grew up in Hohenelbe, a small city at the foot of the Sudeten Mountains and back then part of the Austro-Hungarian Empire, thinks he detects a Viennese accent, and he responds in German.

"We just rent this building."

Stiffly erect in his chair, he quickly gives the address of the Dutchman who has owned the building at 263 Prinsengracht since April 1943.

"Stop playing games with me," the man snarls. His name is Karl Josef Silberbauer. "Who's the boss here? That's what I want to know."

"I am," Kugler says.

"Come with me."

Kugler, a reserved and formal man who strikes many people as utterly unapproachable, has no choice. He has to take the SD men upstairs to the storerooms on the next floor. They ask if there are weapons hidden there. Kugler has to open every box, every barrel, every sack. As he does this, he tries to collect his thoughts. Have they come after *him*? Do they perhaps know that he is in touch with the resistance? That he has a fake identity card . . . ? Or do they know about the people in the secret annex? What if some loose talk has reached the wrong ear? Everything has gone smoothly for two years and a month. Impossible that now, of all times, when the Allies have finally made a breakthrough in northern France and are on the advance, that now, with liberation only weeks away, now, when the tide has finally turned . . .

"You have Jews hidden in this building," Kugler hears one of the Dutchmen say. His hopes fade. These men know. Denial will only make matters worse.

"Where are they?" the others chime in. One of them, Gezinus Gringhuis, is short and obese; another, Willem Grootendorst, has a long, yellowish face. After the war, Kleiman, Kugler, and Otto Frank would identify the third man as Maarten Kuiper, a tall, thin man who has been described as having "a sharp nose in his small face" and "the penetrating gaze of a madman." (They may have been mistaken, however, misled by photos of Kuiper that circulated widely in the press when Kuiper was tried and proved guilty of assassinating resistance fighters during the war. Also, Kuiper could well have been involved in an assassination that took place on the same day as the arrest.)

"Where are they?" The words have the grim sound of a verdict with no possibility of appeal. Silberbauer orders Kugler to lead the way.

Kugler obeys. What else can he do? The men follow him, their pistols drawn. Kugler's brilliant blue eyes seem—more than ever—like an impenetrable wall. But his perfect self-control conceals a feeling of paralyzing helplessness. His mind won't work; his familiar surroundings blur and fade before his eyes. It feels like the final moments before a thunderstorm, muggy, oppressive, threatening. Doubts torment him. Are these men just bluffing the way they are apparently accustomed to during this kind of raid? Is he letting them pull the wool over his eyes? Or have they really gotten a tip-off? Has someone betrayed his charges? A neighbor? An employee? And why today of all days?

Seemingly indifferent, he walks down the corridor that connects the front of the building with the rooms in the rear. One by one he climbs the narrow steps that turn to the right like a circular staircase. The strangers are at his heels. Silberbauer still hasn't gotten used to Amsterdam's terrifyingly steep stairs. Fourteen, fifteen, sixteen. Now they are standing in a hallway whose beige-and-red flowered wallpaper makes it look even narrower than it is. Behind them is the doorway to the spice warehouse, ahead of them a high bookcase: three shelves crammed with worn gray file folders. Above the bookcase hangs a large map of the kind seen in government offices or in schools: Belgium, in 1:500,000 scale.

"Open up." Of course—they know. A yank on the bookcase and it swings away from the wall like a heavy gate. Behind it, a high step leads to a white door about a foot and a half above the floor; the top of the door is hidden behind the map on the wall. The lintel of the door frame is padded with a cloth stuffed with excelsior: it's easy to bang one's head.

Have the Franks heard the loud footsteps and the unfamiliar voices? When Victor Kugler hesitates, the SD men urge him on. Right in front of them, another stairway, barely wide enough for one person, leads to the upper floor of the secret annex. Kugler goes up the left side of this narrow stairway and opens a door.

The first person he sees is Anne's mother, Edith Frank, sitting at her table. "Gestapo," he says under his breath. His dry lips can't form another word. He is afraid she will panic, but she stays seated, frozen. She looks at Kugler and the intruders impassively, as if from a great distance. "Hands up," one of the Dutchmen barks at her, his pistol in his hand. Mechanically, she raises her arms. Another policeman brings Anne and Margot in from the next room. They are ordered to stand next to their mother with their hands over their heads.

Two of the Dutch policemen have run up the stairs to the next floor. While one of them covers Mr. and Mrs. van Pels with his pistol, the other storms the small room next door. He frisks Otto Frank and Peter van Pels for weapons, as if they were dangerous criminals. Then he herds them into the next room, where Peter's parents wait in silence, staring into space, their hands over their heads. "Downstairs with you, and make it quick." The last to appear, with a pistol at his back, is Fritz Pfeffer.

The SD men seem pleased. Eight Jews at one blow. A surprisingly good morning's work. "Where is your money? Where are your valuables?" Silberbauer asks, threateningly. "Come on, come on, we don't have all day." The eight captives appear incredibly calm. Only Margot has tears running down her face, but she is silent.

Otto Frank feels that if they cooperate with their captors everything will turn out all right. The Germans are frightened themselves. They know about the Allied offensive, too. They know the end is only weeks away. Otto points to the closet where he keeps his family's valuables. Silberbauer orders his henchmen to search the other rooms and the attic for jewelry and money. He pulls the Franks' bulky strongbox out of the closet. His eyes search the room. He finds what he's looking for: Otto's leather briefcase—Anne's briefcase, actually, because Otto has given it to his daughter as a safe place to keep her personal papers. Silberbauer opens the briefcase, turns it upside down, and dumps Anne's diary, notebooks, and loose papers out onto the floor. "Not my diary; if my diary goes I go with it!" Anne had written four months earlier. Now she watches impassively. Hermann van Pels tries to bribe the policemen into letting their captives go, but the policemen just laugh at him.

Silberbauer, irritated by how calm his captives seem, empties the contents of the strongbox into the briefcase and bellows, "Hop to it. You've got five minutes to get ready." As if in a trance, all eight get their emergency packs from the next room or from upstairs, rucksacks that have hung packed and readily accessible in case a fire broke out and they had to abandon the building. They ignore the chaos the Dutch Nazis have created in their search.

Oberscharführer Silberbauer, with the SS since 1939, can't stand still. In his heavy boots, he paces back and forth in the small room. People have told him that his marching is intimidating; it also helps him pass the time until everyone is ready to leave. He is thirty-three years old; his pale blond hair is cropped short, in military fashion, over his large, fleshy ears. His lips are pale and thin, his eyes narrowed to slits. An ordinary, rather nondescript fellow: obedient, deferential to authority. It is obvious that his uniform gives him his place in life. He has the upper hand here, he thinks, and beyond that he does not think. He obeys orders. Clearing out this annex is all in a day's work. Until the late fall of 1943, he worked in the criminal division of the Gestapo in his home city of Vienna. Then, although the deportation of Amsterdam Jews had been declared "successfully accomplished" by September, the SS transferred him to the Amsterdam unit of the Gestapo's Department IV B4, the so-called Jewish Division of the Reich Security Headquarters in Berlin, whose job, under Adolf Eichmann's command, is the efficient "solution of the Jewish question." Silberbauer's wife, Barbara, whom he married only recently, has remained at home in Vienna.

Suddenly Silberbauer stops his pacing and stares at a large gray trunk on the floor between Edith Frank's bed and the window.

"Whose trunk is that?" Silberbauer asks.

"Mine," Otto answers. "Lieutenant of the Reserves Otto Frank" is clearly stenciled on the lid of the steel-reinforced trunk. "I was a reserve officer in the First World War."

"But . . ." Karl Silberbauer is obviously uncomfortable. This trunk has no business being here. It upsets his routine. "But why didn't you register as a veteran?" Otto Frank, a Jew, is Silberbauer's superior in military rank.

"You would have been sent to Theresienstadt," Silberbauer says. After the war, Otto Frank would quote this comment of Silberbauer's. People like Silberbauer were apparently willing to believe the Nazi propaganda about humane living conditions in this "Jewish settlement."

Silberbauer's eyes dart nervously around the room, avoiding Otto Frank's.

"How long have you been hiding here?"

"Two years," Otto Frank says, "and one month." When Silberbauer, incredulous, shakes his head, Otto Frank points to the wall on his right. Next to the door to Anne's room, faint pencil marks on the wallpaper record how much Anne and Margot have grown since July 6, 1942. Silberbauer's eyes come to rest on a small map of Normandy tacked to the wall beside the pencil marks. On this map, Otto has kept track of the Allied advance. He has used pins with red, orange, and blue heads, from Edith's sewing basket, to mark Allied victories.

Silberbauer struggles with himself, then says in a choked voice, "Take your time." Is he about to lose his self-control? Has something here touched him? While his assistants guard the captives, he retreats downstairs.

Silberbauer walks through the smaller office, where Victor Kugler was working and where his colleague Johannes Kleiman is now being interrogated, then through the windowless hallway, to the large front office. Beyond the windows that reach nearly from floor to ceiling, sunbeams sparkle on the waters of the canal.

Miep Gies has been left alone in the front office. Her husband, Jan, had dropped by, as he did every day at noon, and Miep had met him at the front entrance to slip him the ration cards she used for the annex residents, then sent him off without his being noticed. The car that brought the SD men had driven away, leaving the entrance to the building unguarded. The warehouseman, Lammert Hartog, seized this opportunity to pull on his jacket and disappear. Though Miep's coworker, Bep Voskuijl, could hardly see through her glasses for her tears, Kleiman sent her off on a couple of errands. She was to take Kleiman's wallet to a good friend of his, the druggist in nearby Leliegracht, and to tell his wife he would not be coming home today. Miep, too, received permission to go, but she chose to stay.

"Miep," Kleiman whispered to her before he was taken away, "keep yourself out of this. You can't save us now, but rescue here whatever you can."

"Well," Silberbauer says to her in German, "now it's your turn." His Viennese accent sounds familiar. Miep was born in Vienna and lived there until she was eleven.

"I'm from Vienna, too," she says in a steady voice.

A fellow Viennese. The Nazi wasn't expecting that. But it's important to stick to routine. Identity card. Standard questions. Silberbauer is in way over his head. "You traitor, aren't you ashamed to have helped this Jewish trash?" he yells at Miep, as if shouting might help him keep the self-control he's on the verge of losing. Since the Allied landing in Normandy, actions against Jews had almost entirely ceased and "Jew hunters" like Kuiper, Grootendorst, and Gringhuis had been transferred to other units. The SD's job now was rooting out resistance cells and preparing for the defense of Holland. But on this morning, Julius Dettmann, the officer in charge of Silberbauer's unit, had made an exception; he simply couldn't ignore the tip the unit had received from an informant. He quickly pulled together a group of experienced men and sent them off. Even Dettmann had not suspected that they would catch eight Jews at once.

It requires all Miep's strength to keep calm, but she does, looking Silberbauer straight in the eye. He finally quiets down, mumbles something about feeling sympathy for her, and says he doesn't know what to do with her. Then he leaves, threatening that he will come back the next day to check on her and search the office.

"For personal reasons, I'm letting you go for now," he says, "but if you leave town, we'll get your husband."

"Leave my husband out of this," Miep replies. "He has nothing to do with this."

"Nonsense. He's mixed up in it, too."

One of the Nazi policemen has in the meantime telephoned for transportation. At last a delivery truck without windows arrives. Carefully guarded by the Nazi policemen, the eight captives come down the stairs from the annex one by one, walk the corridor past the offices, go down another set of steep stairs, and, finally, outdoors. For the first time in two years and a month, they are on the street. Bystanders are watching them; being stared at is painful. The sunlight blinds them. Inside the truck it is dark again.

Miep remains behind with van Maaren. The police have taken Victor Kugler and Johannes Kleiman away with the others. Miep sits at her desk, stunned, exhausted, drained. She could leave now, but she stays. What can she do to help her friends? Is there any way to rescue them? Will the police return?

Minutes pass, or hours—Miep can't tell. Her husband, Jan, finally comes back and rouses her from her stupor. About five o'clock, as Bep and Miep later report, Bep returns. In her distress, she ran about in Amsterdam for hours, fleeing the security service.

Joined by van Maaren and having locked the building, they make their way into the annex. Silberbauer has locked the door behind the bookcase and taken the key, but Miep has a duplicate. Once inside, they are stunned by the mess the police have left behind. They have pulled everything out of the closets, torn the beds apart. The floor of the Franks' room is covered with notebooks and papers. Among them is a little volume with a checkered cover, like an autograph book. It is Anne's diary. With Bep's help, Miep quickly gathers the papers together while van Maaren stands watch at the door. The women grab a few books they borrowed from the library for Anne and Margot. Otto's portable typewriter. Anne's combing shawl. But no valuables to keep for their arrested friends. The police have stolen everything of value.

It's late, but outside the sun is still shining, bathing the facade and the interior of 263 Prinsengracht in the clear golden evening light of a Vermeer. Miep collects Anne's diary and the many loose pages. Without reading a word, Bep and Miep put them in Miep's desk drawer. They don't lock it. That would just arouse the curiosity of anyone who tried to open the drawer. When Anne returns after the war, they will give her back her diary.

2

ANNE IN FRANKFURT

Anne Frank was born in the women's clinic in Frankfurt on June 12, 1929, at 7:30 in the morning, just as the weak rays of the early-summer sun were beginning to seep through the hazy cloud cover over the city. The strength of the baby's first cries reassured her mother. The birth had not gone smoothly. The baby—21 inches long and a healthy 8½ pounds—had had trouble breathing. Anne's crying, a welcome sign of life at first, would continue without stop during the next few weeks and keep Edith Holländer Frank awake most nights.

Three-year-old Margot was allowed to visit her baby sister two days after the birth. She came to the clinic with her maternal grandmother. The Franks had worried that Margot might be jealous of the baby, but Margot laughed with delight when she saw her. Anne's ears stuck out comically, and her wild black hair was silky and soft. When Otto Heinrich Frank went to register the birth of his second daughter and said her full name, Annelies Marie, the clerks were confused. The clinic had recorded "infant Frank" as a boy.

The Franks lived on Marbachweg on the outskirts of Frankfurt. After their wedding on May 12, 1925 (Otto's thirty-sixth birthday), and a honeymoon trip to Italy, the couple had moved in with Otto's mother at 4 Mertonstrasse, a street on Beethovenplatz in downtown Frankfurt. Otto's father, Michael Frank, a banker, had bought the house in 1901, and Otto's mother, Alice Betty Stern Frank, a charming but determined woman, had continued to run the house by herself after her husband's sudden death in 1909. Located in the fashionable Westend, the house was elegant and spacious, with a separate servants' entrance and other features typical of upper-middle-class homes of the period. Otto and Edith Frank lived there for two years; nine months after they moved in, Margot Betty was born. Edith picked the middle name in memory of her older sister, Bettina—or Betty—who had died at sixteen of a ruptured appendix. By happy coincidence Grandmother Frank could feel honored, too. The main reason for the move to Marbachweg was probably Edith's growing need to have a home of her own. Abandoning the parental home ran counter to both her and Otto's family traditions, which took for granted that parents, children, and grandchildren lived together under one roof as an extended family. But times had changed. The younger generation was becoming emancipated, and despite their attachment to their families, the young Franks wanted to lead their own lives. In mid-1927, soon after Margot learned to walk, the family rented its first apartment, at 307 Marbachweg.

If renting an apartment in the city where one's family lived was rather unusual, the Franks' decision to settle in unfashionable Marbachweg was even stranger. But they had their reasons: Otto clearly wanted to satisfy his wife's desire for a small yard or at least a big balcony. She wanted her children to grow up with nature and to play outside in the fresh air as much as possible. Then, too, housing in downtown Frankfurt was scarce, and rents correspondingly high. Apartments on Marbachweg were spacious and affordable. Still, the Franks must have thought twice before they decided to move there. The environment was entirely unlike the upper-middle-class Jewish milieu Otto and Edith were used to. The neighborhood's new residents were government officials, teachers, and white-collar workers, not independent businessmen like Otto Frank. The Franks would be somewhat out of place, but they may have welcomed the opportunity to live in a more socially integrated neighborhood.

The move turned out well. For Margot, the small-town, almost rural atmosphere of Marbachweg was idyllic. The occupants of the two-story houses, each with a pleasant little yard, formed a close community. The Franks had a large apartment in the right-hand half of one of these houses. Actually it was two separate apartments, one above the other and connected only by a staircase, a somewhat inconvenient arrangement, but they adapted to it quickly. The living and dining areas were downstairs and roomy enough to house the Franks' library; though far from being intellectuals, Otto and Edith were well read and interested in many things. The kitchen and bathroom were also downstairs, as was a study for Edith's personal use. It was tiny but large enough for the little writing desk she had brought with her from Aachen and for a bookcase in which she kept her Hebrew prayer books, among others. On the upper floor were the master bedroom, Margot's room, and a room for the housekeeper, Kati Stilgenbauer, for whom the children and their parents would develop a great fondness. Fortunately, there was also a guest room to accommodate Edith's mother and brothers, who often came from Aachen to visit.

Next door, on the ground floor of number 305, lived the landlord, Otto Könitzer, with his wife and three children. A teacher, he had built the house with the help of a loan from the housing cooperative of the Frankfurt teachers association. On the floor above were the Stabs, with their daughters Hilde and Marianne. Mr. Stab worked for the respected building firm Philipp Holzmann. The next house, number 303, had been built by the Naumanns. They had six children, and Mr. Naumann, too, was a teacher.

Despite different social and religious backgrounds the adults were friendly and got along well. In the Westend, 20 percent of the population had been Jews; here the Franks were the exception. There was no synagogue nearby. Otto may not even have noticed this until Edith pointed it out. He had grown up without religious education. She, however, had regularly attended the synagogue in the Westend and would continue to go even after they moved.

As Catholics, the Naumanns and the Stabs also belonged to a religious minority, at least here in Frankfurt. But the neighborhood children played together harmoniously, and Margot, one of the youngest, was readily accepted, as Otto and Edith had hoped she would be. They wanted their daughters to grow up without self-consciousness or prejudice. Fortunately, after years of anti-Semitic agitation, the mood in Germany seemed to have calmed down. Right-wing politicians had blamed the Jews for Germany's defeat in World War I and for the economic and social crisis of the early 1920s. But in recent years the economy had begun to improve.

The children gathered at Hilde and Marianne Stab's house because it had the largest yard, and also a swing and a sandbox. Indoors they often played "church" with great solemnity. Hilde Stab would set up a small altar in her room and, acting as the priest, establish the rules of the game. Margot, five years younger than Hilde, played the part of altar boy. Anyone who wanted to could join in the game. The only children who were not altogether welcome were the landlord's children, Otto, Heidi, and Eva Könitzer, perhaps because their old grandmother was always glaring from the window, ready to scold them at the slightest provocation. The children were, of course, unaware that Otto, Heidi, and Eva's father sympathized with the National Socialist German Workers' Party, the NSDAP, headed by one Adolf Hitler, already known for his inflammatory speeches. But their parents were acutely aware. As far as Otto Könitzer and others were concerned, Jews could not be full-fledged Germans. That was a sentiment few expressed out loud in 1927, but for party supporters like Könitzer, Jews were enemies of the state who took jobs away from Germans. By the same token, though, Jews were rich, which made them reliable tenants. No need to worry that they might not pay the rent, and so he welcomed the Franks as tenants. The fact that they rented two apartments only confirmed him in his prejudice.

Ten-year-old Gertrud Naumann immediately became a special favorite of the Franks. A girl with thick blond braids that hung all the way down her back and a broad, friendly grin, she had watched with great curiosity as their moving van was unloaded; she soon began visiting them often. The youngest of six children, she was crazy about babies, pushing Margot around in the baby carriage, carrying her in her arms, introducing her to the neighborhood kids. But she did not treat Margot like a doll that could be put down when the game began to get boring. Although a child herself, she understood the responsibility involved in looking after a toddler, and Edith, sensing as much, felt comfortable entrusting Margot to her. If Margot was taking her midday nap when Gertrud got home from the Ursuline-run school she attended, she would lie down quietly next to the baby and watch over her. Edith didn't need to worry if she had to run errands after Otto had returned to his office from lunch at home: in addition to Gertrud, there was always Kati, the gentle spirit of the house. She and Edith understood each other and got on well together. "At many points in my life, I looked to Mrs. Frank as my model."

Gertrud often stayed for meals at the Franks'. Their stews of boiled meat, vegetables, and barley tasted better than the ones at home, and Mrs. Frank's wurst seemed to Gertrud the best in the world. Her favorite treat was a bowl of cornflakes with grated apple and cream, an exotic concoction found only at the Franks'. Although Edith had grown up in a kosher household, she did not observe the Jewish dietary laws in her own home; Otto would not have approved. Still, when her family visited from Aachen, she made sure milk and meat were not on the table together, and pork was taboo.

Gertrud was often there, too, when the Franks had guests, relatives, or friends from the Westend with whom they had kept in contact. Otto's secretary, Emeline Margarete Schneider, a heavy, childless woman with thick glasses, would have liked nothing better than to take Gertrud home, teach her to keep house, and, for all practical purposes, adopt her.

Gertrud was no mere babysitter for the Franks but part of the family, almost a daughter to them. Though she loved her own father, a strict and upright man, she responded to Otto's warmth and called him Papa Frank. Edith, on the other hand, was not the kind of person who took children on her lap, nor were they inclined to throw themselves at her. Edith expressed her affection in less demonstrative ways, with kind words or thoughtful presents on birthdays and also at Christmas, even though the Franks themselves never celebrated the holiday. Gertrud got her first watch from them, as well as a necklace, a pretty fur collar, and a silver-plated fountain pen. In 1928 the Franks took her along on their Easter vacation to Bad Soden, a spa in the Taunus mountains. Gertrud shared a room with Margot. There was a reason for their spending their vacation at Bad Soden, only about ten miles from Frankfurt. The Frank family's business included not only banking but also the Soden Mineral Products Company, which produced and marketed "Fay's Genuine Soden Mineral Lozenges," cough drops made from the mineral-rich waters of the springs at Bad Soden. In the late 1920s, Otto Frank was in charge of this branch of the family enterprise. But he was not a natural businessman.

When Edith brought little Anne home twelve days after her birth, Gertrud was just as excited as Margot. The two were looking forward to putting the baby into Margot's doll bed, powdering her bottom, taking her for walks, playing with her, spoiling her. They remained enthusiastic even when Anne kept crying, stopping only when she fell asleep from exhaustion but resuming her heartrending screams as soon as she woke up. A headstrong baby, she was restless during the day, apparently bothered by the heat. She kept her parents awake night after night. "Often has diarrhea and colic," reads one of Edith's laconic entries in Anne's baby book. "Has been screaming all night for the past six weeks." Anne suffered the fate of the second child: for Margot, her firstborn, Edith had commented on every development in loving detail. Now she merely jotted a few words down below the photos of the new baby.

Perhaps the reason why she wrote so little was that she had no time. Edith and Otto had been spoiled by Margot, who from the beginning slept through the night and let her parents sleep. Margot was born with a sunny disposition and, as she lay in her crib, radiated contentment. As a baby, she hardly ever cried, and she had grown into a beautiful girl, whom they often referred to as their "little angel." Anne's strong will, on the other hand, was a challenge, her restlessness exhausting. Her parents took turns taking care of her, and Otto, too, unlike most other men of his class, often got up at night to calm her with gentle words and to massage her belly.

But perhaps the brevity of Edith's entries reflected her concern about other matters, especially financial ones, though at the moment things were going well for the Franks. The family had lost a lot of money after World War I. Restrictions on trade in foreign currency had hurt the family bank, inflation was eating up everyone's private savings, and, like all other good patriots, the Franks had bought war bonds, counting on a German victory. "In these times," Otto Frank had written from the front to his sister, Helene, after she had sold a painting owned by the family, "we have to be content with 'cash' because we still have no idea what is yet to come."

Since Margot's birth, however, the economy had slowly begun to recover, and Edith and Otto felt sufficiently encouraged to hope for greater security. Nineteen twenty-seven was a good year for business in general, and the political parties of the liberal center, which the Franks favored, promised that things would continue to improve. Otto, like most other German Jews, voted for the German Democratic Party, which stood for progress and a growth-oriented economy based on private enterprise, social justice, tolerance, compassion, and individualism. The party was nationalistically oriented, but not dogmatically so.

Otto, who had seen something of the world, was proud to be German. He was a patriot. He had spent some time in Amsterdam and, before that, in New York. Had his father not died so early—one year after Otto finished school—Otto would surely have traveled more. "I used to be teased a lot in school because of my addiction to travel abroad," Otto wrote to some former classmates in July 1918, while in the army. "As you may recall, you all found it especially amusing that I went to Spain one Easter vacation 'to recuperate' and later to England between school and university. I could not bear staying home very long after school and spent the winters of 1909–10 and 1910–11 in New York. But I never intended to live abroad permanently."

After a dull semester studying art history at the University of Heidelberg, where Otto had also taken a few courses in economics, and a year's apprenticeship in the Ferdinand Sander banking house in Frankfurt, he acted on the invitation of his friend and former fellow student Charles Webster Straus to go to New York. At first he held internships in different divisions of Macy's, which was owned by the Straus family. Later, a job was arranged for him at the Manhattan banking firm of L. M. Prince and Co. He spent his evenings going to parties given by his many acquaintances, both Americans and German-Jewish immigrants like the Strauses, Abrahams, and Oppenheimers, and the "Brooklyn branch" of the Rothschilds. Otto had an open mind and was interested in the world, but he loved Germany best. On his return in the fall of

1911, he went to work for a company based in Düsseldorf called Fenestra that made windows and other metal parts for buildings. With the onset of the war in 1914, he was sent to Plettenberg, where he was in charge of horseshoe production for the army.

If Edith had indeed had ominous premonitions, they became reality on Thursday, October 24, 1929, just four months after Anne was born. The crash of the New York Stock Exchange on Black Thursday plunged the whole world into crisis, and a small bank like the Franks', which specialized in international transactions, was particularly hard-hit, its business declining by 90 percent. The Bad Soden company that produced throat lozenges also suffered. People worried about losing their jobs, and the unemployed endured their sore throats and hoarseness without cough drops. Otto was worried not only about his immediate family, for whom money was tight despite the help they received each month from Edith's relatives in Aachen, but also about his mother and siblings, who depended on the family business.

The mood in the country was increasingly disturbing. The steadily declining economy, which brought sharp rises in unemployment, higher taxes, and cuts in social services, spread unrest and discontent. A scapegoat was soon found—the Jews. Now it could be said out loud again: The Jews—who else?—had cheated the honest, upright, and hardworking Germans out of everything they had. "The Jews are our scourge," the demagogues told the jobless, and parents repeated it to their children. Anti-Semitic propaganda appealed particularly to those who felt life had treated them unfairly. In 1928, a year before the stock market crash, the National Socialists had received a mere 3 percent of the vote. In the first Reichstag election, in September 1930, with the Depression deepening, they captured 18 percent of the vote, and by July 1932, their share would rise to 37 percent.

Otto and Edith were realistic enough to take the growing danger seriously but optimistic enough to hope it would pass without casting a shadow on Margot and Anne's happy world. In their home, everything revolved around the two girls, even when there were guests. If the adults were playing parlor games, Margot and Gertrud, if she was there, were allowed to join in.

Anne was too little to play. But even before she could talk she managed to get people's attention. The screaming infant had grown into an energetic toddler. With her natural charm and liveliness she usually got what she wanted. Everyone—her babysitter, her grandmother, and above all her father—found her impish smile and infectious laughter irresistible. The imperfection of her smile—she had inherited prominent eye teeth and slightly buck teeth from her father—made it all the more charming. If snuggling close and gazing up with her big eyes failed to do the trick, she cried piteously. One way or another, she always got what she wanted. "A true little woman," Otto's mother called her youngest grandchild. Anne was willful, much more so than Margot; she was prepared to ignore rules of behavior that Margot obeyed without protest. But the little girl's sauciness and inquisitiveness only rarely exasperated her parents enough to provoke a smack on the bottom.

Otto spent a lot of time with his children. In a world in which most fathers had little contact with their offspring and merely expected them to be obedient and well-behaved, Otto's involvement with his daughters was exceptional. The whole Frank family was unusually attentive to their children, and Otto passed on to Anne and Margot the love and care he had received himself as a child. They called him Pim. People often asked how the nickname originated, but he couldn't remember. Perhaps it came from the French *père.* Or the name may have evolved from one of the family's much-beloved word games, in which "Papa" became "Papim" and ultimately just "Pim." In any case, the nickname stuck.

When his busy schedule allowed, Otto played with Margot and Anne, explaining things to them, and making up stories for them about "the two Paulas." Good Paula gave her parents nothing but pleasure, whereas Bad Paula was always causing trouble. The Paulas were invisible, but if you kept absolutely still and listened intently you could almost always tell where they were hiding at any given moment. Sometimes Good Paula was around and sometimes Bad Paula, depending on how Margot and Anne had been behaving and on what Otto wanted to teach them. Little Anne was more likely to come across Bad Paula.

Otto's mother had invented the two Paulas. Alice Stern Frank was a remarkable and sophisticated woman. She spoke and wrote English and French and was virtually fluent in Italian as well. Following the death of her husband, who was fifteen years her senior, she had taken his place as the head of the family bank, an extraordinary step for a forty-five-year-old mother of four, especially at the time. Margot and Anne called her Omi to distinguish her from Oma Holländer, their grandmother from Aachen. Omi was a modern woman, a strict but kindly disciplinarian, a proud, imposing grande dame. Anne and Margot's cousins Stephan and Bernd, the sons of Otto's sister, Helene, abbreviated Omi to I. For them she invented stories about mice—the church mouse, the country mouse, the school mouse—and she was never at a loss for a new episode.

Oma Rosa Stern Holländer was completely different. (The shared maiden name, Stern, was pure coincidence.) Oma Holländer was reserved and unassuming. Her long dark skirts and round wire-rimmed glasses gave her an old-fashioned air. Like Alice Stern Frank, she was already widowed when Anne was born, Abraham Holländer having died about a month before Margot's first birthday. Edith's older brothers, Julius and Walter, were still single and lived at home. They ran the family firm, B. Holländer, which went back to 1858 and dealt in industrial equipment and scrap metal.

Oma Holländer was known in the family for her angelic temperament, and Margot took after her. Otto and Edith feared that Anne would drive her good-natured Oma to distraction. But the old lady's patience seemed endless. Otto and Edith reproached her for indulging the child and giving in to her whims. She justified her leniency by explaining that her son Julius had also been headstrong and difficult. She said that if people had known more about child psychology when he was Anne's age, his life might have turned out differently. Julius, who is said to have suffered from depression, usually came to visit with Walter, who was three years younger. Both brothers loved the girls, saw them often in Frankfurt, and drove them to Aachen in their car. These trips were always special treats because Otto Frank did not own a car.

A year after the stock market crash, there was no sign of economic recovery. The Michael Frank Bank was doing poorly; costs would need to be cut. It was painful for the family to give up the bank's quarters on Neue Mainzer Strasse, probably the most prestigious commercial address in all of Frankfurt and one it shared with the city's major banks. In 1909, shortly before his death, Michael Frank himself, the founder of the bank, had initiated his firm's relocation from its nearby but less elegant quarters on Hochstrasse to the distinguished banking district. The move represented a major achievement for a man who had come to Frankfurt in 1879 from the provincial town of Landau in the Palatinate and had married into Frankfurt's respected Stern family. He did not live long enough to see his family installed in its new home, a neoclassical villa that had previously belonged to the Du Fays, another leading Frankfurt family.

The bank's new offices at 20 Bockenheimer Anlage, not far from the building where Michael Frank had founded the firm forty years earlier, were attractively located but not especially convenient for business. The area had been a respectable residential neighborhood for the well-to-do, both Jews and Christians, but it had never been a business district. The first floor of the house where the

Franks now had their bank as well as their Bad Soden office was not very prepossessing, and in order to save money they shared the space with another company.

These cost-cutting measures were soon followed by similar ones in the private sphere. Otto Frank terminated his lease on Marbachweg, and in March 1931 the family moved to 24 Ganghoferstrasse. The new apartment, smaller and less expensive, occupied the ground floor of a villa in the so-called Poets' Quarter. The pretty grounds of the villa and the meadows and fields on the edge of the neighborhood looked especially inviting in their spring colors. The place was ideal for the children. It was only a ten-minute walk from Marbachweg, but the milieu was entirely different. Before, the Franks had lived among minor officials and white-collar workers; now, they had liberal-minded doctors, lawyers, and architects—Jewish and Christian—for neighbors. Given the increasingly tense political situation, the Franks felt safer in this upper-middle-class world.

In later years, Otto stressed that he had not been personally subjected to discrimination, but his neighbors on Marbachweg, the Naumanns and the Stabs, for example, saw things differently. The Franks had to move, they claimed, because they could no longer stand the malicious atmosphere in their landlord's house and were frightened by the gangs of storm troopers that marched by singing anti-Semitic songs. The Nazi hoodlums had not yet dared to enter the Poets' Quarter.

Otto Könitzer, the fanatical landlord on Marbachweg, remained true to his prejudices when he looked for a new tenant. He again found a Jewish tenant, this time a stockbroker, who had no sympathy for Orthodox or Zionist Jews and who wrongly assumed that he had nothing in common with "those Jews" who drew the hostility of the right-wing radicals. The anti-Semitism of the National Socialists, he believed, was directed purely at the black-clad,

Playing in the sandbox at Ganghoferstrasse: Anne, age two, and her mother, Frankfurt, 1931.

caftan-wearing, Yiddish-speaking shtetl Jews from Eastern Europe. Certainly not at him.

Anne stayed with the Naumanns while the family moved, sleeping in the crib that had already done service for the six Naumann children—four girls and two boys—and had been kept just in case. Gertrud, now fifteen years old but just as crazy about babies as she had been at ten, bathed, changed, and fed the little girl. Anne obviously felt comfortable with Gertrud, whom she had known since infancy. When the Franks had gotten settled and the attractive blue-gray living room set with its oval side tables was in place, Gertrud visited almost as often as before. The children quickly found new playmates in the neighborhood, but their friendship with Gertrud was special. Sometimes she was even asked to spend the night. She always had presents for Margot's and Anne's birthdays, toys or pretty dresses her older sister, Elisabeth, had embroidered. One of the toys was a diabolo, an hourglass-shaped wooden top that is spun on a string, tossed in the air, and caught again. Another was a board game called Quinto. Edith Frank would later write Gertrud: "Did you know that your Quinto is Anne and Margot's favorite game? Even the grown-ups enjoy it."

But nothing could distract from the political situation, which was never far from anyone's mind. Even though no direct reference was made to it in the presence of women or children, anxieties about political developments were inescapable. The NSDAP was gaining ground. Its program was simple, plain enough for any beer-hall customer to grasp, and therefore likely to succeed. The party was against everything: against liberalism, against socialism, against capitalism, against the middle class, against the elite, against the clergy, and above all against the Jews. The NSDAP would finally put an end to the failed system of the Weimar Republic; people didn't care how. For those who felt they had not had a fair chance, the NSDAP represented new hope. The party's mass assemblies, speeches, and demonstrations mesmerized "the people," *das Volk.* Everything revolved around *das Volk*, "the ethnically pure folk community"; what the NSDAP did, it did out of "love for the people." Few were bothered by Adolf Hitler's megalomania. Here at last, most thought, was someone who would set things straight again. Those who were troubled by Hitler generally told themselves he was a temporary evil.

The first volume of *Mein Kampf* appeared in 1925, the second in December 1926; from 1930 on, the two parts were available as one book. Otto Frank leafed through *Mein Kampf* and read a few passages in it. "No nation can rid itself of this plague [the Jews] except by the sword," Hitler wrote. "Such a process is and always will be a bloody business." At the beginning of World War I, the German government should have "exterminated the Jews mercilessly"; Germany would not have lost the war if "it had gassed 12,000 or 15,000 of them." Like Lieutenant Otto Frank, Adolf Hitler had been awarded the Iron Cross in World War I. How much longer would this man be allowed to promulgate his madness? Otto wondered. How far would people let him go? When would they realize what his intentions really were? What if he actually came to power? What would become of the Jews then? Would the Franks still be safe in Germany? Would Hitler be able to deprive them of their livelihood? There was only one thing Otto felt absolutely certain of and stressed repeatedly to his family and friends: We must not allow this man to deprive us of our German identity. If only the economy would finally pick up.

3

EXODUS

"I was very surprised by your call yesterday and happy to hear all your voices again," Otto Frank wrote to his mother on June 13, 1932. She was in Paris visiting his cousin Jean. "It would have been nice if the occasion for the call had been a more pleasant one. I assume Jean understood correctly what I was saying. The breakdown into ongoing expenses, outstanding debts, and mortgage payments is pretty obvious." Jean Frank, thirty-seven, was a son of Michael Frank's younger brother Léon, who had emigrated to Paris, married his niece Nanette, the daughter of his eldest sister and a rabbi from Philadelpia, and done very well as a stockbroker. Alice Frank's main reason for going to Paris seems to have been to ask her extravagant nephew for help. The fortune he had inherited after his mother's death in 1909 and his extraordinary talent as an interior decorator and furniture designer had provided him entry into the artistic circles of Stravinsky and Diaghilev and of the Surrealists around Aragon, Éluard, and Picasso. Under their influence, he had been drawn to Communism. He maintained a lifelong friendship with Jean Cocteau; he worked together with the Giacometti brothers and with Dali. Experimenting with drugs was routine for these artists.

By mid-1932 the Franks' financial position had become precarious. Not only was the bank on the brink of disaster, but income from the springs at Bad Soden threatened to cease altogether. "We lack the most basic means. . . . My pessimism and worries of the last few months were only too well founded. I have to ask whether it still makes sense to hold onto the house on Mertonstrasse," Otto wrote. "I am speaking from an economic and political point of view." About his younger brother, Herbert, he wrote: "Herb will try to get away from Frankfurt and find a job elsewhere. There is not much he can do here." Two months earlier, in April 1932, Herbert Frank had been arrested and imprisoned for several weeks. The bank had "violated regulations governing international trade in securities," tax investigators in Frankfurt had declared. As the "partner with a controlling interest," their letter stated, Herbert Frank was held responsible.

Herbert, or Herbi, as he was sometimes called by his family, was a cheerful, warmhearted person, uncomplicated and optimistic, though sometimes a little cynical. He enjoyed life's pleasures more than Otto did and was not easily depressed or upset. On April 12, 1922, against the wishes of his family, he had married a non-Jewish American woman named Hortense Schott. He had been a partner in the bank since 1923 and was reluctantly acting as its president, but his brothers, Robert and Otto, felt even less qualified than he. In the winter of 1931–32 a man he did not know who identified himself as a stockbroker from Karlsruhe had offered him stock in German industrial firms worth over a million Reichsmarks. Herbert was to act as middleman and sell the shares to various Frankfurt banks for a lucrative commission most welcome to the faltering Michael Frank Bank. Herbert arranged the apparently routine transaction without recognizing that there was a problem. The shares and bonds the man had given him to sell had been issued abroad, and trade in foreign securities, that is, securities issued abroad, had been strictly illegal in Germany since 1931.

It made no difference whether the headquarters of the companies whose securities were sold were in Germany or elsewhere.

Herbert had charged fees and commissions no higher than were customary, and—as he did with every transaction—he had kept careful records that could easily be checked. This, too, suggests that he was acting in good faith; if he had planned to do something illegal, he would have tried to conceal the facts. He had trusted the dealer, who seemed like an honest businessman, and it had evidently never occurred to him to ask where the shares had been issued.

On May 14, 1932, Herbert was released from jail, where he had been awaiting trial, but for the time being he was unable—and unwilling—to appear in the Frankfurt banking world. Regardless of whether the upcoming trial found him innocent or guilty, his reputation was tarnished. This setback was all the more frustrating because trade in stocks was apparently picking up again. The Frankfurt Stock Exchange had been closed for almost a year as a result of the worldwide Depression, but it had just reopened in April. Taking this as a clear sign of an economic upswing, Germany's financial community was cautiously optimistic.

The court took its time scheduling the trial. In the summer, Herbert resigned as president of the Michael Frank Bank and decided to leave Germany. His wife had left him in 1930—the family's intuition had proved correct. In August 1932, the divorce was finalized. When his case finally came up in October 1932, he was already settled in Paris and had no intention of returning for the proceeding. His lawyer justified his absence by pointing out that his client had already spent time in prison and that the needless delay from April to October had caused him "not only material but also mental harm" from which he had not yet recovered.

Otto Frank, convinced that "not much would come of the matter," represented his brother in court and to the press. The bank, he said, had made a mistake in trusting the stockbroker and assuming that his being German meant that he could be depended on to respect German securities law. Unfortunately, this individual was not available for questioning because he had left the country. The case against Herbert Frank was closed. The court must have realized that he had been the victim, not the perpetrator. It was never determined who had instigated the investigation into the bank's affairs barely four months after the ill-fated transaction. If someone had wanted to harm the bank, to deliberately ruin its reputation, he succeeded: the negative publicity sped the ailing bank's decline toward collapse.

"We have no idea where we will end up," Otto concluded his report of bad news to his mother, "but the main thing is that we stay healthy and that you have enough to live on. We are younger and better able to deal with adversity. It is important to see things as they are and to act accordingly." Otto, who would officially assume the position of bank president on October 1, 1932, felt himself no more able than Herbert to restore the bank's fortunes. More sober and cautious than his younger brother, he was realistic enough not to indulge in false hopes. "We will try to hold on to the business as long as we can. We will have to discuss later what the solution should be. . . . But dissolving the firm seems pointless at this time."

Somehow things had to go on. And somehow they did. On June 13 it seemed that the firm would no longer be able to meet its obligations, but on the fourteenth, before Otto's letter could even have reached his mother, good news arrived from Paris. "I have just received your telegram, which I read to the effect that the July mortgage payments will be met. I hardly need tell you how great my relief is, since it would have been impossible to keep the house otherwise. Jean has behaved admirably, and we cannot thank him enough," Otto wrote. Cousin Jean Frank (known professionally as Jean-Michel Frank) had turned his artistic talent into a successful international business. His plain, functional style had set new standards in modern design, and collectors avidly sought out his avant-garde furniture that made use of unusual, experimental materials. In the early 1930s he did the interior decoration for New York's newly built Rockefeller Center.

Jean's help arrived just in time. The infusion of money, however, could only relieve the acute symptoms of the illness, not cure it. "Business is bad," Otto had written to his sister, Helene, two months earlier on April 2, 1932. "There is no telling where we're heading. The only bright spot is the children, who are sweet and take my mind off our troubles."

Margot, with her dark, expressive eyes, had grown into a beauty. Polite and shy, she was almost a little too serious, an exemplary child who never teased and was the delight of all the relatives. Even when she laughed and played, she was always well-behaved. At six, she was a model sister for Anne, whom she cared for with touching devotion and whose high spirits she balanced with her own reserve.

In the spring of 1932, Margot started school. Anne was envious. The Franks had decided to send their children to the Ludwig Richter School on Eschersheimer Lindenbaum. The school was close to where they lived, and many children whom Margot knew went there, children from different social and religious backgrounds, Protestant, Catholic, and Jewish. Moreover, the school, named for Ludwig Richter, a Dresden painter of idyllic old-German scenes, subscribed to progressive teaching methods. It was the type of school Edith and Otto had hoped to find. The building, which had been designed as part of the "New Frankfurt" urban program, was only three and a half years old. The classrooms were modern and sunny. Instead of traditional heavy desks, the rooms had lightweight, movable ones that could quickly be arranged in rows, clusters, or a U-shape; there was also an outside play area, and in good weather, classes were held outdoors. Nature and learning were no longer considered mutually exclusive.

The principal, Walter Hüsken, was a progressive educator who in 1930 had been one of the founders of the Radical Democratic Party. The party was in fact radical in only one sense: it was fundamentally opposed to radicals of both the right and the left. It regarded itself as the successor to the German Democratic Party, which had moved to the extreme right, and it consistently spoke for the liberal center, whose views Otto Frank supported.

Walter Hüsken wanted to democratize the school system. He opposed authoritarian teaching methods; instead of merely listening until they practically fell asleep, children should participate more actively in the learning process. His teachers were no drill masters wielding canes but kindly, trustworthy adults ready to hear what their pupils had to say. Less coercion and more freedom was the motto.

The concept was promising, but the Depression made its realization difficult. There were forty-two girls in Margot's class, too many for one teacher to attend to individually, but the budget did not allow for smaller classes or more classrooms. Schools, too, were feeling the effects of the Depression.

Margot brought home her first report card in the fall of 1932. She was a "good" pupil with excellent marks for diligence. She liked school. There were only five Jewish girls in her class, but the other thirty-seven hardly noticed. Nor did the teachers care. Twice a week she went to a class in Jewish religion, as her mother wanted. But nobody thought her strange or exotic. After all, the Catholic girls didn't have the same religion teacher as the Protestants. Margot was no different from anyone else. Her best friends were baptized. All was still bright in her child's world.

But the adults' world was rapidly darkening. Many in the privileged Poets' Quarter still believed—or chose to believe—that all was well, but they knew that in other parts of the city the National Socialist Bund Deutscher Mädel (BDM), or League of German Girls, was gaining in popularity. The girls in the Bund were taught to be proud of their race: they were the future "German

On the Hauptwache Plaza: The last photograph of Anne, Edith, and Margot Frank together in Frankfurt, 1933.

women," disciplined, obedient, and dutiful. Contact with Jews was forbidden.

The BDM, like all the other Hitler Youth groups, was a relatively harmless indicator of the changing political climate. Paralyzed, the liberal center watched the NSDAP's rapid rise from a marginal group, an insignificant political party, to the country's most powerful political entity. The party could no longer be ignored. In the election on September 14, 1930, more than 6.4 million people had cast their vote for Hitler's party, raising the number of Nazi representatives in the Reichstag, Germany's parliament, from a mere 12 to 107 and making the NSDAP the second-largest faction. In the electoral district of East Prussia it was already the biggest.

By May 1932, almost six million Germans had lost their jobs—and their faith in democracy. In the Reichstag election of July 31, the NSDAP scored its greatest triumph. It won 37.3 percent of the votes and doubled its seats in the parliament. Terror reigned. The SS and the SA, the storm troopers, who had been temporarily banned in April, could now march again and vent their fury against their political opponents. For a while, the brutality and cynicism of these organizations frightened even some of the NSDAP's supporters. In the next election, on November 6, the party received two million fewer votes than it had in July. Alienated voters had cast their ballots for the German Nationals or for the German Communist Party on the extreme left.

But only the shortsighted could see these developments as a hopeful sign or a cause for relief. The Weimar Republic's opponents on the extreme right and the extreme left made up 58.5 percent of the population and thus were already in the majority. Germany had become impossible to govern.

Many people managed to convince themselves that this couldn't be happening—but not Otto Frank. The Führer, as Nazi party members had been calling Hitler since 1921, had issued his warning, and Otto took it seriously. If Hitler and his party came to power—which seemed increasingly likely—the Jews could be in real danger. In that case, the Franks would have to leave Germany. What other choice did they have? Even an economic recovery would not save them. Besides, there was no sign of recovery, at least not for most people. The Franks had always been considerably better off than the average, but now their scant resources were almost depleted.

Under the circumstances it seemed foolish to keep paying rent month after month when there was plenty of room for everyone at Otto's mother's house. They had to be sensible and set aside their preferences and reservations. At the end of 1932, Otto informed his landlord that "because of the changed economic situation" he unfortunately had to terminate his lease. At the end of March 1933, after the stipulated term of notice had expired, he and his family moved back into the house they had left exactly six years earlier, in March 1927, to build a life of their own.

Since January 30, 1933, at the latest, it had been clear to Otto that the return to Beethovenplatz would not be a homecoming but a brief layover. On that day, his fears were confirmed. Reich President Paul von Hindenburg—once a powerful, respected figure but now a sick man barely able to stand, a puppet easy to manipulate—appointed Hitler chancellor of the Reich. The Nazi leader had achieved what he wanted.

In his inaugural speeches Hitler announced his intention to revive Germany and defend it against the cancerous growth of democracy. Once in power, he issued emergency decrees stripping the opposition parties in the Reichstag and in the diets of power, steps taken "for the protection of the German people," as these proclamations grandiloquently declared. He used the burning of the Reichstag on the night of February 27–28, 1933, as a welcome opportunity to defeat his most powerful enemy, the Communist Party. Freedom of assembly and freedom of speech were suspended. Realizing that they would soon be at the mercy of a dictatorship, people reacted with uncertainty and fear. They hunkered down, kept quiet, and waited.

Meanwhile, the supporters of the NSDAP were making plenty of noise. There were processions and marches day and night; battle slogans rose up from the crowds and blasted from loudspeakers. SA men marched wherever one looked; clad in their brown uniforms, they were used as auxiliary police squads. Many of them were out-and-out hoodlums, loudmouthed thugs recruited from the ranks of malcontents in all classes of society.

As early as February and March 1933, there were rumors of attacks against opponents of the Nazis—members of left-wing parties, liberals, intellectuals, Jews. On March 11, the mayor of Frankfurt, Ludwig Landmann, resigned—voluntarily, according to the official statement. And—again voluntarily—he fled the city, which had, after Berlin, the largest Jewish population in Germany. In reality, of course, he was fleeing from the Nazis, who had threatened to arrest him. Landmann was not only a political opponent but was also of Jewish background, although he had renounced the Jewish religion and considered himself an atheist and a German. The Nazis cared only about his "race." He was a Jew.

On March 13, having won the local elections in Hesse the day before, the National Socialists hoisted the swastika atop the Römer, Frankfurt's city hall and a building rich in historical associations. The Nazis' opponents were still keeping quiet, partly because, without being aware of it, they had long since been silenced and partly because they did not yet realize just how threatened they were by this totalitarian terrorist regime. Hitler's speeches about blond fellow Aryans, about subhumans—Slavs, Gypsies, homosexuals, and Jews—and about blood, soil, and honor were so insane and illogical he couldn't possibly stay in power very long. "Those who will not change their ways will be bent and broken. . . . Capital punishment for betrayers of their country and people," Hitler proclaimed. Were these the hysterical threats of a madman or a warning to be taken seriously?

Otto Frank suspected the truth, that this was only the beginning. It was just a matter of time, he feared, before the town of Bad Soden would revoke the Franks' license to use the mineral springs and before the Franks' bank would be boycotted. How, and above all where, could they make a living? He was convinced his family would have to leave Germany. How long would they have to stay abroad? Where should they go? To Switzerland, where his sister, Helene, had been living with her family since 1930? Should they join their relatives in Paris? What about London, where his younger cousin Milly Stanfield lived? Or Amsterdam, where he still knew people? Or the United States, where he would have to revive contacts from even farther in the past? Wherever they went, he needed work. There were not enough savings to finance life in exile for any length of time; besides, no foreign country would grant him a residence permit unless he had a job.

Otto's brother-in-law, Erich Elias, came up with the best idea. The two men had known each other since the winter of 1919, when Erich had worked at the Frankfurt Stock Exchange as an agent and stockbroker for the banking firm of Heichelheim Brothers. As a partner in the Michael Frank Bank, Otto had done business with him and come to appreciate him not only as a capable banker but also as a sympathetic and serious person. It is likely that Otto introduced this business friend to his family and his younger sister, Helene. Lunni or Leni, as the family liked to call her, was very close to Otto. He felt responsible for her—almost like a substitute father—and he thought they were alike in temperament. "You, more than the others, are the kind of person who likes to act on feeling, who needs love in order to flourish, and who is able to give love," he had written to her in May 1917. "I am very similar in this respect." He had vehemently talked her out of an earlier infatuation. "Ideals are ideals because they are not realizable," he had impressed on her in one of his regular letters from the front, and he had repeated the warning in a later one: "Don't go too far with this. It really doesn't make sense and can only do harm. You've got to be reasonable."

He had no objections to Erich Elias. On the contrary, he was pleased that his sensitive sister, who loved the arts, especially music and the theater, and spoke four languages, felt drawn to this serious, reliable, and obviously competent man. Erich would be the stable element the impulsive Helene needed in her life.

At the end of 1920, Erich Elias left Heichelheim Brothers, and on February 3, 1921, he joined the Michael Frank Bank as a partner. The wedding took place two weeks later, on February 16. (Otto felt so close to Elias that he chose him for his best man at his own wedding four years later.)

Eight years later when Erich Elias accepted a position in Basel the bank was in serious financial trouble. His job was to establish a Swiss branch of Opekta, a subsidiary of the Frankfurt concern Pomosin-Werke. Since 1911, the Pomosin-Werke had been manufacturing pectin from apple pomace and had enjoyed a monoply in Europe in providing this jelling agent to the jam industry. Opekta had been formed in 1928 to open up the private, or "housewife," market, and though it was a subsidiary of the Pomosin-Werke and distributed the liquid pectin produced exclusively by Pomosin, it had to make its way independently in the marketplace. Pomosin could not afford to offend its major industrial customers.

"Opekta Jell-Aid" was something of a revolutionary product. Convincing housewives of that, though, was a difficult job at first, and the business got off to a slow start. But for the banker Erich Elias, the planned expansion of Opekta into neighboring European countries was nonetheless an interesting opportunity, and for the bank it was a relief. There was now one less family to feed.

In early 1933 Erich told Otto that Robert Feix, the financial director of the Pomosin-Werke and a stockholder in the company as well as the founder of Opekta, was dissatisfied with how the business was doing in the Netherlands. He wanted Opekta to become a brand name there. The company's present agent in the Netherlands, a Victor Kugler, hadn't made much headway. Wouldn't this be an appealing challenge for Otto? Holland was not far from home and, like Switzerland, had remained neutral during World War I. The Dutch were a liberal and tolerant people who would also stay out of future political conflicts. The Jews in Amsterdam—10 percent of the city's population—were a thoroughly integrated and accepted minority. Otto's familiarity with Amsterdam and with the Dutch language would be an added advantage.

Otto Frank had done business in Holland ten years earlier, when the ailing Michael Frank Bank had decided to open a subsidiary in Amsterdam. Otto was chosen to manage it because of his training in New York; of all the men in the family, he had the most experience working abroad. On December 31, 1923, he registered the firm M. Frank & Zonen (M. Frank and Sons), located at Keizergracht 604, with the Dutch Chamber of Industry and Commerce as a company engaged in banking and currency transactions. In addition to Otto, who had, for this purpose, moved his primary residence to Keizersgracht in Amsterdam, the partners listed were Herbert Frank, Erich Elias, and the Frankfurt parent company, Michael Frank.

This was a popular maneuver at the time. Many German banks were trying to improve their positions by setting up branches in Amsterdam, which since World War I had become the European center for currency trading. But these branches were subject to certain restrictions. To protect themselves against unwelcome competition, the Dutch banks insisted that these new subsidiaries specialize in handling the capital Germans had transferred to Holland for tax reasons. They were not allowed to attract Dutch clients.

The Franks' plan failed. After only one year, on December 15, 1924, Otto had to give up. Risky currency speculations had proven so damaging that Frank & Zonen had to be liquidated. But no bankruptcy was declared; apparently the bank assured its creditors that it would pay them back in installments. It took a good four years for everything to be settled. The liquidation was not completed until the end of January 1929—six months before Anne was born—when the firm's name was finally struck from the registry of the Dutch Chamber of Industry and Commerce. Otto Frank could not know then that he would soon be returning to Amsterdam.

By early April 1933 the situation of Jews in Germany had worsened dramatically. On March 27, the city government of Cologne had announced: "Jewish firms are henceforth ineligible to submit bids or form contracts, etc." Two days later, on March 29, the president of Hesse had declared: "It is a matter of honor to the German and Hessian press to eliminate any foreign, international, and Jewish influence on the news, entertainment, and advertising sections of newspapers and magazines." This announcement was part of an inflammatory campaign designed to set the stage for the first organized boycott since Hitler's assumption of power. On Saturday, April 1, 1933, at 10 a.m. precisely, so the party order ran, uniformed and, in some cases, armed Nazis were to block the entrance of every Jewish store and business in Germany and prevent customers from entering. "German citizens! Defend yourselves! Don't buy from Jews!" In many places those who ignored the guards and insisted on entering a store were photographed and their pictures published in the newspaper the next day. The boycott was aimed not only at store owners but at Jewish professionals, such as doctors and lawyers, as well. For the time being, banks were left alone because even the reckless Nazis did not want to cause an international banking crash.

The most fanatic anti-Semites, especially Julius Streicher, editor of the magazine *Der Stürmer*, and Heinrich Himmler, were disappointed with the response. The general public, it seemed, still resisted being mobilized. Nonetheless, they looked the other way and let things happen without protest. A letter by the head of the Jewish Community of Frankfurt in the April issue of that organization's newsletter offered but meager comfort to his fellow Jews. "Nothing can rob us of our thousand-year-old connection with our

German homeland, and no hardship or danger can alienate us from the faith we have inherited from our fathers," it read. "If no voice speaks up for us, may the stones of this city testify on our behalf, this city whose prosperity owes so much to the efforts of the Jews, this city where so many institutions attest to the communal spirit of the Jews, this city where relations between Jews and non-Jews have always been exceptionally close."

The boycott of Jewish stores was merely a dress rehearsal. It was the prelude to a flood of anti-Jewish edicts that excluded Jews from all areas of public life, a prelude to isolation. The principle of equality for all citizens, embedded in the German constitution since 1871, was abolished. In Frankfurt, as in other cities, the income of Jewish businesses fell precipitously after April 1; many were forced to declare bankruptcy or to sell their assets below market value. In the month of October alone, 536 Jewish enterprises closed in Germany, and the number of unemployed Jews rose sharply.

A law enacted on April 7, 1933, entitled Reform of the Civil Service, decreed that all institutions of the Reich, of its states and municipalities, including schools and universities, were to be "cleansed." Jewish teachers and those who held political views opposed to Nazi ideology were deemed enemies of the Reich and could be dismissed immediately. Walter Hüsken, Margot's principal at the Ludwig Richter School, was one of the first to be fired by the Nazis, and Margot's teacher did not return after Easter vacation either.

The Franks, having moved back to the Westend, had already transferred Margot from her old school to one called the Varrentrapp School. The quiet, reserved seven-year-old had to adjust to a new setting, new schoolmates, and a totally different educational approach. Jewish pupils, moreover, were now obliged to sit together in one corner of the classroom, strictly segregated from their Aryan classmates. It seemed likely that both Margot and Anne, who was now kindergarten age, would soon be prohibited from attending the public schools. Otto's and Edith's worries about their daughters' educations must have intensified their desire to emigrate.

On May 10, 1933, National Socialist student groups marched "against the un-German spirit" and burned "un-German writings" in street actions designed to attract publicity. By now it seemed inevitable that the Franks would emigrate to Amsterdam. "When the Jews write in German, they lie," the Nazis had proclaimed. The works of Thomas, Klaus, and Heinrich Mann, of Arnold and Stefan Zweig, of Kurt Tucholsky, Erich Maria Remarque, and Franz Werfel, not to mention the Communist writings of Marx and Engels and the books of Bertolt Brecht and many others, were tossed into the flames in many German cities to the accompaniment of shouted slogans; it was as though the demonstrators wished to burn the authors themselves at the stake. Otto Frank's favorite poet, Heinrich Heine, whose poem "Lorelei" every schoolchild knew by heart, was declared a nonperson. In future textbooks, "Poet unknown" would replace the name of Heinrich Heine, a poet who had written a hundred years earlier, "Wherever they burn books they will also, in the end, burn human beings."

In midsummer of 1933, Otto had decided to emigrate to Holland rather than any other country, and he went to Amsterdam to prepare for his family's move. Edith and the two girls had gone to Aachen to stay with Oma Holländer and their uncles Julius and Walter. Otto wanted to set up his new business and find lodgings before Edith and the children joined him. In the meantime, Edith would go back and forth between Amsterdam and Aachen, which was conveniently located near the Dutch border. In an emergency Edith and the girls could quickly reach safety in Holland.

Otto's fresh start in business did not go smoothly. Forty-four years old by now, he had originally been sent to Amsterdam as a trustee to form a subsidiary of the Rohstoff Verkehrs AG (Raw Materials Trade Company), or Rovag, which for tax reasons had established its headquarters in the Swiss canton of Glarus. Since 1929, the Opekta operation in Cologne and several Opekta subsidiaries abroad had been consolidated under Rovag, which was headed by Erich Elias. Various legal problems had emerged, however, and the owners of the Pomosin-Werke found themselves obliged to change their plans, at least as far as their foreign subsidiaries were concerned.

"Pomosin Import Utrecht" had been marketing Pomosin-Werke pectin in Holland since the 1920s. Its manager, Frans J. M. van Angeren, a successful restaurant owner who dealt in pectin on the side, felt that the demand for pectin in Holland was not large enough to support more than one supplier. He was unwilling to take on a competitor—especially if the competition came from a subsidiary of his own parent company—nor was he willing to accept a board member in his business who had been named by headquarters in Frankfurt, a position Robert Feix had apparently intended for Otto Frank to assume.

On August 5, 1933, Otto Frank informed his brother-in-law of the turn their plans had taken: "After it became clear that the complications raised by Mr. van Angeren made it impossible for me to establish an Opekta subsidiary in Holland, I decided to form an Opekta company under my own name." Just what those "complications" were can no longer be determined. According to Otto, van Angeren was at odds with customs officials. Why this point had any bearing on why "Dutch Opekta" had to be "a purely Dutch enterprise" in which Rovag could have no role also remains a mystery.

It is clear, at any rate, that management at the Pomosin-Werke and Opekta wanted to retain Otto Frank merely as a legal front man and to claim a share in Opekta Amsterdam's business. Otto Frank, however, no longer regarded himself as their trustee and considered himself "completely independent."

For permission to use the trademark Opekta he had to pass on 2.5 percent of his profits to the Frankfurt company and "to purchase all his pectin from Pomosin-Werke." A further rather disappointing condition, doubtless insisted upon by Pomosin Utrecht, was that Otto had to agree not to infringe on Pomosin's business and to sell his pectin only to end users. Pomosin Utrecht would continue to supply Dutch canning companies and jam producers. Neither Frans van Angeren nor his brother-in-law Joop Hofhuis, whom he had engaged as his head manager, had any interest in the "housewife" market. (This fact would explain the trusting and, indeed, friendly relationship that developed between the Hofhuis and Frank families, of which more will be said later.)

Otto Frank was now set up as an independent businessman, but he lacked the necessary start-up capital. His brother-in-law lent him 15,000 Dutch guilders in the form of an interest-free loan, secured by shares in Opekta Amsterdam. Otto would either pay the loan back within ten years or pay it off with a transfer of shares. The money for the loan actually came from Rovag. "Because Mr. Frank cannot conclude any agreements directly with Rovag himself," Erich Elias wrote on August 13, 1933, "I have made this agreement in my own name but in the interests of Rovag and solely on its behalf."

Just one day later, according to an entry in the Registry of Residents, Otto and Edith Frank moved to Amsterdam, and on September 15 Otto registered the firm with the Dutch Chamber of Industry and Commerce under the name of Nederlandsche Opekta Maatschappij N.V. (Dutch Opekta Joint-Stock Company). Its business was described as the "production and sale of fruit products, especially pectin." Otto was the sole shareholder. In July 1934, he had the notation "*in oprichting*" (in formation) deleted. The Michael Frank Bank, meanwhile, had been officially dissolved at the end of January 1934. In Otto's absence, an attorney had arranged the liquidation of the Soden Mineral Products Company. (The municipality of Bad Soden still manufactures lozenges today.)

Otto had little time to look for a place for his family to live. Immediately after his arrival, he had moved into a sublet apartment on the third floor of 24 Stadionkade, and on August 16, 1933, he had his and Edith's names entered in the municipal registry of residents. "I've been here four weeks already and am very busy. I hope to see you here sometime if everything works out," he wrote to Gertrud Naumann in Frankfurt on September 4. During a walk they took together shortly before he left Germany, he'd given her the following advice: "Take your children seriously, so that they can take you seriously. If you promise them something, you have to keep your promise; otherwise they will lose faith in you."

Edith traveled back and forth between Aachen and Amsterdam to assist her husband. Otto was under great pressure at work, so it was her responsibility to look for suitable living quarters. "Dear Gertrud," she wrote on November 3 to her young friend, who was saddened by her separation from the Franks. "My husband enjoyed your lovely letter very much and will write to you as soon as he has more time. I am busy looking at apartments and don't know yet when I will get back to Frankfurt. The children are having a good time in Aachen." As a return address she gave 120 Nieuwe Zijds Voorburgwal, the original location of Otto's firm. It was a small two-room office in a strikingly modern nine-story building in the old city. In the Amsterdam of that day, it looked practically like a skyscraper.

Two weeks later, on a postcard dated November 16, Otto reported success. "We'll soon have a place to live. Winter will pass, and perhaps we'll see you here sometime next year," he wrote to Gertrud. The next sentence explained the brevity of his message. "I have a lot of work to do and am quite tired and nervous but otherwise, thank God, in good health."

To the physical exertion required to establish a new business was added the emotional strain of having to leave his home, his relatives, and his friends to start all over in an unfamiliar world. Otto kept insisting that his emigration to Holland was not a flight. But it was hardly a voluntary move.

In February 1916, Otto had written to his sister, Leni: "I often feel and have often felt that one's mother and one's siblings are the only truly reliable people; at least that is the way it is with us Jews." Now he was considerably older and had a family of his own, which was at once a responsibility and a source of support. But he still missed his brothers and sister, whom necessity had scattered to four different countries.

Herbert Frank had remained in Paris since his involuntary emigration in 1932. There he felt "very isolated and lonely," Edith later said. Otto's brother Robert, or Robbo, the clown of the family, had decided to move with his non-Jewish wife, Charlotte, or Lotti, to London, then as now a center of artistic activity. Since childhood he'd had a passion for art. He had a talent for drawing and impressed the family with his illustrations. He even wrote and illustrated a delightful children's book for his nephew Stephan Elias. In 1907, Michael Frank had bought an art dealership, perhaps in the hope of providing a livelihood for his eldest son, who was even less drawn to banking than his younger brothers. Robert became a deputy manager of the enterprise, and later, when money became scarce as World War I dragged on, he arranged for the sale of paintings from the family's private collection. "Robert has sold the painting *Adam and Eve* and is very sad about it," Otto commented in a letter from the front. "But I'm glad the picture left the house for such a good price." In London, too, Robert dealt in art.

Alice Stern Frank left Frankfurt about two months after Otto, but she emigrated to Basel. Her daughter, Helene, who had followed her husband there in 1930, had already settled into her new home. Helene and Erich Elias were financially secure, and their living situation was stable. Alice's grandsons, Stephan and Bernhard, or Bernd, adored her. They loved Sunday mornings, when she told them her fanciful mouse stories with classical music playing softly in the background. Stephan, who was two years older than Bernd, had stayed with her for several months to finish out the school year after his parents had left for Switzerland.

In the late summer of 1933, Alice Stern Frank rented a four-room apartment at Schweizergasse 50 in Basel. Her son-in-law's apartment at 139 Gundelingerstrasse was already accommodating not only his wife and sons but also his mother, who had moved to Basel with them. Alice liked her new home well enough, but it could not compare with her Frankfurt home on Beethovenplatz, where she had lived for over thirty years. She had sold that house with great regrets but at a good price. At least she had been able to take her most prized pieces of furniture with her to Basel, and her new kitchen was even bigger than the one in Frankfurt.

But she was not happy in Basel, and she missed Frankfurt. Her family could trace its roots back to the early sixteenth century; her

Alfred Holländer's bar mitzvah celebration, Oberhausen, 1912; back row, from left: Max Moses Holländer, Abraham Holländer; far right: the bar mitzvahed Alfred Holländer; front row, from left: Mathilde Berg Holländer, Bertha Baer, Rosa Stern Holländer.

ancestors both on her father's side—the Sterns—and on her mother's side—the Cahns—had always lived in Frankfurt. Her mother (Margot and Anne's great-grandmother) had been named Cornelia, a popular name among Frankfurt's middle class (Goethe's sister was named Cornelia, and Goethe was born in Frankfurt) and an indication that some time back the family had already felt connected more to Germany, and to Frankfurt in particular, than to the Jewish world. Hebrew tradition clearly played a minor role in the Sterns' life. Anne's great-grandfather, too, a man who made his fortune dealing in "silver-plated merchandise," was concerned more with assimilation than with his Jewish background. Almost as if they knew this in advance, his parents had named him August Heinrich, which was the name of Goethe's son.

Gertrud Naumann received her first detailed letter from Alice Stern Frank in November 1933. "I know how sad you were because we all left Germany, but I hope very much that your affection for our family will not fade," she wrote. She emphasized the positive aspects: the street she lived on was quiet, and the city, though small—nothing like Frankfurt or Amsterdam—had some lovely spots. She admitted that the language was difficult: "Swiss German is not a beautiful language; it is very hard to understand." Edith Frank was not fooled by her proud mother-in-law's confident tone. "Omi is homesick in Basel and suffering from being separated from her children," she realized.

According to statistics assembled in 1941 by the Central Association of Jews in Germany, approximately 63,000 Jews had emigrated by the end of 1933. But Edith's relatives had no intention of leaving Germany. "Her two brothers shared the delusion of many others," Otto Frank would say in retrospect. Julius and Walter continued to run B. Holländer, the Aachen enterprise, as best they could. Anne's great-grandfather Carl Benjamin Holländer, an extremely religious man born in the small town of Aldenhoven near Aachen, had founded it seventy-five years earlier, and her grandfather Abraham had built the secondhand rags-and-scrap-metal business into a respectable wholesale company dealing in metals of all kinds and one of the leading businesses in Aachen. Over time he prospered and distinguished himself in the Jewish community and the city at large. He took his father—who died blind at ninety-four—into his home, but survived him by less than four years. Abraham's brother, Max Moses, fourteen years younger, had established a branch of the company in Oberhausen in the Rhineland. Business was no longer going well anywhere, however, and the Nazis had made their presence felt even in peaceful Aachen. But Julius and Walter wanted to believe that things would soon improve. So did the many uncles and aunts and cousins Edith had grown up with. Her father, Abraham, had been one of nine children, and Edith had gone to school in Aachen with a

Abraham Holländer, Anne's grandfather (1860–1928)

Carl Benjamin Holländer, Anne's great-grandfather (1830–1924)

number of her cousins—Meta, Frieda, Irma, Ilse, and Elsbeth. After she married and moved to Frankfurt, Edith hardly ever saw them but never completely lost touch. In 1931, Elsbeth committed suicide, leaving two small children. Meta, born in 1900 like Edith, wanted to become an opera singer and later appeared on the stage of the Metropolitan Opera in New York. When Edith and her cousin Irene Holländer, who had grown up in Oberhausen, were young, they used to play tennis. Irene was modern and emancipated, trained in business, and one of the first women in Germany to get a driver's license. She was the brain of the family, her relatives said. She divorced her husband in October 1933 because he had had an affair with his secretary, but for the time being she had no intention of leaving Dortmund, where she lived with her two daughters. It was not political naïveté alone, however, that kept her from leaving Germany with them. For her, as for many others, emigration was a question of money as well.

For Edith Frank, the move to Amsterdam meant that at least she could stay near her family. Aachen was about halfway between Frankfurt and Amsterdam, and she would be able to visit her mother and brothers as often as before. The apartment she and Otto had found was not as grand as what they were used to, but there was room for guests.

"Our apartment is similar to the one on Ganghoferstrasse, only much smaller," Edith wrote of her new home on Merwedeplein, in the midst of a modern development south of the old inner city of Amsterdam. The neighborhood was called Rivierenbuurt, or the River Quarter, and many of its wide and well-laid-out streets were named after rivers. According to the municipal registry of residents, the Franks moved into their new home on December 5, 1933. The apartment was not only reasonably priced but also, by Dutch standards, quite large—a fact Edith may not have fully appreciated. "There is no room in our bedroom for anything except the beds. No cellar, no pantry, but everything is bright, convenient, and warm, so that I can manage easily without a maid." On December 7, Otto registered Margot and Anne as well. But Edith wanted to get settled in the new apartment before she went to get the girls; she wanted to have everything in place first. In the meantime, the girls were in good hands at their Oma Holländer's in Aachen.

Anne was used to spending time in Aachen. As early as September 1929, Edith had noted in Anne's baby book, "When someone—usually Uncle Julius—enters her room in the morning she is delighted and loves to clown around." Edith's brothers loved Anne as if she were their own, and Oma, the ideal grandmother, didn't hesitate to spoil her grandchildren. Her patience with Anne,

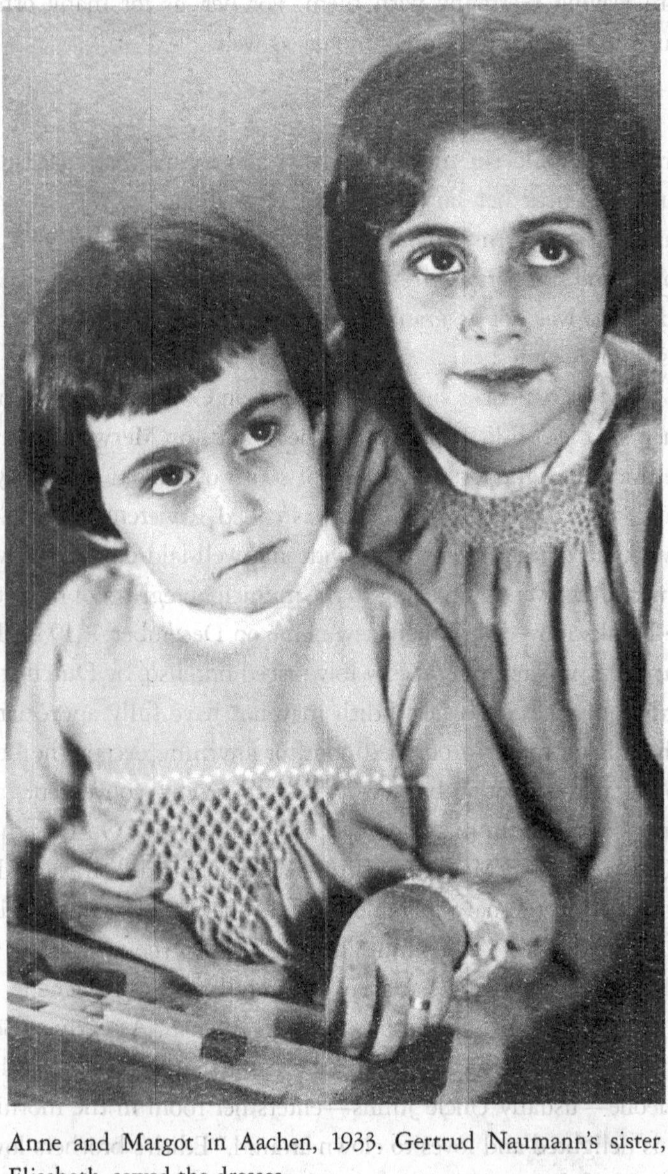

Anne and Margot in Aachen, 1933. Gertrud Naumann's sister, Elisabeth, sewed the dresses.

by now a 4½-year-old live wire, was inexhaustible. Anne was already outspoken. "Won't someone offer a seat to this old lady?" she is said to have asked when she and Oma got onto a streetcar and found all the seats taken. She was certainly not shy, but her request for a seat for her grandmother was not necessarily a sign of forwardness, let alone impertinence. It was likely an expression of affection and social thoughtfulness not only for her beloved Oma but for the elderly in general, feelings she would retain as she grew older.

Shortly before Christmas 1933 Edith wrote again to Gertrud Naumann: "Tomorrow the two uncles will bring Margot and stay here over the holiday." Edith wanted Margot to have a chance to adjust to life in Amsterdam before starting school on January 4, when the Dutch children returned to classes after Christmas vacation. Edith could well imagine the temper tantrums Anne would have when the three left her behind. "Anne will want to come too. Oma will have a hard time keeping her there another few weeks."

4

A NEW HOME

Anne Frank was not a retiring child. She demanded constant attention—or so it seemed to her parents. She was inquisitive, asking one question after another and refusing to be put off with partial answers. If she asked "Why?" she expected a full and detailed response; if she didn't get it, she was deeply hurt. But when Anne the tormentor tilted her head to one side, lowered her eyes, faked a bashful smile, and batted her eyelashes, no one could resist her, least of all her father. Curiosity, humor, and an adventurous spirit sparkled in her big greenish eyes, made all the more expressive by their dark brows and long lashes. She loved company, fun, constant activity. Otherwise, she grew fidgety. She was headstrong and mercurial. Thwarted, she'd resort to tears in order to get her way.

On Tuesday, June 12, 1934, she was even more excited than usual. It was her birthday, her fifth, and the first she would celebrate in her new home. In the afternoon, she had her new friends over for a birthday party—a family tradition the Franks brought with them from Frankfurt. Among the guests was Hanneli, with whom Anne attended kindergarten; Sanne, who lived around the corner; and Juliane, who was two years younger and lived one flight up from the Franks. Margot had also invited her classmate Barbara, Sanne's older sister. Each of the girls brought Anne a present and received a little favor in return. Juliane, for example, took home a tin tea service for her doll kitchen.

Anne was the perfect hostess. She swept the others along with her enthusiasm and her infectious giggling. Her lively prattle was still mostly in German, but Dutch words had begun to crop up in her speech.

She had come to Amsterdam from Aachen only four months earlier, as a surprise for Margot, who had been living in Holland for two months. Margot had celebrated her eighth birthday on February 16, and when she came into the living room she found her little sister all dressed up and sitting on the table along with

Children's party in Amsterdam, February 1934: Anne Frank (front right), Margot (back right), and Barbara Ledermann (left of Margot).

the other gifts. In a white tutu, and with her hair cut short like that of a street urchin, Anne took part in Margot's little birthday party. She was remarkably quiet and reserved, awed by the new faces and new surroundings.

But her shyness did not last long. "Anne has made the adjustment better than Margot," Edith Frank wrote in July to Gertrud Naumann, with whom she continued to maintain an active correspondence. Anne's first weeks had not been easy. Edith Frank did her best to make the transition as smooth and painless as possible. She hoped their lives would settle down and that her children's routine would quickly resume. But whereas Margot went to school every morning and came home happy and full of stories, Anne was lonely for her friends in Frankfurt and Aachen and the company of other children. She begged her mother to let her go to kindergarten, but it was already full. To keep her busy, Edith sent her back to Aachen several times to visit her grandmother and uncles.

By May, however, there was room for Anne in the kindergarten and she began attending the Montessori school on Niersstraat, a ten-minute walk from home. On her first day there she made friends with a girl named Hanneli Goslar, who spoke German and, like her, had been living in Amsterdam only a short time. Anne had already seen her and her mother in a shop a few days earlier. Anne's mother and Ruth Goslar, delighted to find that they both spoke German, had struck up a conversation and discovered that they lived next door to each other on Merwedeplein. The children, in the meantime, had eyed each other with interest.

When Hanneli arrived at the *Kinderhuis*, as the preschool classes at the Montessori school were called, Anne was already there. Among the many unfamiliar children speaking an incomprehensible language, Hanneli was relieved to find not only one she knew but also one who spoke German. She headed straight for Anne, who gave her a welcoming hug. Absorbed in each other, the two girls completely ignored their worried mothers, who had braced themselves for whining and tears. "Anne really enjoys going to kindergarten now," Edith could report.

In no time Anne had made many friends. Her cheerfulness, inventiveness, and love of mischief made her popular. She showed her domineering and possessive side only when she didn't get her way. Anne's best friends, Hanneli and Sanne, probably didn't mind Anne's taking the lead. Hannah Elisabeth Goslar—Hanneli to the other German children but Lies to her Dutch schoolmates, who could not pronounce Hannah—was six months older than Anne. She was considerably taller but just as delicate—indeed, skinny—and wore her brown hair in ringlets. She was extremely gentle and shy. Susanne Ledermann, whom Anne called Sanne but whose parents and sister continued to call her the more German Susi, was also about six months older than Anne. A quiet, intelligent child, Sanne was less volatile and playful than Anne; even when she smiled her dark eyes seemed serious. The trio of girls, soon inseparable,

Hannah Goslar, Anne Frank, Dolly Citroën, Hannah Toby, Barbara Ledermann, Sanne Ledermann (from left to right), Amsterdam, 1937

was known as Anne, Hanne, and Sanne. Their parents were pleased that they had developed a close friendship that transcended the common circumstances that had brought them together.

Merwedeplein was the center of the River Quarter. Unlike the leafy neighborhood around Ganghoferstrasse in Frankfurt, which was a paradise for children, this triangular plaza was urban and rather bare. At the point of the equilateral triangle stood *De Wolkenkrabber*—the skyscraper—which rose a staggering twelve stories, twice the height of the other buildings. Its upper stories afforded a view over the entire quarter. The buildings to the left of the skyscraper were odd-numbered, those to the right even-numbered. Each building was like the next, its simple facade sand-colored brick, its shutters a plain white, its balconies in back just large enough for two chaise longues. This was modern city planning, uncomplicated, versatile, inexpensive, without history and without profile—and perhaps for those very reasons perfect for people who had to start afresh. The Franks lived on the third floor of the fifth house on the left side of the street, at 37 Merwedeplein, the number—as was customary in Holland—indicating the apartment rather than the building.

The skyscraper, at the base of which people could keep their bicycles for a monthly parking fee, was the meeting place for the older children. The younger ones congregated in the middle of the plaza, which—like other parts of the quarter—was still under construction in 1934 and resembled an oversized sandbox in which the children could build sand castles, dig tunnels, bake sand cakes, and fight sand battles.

Later, the plaza was landscaped. Symmetrically placed shrubs and trees separated the asphalt of the street from the lawn in the center. The grass was not, however, a delicate decorative variety but a rugged turf suitable for a playground. On Amsterdam's rare sunny days, the neighborhood children would be out on the Merwedeplein, those who lived on the left side in a separate group from

Merwedeplein with the "skyscraper" in the background, Amsterdam Zuid, ca. 1936. The Franks lived in the third-story apartment marked in the right foreground of the picture.

those who lived on the right. It was not particularly easy for newcomers to join in, unless they happened to be as outgoing and self-confident as Anne.

A child who wanted to pick up a friend to play would not knock on the door or ring the bell but whistle a tune agreed upon beforehand. Anyone who could not whistle—and Anne, with her overbite, could not—had to resort to something else. If Anne wanted to call a friend to play, she had to sing the tune.

In the trees and shrubbery and on the grass in the middle of the plaza, the children played hide-and-seek, tag, and catch, and shot marbles. There were always enough children for games like stickball. The girls did handstands and cartwheels and jumped rope. On the sidewalks they played hopscotch, raced about on scooters and roller skates, and rolled hoops, whipping them along with small sticks.

Starting in 1933, many Jewish families moved into the neighborhood, most of them immigrants from Germany and, from 1938 on, from Austria as well, all of them in search of reasonably priced lodgings. When the Franks moved into their apartment on Merwedeplein, many others in the quarter were still empty. Eventually, though, 50,000 people were living in the River Quarter of Amsterdam, 32 percent of them Jews.

The parents often became acquainted through their children, and most of the people they met were fellow exiles. Their common fate bound them together, eradicating differences in background and social class. The Dutch population, however, greeted the influx of foreigners, non-Jews as well as Jews, with mixed feelings. As the number of immigrants increased, tolerance and a willingness to help them began to give way to fears of being overwhelmed by this alien element. As early as January 1934, Dutch immigration authorities had registered 4,200 Jewish refugees from Germany, and the numbers grew in the next few years.

German dominated on the streetcar lines connecting South Amsterdam with the center of town. Even the conductors spoke German, and these lines were nicknamed the Orient Express. The Dutch were not amused, and many of them chose to keep their distance; a German was a German, after all, whether an Aryan or a Jew. (The popular Dutch term for Germans was *Moffen*, or muffs, a pejorative whose meaning and derivation are unclear.) But the Jews, for their part, were intent on becoming part of Dutch society, and with time, contact with their Dutch neighbors increased. Once again, the children—who picked up the language more quickly and attended school with Dutch children—were the ones to break the ice.

Edith and Otto Frank cultivated friendships with families they knew from Frankfurt but actively developed new ones. They soon became close friends with the Goslars and the Ledermanns. A few months after the Franks, the Goslars, too, had emigrated to Holland and moved to Merwedeplein. Hans Goslar was Otto Frank's age. From 1919 to 1932, he had run the Prussian government's press office. Ruth, twelve years younger than her husband and therefore about Edith Frank's age, was the daughter of a Zionist lawyer and had worked as a teacher before her marriage.

As director of the press office, Hans Goslar had been a high-ranking official with correspondingly imposing titles: Prussian press chief, governmental councillor, and, from 1926 on, ministerial councillor. "Without Goslar," the Prussian minister of the interior, Carl Severing, had said, "we would have remained stymied on many occasions. He is not only a man of indefatigable energy but also one with extraordinary knowledge and a phenomenal memory. To the Nazis he is enemy number one. Their hatred can only raise him in the esteem of a democrat."

In 1932, Goslar was relieved of his post without notice. Hitler had not yet assumed power, and yet a Jew like Goslar—who throughout his years of government service observed the Jewish Sabbath but spent every Sunday working alone in his office—must have been an unwelcome annoyance to those who were already obeying their future masters. Many a political party chose to remove its Jewish members from prominent positions at this time.

Like Otto Frank, Hans Goslar had been raised in an assimilated family; unlike the Franks, though, his family put up a traditional candle-lit Christmas tree every year. In Eastern Europe, where he served during World War I, he became acquainted with the emotional power of Hasidism. A Social Democratic Zionist when he left, he came back to Berlin a religious man who saw it as his duty to "immerse himself in the spirit and rituals of Jewish theology."

In 1933, a professional opportunity presented itself. The Unilever company in London offered him an attractive job, and the Goslars moved to England. But when it turned out that his new employers could not—or perhaps did not want to—grant him his

Sabbath, he chose to give up his secure position and income. Moving next to Amsterdam, which he regarded as an interim station on the way to Palestine, he established a consulting business for Jewish emigrés. To save on rent, he set up his office in the family apartment at 31 Merwedeplein in the building next to the Franks, and his wife, Ruth, took on the job of office manager. Franz Ledermann, an attorney and notary, became his partner. Ledermann was the same age as Otto Frank and Hans Goslar; his wife, Ilse Citroën Ledermann, was Dutch by birth and four years younger than Edith Frank. With their daughters, Barbara and Susanne, they, too, had emigrated to Amsterdam from Germany.

For many years, the Ledermanns had spent their summer vacations visiting relatives in Holland. In 1933, a brother-in-law of Ilse's, a journalist with the newspaper *De Haagse Post*, warned them against returning to Germany. Nine years earlier, he had covered Hitler's trial for treason in Munich and had fully grasped the situation even back then: this man, who had led the November 1923 putsch against the federal government and the march on the Feldherrnhalle (field marshals hall) in Munich, was not one to be stopped by a prison sentence. On the contrary: it would only make him more dangerous. At the trial, the Bavarian judges hadn't even interrupted his demagogic speeches and his attacks on the Weimar Republic. Now that this rabblerouser had become Reich chancellor, he would make good on his threats, of that Ilse Ledermann's brother-in-law was sure.

Ilse Ledermann would have preferred to stay in Holland, but her husband balked at the idea. His practice in Berlin was flourishing, they were enjoying great prosperity, they moved in the best social circles. In Holland, he would not be admitted to the bar. He knew only a few words of Dutch. And he was a German, after all. He knew many decent Germans. They would never let things get out of hand. But by mid-1933, Franz Ledermann began to feel the effects of the boycott against Jewish lawyers. He lost his most

Sanne, Ilse, Barbara, and Franz Ledermann, Noorder Amstellaan, ca. 1936

important clients and was only allowed to represent Jews. When his income plummeted, he agreed to emigrate. Now, together with Hans Goslar, he was helping his fellow immigrants deal with their financial and legal problems. Among other things, the two of them tried to help German immigrants trade the property they owned for real estate in other countries. Meanwhile, Ledermann studied Dutch law, and after three years he was admitted to the bar in Holland.

That the three families had moved in separate circles at home hardly mattered in this new country. The Franks were invited to the Goslars every Friday evening, sometimes for tea or coffee after dinner and often for dinner. The Sabbath candles would already have been lit, and Hans Goslar would have just returned from services at the synagogue and blessed his daughter, Hanneli. It meant a great deal to Edith Frank to participate in the Sabbath ritual at the Goslars. Hans Goslar pronounced the Hebrew blessing over the kiddush cup before the Sabbath meal, washed his hands in the special bowl, and, finally, blessed the two braided Sabbath loaves and passed pieces to everyone at the table. These were the same Friday-evening rituals Edith's parents had observed in her Aachen home. She had not missed them in Frankfurt, but now, in exile, they gave her strength and a sense of continuity in this alien, bewildering environment. Otto, however, was unfamiliar with religious Judaism and did not understand the Hebrew blessings. He had not even been bar mitzvahed. Nonetheless, he listened attentively and respectfully on these Friday evenings. "I see what a firm foundation religion provides a person," he admitted later, "but it just doesn't speak to me."

Edith would have liked to invite the Goslars to her home, but Ruth Goslar, at her husband's request, kept a kosher household, and the Goslars could not have eaten anything at the Franks'. In fact, Ruth Goslar rarely attended the afternoon coffee circles that the immigrant wives held at the Franks' and in other apartments, though not, primarily, for religious reasons but because she worked all day as her husband's secretary and had no time for such small pleasures.

For most of the other wives, the majority of them upper- and middle-class Germans accustomed to the help of housekeepers, cooks, and governesses, these gatherings were welcome opportunities to vent their frustrations. Their husbands, anxious about the future, were busy trying to establish themselves professionally and their children were attending school, some of them initially a special program in the Rivierenbuurt designed for German-speaking newcomers. The children slipped effortlessly into their new lives and learned their new language easily.

At first the German children had some problems with Dutch words that looked like German ones but meant something different. The notice "*3 x bellen*"—"Ring 3 times"—often appeared under doorbells. But instead of ringing three times, as the residents intended their visitors to do, the German children would bark three times like little dogs. (*Bellen* means "to bark" in German.) And the door sign that read "*Aan de deur wordt niet gekocht*" left them weak with laughter. "At the door nothing is cooked," they joked, although they had all long since learned that *gekocht* was the equivalent of *gekauft* in German. "Here nothing will be bought" was the meaning. In other words, "No solicitors."

But the children's mothers were having a hard time adjusting. Their sorrows and complaints varied, but they all agreed on certain things. The Dutch domestics, for one, were a catastrophe: Mrs. X's girl had done this or that wrong, Mrs. Y's simply could not be relied on—these ladies, strikingly well dressed by Dutch standards, rarely bothered to refer to maids by name. There was nothing wrong with Amsterdam—it was a pretty city, quite pleasant and friendly—but in Germany, things had been far superior. The ladies could not wait to return home. All of them had had to abandon their former standard of living and learn to make do. As for the language, well, it *wasn't* a real language; it was—and here they clutched their throats—an affliction of the larynx. Dutch did have one advantage: it was easy to learn—for anyone who wanted to learn it, that is.

Like many other German immigrants, Edith Frank seems to have been incapable of mastering the pronunciation. Her wooden-sounding German accent embarrassed her children and made them feel that their parents were at a total loss with the language.

Whether Edith Frank gave up her intensive course in Dutch after the second lesson, as people maintain even today, is uncertain. But her written Dutch, apart from a few Germanicisms, was soon quite passable. A note she wrote in late June 1935 to Bep Hofhuis, the wife of the Pomosin Utrecht director, to congratulate her on the birth of their son Frans confirms this. The Hofhuis family lived around the corner from the Franks on Noorder Amstellaan, the present-day Churchillaan. Edith frequently invited Bep over for a

Sunday coffee klatch. The two women from very different backgrounds got along well. Bep was amazed at Edith's seriousness and religiousness—also by her beautifully embroidered tablecloths and her handsome silver. The families remained in touch even after the Hofhuises moved to Hilversum two months after the baby's birth.

"Imagine. Today I have to register Anne at school," Edith Frank wrote to Gertrud Naumann on March 26, 1935. "Anne will probably continue on in the Montessori school." The pedagogical principles that Maria Montessori had developed thirty or so years earlier, with their emphasis on self-motivation and individuality, were perfectly suited to a strong-willed and obstinate child like Anne Frank. Eschewing the conventional division of children into grades, the system allowed more tolerance both for those who were ahead of their age group and for those who were behind. At the start of each school day pupils chose what they would do, whether alone or in a group. Anyone who wanted to draw could draw, anyone who

Otto Heinrich Frank in the sixth year at the Lessing Gymnasium, Frankfurt, 1904.

wanted to do arithmetic could play with an abacus; the main thing was that the pupils concentrate on whatever they had chosen to do. Anne read a lot. She had begun reading a few months earlier, probably imitating Margot. In January 1935 Edith Frank had written to her family, "Anne is learning to read with great difficulty." "With great difficulty" was underlined.

We do not know if Edith and Otto Frank studied the writings of Maria Montessori. They themselves had been educated in the best German tradition. At the humanistic Lessing Gymnasium in Frankfurt, Otto Frank had learned Latin and Greek and in the spring of 1908 had passed his final exams, the only Jewish pupil in his class. Starting in 1906, Edith had attended the Victoria School in Aachen, a privately chartered Protestant girls' school supported in part by the Women's Educational Society of Aachen and Burtscheid. The school's charter made explicit provision for enrolling non-Protestant pupils. Edith's first foreign language was French. She also studied English and, as part of obligatory Jewish religious instruction at school, Hebrew. She graduated in 1916.

Edith Frank (back row, fourth from left) in her class graduation picture, Victoria School in Aachen, 1916.

For Margot, who could tolerate regimentation more easily than Anne, the Franks thought a traditional education similar to their own was appropriate, and they sent her to a conventional elementary school, the Jekerschool; perhaps they feared that their obedient, diligent, retiring daughter would be overwhelmed—and overlooked—in the freewheeling environment of the Montessori school.

Every morning Margot and Barbara Ledermann rode their bicycles side by side to the elementary school on Jekerstraat, two little beauties, admired and envied. They were nicknamed Snow White and Rose Red, though Day and Night would have suited them just as well, for Barbara, with her blond hair and inquisitive blue eyes, was a rebel from early childhood, while Margot with her dark, gleaming pageboy and her innocent gaze was a dutiful, good-natured, and hard-working girl. Margot was a model pupil; Barbara, by contrast, was a hopeless case academically.

Like the other immigrant children accustomed to the German school system, they both tried hard to make a good impression. Where they came from, pupils had to stand when they were called on, and so they leapt to their feet and stood at attention whenever the teacher said their names. Their Dutch classmates made fun of them, and the teachers, too, had trouble suppressing their laughter.

But they soon adapted to the more modern ways in Holland. The language was harder to adjust to. On her first dictation, Barbara made forty mistakes. Even Margot got back a paper with about twenty-five corrections on it. Margot worked hard, however, and soon became one of the best students in her class. But Barbara—who liked nothing about the school day except the moment when it ended—might not have been promoted without the help of her conscientious friend.

When Anne entered the Montessori school, the pedagogical theory and practice of "the most interesting woman in Europe," as the innovative educator had been dubbed in the United States, was already forbidden in Germany; Montessori education was hardly compatible with Nazi totalitarianism. In Aachen, Helene Helming, the supervisor of the Catholic Montessori teachers, had been forbidden to work. Montessori schools had been closed all over the country because their principals had refused to observe the government-prescribed "Jewish quotas." In Berlin, two Socialist Montessori teachers had disappeared without a trace, and Montessori's writings had been burned. From 1933 to 1939, Maria Montessori herself would live in Holland because, after a stay in Barcelona, she was no longer permitted to work in Italy, her now-Fascist homeland.

Anne, playful, lively, and easily distracted, enjoyed school and the freedom her teacher, Jan van Gelder, a moderate Communist, gave the children. They were allowed to do almost anything and were required, so it seemed, to do very little. In Anne's class, almost half the children were Jewish, many of them from German families. The school made considerable allowances for these children, who were slowly ridding themselves of their accents. The teachers did not make excessive demands of them but gave them time to adapt to their new surroundings. Anne—Annelies to her Dutch schoolmates—was not forced to struggle with arithmetic much, for example. Nor was Hanneli Goslar or their mutual friend Kitty Egyedi. There were plenty of other things to do. Anne began writing stories very early. Kitty displayed a remarkable talent for drawing and liked to arrange words and letters in patterns that suited her playful visual imagination, sometimes running all the words in a sentence together, other times spacing the letters far apart. The Montessori school not only tolerated such unorthodoxy but encouraged it. When arithmetic was the order of the day, it was taught in the form of a game. If, for example, Mr. van Gelder asked the children what two times one was and no one knew the answer, he would take the children by the hand one at a time and hop with them up and down the rows of desks, counting as they went. Two hops times one was two. Three hops times two was . . . six. There would be smiles all around.

Children from Orthodox families were not required to attend school on Saturdays. Sol Kimmel was among them, a small, chubby boy with blond hair and blue eyes. Even as a five-year-old, Anne was drawn to him, perhaps because he had no father and she felt sorry for him or because he could be very funny; at any rate, she decided she would marry him. His cousin, Ab Reiner, was slim and dark-haired and clearly the more attractive. He, too, was absent from school on Saturdays, as was Hanneli Goslar, with whom Anne, once she was considered advanced enough for nightly homework, made an agreement that she kept for the rest of their time in school. They never saw each other on Saturdays, which Hanne spent with her Sabbath friend Ilse Wagner and Anne spent with Sanne, who, like Margot, attended the Jekerschool. But every Sunday, after Hanne had come home from her religion lesson, Anne gave her the previous day's assignment. Then they played together, either at the Goslars' or at the Franks' apartment.

The Franks kept a warm, hospitable home where their daughters' Dutch and immigrant friends were always welcome. Children loved to visit the Franks' house: life seemed more elegant than it was at home. Mrs. Frank served delicious rolls topped with cream cheese and chocolate bits, cold lemonade, and bottled milk, a particular treat. Ordinarily, grocers ladled milk from a large can into jars that customers brought with them to the store; bottled milk was more expensive. The Franks even had central heating—a rare luxury. And if you stayed for a meal, the dining table was equipped with a lazy Susan you could spin around and choose your dishes from. Water was served with the meal. That in itself delighted Hanneli, who at home was allowed to drink water only after meals. At Anne's, too, she could be freer about the Jewish dietary laws, which her parents did not expect her to observe as strictly as they did.

The greatest delight of all was Mr. Frank. His wife was always there and always friendly, but the children hardly noticed her; they took such things for granted in mothers. But Otto Frank, at almost six feet a tall man for those days, was special. With Mr. Frank you could talk and joke about anything. He made up games, told stories, always had a comforting word, and seemed to forgive Anne everything, even when she was stubborn and insisted on having the last word. Margot and Anne adored their father, whose close-cropped moustache and fringe of thinning hair were already turning gray. Their adoration was well-founded. Otto's high spirits were truly infectious. And when he was at home he spent more time with his children than most other fathers did.

What they could not know, both because Otto Frank knew how to keep some things to himself and also because he was blessed with a truly optimistic nature, was that he was working harder than ever before and had more than his share of worries. "I'm under way almost daily and come home only in the evening. It's not like it was in Frankfurt, where I came home at noon and could rest a bit. There's no letup all day," he wrote to Gertrud Naumann, probably in 1934.

His business was off to a slow start, hampered by its seasonal character: when he launched it in the fall of 1933, the fruits for making jams and jellies had long since been harvested, and Dutch housewives had already put up their strawberries and apricots, as they'd done for years, without the help of Opekta pectin. Extended trips throughout Holland, like one he made in October 1933 to a weeklong fair for household goods staged by the magazine *Dameskroniek* in Rotterdam, were wearying but essential for his young business, but they brought only modest returns.

In this start-up phase of his enterprise, Otto Frank received urgently needed support from his uncle Armand Geiershöfer, a glove manufacturer in Luxemburg who twice in the course of 1934 transferred funds to Otto's business account. Help amounting to at least "80,000 Gulden in the form of advertising" as well as in "cash" came from Rovag in Switzerland.

"Business prospects are unfortunately very poor," Edith complained year after year, "but we mustn't lose heart." Even establishing a distribution network proved arduous. The new product, available as a liquid or a powder, was to be sold primarily in drugstores, especially in rural areas. Otto had to be a high-powered salesman on two fronts: first, he had to convince skeptical housewives of his product's effectiveness and, second, he had to convince retailers that housewives would actually buy it. Unable to afford a large office staff or representatives, he had to travel a lot himself. "Papi left again Monday for a whole week," Edith wrote in October 1934. And again: "Mr. Frank hasn't taken any time off and looks thin and tired."

When Otto was away, Victor Gustav Kugler ran the office. This trained electrician and mechanic knew the business better than Otto did and was also someone with whom Otto could speak in his native language. Born in Austria in 1900, Kugler had lived in Utrecht since 1920 and had spent several years working for Pomosin Import Utrecht. Kugler, whose impeccable grooming and clothing reflected a somewhat rigid nature, had originally been designated to establish Opekta Amsterdam himself. Apparently that plan was not progressing quickly enough to suit Opekta's founder, Robert Feix. When Feix therefore decided in favor of Otto Frank, Kugler agreed to go to work for Frank and from then on commuted daily between his residence in Hilversum and the office in Amsterdam.

A young Austrian woman soon proved to be a great asset to the new business. When the first secretary Otto hired fell ill in the fall of 1933 and was absent for days at a time, he had to find a replacement for her. One of his sales representatives knew that her neighbor's daughter was looking for a job and passed Otto's business card on to her. He took an instant liking to Hermine Santrouschitz, who was born in Vienna. "She is a very unselfish person," Otto Frank soon realized

A petite woman in her midtwenties with dark blond, wavy hair and a round face, she was unassuming yet confident, calm, and forceful, an able assistant who did not stand on ceremony but settled right down to work. Shortly after World War I, when she was eleven, she had been sent to Holland as part of a program for ill and undernourished children. The emaciated child was to have stayed only a few months until she recuperated from the effects of postwar poverty in Austria, but she remained for the rest of her life. Once she had recovered from the initial shock of leaving home, she felt happier with her foster parents than she had with her own. Her return to Austria was postponed again and again, her foster parents changed her name, Hermine—difficult for the Dutch to pronounce—to Miep, and when she turned sixteen and had to decide whether she would remain in Holland for good, it was an easy decision.

Miep quickly became the mainstay of the office. She handled the correspondence, did the billing, made coffee, responded to customers' telephone and written queries and complaints, tirelessly explained the proper proportions of Opekta pectin to fresh fruit, and placed ads in magazines and newspapers. When Otto hired women to demonstrate his product to housewives around the country, Miep sometimes trained them and accompanied them on their travels. Today one would call her a marketing consultant.

Gradually, the employer-employee relationship evolved into a less formal one verging on friendship. Otto Frank, for his part, could depend on Miep not to overstep the bounds of propriety; for hers, he was a cultivated, educated upper-middle-class gentleman, kind and considerate and therefore all the more worthy of respect—an employer, in short, whom she held in high esteem but to whom she did not feel subservient. She was pleased when Otto Frank invited her and her boyfriend, Jan Gies, for dinner.

At the Franks' hospitable home, Miep and Jan noted the contrast between the elegant, expensive furniture the family had brought from Germany—Edith's graceful little writing desk, the stately grandfather clock, the extensive library—and the cheerful clutter of dolls and toys, crayons and children's drawings; it was clear who ran the household: the two charmingly dressed, well-behaved little girls. However self-confident and forward Anne may have been among family and friends, she was initially shy around strangers. But soon she warmed up and began asking lots of questions and making people laugh with funny faces. Though Jan and Miep spoke Dutch with the two girls, they spoke German with Otto and Edith, who were still struggling with the language.

Edith usually greeted people visiting for the first time with a polite reserve that could easily be misinterpreted as aloofness, coldness, indeed snobbery, but she, too, soon warmed to her guests in the course of conversation. Those who knew her better regarded her as witty and quick. Despite her elegant clothes, she made a somewhat frumpy impression. She had worn her hair in a modern pageboy cut for years, but in Amsterdam she had let it grow and now gathered it in a knot at the nape of her neck, an unstylish hairdo for a woman of only thirty-five. She seemed to be turning from a vital young woman into a stodgy matron. Edith was not happy; that was obvious. But when she spoke of Germany, of her youth in Aachen, of her experiences as a young mother in Frankfurt, and of her family at home, the nostalgic smile that crossed her face made her look years younger.

Edith had good reason to feel lonely and isolated. Preoccupied with his work, Otto was seldom home and struggling, as he said, "to put food on the table and get ahead." Anne and Margot had long since adapted completely to Dutch life and remembered little about their earlier home. Of course, Edith had enough household chores to keep her busy. Like her immigrant friends, she had always been able to rely on the help of a housekeeper, cook, and governess, but now she had to do everything herself. "We haven't had any household help since October," she wrote to Gertrud Naumann in June 1935, "and the children, whom you taught so well, are helping me." She was also a busy hostess. Unobtrusive, almost unnoticed, remaining in the background, she was nonetheless responsible for the pleasant domestic atmosphere. And she was constantly concerned about Margot's and Anne's health.

Anne especially was prone to illness and often bedridden. "Anne still has to spend time in bed because of a lingering flu she came down with in October," Edith wrote on December 27, 1935. "But fortunately she has recovered well in recent days. She gets up often during the day, enjoys being spoiled, and doesn't miss school much. Her teacher, an extremely nice man, came to visit her not long ago." But the delicate girl—who, despite her rambunctious temperament, had acquired both at home and at school a nickname of Otto's mother's devising, *Zärtlein* (fragile one)—was often absent for weeks at a time. At first she had the usual childhood illnesses—whooping cough, chicken pox, and in December 1936, measles. Then came a constantly recurring fever that, though mild, nonetheless sapped her strength. Anne had heart trouble, some people said. Maybe she had been a blue baby, others theorized. Still others suspected rheumatic fever.

At the beginning of 1937 Anne was sick again, but on January 18 Edith could write, "Anne was out on the street for ten minutes today for the first time, and we hope she'll continue to recover well." But not until a year later, in the spring of 1938, could her mother breathe a sigh of relief. "We're delighted that Anne is somewhat stronger now." Still, the frail-looking child had to be careful. In gym she almost always sat on the spectators' bench, though not entirely because of her fragile constitution. She had a trick shoulder and couldn't do somersaults or cartwheels for fear of dislocating it.

But throwing her shoulder out was evidently painless, because once she had mastered the art of popping it in and out, she entertained her friends with her new talent. She liked astonishing her schoolmates—and making them wince. Most of all, she liked being the center of attention.

Still hoping that she would soon be able to return to her homeland, Edith Frank kept in close touch with her family in Germany. She wrote detailed letters to them when time permitted, and she was delighted when a relative, her mother in particular, came to visit. Oma Holländer usually stayed for several weeks and assisted with the household. "We are very much looking forward to mother's visit. I can really use her help," Edith confessed. When her mother wasn't helping out, she sat quietly in a comfortable chair, as unobtrusive as a tasteful piece of furniture that no one noticed at first but that made everyone in the room feel warm and content. Edith and her mother were particularly close, surely in part because the death of Edith's older sister, Betty, at sixteen had brought them together.

There were also visits from Otto's relatives, among them his younger brother, Herbert, who continued to struggle, unsuccessfully, to establish himself in Paris. Anne delighted in calling him Uncle Blue Dot after she discovered a tiny birthmark to one side of his nose. Otto's cousin Arnold, who had worked in the family business in Frankfurt, also came, as did his cousin Milly Stanfield, a gifted cellist who had studied at the Royal Academy of Music in London and the Ecole Normale de Musique in Paris and had made a name for herself as a music critic.

Family members from Basel came often, among them Stephan Elias. A letter he wrote home described the easy relationship between Otto Frank and his children. "Anne is awake by six in the morning. Then we have a chat. Otto comes and crawls into bed with Anne, and Margot comes downstairs."

On another occasion Stephan arrived with his mother, Aunt Leni. "Do you sometimes think back on the summer you were in Zandvoort?" Margot wrote to him on his birthday on December 20, 1936, referring to a favorite seaside resort not far from Amsterdam where he had gone with her.

Another visitor was Otto's mother, whose imperious manner Anne's friends found intimidating. In a stern, reproachful, not entirely grandmotherly tone, she would say, "Good morning, Hanneli, good morning," if Hanne, who had come to play, neglected to greet her first. And Hanne often neglected to do so, not out of rudeness most likely but simply because she was shy.

Edith Frank heard from her aunts and cousins that their circles were shrinking, that they felt more cut off every day. Those of her relatives who had opportunities abroad and could afford to leave were abandoning Germany, driven out by the increasingly harsh measures against Jews. They were no longer granted rights or their individual identities. The Franks, it seemed, had emigrated just in time. The Reich's Law of Citizenship of September 15, 1935, had declared Germany's Jews aliens in their own country. They were not even second-class citizens; they were last-class citizens, unable to vote. That same day the Nuremberg Laws were promulgated to "protect German blood" from all "alien blood." In the interest of "preserving the purity of the German nation," the Nuremberg Laws spelled out in detail the definitions of "Aryan and Jewish, half and quarter Jewish, related to Jews by marriage, and racially pure." To discriminate against Jews, to persecute them, was thus legally sanctioned. Germans were now free to indulge their bigotry and hatred knowing they were in compliance with the law, a reassuring feeling for people with a strong traditional respect for governmental authority.

Every government agency and every official document noted the degree to which an individual was "Aryan," "Jewish," or "related to Jews." Marriage between Jews and non-Jews, branded as "racial defilement," was prohibited and punishable by law. Jewish lawyers could have only Jewish clients; Jewish doctors could treat only Jewish patients. Jews who employed Christians as domestics were liable to prosecution. Jews who raised a German flag could be arrested. Forced labor, concentration camps, Dachau, Sachsenhausen-Oranienburg—all became fear-inspiring words, the weapons of a system of organized oppression. Respectable "Aryans" had been persuaded that contact with Jewish parasites was harmful to the German people. And in fact a frighteningly large number of "good" German citizens informed their Jewish friends and acquaintances that they could no longer associate with them. Fearfully, obediently, they asked their Jewish neighbors not to say hello to them anymore on the stairs in their apartment houses, much less on the street.

In October 1937 Ursula Kronheim, the elder daughter of Edith's cousin Irene, made a stop in Amsterdam on her way to join her family in Peru. Irene had sold the expensive furnishings of her apartment to an "Aryan" for barely a quarter of their value and in February 1937 had left Dortmund with her younger daughter, Dorothée, and her mother, Mathilde Berg Holländer. She had not been able to get a visa for the United States, but her brother was already in Peru and expecting them there. Irene had only been able to get three tickets for the boat. She decided to leave twelve-year-old Ursula—or Ulla, as she was known—in the care of her aunts until a fourth ticket could be procured.

Now Ulla was about to sail. With her hand luggage, twenty dollars in travel money, and the Franks' telephone number in her purse, she had set out for Amsterdam from Cologne, where she had been finishing out the year at the Jewish school. It had been arranged for her to spend the night with the Franks and board her boat the next day. Otto was to take her to the port at Rotterdam. But Ulla's divorced father had followed her to Amsterdam and tried to keep her from leaving. A scene ensued, with angry words and shouting, horrifying to an insecure girl scarred by the anti-Semitic hostility she had experienced in Germany. A Jewish attorney who had lost an arm in World War I, Walter Kronheim was dependent on an ever-shrinking Jewish clientele and far in arrears with his child support; no doubt desperate, he would not give in until Otto Frank threatened to call the police. Ulla departed on the steamer, traveling first class but alone. A long time would pass before she could put the incident behind her, overcome her fear, mistrust, and suspicion, talk about her childhood in Germany, and make peace with her family.

The Franks waited in vain for a visit from their Frankfurt friend Gertrud Naumann. After having worked as a secretary for a Jewish textile firm, she now had a job with I. G. Farben, the chemical manufacturers. "I hope to see you here sometime, if everything works out," Otto Frank had written to her soon after his arrival in Amsterdam, and he had extended the invitation again in subsequent years. But the trip was out of the question for Gertrud. Her mother was often ill, and her father, as a devout Catholic and a democrat, was under attack. Nazi aggression was directed not only at Jews but also at political opponents; anyone who did not believe in the Third Reich or who opposed its laws was an enemy. Anyone who refused to greet others with "Heil Hitler!" was an enemy, too. Criticism or jokes about the government—even the expression of the most tentative doubts—were regarded as treasonous.

"A centrist hypocrite lives here! Subversive politics from the pulpit!" The Nazis scrawled these slogans on the wall in front of the Naumanns' home at 303 Marbachweg, denouncing Gertrud's father as a Catholic rather than as a teacher. In the school where he taught, he was regarded as an enemy of the regime, and the administration was constantly looking for an excuse to get rid of him.

They soon found one. In a manual-arts class, he had asked his students to bring in newspapers for a bookbinding project. Word reached the school administration that one student had used pages from a Communist newspaper. Accused of being responsible for this outrage, Naumann was dismissed immediately, and the Gestapo searched the family's apartment. Thereafter he could work only as a substitute teacher in various schools.

The Franks learned all this only later. Afraid of the censors—a justified fear, as it happened—the Franks and their correspondents wrote only innocuous letters, chatting about this and that, sending good wishes, and exchanging gifts and sometimes photos. Otto's former secretary, Emeline Schneider, was commissioned to find nice birthday presents for Gertrud on the Franks' behalf. Gertrud sent back handmade gifts for the children. "The little combing shawls are utterly charming. Many thanks," Edith wrote in January 1938, delighted with the garments Gertrud had sewn from a flower-print material and trimmed with delicately scalloped red ribbon. Gertrud called the fine stitches she used "mouse-tooth stitching."

Still, there were a few opportunities to meet after 1933. "We have at least seen each other and had a chance to talk. Let's hope we'll have another chance again soon," Edith wrote after a short visit to Frankfurt in October 1936. A year earlier she had sent this message to Gertrud: "Just think! My husband and Margot may travel to Basel by way of Aachen and Frankfurt. They'll have only one day in Frankfurt, but they will want to see you no matter what and will let you know well ahead of time."

In December 1935 Otto and Margot went to Switzerland for Alice Stern Frank's seventieth birthday, although it is not known whether they stopped in Frankfurt. From Basel they continued on to the resort town of Adelboden in the Bernese Oberland. Margot learned to ski, and her cousin Bernd Elias taught her to skate. "This morning and afternoon I was on skis for the first time," she wrote in a postcard to a school friend, Edith Jacobsohn. Anne does not seem to have gone along on this trip. She was recovering slowly from a bad case of flu and probably spent the New Year's holiday with her Oma in Aachen.

But a few months earlier, in June 1935, six-year-old Anne, too, had visited Switzerland. "Anne has gone to Basel with Omi," Edith wrote, after her mother-in-law had left Amsterdam and she herself had gone to Aachen. Anne spent a few sunny days with her grandmother in Sils Maria in the Oberengadin. It was so warm that she could take off her blouse and play outdoors with just her skirt on. Anne seemed happy and relaxed. She stayed in the Villa Larêt, a luxurious country house that belonged to a relative, Olga Wolfsohn Spitzer, a second cousin of Otto Frank's. Born in Paris, Aunt O, as the children called her, was French to the core, rich, educated, and

Anne Frank, Sils Maria, 1935

generous. Her father had been a stockbroker; her husband, Arthur Spitzer, originally from Vienna, had founded the Spitzer Bank in Paris and, about 1910, had built the Villa Larêt for his wife. Socially and politically active, she had founded an organization called Le Service Social de l'Enfance en Danger Moral in the 1920s to provide aid to children and young people at risk. Later, she was instrumental in establishing France's first courts for juvenile offenders. The profession of *assistant social*, or social worker, in France can be traced back to her efforts.

Year after year, Olga, who knew hardly a word of German, invited her German relatives to Sils Maria for summer holidays. Villa Larêt was a welcoming house, grander than the Franks were accustomed to but by no means ostentatious. Manners were more formal there but not impossibly stuffy, and the staff, in uniforms and white gloves, were friendly though correct.

Anne visited Sils Maria again in the summer of 1936, this time with her mother and Margot, and she remembered it fondly. "How are things with you?" she wrote to her grandmother in July 1941, when the Franks could no longer go abroad themselves. "Is it nice in Sils Maria?"

When Anne went to Basel, she spent her time with her cousin Bernd. Although he was four years older than she, they got on famously. His parents called him Buddy, but to Anne he was Bernd. He had wheeled her through the streets of Frankfurt in a baby carriage, one time taking a curve a little too fast and tipping the carriage over; Anne was unharmed. After the Elias family moved to Basel, the children saw each other only occasionally, and Anne most likely had little memory of him. Now they became reacquainted, and the difference in their ages didn't seem to matter. They were much alike—sassy, playful, imaginative, and tireless. They were constantly thinking up new pranks and inventing games. They raided their grandmother's closet and dressed up in her clothes or entertained the adults with puppet shows and skits in German. Bernd didn't hit it off nearly so well with Margot, even though she was closer to his age and they had often played together in Frankfurt. Margot was too serious and had no talent for silliness. She was a little lady who didn't get dirty. Anne could be enlisted for any crazy scheme.

It may also be that Anne was more impressed with him than Margot was. She particularly admired his virtuosity as an ice skater, the way he could dance and do gymnastics on skates and the way he got up laughing after falls that would have left anyone else lying on the ice in pain. Back home in Amsterdam, Anne, too, enjoyed skating, and in a letter to her relatives in Basel in early January 1941, she dreamed of future triumphs on the ice, hoping one day to skate as well as Bernd. "Perhaps we could appear together," she suggested to them, "but then I'll have to train very hard to get as good as you."

Probably she never skated with Bernd, although she did go to Switzerland once in the winter, most likely in 1937. "Last week my husband had to go to Basel and, to Anne's great delight, he took her with him," Edith wrote in a letter she dated December 22 without noting the year. "For two years she has been hoping to take a trip with her Papi . . . and since Uncle Robert and Uncle Herbert are there too, the timing could not be better."

In 1938, as the situation for Jews in Germany was becoming increasingly threatening, Otto Frank again visited the Naumanns on Marbachweg. Everyone had much to tell—Otto about Anne and Margot, Edith, and life in Amsterdam, the Naumanns about the political situation in Frankfurt, Gertrud's progress at her job, and her desire for a husband. When Gertrud accompanied Otto to the streetcar stop, he suddenly became nervous. All it took these days was for one malicious person to spy a Jewish man and a young Gentile woman together. If they catch us, he whispered to her, we'll both be arrested.

5

GROWING DANGER

It was one of those typical damp, cold days in Amsterdam when autumn finally gives way to winter, a gray afternoon near the end of November 1938, and nine-year-old Anne was on her way home from the Montessori school with a group of girls that included Hanneli Goslar and a Dutch schoolmate, Iet Swillens. Indifferent to the wind and cold, the girls meandered along Niersstraat, turned right onto Maasstraat, then left onto Zuider Amstellaan, the wide boulevard (now called Rooseveltlaan) that angles through the River Quarter, passing the Merwedeplein. The route probably can be covered in five minutes, ten at most, but as usual the girls let themselves be sidetracked. They ran into a friend, discovered something intriguing in a store window, played one more quick game of marbles or hopscotch.

Anne, a tireless chatterbox, usually dominated the conversation. Amusing and fun-loving, she was nevertheless too sharp-tongued for some, too combative and know-it-all for others, and her disarming honesty was sometimes too direct. She was quick to catch on but distractable, curious but easily bored. A skinny child still, she wore her thick dark brown hair shoulder length now, parted and held back with an inconspicuous metal barrette.

The harsh winter weather had its positive side: the children would soon be able to go skating again. Anne could hardly wait; next to swimming, skating was her favorite sport. Hanneli Goslar

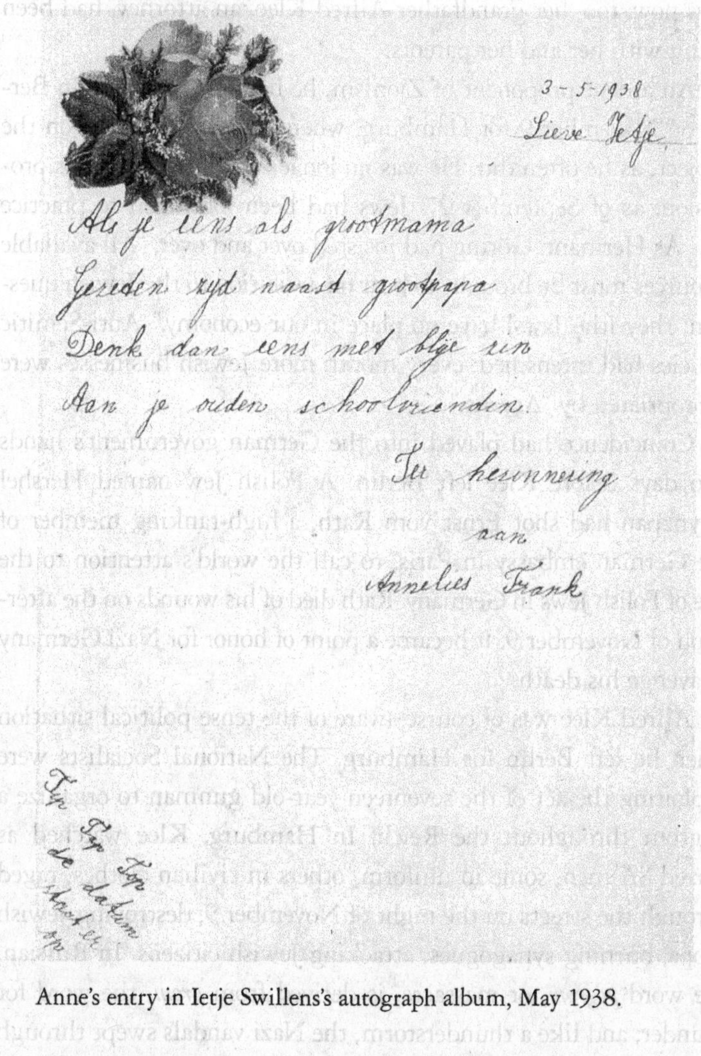
3-5-1938

Lieve Ietje,

Als je eens als grootmama
Gezeten zyd naast grootpapa
Denk dan eens met blije zin
Aan je ouden schoolvriendin.

Ter herinnering
aan
Annelies Frank

Tip Top Top
de datum
staat er
op

Anne's entry in Ietje Swillens's autograph album, May 1938.

couldn't join her because she had no skates. Her father had plenty of work in his office for German refugees, but he was reluctant to ask more than a minimal consulting fee from his hard-pressed clients. Consequently, money was in short supply in the home of the former Prussian press chief, and there was none to spare for luxuries like skates or bicycles. Hanneli had to accept that. For several days now, too, her grandfather Alfred Klee, an attorney, had been living with her and her parents.

An ardent proponent of Zionism, he had left his home in Berlin on November 9 for Hamburg, where he was to lecture on the subject, as he often did. He was no longer able to work at his profession: as of September 27, Jews had been forbidden to practice law. As Hermann Göring had insisted over and over, "All available resources must be brought to bear on a solution to the Jewish question; they [the Jews] have no place in our economy." Anti-Semitic policies had intensified; every month more Jewish businesses were expropriated by "Aryans."

Coincidence had played into the German government's hands two days before Klee left Berlin. A Polish Jew named Hershel Grynzpan had shot Ernst vom Rath, a high-ranking member of the German embassy in Paris, to call the world's attention to the fate of Polish Jews in Germany. Rath died of his wounds on the afternoon of November 9. It became a point of honor for Nazi Germany to avenge his death.

Alfred Klee was of course aware of the tense political situation when he left Berlin for Hamburg. The National Socialists were exploiting the act of the seventeen-year-old gunman to organize a pogrom throughout the Reich. In Hamburg, Klee watched as crazed SA men, some in uniform, others in civilian clothes, raged through the streets on the night of November 9, destroying Jewish shops, burning synagogues, attacking Jewish citizens. In Russian, the word *pogrom*, or massacre, is derived from *grom*, the word for thunder; and like a thunderstorm, the Nazi vandals swept through

Germany, leaving no city untouched. These attacks, organized by the party leadership, were supposed to appear spontaneous, as if the *Volk* had risen up of their own accord, motivated by a sense of national outrage. But as the fanatical vandals and arsonists set to work on what became known as *Kristallnacht*, Germany's citizens were fast asleep. Not until morning did spectators begin to gather on the streets, many of them shocked and horrified at what they saw. But the threat of arrest hung over anyone who openly disapproved.

Early on November 10, Alfred Klee called his son in Berlin and asked whether he could return home safely. His son's answer was "You have a little granddaughter in Amsterdam," an answer stated so emphatically that Klee took it as a coded warning. Hanne's birthday was in two days. A surprise visit from her grandfather would surely be a great treat for her.

On the morning of the twelfth, a Sabbath, Alfred Klee was waiting on the steps of the Goslars' apartment house when the Goslars came home from synagogue. Next to him was the little suitcase he had packed for his brief business trip to Hamburg. He had nothing more with him, and there was no going back for this illegal refugee. When Hanneli saw her grandfather, she rushed into his arms. It was a wonderful birthday surprise, completely unexpected. She would have to tell Anne right away.

The chattering girls arrived at the building on Zuider Amstellaan where Iet Swillens lived. Iet—or Ietje, as she was called—was only a month older than Anne but markedly taller and sturdier. Before Iet went inside, Anne quickly told her friends that her mother had been upset for the last few days. Something awful had happened to her brother, Anne's uncle Walter. He had been arrested, and Anne's mother did not know where he was being held. Anne's voice was hushed, but a note of excitement was audible in her dismay. Indeed, Iet noted little evidence of real concern; the children's world, after all, was tiny and still intact. Anne's life, like that of any other sheltered child, revolved around herself, her school and her lessons, her friends, her vacations, her free time, and her pleasures. Her parents didn't discuss their problems in front of her, and she had picked up only occasional snippets they let drop. Anne had no idea what had actually happened to her uncle. Iet knew even less. Nonetheless, Anne's words—and her tone—would stick in Iet's memory.

Walter Holländer had in fact been a victim of the November pogrom. In a secret communiqué of November 9, 1938, to all the regional party chiefs in Germany, Heinrich Müller, head of the Gestapo, had written: "Prepare to arrest about 20,000 to 30,000 Jews throughout the country. Select in particular well-to-do Jews. Further orders will be issued in the course of the night." Until that night of terror, Aachen had been regarded as one of the few German cities where Jews—although in fact as devoid of civil rights as Jews anywhere else in Germany—could nonetheless live more or less in peace, provided they kept a low profile. But now, even in this provincial city tucked away in the corner between Belgium and Holland, the reprieve was suddenly over.

On the evening of November 9, the Aachen municipal theater—long since declared off limits for Jews—had staged Verdi's *Il Trovatore*, the performance billed as a memorial to the "victims of the Feldherrnhalle in Munich"; on this date fifteen years earlier, Hitler's "national revolution" had come to an inglorious end before the Feldherrnhalle with sixteen people dead, many wounded, and Hitler under arrest. Only a few hours after the end of the performance, the synagogue on Aachen's Promenadenstrasse was in flames. As a witness reported later, it appeared that the fire department was trying to put out the blaze, but in fact the firemen on the roof were spraying chemicals that ensured the total destruction of everything inside. The Aachen synagogue, consecrated in 1862, was one of over four hundred that Nazi gangs burned in Germany that night.

Until late the next morning they went about destroying homes and businesses throughout the country. With wrecking bars, sledgehammers, and picks, they smashed windows and broke down doors; they threw furniture and machinery out into the street, painted anti-Semitic slogans on walls, and attacked Jewish citizens. While the Nazis in other major cities were robbing and beating thousands of Jews, killing about a hundred, they behaved in a relatively civilized manner in Aachen. No physical assault, no robbery. Their orders must have called for some restraint. But many Jewish men were arrested, randomly plucked off the streets or intentionally taken from their homes and transported in trucks to a building on Theaterplatz. Kept in the cellar, they waited, some for several nights, to see what their captors had in store for them.

In total, 248 Jewish men from Aachen and environs were arrested and jailed on November 10 and in the days that followed. The police had to meet their quota. "On November 12, 1938," Walter Holländer recalled in 1954, "I was arrested by the national police during the persecution of the Jews." Whether he was in fact arrested two days after the night of rioting or just forgot the exact date after all the chaotic years that ensued cannot be determined, nor does it matter. What does matter is that he was taken three days later, on November 15, to the Sachsenhausen concentration camp less than ten miles outside Berlin, one of 113 Jews from the Aachen area. The other 135 prisoners from Aachen were taken to Buchenwald. All of them were to be held temporarily in order to humiliate them, isolate them, prove to them how powerless they were, and ultimately force them to emigrate.

In Sachsenhausen, one of the first camps built and originally intended for political enemies, conditions for Jews were particularly harsh. They wore striped convict uniforms made of cotton, much too light for the cold November weather. A yellow triangle for "Jew" was sewn on their jackets and, if the whim of their captors so dictated, a red one for "political prisoner." Strong or weak, healthy or sick, they were forced into hard labor and worked to the point of exhaustion. They were not allowed to receive as many letters and packages as other prisoners and had no opportunity to improve their situation. If the SS men in charge of the camp were in the mood for some sport at the prisoners' expense, they selected Jews to harass. Individually or in groups, hundreds of Jews were humiliated, mistreated, or tortured to death. It was all, of course, a secret.

Walter Holländer was hard pressed to keep up his spirits. His brother, Julius, whom the Nazis had arrested the same day, had not been sent to a concentration camp. He was a veteran of World War I, and a wound to his elbow had left him with a stiff arm. At a later selection, this handicap would have cost him his life: unable to work, he was useless. But now it saved him. Walter had not been a soldier and was therefore at a particular disadvantage. He was told that he would be freed only on condition that he leave Germany immediately. But to prove that he would leave, he had to produce an entry visa for a foreign country.

Those like Julius and Walter Holländer who wanted to emigrate to the United States had, first, to show an affidavit from a relative already living there, guaranteeing support. Then they had to sit back and wait. The list of people seeking American visas was long. By the beginning of 1939, the consulates had received about 300,000 applications, many too many for someone waiting in a concentration camp until his name came up. The government of the United States, like those of all the other important countries for émigrés—Holland, France, England, and Palestine—held strictly to its quotas. The persecution of the Jews in Germany, these countries kept telling themselves, was an internal matter. Why should other countries burden themselves because of it? The U.S. official annual immigration quota for Germans and Austrians was a little over twenty-seven thousand. After the November pogrom and the subsequent mass arrests, this quota was suddenly filled for the first time; about 90 percent of the immigrants were persecuted Jews.

Julius, who had already signed a guarantee that Walter would leave Germany immediately, took the next logical step. In mid-November 1938, he applied to the Dutch embassy. After all, his sister and his brother-in-law, a businessman with a steady income, had been living in Amsterdam since 1933. Well before the November attacks on Jews, Julius had consulted with Otto and applied for a residence permit in Holland not only for his mother, Rosa, but also for his brother and himself. Because this Aachen family was "respected and well-to-do," the German authorities were particularly hostile toward the Holländers, and the pressure on them was now all but intolerable.

The uncertain future that emigration to the United States presented would have placed physical and emotional demands on Rosa Holländer that her family felt they could not impose on her. And for Anne's uncles, bureaucratic barriers made that destination virtually impossible. The only reasonable action was to find a different refuge.

Unbeknownst to Julius Holländer, the Dutch authorities had already determined the family's fate. On November 17, 1938, the Ministry of Justice in The Hague had communicated to the "General Counsel of the Amsterdam Police Department" in a letter that was sent out by the hundreds in those days that Rosa Holländer, née Stern, was "granted temporary residence in Holland," under the following conditions: she could not become a financial burden on the Dutch government, nor could other family members, namely, her sons, Julius and Walter, take up residence in Holland. Violation of these terms would mean deportation for Rosa Holländer.

Contrary to Julius's expectations, an entry visa for his imprisoned brother was not so easy to obtain. The worldwide Depression had come to Holland quite late, but when it came, it came with full force. Arguing that the immigrants would become a burden on the state, the Dutch conservative camp—chiefly Catholics but some Protestants and even some liberals—had voted in May 1938, right after Germany's annexation of Austria, to treat refugees as an "undesirable element," despite the objections of the Social Democrats, the Communists, and the liberal Protestants. Only those who could prove they were in mortal danger would be permitted to enter the country and remain there. The minister of justice, C. M. J. F. Goseling, was assigned the task of determining life-threatening circumstances. This practicing Catholic had met on November 13, 1938, with high-ranking members of Amsterdam's Jewish community and two days later announced in Parliament that asylum would be granted to several thousand persecuted Jews; he was apparently not capable, however, of recognizing the danger the German concentration camps represented. (Ironically, he himself would die in Buchenwald just a few years later.)

After the November pogrom, between forty and fifty thousand Jews from German-speaking countries applied for entry visas to Holland. About eight thousand Jews were ultimately permitted to enter the country legally, not as new citizens, however, but as refugees; most were allowed to stay only temporarily on their way to other countries. Walter Holländer was among those admitted. He received notice that Zeeburg, an internment camp on the east side of Amsterdam, would take him in. That he had family in Amsterdam did not matter. But he did not complain. He was saved. On December 1, 1938, "the Jew Walter Holländer" was released from the "state concentration camp Sachsenhausen" and ordered "to notify the police of his place of residence immediately." The message the camp administration impressed on its prisoners upon their release was a threatening one: If a single one of you tells anyone on the outside what you have seen here, we'll find you and bring you back immediately, no matter where in the world you happen to be.

Was Holland safe, and if so, for how much longer? Who could guarantee that Adolf Hitler, having annexed Austria, would not bring Holland "home to the Reich"? Weren't ambitious German ideologues stressing that the Dutch, too, were "Germanic" people and Dutch only a dialect of High German? Didn't they also claim that the separation of Holland from the German empire in 1648 after the Thirty Years War had been "illegal" and that a reclaiming of this "stolen territory" would therefore be legitimate? Could German Jews still feel certain that they would not be subject to anti-Semitism in Holland?

It was true that Dutch Jews, who made up about 1.5 percent of the population, had been granted complete civil rights in 1796, more than fifty years earlier than in Germany. They were almost totally assimilated and felt completely safe in their tolerant homeland. The prejudices and the latent hatred for Jews that had periodically erupted in Germany were unknown in Holland. Ten percent of Dutch Jews were traditionally employed in the diamond industry, a few as wealthy dealers, most of them as poorly paid cutters. In Amsterdam, a small class of very prosperous Jews, mostly of Sephardic background, whose ancestors had immigrated from Spain and Portugal as early as the sixteenth century, held leading positions in the country's economic and cultural life and stood apart from the great majority of Dutch Jews. Most of the Jews in Holland were Ashkenazim of East European origin who worked in factories and on the docks or earned their livings as street peddlers, dealers in used goods, or artisans; many were leaders in the labor movement. Dutch Jews were not just tolerated but integrated and respected.

There were, however, anti-Semitic "terror groups" like the radical right-wing IJzeren Garde (Iron Guard), and their acts of vandalism kept the courts busy. But these acts were regarded as isolated cases. The perpetrators were, as one judge put it, "young louts who ought to be in juvenile court" and who were "acting not on their own but under the influence of a dangerous individual [Franz Theodor Look]."

Twenty-two-year-old Anton "Tonny" Christiaan Ahlers was one of these "louts." He and his friends attacked Jewish sales personnel and their Jewish customers in Amsterdam's Bijenkorf department store; they distributed anti-Jewish pamphlets; they smashed the window of the Jewish Refugee Committee; they defaced the memorial to the Jewish playwright Herman Hewijermans.

Their fanaticism, their capacity for provocation, and their readiness to engage in violence had greater significance than was appreciated at the time. Particularly in the case of the unemployed Tonny Ahlers, who would tell the police on one occasion that he was an office worker and on another a student, these characteristics demonstrated an increasing unscrupulousness in the name of National Socialism. He was jailed and probably spent several months in prison. Nevertheless, the Dutch regarded him and his ilk as a fringe group and did not take them very seriously.

Then, too, it seemed by 1938 that the Fascist parties that had formed in Holland in the early thirties in imitation of Germany's NSDAP were losing ground. The Nationaal-Socialistische Beweging (National Socialist Movement), or NSB, had won 7.94 percent of the votes in the parliamentary elections of April 1935, making it the fifth-strongest party in the country, but in May 1937 it garnered only 4.22 percent and in April 1939 less than 4 percent. Many of the party's supporters disliked the fact that its founder, Anton Adriaan Mussert, a government employee of lower-middle-class background who had married an aunt fifteen years older than he, was cozying up to Hitler's Germany.

As Jews, the Franks had no reason to fear the growing intolerance of the Dutch, but as Germans they did. When Otto's cousin Milly Stanfield came to visit in 1938, she noticed that the family never spoke a word of German on the street even though they spoke a mixture of Dutch and German at home. Milly concluded that Otto had instructed his children to speak Dutch in public so as not to cause offense in the country that they had made their home. What Milly did not realize was how unnecessary this warning was, for Anne and Margot were by now fluent in Dutch. Indeed, Dutch was more familiar to Anne than German.

The looming uncertainty plagued not only the Franks but everyone in Holland. Would Hitler actually dare to claim their country as Teutonic territory? Whatever happened, he would not be able "to march in to the cheers of a friendly population," as he had set out to do in Austria on March 13, 1938. The Dutch aversion for the Germans was much too great for that.

In any case, Otto Frank was among the majority who thought Hitler, for all his megalomania, would nonetheless respect Dutch neutrality. He also hoped that the German people would refuse to put up with the madness of National Socialism much longer. Optimistically he compared the November pogrom to the crisis of an illness and its accompanying high fever, after which Germany would finally recover its mental health and common sense. But news of that terrifying night probably robbed Edith Frank of whatever emotional equanimity she had left. For Otto, the brutal attacks on German Jews may well have remained abstract and incomprehensible. None of his close relatives had been affected; they had all left the country in time. Edith, however, was feeling the direct impact of these events. Her brother had been imprisoned in a concentration camp a mere 150 or so miles from Amsterdam and treated more severely than a hardened criminal. And now, since December 26, 1938, as a refugee without rights or possessions, this former businessman was forced to stay in a "quarantine institution"—as the Zeeburg camp was identified in its letterhead—where living conditions were primitive and the food poor. "We were cut off from all contact in this refugee camp and kept under police supervision. We were not allowed—nor was it even possible—to engage in any income-producing work," Walter Holländer would later write, "but we had to pay for our stay in the camp. If I wanted to leave for any reason, I had to obtain written permission from the police officer in charge."

It seems likely that Walter did obtain "passes"—rare though they probably were—to visit the Franks, though we have no documentation of this. We do know that Walter was permitted to go to the Huize Oosteinde, a kind of German-Jewish cultural center that had opened its doors in January 1937 and quickly become a favorite gathering place for immigrants. Books and newspapers were available there, and visitors could engage in various sports, take part in discussions, and study English or Hebrew. Since he had to wait a whole year for his visa to the United States, Walter Holländer probably took a course in English.

Walter's situation may have been far from ideal, but he was at least safe from the Nazis for the time being. Edith's mother still had some bureaucratic hurdles to clear in both her old and her new homes before she could be rescued from Nazi Germany. Edith had long weeks of anxiety still before her.

On January 30, 1939, the sixth anniversary of his assumption of power, Hitler once again summoned his rhetorical fervor to stir up fear of the Jews in the German population. If another world war broke out, Hitler said, it would be the fault of the Jews. "I have often proved a prophet in my lifetime," he declaimed in his usual melodramatic manner, "and most of the time people have laughed at me. . . . But today I am going to be a prophet once again. If the international Jewish financiers in Europe and beyond should succeed in bringing another world war down on us all, the final result will be not a Bolshevist triumph over the earth and a victory for the Jews but the destruction of the Jewish race in Europe."

That day Rosa Holländer received her new passport.

But what about Edith's older brother, Julius? He, too, wanted to leave Germany as quickly as possible. But which country would accept him? That the Dutch government did not want him was clear. Would the United States take him? And what would become of the family's business? Its home and property?

The firm of B. Holländer was still showing respectable profits of about 33,000 Reichsmarks annually, but immediately after Walter's arrest in November 1938 the National Socialists ordered the firm to close its doors. The order was not the isolated act of a particularly anti-Semitic Aachen party member; it was backed up by a law, the First Decree for Eliminating Jews from German Commerce, passed on November 12.

An entry of January 26, 1939, in the Aachen commercial register reads: "The firm of B. Holländer has been dissolved." The closing down of the family firm was now finally official and entered in the record books—forty-three years of work destroyed with a stroke of the pen. But at this point the loss of the firm was the least of the Holländers' worries. The Holländers had finally understood that the Nazis had stripped them of their last defenses under the law.

Julius Holländer's application for entry into the United States was quickly approved. His cousin Ernst, who had been living there for some time, signed an affidavit guaranteeing his support. On February 24, 1939, Julius received the necessary visa, and on March 25 he boarded the *Veendam* of the Holland-American line in Rotterdam.

Before Julius Holländer left his homeland forever, he saw to it that at least a few items from his family's home in Aachen made their way to Amsterdam, pieces, he later said, "that had been in the family for a long time and therefore had sentimental value for my sister": a chest of drawers, a grandfather clock, a desk, a wardrobe, armchairs, a carpet, some paintings. Jews had long since been denied control of their own possessions, and export permits were expensive. On February 27, 1939, Julius transferred 1,470 Reichsmarks to the account of the Reich Ministry of Commerce in the Gold Discount Bank of Berlin; the same day he paid 280 Reichsmarks in Walter's name, then two weeks later an additional 400 Reichsmarks. The Nazis' perverse legal system registered these payments as a "tax on abandonment of the Reich" designed to bleed Jews financially dry and make them as unattractive as possible to host countries. Who wants to take on the burden of indigent immigrants?

The family had to leave behind most of the furnishings and hundreds of books in the spacious apartment they had rented at 1 Pastorplatz—three living rooms, three bedrooms, and various extra rooms—where Rosa, Julius, and Walter Holländer had lived since 1935 and where Anne Frank had spent several happy vacation weeks. "It was impossible for us to realize any value from the furniture. We just had to abandon it," Walter stated many years later. The Holländers had sold their house on Liebfrauenstrasse and moved into an apartment in 1932, apparently for economic reasons and in any case with the agreement of Otto and Edith Frank. Their first move was to an imposing town house at 42-44 Monheimsallee, where Anne stayed with them almost an entire year in 1933 and 1934; the second was to Pastorplatz.

The Holländers were never informed as to what became of the property on Grüner Weg that had housed the family business ever since Anne's grandfather Abraham Holländer had acquired it in 1913. They had neither the time nor the opportunity to sell it before they left the country. The National Socialists "Aryanized" it by the usual method—selling it off in a perfectly "legal" forced auction. The lot, measuring 17,916 square meters, carried substantial but by no means extraordinary mortgages held by the Dresden and German banks; the Aachen registry of deeds contains a December 1925 entry that reads: "As security against all claims, past or future, that have been or may be made on the Dresden Bank in Aachen and on the Aachen branch of the German Bank in consequence of their business relationship with the firm of B. Holländer." Now that the Holländers had closed their business and left

B. Holländer,

(Inhaber: Abraham Holländer)
gegründet 1858,
am Bahnhof Aachen-Nord.
908 u. 909. Privat- 858.

Eisenschrot und Altmetalle.

Ankauf, Verkauf,
Abbruch industrieller Anlagen.

Lager
in Dampfkesseln, Maschinen, Maschinenteilen, Trägern, Säulen, Schienen, Bassins, Baueisen, Rohren, Ventilen, Transmissionen, Fenstern, Treibriemen, Rädern, Kaminen und allem möglichen Nutzeisen.

Belagplatten, Knotenbleche und Bleche aller Art in eigenem Scheren- und Walzenbetrieb nach Maß und Zeichnung geschnitten.

Fallhammerbetrieb.

Rohprodukte für Papier-, Kunstwolle- und chemische Fabriken. Lumpen-Sortieranstalt.
Eisenbahn-Gleisanschluß Aachen-Nord.

Listing of the B. Holländer firm in the Aachen address book, 1914.

the country their mortgage payments were left outstanding. It was only to be expected that their creditors would move as quickly as possible to collect what was due them.

"Compulsory auction of the real estate listed in the registry of deeds of the City of Aachen, volume 169, page 6724, in the name of the B. Holländer Company is hereby ordered," the Aachen district court announced on May 4, 1939. Included in the auction were the family's former residence, the office and adjoining courtyard, as well as the packing hall and courtyard, sorting hall, canteen, stables, lavatories, general warehouse, smithy, a warehouse for bundles of rags, and the concierge's booth. The total assessed value was 103,900 Reichsmarks, the best offer 54,000 Reichsmarks. "In accordance with the final decision of the Aachen district court of July 27, 1939," the Aachen branch of the German Bank was recorded as the new owner in the registry of deeds. The bank had been the only bidder, and a little over a year later it sold the property to an "Aryan" without realizing any further profit on it.

The Franks probably learned of this only piecemeal, and that was doubtless a good thing. They had troubles enough as it was. "What can one say in a birthday letter in times like these?" Otto wrote to his mother in December 1938. "We have to be grateful for what we still have—and not give up hope! It is miserably cold here, too, and we think constantly of those who, unlike ourselves, have no warm place to stay."

And how was Rosa Holländer standing up? She was among the exceptions who in late March 1939 were allowed to enter Holland and remain there. Before Julius Holländer—himself in possession of only a transit visa—continued on to Rotterdam, he took his mother to Merwedeplein a nearly mute, broken woman in a state of shock.

Was Holland safe, and if so, for how much longer? In early 1939 the Franks continued to ask themselves this question. It seemed they were facing the same situation they had confronted in Germany in 1933. Should they leave Amsterdam and start all over somewhere else? Could they uproot Anne and Margot again? Both girls were totally at home in Amsterdam now. How would they respond to another country? And what would that country be? Switzerland?

Wasn't Holland just as safe? Palestine? No, they had neither Zionist nor religious inclinations. Sanne Ledermann's father had been there in 1934, hoping to establish business connections, but he had come back to Amsterdam frustrated. Nothing but flies and Arabs there, he had groaned, absolutely unbearable. South America? They had friends and relatives in Peru and Argentina. And then there was England. But regardless of what *they* wanted, what country in the world would still be willing to accept them? The borders not only in Europe but everywhere else had become tighter than ever. As early as December 1937, almost a year before the November pogrom, Edith Frank had expressed her worries in a letter to Willi and Hedda Eisenstaedt, a couple who had moved on from Amsterdam to Buenos Aires: "I think every German Jew must be combing the world in search of a refuge and not finding one anywhere. . . . Perhaps we too will move on (but this is just a vague possibility we have talked about only with the Goslars)." She added a melancholy note: "We realize that we would feel much the way you do and that our hearts would yearn again for Amsterdam."

As in 1933, the family's personal finances—profits from the sale of jelling agent were still nowhere in sight—and the uncertain political situation conspired to leave Otto Frank constantly troubled. "I always tried to get away from here," he would write (in English) in April 1941. But his cautious nature and financial situation did not allow Otto to leave Holland without having solid business prospects in a new country. Otto traveled frequently to London, presumably on behalf of the Pomosin-Werke. "Papi is going to England again today," Margot wrote to Grandmother Frank on December 2, 1937, "and I hope he won't stay away too long." Edith, too, noted in her letter to the Eisenstaedts that since September Otto had been away most of the time and was "working intently on something in England. . . . Whether it will turn out is uncertain. Unfortunately, we are not satisfied with how the business is going and need to supplement it somehow."

For a while, Otto had had his eye on an opportunity in North America. "Shortly before the outbreak of the war I had an arrangement with a strong group to open a new factory oversea, where I had to be one of the directors," he wrote in his imperfect English. As early as 1938 he had applied in the American consulate in Rotterdam to emigrate to the United States. But like thousands of others, the Franks did not find a place in the quota of emigrants admitted from Germany.

We cannot know how much hope Otto Frank had for his application. What is certain is that Edith, until her brother emigrated to the United States, resisted the idea of moving still farther from Germany. She wanted to stay nearby, Otto explained later. "I am worried about my family," she said. But as their anxious thoughts turned toward America, Edith, too, felt the need to leave Holland. It is also clear that Otto Frank was not betting everything on a single card but, to the extent he was able, kept several options open. Even though his attempts to emigrate were entirely serious, he worked diligently to build up his business in Holland, which did finally seem about to take a turn for the better. As Edith put it in one of her last letters to Germany, "My husband is very tired and in desperate need of a few days' rest. The business is a constant struggle, but otherwise things are going smoothly for us."

Although the income from pectin sales had remained low, Otto had expanded his business. Since October 1938 he had been running, in addition to Opekta, the small firm of Handelsmaatschappij Pectacon N.V., which was registered as a "producer of and dealer in chemical products and foodstuffs." The company made, and supplied to meatpackers, mixtures of spices used in the preparation of different kinds of sausages. It is not clear whether it was Otto's idea or that of his old friend Johannes Kleiman to diversify into the spice business. The two men had known each other since the spring of 1923. Kleiman had worked as a deputy manager in Otto's Amsterdam branch of M. Frank & Zonen and then, together with the Belgian Jacques Hauskin, had become a partner. After Otto returned to Amsterdam in 1933, they were probably in constant contact.

Johannes Kleiman had earned Otto's complete confidence in the 1920s, for, when the bank had to liquidate in 1925, Otto had given the young Dutchman, seven years his junior, full power of attorney and had moved the firm to Kleiman's apartment. A business without income could do without paying rent. While Kleiman saw to the orderly dissolution of the business, Otto had returned to Germany, where he commuted back and forth between Frankfurt and Aachen and married Edith on May 12, 1925.

For the first five months of its existence, the newly founded Pectacon again listed Kleiman's Amsterdam apartment as the company's official address, and Kleiman was its director. When the business moved into Opekta's offices, Otto Frank named himself director and Johannes Kleiman supervisory director. Kleiman took over the bookkeeping for both Pectacon and Opekta.

A lean man with a thin face, sunken cheeks, and a strikingly high forehead, Johannes Kleiman suffered from chronic stomach problems and probably knew as little about spice mixtures as Otto Frank did. But they had found a specialist in the field, Hermann van Pels, a man who—as Otto's secretary, Miep, said with admiration—had an infallible nose for spices.

Van Pels needed only a quick sniff to identify an herb or root. In Osnabrück, Germany, he and his father had been suppliers of items for the butcher and meatpacking trade, including the spices and casings for sausage making. In the summer of 1937, he and his wife, Auguste, née Rottgen, and their eleven-year-old son, Peter, had fled to Amsterdam with the intention of moving on as quickly as possible to the United States but with no greater prospects for success than the Franks had. Otto Frank knew that Hermann van Pels "had emigrated [to Holland] with 3,000 Reichmarks and had lost them in 1938–39." Though of Dutch extraction, van Pels had grown up in Germany. He was an uncomplicated man, a bit of a joker, agreeable and easy to work with. He was louder, more gregarious, and less sensitive than Otto Frank, and a heavy smoker. His expertise made him essential to the business. Otto treated him more as a partner than as an employee. "In 1940–41 he earned so much working for me that he could get a nice apartment and live well. He was incapable of saving."

Van Pels and his wife, who married in 1925, were frequent visitors at the Franks'. At regular intervals Otto and Edith invited people over for Saturday afternoon coffee. These were mostly German refugees, some of whom had not fled to Amsterdam until 1938. Among them were the dentist Fritz Pfeffer and his companion, Charlotte Kaletta, but there were Dutch guests as well, such as Miep Santrouschitz and her fiancé, Jan Gies, and the Hofhuis family. Good neighbors and a circle of loyal friends helped everyone cope with life in a foreign country. Someone would always lend a sympathetic ear; solidarity and an unquestioning willingness to help one another were taken for granted, even at times of financial need. In fact, the Franks were anything but well off; they were even renting out a large room in their apartment to help make ends meet. But compared with the many immigrants who had left Germany later, unable to bring anything with them, they were living very well indeed. Edith never hesitated to share food, and Otto readily loaned modest amounts of money to his close friends even when there was little hope of being repaid anytime soon. "Giving never made anyone poorer" had been his mother's adage and lifelong guiding principle, and he made a point of impressing it on Margot and Anne.

Conversation over coffee, tea, and cake focused primarily on the political situation and worries about the future. All the guests watched Hitler's every move. A half year after the annexation of Austria, he occupied the Sudetenland with the acquiescence of Paris and London. The Franks and their friends could at least see some minimal justification for that invasion, which they chose to interpret as nonthreatening: Hitler claimed to have "liberated" the Sudeten Germans, who comprised more than 50 percent of that region's population. But it was obviously more than just happy coincidence that Czechoslovakia's military fortifications were located there and that Hitler's annexation had, in effect, paralyzed the Czech army.

Everyone knew it was serious when Hitler's troops then marched into Prague on March 15, 1939. England now seemed to regret its earlier acquiescence and with French support issued a guarantee of mutual defense to all the central European countries between Germany and the Soviet Union. Would Hitler continue to pursue his expansionist policy despite that guarantee? What would he do next? Would he really dare go to war?

Political discussions at the Saturday afternoon coffees ceased abruptly if Anne or Margot entered the room. The children needed a sense of security and stability. Almost all the parents agreed on that, and by preserving the appearance of harmony and safety for their children's sake, they preserved it for themselves as well. The normality of their everyday lives helped them maintain their equilibrium. The day's small pleasures and problems distracted them from their fears about the future and about their very survival.

The Franks took trips, spending the summer holidays of 1937 in the Belgian seaside resort of Middelkerke. They went on outings, bicycled in the country, swam at the shore. In March 1938—a photograph documents this—they explored the Dutch lakes aboard a *salonboot*, a Dutch excursion boat. Edith taught her daughters to knit and sew and tried to interest them in religious instruction. The liberal Jewish congregation on Tolstraat, which had been founded in the early 1930s and had grown with the influx of German-Jewish immigrants, had become an important part of Edith's life. Most German Jews did not feel comfortable with the Orthodox Judaism that dominated in Holland, aligning themselves with the liberal Reform movement instead. Like Otto Frank, they had rarely entered a synagogue in Germany, and they regarded the Amsterdam congregation more as a community center. Indeed, until the Nazis had forced Jewish identity on them, they had given it little thought.

Edith went to services at the synagogue, and she helped organize children's festivals there. The children whom she lined up in double rows and presented with brightly colored little flags were struck by her reserved ways but could sense her affection and sympathy for them.

Margot stuck with her mother, and she shared the enthusiasm of most of the immigrant girls for the young rabbi, Ludwig Jacob Mehler, who came from Berlin. Before arriving in Amsterdam in 1934, he had had a post in Frankfurt am Main. He was an excellent teacher, and Margot took religious instruction from him every Sunday morning.

Anne's rare visits to the synagogue were of little importance to her, and she took a skeptical view of the popular rabbi. When he told a story one day about Abraham, she caused a stir among the pupils by asking impudently how he could know where Abraham put his feet.

Edith let Anne have her way. What else could she do? Otto maintained minimal contact with the congregation, and Anne adored him above all others. For all the difficulties Otto was facing, when he was with his children, he was all theirs. He served as adviser, friend, and entertainer, not only to them but to their friends as well. He revived the two Paulas and loved to tell other stories and to make up funny songs, including a "Chinese" one Anne and Hanneli couldn't get out of their heads for weeks:

Yo, di-vi-di-vo,
di-vi-di vaya, kasch-kaya, kasch-ko,
di-vi-di-vo, di-vi-di vitsch-vitsch-vitsch-vo.

Laughing as they struggled with the words, they returned again and again to the refrain:

Yin-yang, yin-yang, vosch-kai-da-vitschki,
yang-kai, vi-di-vi, yang-kai vi-di-vi,
Yin-yang, yin-yang, votsch-kai-da-vitschki,
Yang-kai vi-di-vi, aya!

Anne's friends envied her. Mr. Frank seemed to Hanneli always to be in a good mood. He even took the time to attempt to teach her how to ride a bike. Using Anne's bike, since she didn't have her own, she pedaled as Otto held on to the rack behind the seat and ran up and down the sidewalk of Merwedeplein with her. But to no avail—Hanneli was uncoordinated and afraid of getting hurt, and lacking a bike of her own, she never learned to share Anne's enthusiasm for this popular Dutch pastime. Otto was kind enough to console the girl, even for this minor defeat.

He never lost his patience with Anne, Hanneli noticed, though Anne could be quite difficult. Combative by nature, she insisted on getting her way even if she wasn't altogether clear about what it was she wanted. She did not accept criticism gracefully. Margot's friends often found Anne's brashness irritating. At thirteen Margot was still obedient and forbearing, also slightly plump and stolid, as if her figure reflected her personality. She showed not a trace of adolescent rebellion. Anne was just the opposite, eager to lead the pack even at nine and ten, stormy and demanding, but for all that, she was basically reasonable and not excessively stubborn. Good people and bad people have one thing in common, her father told her. They both make mistakes. But good people can admit their mistakes, discuss them with others, and learn from them. "My dear little Anne," he wrote on May 12, 1939, his fiftieth birthday and fourteenth wedding anniversary, "things haven't always gone as smoothly for you as they did for your sister, though in general your sense of humor and your amiability allow you to sail through so much so easily. I have often told you that you must educate yourself. We have agreed on 'controls' with each other and you yourself are doing a great deal to swallow the 'buts.' And yet you like to spoil yourself and like even more to be spoiled by others." None of which was so terrible, Otto added, if Anne remained as good, decent, and lovable as she had always been. "You are not obstinate and so, after a few tears, the laughter is soon back again. 'Enjoy what there is'—as Mummy says. May this happy laughter stay with you, the laughter with which you enhance your, our, and other people's lives." Anne would copy this "marvelous letter from Daddy" into her diary on June 19, 1942.

Despite her high spirits, Anne was easily upset. "The nervous little thing has to have plenty of rest," Edith observed. Perhaps it was justified concern for Anne's health that made Otto so indulgent. His motives didn't matter to Anne's friends. They saw in Mr. Frank a cheerful, kindly man they respected but were never afraid of, someone they could ask any question at all because he would always take the time to answer. He was the father every child longed for.

When it came to humor, Hanne's father was not without talent, either. On the Jewish festival of Purim—the year must have been 1938 or 1939—the Goslars gave a party. Purim celebrates the salvation of the Jewish people from persecution under the Persian king Xerxes, and those at the Goslars' party must have been vividly aware of the historical parallels with their current situation. The Old Testament tells how Xerxes' queen, Esther, courageously intercedes with her husband to save her people from the tyrant Haman and his plan of destruction. The day of the Jews' deliverance is celebrated with dancing, song, and festive meals. Costumes and disguises figure importantly, perhaps signifying the change in the status of the Jews—from persecuted to protected, from scorned to honored.

At the Goslars' Purim celebration, the adults as well as the children dressed up. Hans Goslar parted his hair to the side and drew a tiny black moustache on his upper lip. Then he put on his raincoat, went next door to the Franks', and rang the bell. When the door opened, he straightened up stiff as a board, put his left hand on his hip, and, his lips pressed tightly together, stared at Otto and Edith with the intent gaze of a hypnotist. Delighting in their momentary fright, he held his pose for the few seconds it took them to catch on and dissolve in laughter.

In the early hours of September 1, 1939, Hitler's armies attacked Poland, and the Western powers began to mobilize. If Germany did not immediately withdraw its troops, England and France warned, they would, as agreed, come to Poland's aid. Hitler did not budge, not even when the English issued an ultimatum at nine on the morning of September 3 or when the French followed suit at five that afternoon. The English and French declarations of war that followed were mere formalities. World War II had begun.

The efforts of the French and English did little to hamper Hitler's rampage. In his first blitzkrieg, he brought Poland—and well over two million Jews—under his control. He wasted no time. In a special order dated September 21, Reinhard Heydrich, head of the SD, the security service, instructed "action forces" experienced in carrying out pogroms to "consolidate" the Polish Jews. All over Poland, Heydrich's men beat, robbed, and humiliated Jews. They cut off the beards of Orthodox Jews, forced the men to their knees, and made them turn somersaults. Discriminatory regulations followed this wave of terror.

In Holland, people were horrified by these developments. The Dutch press, however, was restrained in its reporting. In the interests of Dutch neutrality, it did not want to needlessly "irritate the Third Reich." In his "Directive Number 1 for the Conduct of the

War," issued on August 31, 1939, Hitler had stressed that the neutrality of Holland, Belgium, Luxembourg, and Switzerland was to be "scrupulously observed," and Holland's prime minister, Hendryk Colijn, referred to this order when he assured his worried citizenry that their country was not in immediate danger and that they could sleep in peace.

Neutrality was the word that people in Holland clung to now, no group more desperately than the immigrant German Jews. Otto Frank, ever an optimist, argued against the fears of many of his friends by pointing out that Holland had remained neutral in World War I; surely it would remain neutral now. But even he must have harbored grave doubts, and he expressed his worries in a letter to his cousin Milly Stanfield in London. What if Holland should be attacked after all? he asked. Would he be able to keep Anne and Margot safe?

He tried to hide his concern from his two girls, but he could not dismiss the tense situation entirely because Margot, who was fourteen, was already feeling its effects herself. "We often listen to the radio as times are very exciting, having a frontier with Germany and being a small country we never feel safe," Margot wrote in English in late April 1940 to a fourteen-year-old American pen pal named Betty Ann Wagner, who lived on a farm near Danville, Iowa. Working through a pen pal project, Betty Ann's teacher and a teacher in Amsterdam had exchanged their pupils' addresses. Margot explained to Betty Ann why she could no longer visit her cousins in Basel: "We have to travel through Germany which we cannot do or through Belgium and France and that we cannot either. It is war and no visas are given."

Anne, whose eleventh birthday was a month and a half away, showed no signs of concern in her letter to Betty Ann's younger sister, Juanita. She chatted about her life at school, her postcard collection, her approaching birthday. Otto helped Anne translate her letter into English, and she then wrote it out herself. "In case you and Betty get a photo do send a copy as I am curious to know how you look." There was no mention of the worsening situation in her native country. On the contrary, she signed her letter, "Hoping to hear from you I remain your Dutch friend Annelies Marie Frank." Juanita's reply never reached her.

6

TRAPPED

Caught! They had not been able to outrun the Nazi danger. The invasion of Holland by German troops shocked the Franks as it did their compatriots.

Shouldn't they have foreseen this? For months a German attack had seemed imminent, yet there had always been some cause for hope. Twenty-nine times over the past six months a German colonel had leaked to the Dutch government the date Hitler planned to invade Holland, and twenty-nine times the alarm had been false. Twenty-nine times the appointed day had passed uneventfully, thanks presumably to bad weather. Indeed the winter of 1939–40 had been the coldest in eleven years. To the delight of skaters, the canals had remained frozen for weeks on end. The spring had been typically rainy.

After twenty-nine false alarms, hardly anyone in the Dutch government took the warnings seriously anymore. Most Dutch officials had come to the reassuring conclusion that Hitler was trying to provoke their country into violating its neutrality.

The early days of May 1940 turned delightfully warm and sunny, ideal weather for an invasion, and this time the attack ordered on May 9 actually occurred. Germany did not declare war on Holland. Hitler claimed that his troops came to protect this neutral state from the danger that the Allies might use the Netherlands as a beachhead for an attack on the Ruhr. Then, too, Hitler argued, Holland had long since violated its neutrality by allowing English planes to fly through its air space. The truth was that Hitler needed airports near the North Sea himself.

At dawn on May 10, 1940, German troops and planes swooped down on Holland. It was still dark when a distant roar became audible in Amsterdam. Some must have thought it was an approaching thunderstorm and gone back to sleep, but many people quickly realized that the threatening growl came from airplanes, and they leapt out of bed to turn on their radios. What was going on? Were those English planes or German ones? "Airborne troops have landed near Gouda . . . German troops have crossed the Dutch border at several places and are moving westward . . . Still other airborne units have surrounded Edam . . . North of Wijk an Zee, more airborne troops . . . Some German troops are in Dutch uniforms . . . in farmers' overalls . . . dressed as ambulance crews . . . riding bicycles." Confusing reports and unsubstantiated rumors filled the air. Amsterdam's Schiphol airport had been bombed.

Early that morning, the queen of the Netherlands came on the radio and urged people to stay calm. Her speech did little to calm anyone, least of all the Jews. Everyone realized that the Dutch army was no match for the Germans. But, Queen Wilhelmina told her people, Holland would not give up without a fight.

Some yielded to panic, others to paralysis: What would the Germans do? People waited helplessly for the latest news and instructions. Mothers were the first to find a way to deal with the crisis. Breakfast—their children had to have breakfast. Resuming the daily routine was one way to overcome fear. If everyday life could go on as usual, life itself would go on.

Parents discussed whether their children should go to school.

The war had still not reached Amsterdam. Only the empty streets and the radio reports indicated that anything was wrong. The children would stay home. So Anne did not go to school that day, and she no doubt shared the feelings of all children her age: though worried by what she had heard at breakfast, she probably welcomed the prospect of no school and a three-day weekend, for May 10 fell on a Friday in 1940.

Otto Frank most likely went to his office as usual. He, too, resorted to his daily routine in an effort to calm his fears, for strong and confident as he may have seemed at home for the sake of Edith, the children, and frail Oma Holländer, he was in fact deeply disturbed. He should have known. They all should have known. Only a few weeks earlier his cousin Milly had urged him to send Anne and Margot to England. She and her mother had offered to take care of the girls until the war in Europe was over. He had refused. Neither he nor Edith could imagine being separated from their children, no matter what happened. And now the Nazis had caught up with them all.

The sun, which had, ironically, shone with particular splendor on this blackest of all Fridays, set over a country in chaos. Telephone service was interrupted. Worried about food supplies, people were storming the stores. Some months earlier, just after war broke out in Poland, the government had ordered the rationing of various basic foodstuffs, making them available only in exchange for stamps good for limited periods: pink stamps for bread, blue for milk, and so on. At first it had seemed an annoying bureaucratic measure. Everyone still got enough to eat, but stamps could be had only by those with a basic gray card issued to both adults and children, and food could be purchased only if the appropriate stamps were redeemed while they were still valid. If you didn't have a valid sugar stamp, you got no sugar; no valid meat stamp, no meat. The system proved an important educational measure: people had to learn to buy only a reasonable amount of supplies, to pay close attention, and to be extremely flexible. Posters everywhere carried the slogan "Hoarding hurts your country." Because *hoarding* in Dutch literally means "hamstering," the illustrations on these posters were of greedy rodents. But now, panicked by the German invasion, people were rushing to stores to get whatever nonperishables were available.

Repeated air-raid alarms, announced by the earsplitting yowl of sirens, kept people constantly on edge. In previous months, the residents of Merwedeplein had had to take part in fire and air-raid drills and had shared words of comfort and encouragement during those exercises. Now, though, things had turned serious. Every alarm seemed to bring the war closer and to increase their fears. But still nothing happened.

People kept their radios on all day, waiting for the latest instructions. An 8:00 p.m. curfew was imposed, and everyone was cautioned to reinforce their windows with tape and to cover them with blackout paper. No point in lighting the enemy's way.

In one day, the social structure of Holland had been transformed. Where once there had been rich and poor, an upper and a lower class, a right wing and a left wing, and various religious blocs, now only one criterion distinguished good from bad, friend from enemy: was a person anti-German or pro-German? Anyone suspected of sympathizing with the German National Socialists was arrested. Well before the invasion, a list of the leading Dutch Nazis had been compiled. All native Germans, even German Jews, were considered "enemy aliens" and placed under house arrest. The lucky ones had Dutch friends or neighbors who kept them supplied with food. Germans—Jews and non-Jews alike—who came to the attention of the police for any reason were arrested, regardless of their political persuasion. The point of these measures was to ensure maximum security for the Dutch population, and they were no doubt enacted with the best of intentions. But in retrospect they can be excused only in the light of the general chaos, which afforded people neither the time nor the presence of mind to make fine distinctions and accounted for all sorts of absurdities. For no one was in greater despair over Hitler's invasion than the German Jews who had emigrated to Holland.

Many of them refused to sit by and wait for further developments. Some—and sometimes even entire families—saw suicide as the only alternative. They took overdoses of sleeping pills, hanged themselves, or—hoping to die in their sleep—turned on the gas jets and closed the windows. Sanne and Barbara Ledermann watched from the balcony of their apartment as a man in a building across the street from theirs was rescued at the last minute from his gas-filled apartment. They probably told Anne and Margot about the incident.

Many other Jews tried to leave Holland. The few who had cars drove toward the sea, to ferry ports like Ijmuiden and Scheveningen. Others went by bicycle because no trains or buses were running. Rumor had it that the Dutch government was providing ships to take Jewish refugees to England.

But in the turmoil of conflicting orders and vague announcements, very few managed to leave the country. Some people were stopped at checkpoints and turned back; others reached the ports but found the ships already full. All returned home discouraged.

The Franks stayed in Amsterdam. They didn't have a car, and their chances of getting through as a family of five with two young daughters and an ill and elderly grandmother were slim. Otto Frank assessed their situation correctly. They waited and did as most of their Jewish friends did: they tried to shield their children from the terrifying reality.

Life went on, even after it became known on May 13 that Queen Wilhelmina had fled the country on an English destroyer, taking her cabinet with her. The queen, who had been ruling her country for forty-two years and whose presence was regarded as a symbol of stability, had left her people in the lurch. It would take quite a while for them to get over their rage and disappointment and give Wilhelmina's decision their blessing. As an exile in London, she might be able to help her people. As Hitler's prisoner, she would have been powerless.

"Think of our Jewish compatriots," the sixty-year-old queen had urged in the last radio address she gave in Holland. A year earlier, she could have used some of her own advice. After searching for a suitable place to locate a camp for Jewish refugees, the government had notified her that it had selected a parcel of land in the Veluwe nature preserve near Elspeterveld. Her "regretful" response—expressed with appropriately royal tact—was that the parcel was much too close to her summer residence. And so, instead of being seven miles from the royal hunting lodge, the camp was finally built far away in swampy Westerbork in the damp, cold northeastern corner of the country.

Life went on, even after it was announced at 7:00 p.m. on May 14 that Holland would surrender. The Dutch had fought bravely for three days against the overwhelmingly superior forces of the German Goliath. But then Germany had issued an ultimatum that left the Dutch no choice: surrender and turn Rotterdam over to the German forces or the port city and various other targets would be bombed.

Hitler would later blame faulty radio communications for Germany's failure to hold to the terms of the ultimatum. Even as the surrender negotiations were in progress, the Germans were bombing Rotterdam's old city, killing about eight hundred civilians and destroying innumerable buildings, among them the American consulate. Several thousand immigration applications waiting there for processing went up in flames, among them probably the application of the Frank family.

Leaflets dropped on Amsterdam and Utrecht, warning of more

bombings, put the Dutch government under even greater pressure. On May 15, it signed the surrender agreement. Only five days, and the war was over; Holland was an occupied country. The people of Amsterdam watched in horror as columns of German soldiers in gray field uniforms and potlike helmets marched through the River Quarter in time to their military songs and headed into the Old City, noisy and fear-inspiring yet at the same time eerily obedient and disciplined. For the Jews of Holland, the war had just begun.

And still, life went on. Shops reopened, children went back to school, adults returned to work, and in June 1940 the American consulate in Rotterdam reopened. There were no attacks on Jews of the kind reported from Poland, no persecution, no discriminatory regulations, no pogroms. Despite the uncertainty, people breathed easier. The hated Germans made their presence felt everywhere, of course. They even replaced the customary white-and-blue traffic signs with yellow-and-black ones that served as a constant and conspicuous reminder of the occupation forces' presence. But one could get used to different traffic signs.

Soldiers in German uniform became an everyday sight on the streets, but they behaved courteously and were even friendly, tempting the Dutch to believe, though they knew better, that the Germans actually were what they claimed: protectors, not occupiers, of the country.

Books by Jewish authors were, of course, removed from the schools, but if that was the worst step taken against the Jews, they could live with that. Immediately after Holland's surrender, many Jews—anticipating such a measure and fearing their homes would be searched—had rid their apartments of any books by Jews or Communists. Franz Ledermann, for example—to Sanne and Barbara's horror—had filled a big laundry basket full of books he had brought from Berlin, then destroyed them in his own private book burning.

And yet in fact, in his inaugural speech of May 29, 1940, Arthur Seyss-Inquart, an Austrian whom Hitler had appointed Reich commissioner for the occupied Netherlands, had adopted a conciliatory and antiauthoritarian tone. "We Germans have not come to subjugate this country and its people, nor do we seek to impose our political system on them," Seyss-Inquart said. As Austrian minister of the interior, he had done his best to lend Germany's annexation of Austria at least the trappings of legitimacy. Hitler had his reasons for appointing him to the new post. A father of three who walked with a pronounced limp, the result of a near-fatal mountaineering accident, Seyss-Inquart was courteous, correct, and reserved. In other positions, his leadership style would not have been aggressive enough, but for the job of Dutch Reich commissioner he was just the man Hitler was looking for. On Hitler's express orders and in contrast to German policy in other occupied territories, Seyss-Inquart formed a civilian government, and he assured the Dutch people that it would continue to function alongside the German occupation administration.

Could he be taken at his word? An attorney who was said to have won his cases "by keeping quiet, not by talking," Seyss-Inquart had been assigned to create order in Holland and placate its infuriated citizens. He stressed that there was nothing to prevent the German people and their "close relatives," the Dutch, from "meeting on terms of mutual respect." Seyss-Inquart was a practiced political tactician, and the purpose behind his initial restraint would soon become all too clear. The Jews found it reassuring that his speeches made no mention of the "Jewish question." But that omission was, of course, simply part of his strategy.

And so life went on, for the Franks, too, almost—though not quite—as if nothing had happened. Anne and Margot had to concentrate on their schoolwork. Only a few weeks were left until final report cards and the beginning of summer vacation. Anne was outraged that Holland had surrendered. Surrender was a concept she was hearing about for the first time, and she didn't like the sound of it. It didn't suit her character.

Naturally, she was affected by the uncertainty all around her, and often she was afraid. But her fear was not the oppressive anxiety that haunted her mother and grandmother. Anne's was a child's fear, concrete and momentary. It sent her in tears to the haven of Otto's bed when the night sky filled with the earthshaking drone of bombers, but it disappeared again quickly once quiet had returned. "Sleeping with Daddy is very nice, but I wish that there was another reason that I could sleep downstairs and that the times were normal again," Anne wrote to her grandmother Alice Stern Frank.

Anne joined her Dutch schoolmates in cursing the Germans. Because of them her birthday had not been celebrated as grandly as she had expected and she would not be able to go to Switzerland in the summer. But she could still go to the swimming pool in Amsterdam and perhaps even to the shore. Margot would play tennis and go rowing. These were things Anne couldn't do—she still had to be careful with her shoulder. A brief visit with Abraham and Isa Cauvern in Laren provided a change for her, as one the previous July had as well. The solid friendship that had grown up between Isa and Otto Frank since she began working for him in 1935 made it possible for him to entrust Anne to her care with full confidence.

The possibility of leaving Holland continued to preoccupy both Edith and Otto Frank, but they realized that their chances were almost nonexistent. Even Switzerland, a neutral country, had closed its borders. Otto's brother-in-law Erich Elias had a brother, Paul, who had been trying to obtain a Swiss visa since the spring of 1939. But he had been repeatedly turned down, even though Erich—before he lost his job as head of Rovag in Switerland and the family had to rely on his wife's business in secondhand goods—had guaranteed Paul's support in Switzerland as well as funds for his passage to Bolivia. If Paul could not get a visa, a family of five would have no chance at all.

Instead of giving himself over to unrealistic hopes, Otto Frank decided to make the best of things in Holland, and things indeed seemed to be falling into place for him. Business was finally improving. Hermann van Pels was teaching Victor Kugler the art of spice mixing, and in June 1940 Otto promoted his oldest employee to the position of proxy for Pectacon. Thanks to Pectacon, sales were significantly better than in previous years. Then, too, Opekta and Pectacon were able to save on overhead because both were using the same building, as well as the same office and warehouse personnel. The two businesses benefited from the general economic upswing in Holland and showed a profit for the first time.

Among Pectacon's many customers, though not one of the more regular ones, was the German Wehrmacht. That is evident in the company's order books, in which deliveries to the Wehrmacht's supply office in The Hague, to the N.V. Sunda Compagnie on behalf of the supreme command in Berlin, and directly to the Wehrmacht are recorded. Miep Gies would later confirm that Pectacon sales representatives traveled all over the country bringing in additional orders to Prinsengracht and that some of the orders were from German garrisons.

It was customary for the Wehrmacht's quartermaster offices in The Hague to order from wholesale dealers like the N.V. Sunda Company in The Hague, which then procured the items from smaller suppliers. An entry in Pectacon's order books dated June 5, 1940, just three weeks after the German takeover of Holland, documents just such a purchase. An insert from the Wehrmacht supreme command spells out the terms that all contractors dealing with the German occupation had to adhere to.

Did Otto Frank know at this point that he was supplying goods for the German army?

Sales representatives working for Pectacon on a commission basis—Mr. Oldenboom, Mr. Van der Held, and Mr. Kolle—seem to have dealt openly with the Germans. On September 17, 1940, Oldenboom and Van der Held took a large direct order on which they earned a 1 percent commission. This is the only order of its kind recorded in the books. Two days later, Pectacon delivered to the Wehrmacht quartermaster five hundred kilograms (eleven hundred pounds) of white pepper, five hundred kilograms of black pepper, and five hundred kilograms of nutmeg, all packed in handy metal containers. These spices were then distributed to individual companies.

How often Otto Frank supplied goods for the Germans cannot be documented. Most of the relevant records can no longer be found, and the remaining ones do not show any further direct transactions with the Wehrmacht. A statement by the later warehouse foreman, Willem van Maaren, however, indicates that business with the Wehrmacht was transacted indirectly: "During the occupation period, Pectacon did a lot of business with the Wehrmacht, but these deals were conducted by middlemen." He seems to suggest further that not only Pectacon but Opekta as well dealt with the enemy. We have no proof of this, nor can we assume it with any certainty. Opekta was merely one of Frankfurt Pomosin-Werke's distributers. Pomosin's "half-Jewish" owners had—in Nazi jargon—"apparently Aryanized" the business in 1937 and maintained cordial relations with Nazi bigwigs like Martin Bormann and the Frankfurt police chief Adolf Heinz Beckerle.

As producers of "goods essential to the war effort," the Pomosin-Werke did in fact enjoy special status. In the 1930s and 1940s Pomosin developed a dehydrated jam for the front and did research on the pharmaceutical uses of pectins, as coagulents to aid in blood clotting, for example ("Sangostop" had existed since World War I), as stabilizers, as detoxifying agents in cases of poisoning with heavy metals, and as ingredients in medicines for treating diarrhea. Otto Frank had nothing to do with these branches of the business. As Miep Gies reported: "[Our] pectin . . . made jam jell quickly. It was not used for any other purpose."

Was Otto Frank ever troubled by the thought that he had helped the enemy? Did he ever learn that he was denounced as "a profiteer and traitor" after the war? He never made any public statement to that effect. However, it is documented that between 1941 and 1942, in Amsterdam alone, fifteen hundred Dutch businesses had dealings with the occupation. To refuse German orders by, for instance, faking a lack of inventory was possible but extremely risky and therefore not advisable. As a businessman and especially as a Jewish businessman, Otto Frank would have not only endangered his business but also risked exposing himself and his family to the whims of the Germans.

By late 1940, the improvement in business made larger quarters desirable. The office and warehouse space Otto Frank had rented at 400 Singel had become too small, and on December 1, 1940, seven months after the German occupation began, Opekta and Pectacon moved into new quarters, a modest early-eighteenth-century building located on a canal and fifty yards from Amsterdam's best-known landmark, the Westerkerk. The narrow four-story structure had a plain facade of dirty red brick and fit inconspicuously into the densely packed row of buildings along the canal. It actually comprised two buildings, which had formerly housed the offices and workshops of several small businesses: a dressmaker's shop, a manufacturer of rolls for piano players, a printing shop, a wine and spirits dealership. Now Otto Frank's businesses with their eleven employees occupied the front one. The warehouse was on the ground floor, the offices on the second, and additional storage rooms on the third and fourth. Otto Frank sublet part of the rear building, which was accessible through a narrow corridor, to a Jewish acquaintance of his named Arthur Lewinsohn. This pharmacist, chemist, and inventor—known to his friends as Apo, for *Apotheker*—had been forced in 1933 to sell his pharmacy in Berlin-Kreuzberg to a former employee for well under its market value. Before fleeing Germany at the end of November 1938, he had continued to develop new products—a depilatory, a mouthwash, screw anchors, tooth cement, a hardening compound for steel and iron—but had to let the patents to them go to "Aryan" colleagues for paltry amounts. In early December 1938 he was unable to cross the border into Holland, lacking the necessary documents. An old friend of his from Scheveningen, however, was able to arrange a refugee's entry visa and residence permit for him and prevent his being forced to return to Germany.

Like so many other refugees, Lewinsohn remained stuck in Holland because he could not obtain a visa to any South American country. Despite the ban preventing refugees from working in Holland, Lewinsohn tried to establish himself there as an inventor. He set up a laboratory in the space he rented in the annex and plugged away at his experiments there. Thanks to his usually high spirits and his ready store of jokes, he also made himself well liked. The other rooms and an attic under the steep gabled roof remained empty. The neighboring buildings at the new address, 263 Prinsengracht, were occupied by small businesses like Otto Frank's. Meanwhile, members of the Weerbaarheidsafdeling (defense section), a paramilitary branch of the NSB, were setting up a flag hall at 400 Singel, Opekta's former address.

Earlier, Anne had sometimes joined her Pim at his office on weekends, and she occasionally went to Prinsengracht, too. On a Saturday morning in the summer of 1941, she watched him cooking up a batch of jam. From time to time, he experimented with different quantities and recipes. "While her father was in the middle of preparing a second batch, he was called away to attend to other business, but no problem: Anne had paid close attention and finished the project by herself," Johannes Kleiman reported later. "Her whole manner said: 'I can handle this.' [Anne] was really interested and eager to learn. She wanted to know how to do things herself." Sometimes Hanneli or another friend accompanied Anne. Playing at the office was fun. The girls could telephone from room to room on the intercom, type on the typewriters, use the various stamps to print comical figures made out of letters, or pour water out onto the street from the windows of the second-story office where Miep, her young colleague Bep Voskuijl, and Johannes Kleiman worked. Anne giggled so widely and infectiously over her pranks that it was almost impossible to be angry with her. When she opened her mouth to laugh, one noticed that her right front tooth stuck out, just as Edith Frank's did, giving her an impish look all the more lovable for its imperfection. But Anne didn't like to hear that she shared any features with her mother.

Now, however, she did not go to the office as often as she had in the past. Since the birth in October 1940 of Hanneli's sister, Rachel Gabriele Ida—or Gabi, as she was called from the start—the girls' Sunday ritual had changed. Anne was crazy about little children. She spent as much time as she could at the Goslars', often with Margot, watching Ruth Goslar bathe, powder, and feed the baby. Then, after begging permission to take Gabi out for a stroll, she would proudly push the baby carriage around on Merwedeplein. "Anne and I love to go visit the Goslars' baby," Margot wrote to her grandmother in December 1940. "She laughs now and grows cuter by the day." Omi Frank in Basel had to celebrate her seventy-fifth birthday without her granddaughters. "We hope that this has been the most unpleasant of birthdays," Anne wrote in her congratulatory letter, an oblique reference to the war and the only one we have from the eleven-year-old Anne. Otherwise, she wrote in a carefree tone about her activities at school; either her parents had succeeded in sheltering her from their worries or they had impressed on her the need to write only about "harmless topics," because of the threat of censorship. "I had dictation this afternoon and made no less than 27 mistakes. You will surely laugh, but this should come as no surprise because the text was very hard and I'm no star at dictations." She wrote, too, about her favorite winter sport: "I'm really looking forward to tomorrow, when I'll go skating at the rink (for the first time this year)." On January 13, 1941, she sent her relatives in Basel, especially Bernd, the family's best skater, a detailed report on her skating experiences. "I spend every free minute I have at the rink. Until now I'd been using Margot's old skates that I had to attach to my shoes with a key. All my friends at the rink had real figure skates with the blades attached to the shoes with little nails so they can't come off." Anne must have begged and pleaded for new skates so relentlessly that her parents finally gave in. "After pestering my parents for a long time I got new skates, and now I'm taking lessons in figure skating. We're learning to waltz on skates, to jump, and all kinds of other things. I gave my old skates to Hanneli, and she is very pleased with them, so now both of us are happy." At the end of her letter she wrote about little Gabi Goslar. "Hanneli's baby sister is very sweet. I'm allowed to hold her sometimes. She smiles at everyone, and all the children envy Hanneli."

Life went on, almost—but not quite—as if nothing had happened. Every week the German administration came up with new regulations. At first these applied to everyone, but more and more of them were directed specifically at the Jewish population.

"To protect the Dutch population from false news reports," the occupation forces had decreed as early as July 4, 1940, the people would henceforth be allowed to listen only to radio programs broadcast either "by stations located within occupied Dutch territory" or "by stations of the Greater German Reich, inclusive of the Protectorate of Bohemia and Moravia and of the General Government of the Occupied Territories of Poland." Anyone caught listening "intentionally" to other stations would be subject to a heavy fine or, in more serious cases, up to ten years in prison.

This prohibition was, of course, directed against the BBC and Radio Oranje, a program named for the Dutch royal family and broadcast by the BBC. Starting at the end of July 1940, the queen spoke to her people every evening from her exile in London. There could be no compromise, she said, with Hitler and his henchmen; this was a war between good and evil, and good would prevail. Her impassioned speeches helped keep up her people's spirits, but for the Dutch population they must have rung hypothetical and hollow. What constituted compromise? Was a butcher who sold to German soldiers guilty of compromising? What about Otto Frank, who was responsible not only for his family and himself but also for his employees and who therefore filled orders for the Germans? Who can dare to pass judgment on him? As the war continued, the occupiers of course assumed ever greater control of the Dutch economy. By 1944, the fact is that about half of all Holland's businesses were providing goods and services to the occupation. Still, it would be no exaggeration to say that—apart from the small number of Dutch National Socialists—nearly every adult in Holland, including the Franks, listened to Wilhelmina and her newscasters every day and took courage from them.

On July 16, 1940, the Germans directed their first blow against the Jews in Holland—but without even using the word *Jews.* The law for the "Prevention of Cruel Practices in Slaughtering" forbade the slaughtering of cattle and poultry in accordance with Jewish religious law. Only the relatively small group of Jews who kept kosher households were affected: from now on, they would have to be vegetarians. Most Jews took little notice of the regulation. If this was the worst they had to put up with, there was no cause for distress.

The next order came in August. All German Jews who had immigrated to Holland after January 1, 1933, were required to register with the Office for Resident Foreigners. A routine registration, people were assured, nothing to worry about. Otto Frank obeyed the summons and registered his family as "German Jews." Anne and Margot knew nothing of this. Individuals were not required to appear in person. Who knows whether the summons gave Otto an inkling of how dangerous his situation was, whether he realized that from now on the Germans could keep track of him? Or did he, like most others, see the measure as essentially unimportant? In retrospect it seems clear that the Germans had taken their first step toward solving the "Jewish question" in Holland.

Otto must have seen through the next seemingly harmless regulation. On October 22, 1940, Arthur Seyss-Inquart, whose wife was an adamant, indeed a fanatical, anti-Semite, ordered all businesses that had more than 25 percent Jewish ownership or at least one Jewish director or legal representative to register with the Bureau of Economic Investigation. Otto's quick response suggests that he had already made plans for such an eventuality. He realized that the decree was only the first step in the total "dejudification of commerce" and that it would be followed by measures similar to those by which Jewish property had been "Aryanized" in Germany. He had watched his wife's family lose everything they had, and he was determined that the same thing not happen to him.

The complete reliability of Otto's employees was of inestimable value to him. They admired his calm, courteous, and modest ways, his keen sense of justice, his paternal interest in each of them, and they repaid him with unquestioning loyalty. Otto and his employees must already have made plans to thwart the forced "Aryanization" of the business, for the day after the decree was announced, Victor Kugler and Jan Gies founded La Synthèse N.V., temporarily located in Kugler's hometown of Hilversum, a firm whose purpose was "to manufacture and trade in chemical and pharmaceutical products, foodstuffs, and table luxuries, as well as to participate in similar undertakings, all in the broadest sense." The former deputy director, Victor Kugler, was named managing director and Jan Gies, by now a trusted friend, supervisory director. They also put up the necessary initial capital, supplied, of course, by Otto. So there it was: a purely "Aryan" enterprise, totally legal, which was then ready to move its headquarters to Prinsengracht in December 1940.

In all other respects Otto obeyed the regulations laid down by the occupation forces. To do otherwise would only have jeopardized him and his employees. "Violations of military or political regulations," Seyss-Inquart had threatened, carried a minimum sentence of up to six months in prison and a fine of a thousand guilders; violation of the registration requirement for Jewish businesses could bring as much as five years. On November 27, 1940, Otto Frank therefore gave the Bureau of Economic Investigation the required details concerning his two enterprises. At that time he owned a 100 percent interest in Opekta and only 20 percent in Pectacon, claiming that the remaining stock in this young company was yet to be issued. That unissued stock left Otto with an escape hatch that he made use of four months later: in early April 1941, in accordance with decisions reached at a fictitious board meeting supposedly held on February 13, the previously unissued 80 percent of the company's stock was registered in the names of Johannes Kleiman and Otto's non-Jewish attorney, Anton Dunselman. (Otto Frank had been working with Dunselman since the 1920s.) So now Pectacon, at least, was in "Aryan" ownership. Otto would deal with the Opekta problem later. For the moment, it was under the protection of the Frankfurt Pomosin-Werke.

"Strike! Strike! Strike! Protest against this abominable persecution of the Jews!!!" Some members of the Dutch Communist Party made this appeal to Dutch workers in a leaflet distributed on February 24, 1941. "On Saturday and Sunday, the Nazis plucked hundreds of Jews off the streets and hauled them away to unknown destinations in paddy wagons. . . . Workers of Amsterdam, can you tolerate that? No, a thousand times no!!!! Organize a protest strike in every place of business!!! Join in solidarity to fight against terror!!! Demand the immediate release of the imprisoned Jews!!!! Demand the disbanding of the WA [Weer Afdeling, or Defense Department, a paramilitary NSB organization] groups!!! Organize for your self-defense in factories, in all quarters of the city!!! Show your solidarity with the sorely mistreated Jews, working men and women like you!!! Take Jewish children away from the Nazis and into your homes!!! Make use of the vast strength your unity gives you. This strength is much greater than that of the German military occupation. Strike!!! Strike!!! Strike!!! Join together!! Take heart!! Strike for the liberation of our country!!!"

The appeal proved effective. On February 25 at ten-thirty in the morning the streetcars of Amsterdam came to a halt. Hundreds of thousands of people throughout the country stopped working. In shops and restaurants, salespeople, waiters, and waitresses refused to serve anyone. In factories, shipyards, railroad stations, newspaper offices, and print shops, the roar and clatter of machinery—from typewriters to riveting guns to locomotives to printing presses—fell silent. The most widespread strike Holland had ever experienced was the people's collective response to a series of increasingly brutal Nazi attacks on the Jewish population, a response that was and that remains to this day unique in the world in both its intent and its scope.

The unexpected announcement on January 10, 1941, that all Jews in the country now had to register, as the German immigrants had had to do a few months earlier, had caused some uneasiness, but still the Jews did not perceive it as an immediate threat. Most of them dutifully obeyed the new regulation. Written in the Nazis' typically high-handed, arrogant, and verbose bureaucratese, the registration order included the following requirement: "The individual registering will pay in advance a fee of one guilder to

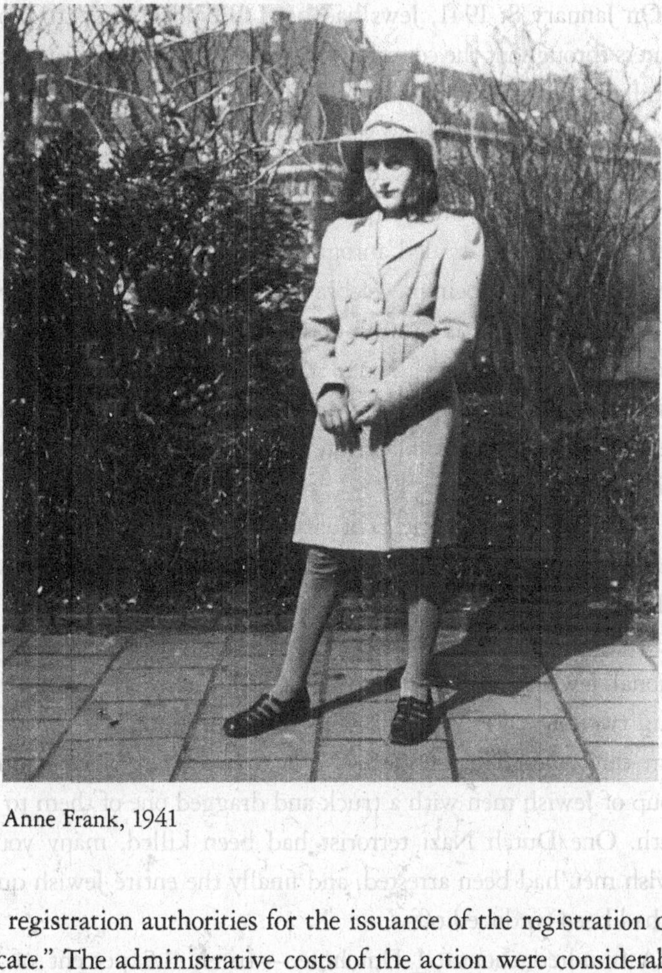

Anne Frank, 1941

the registration authorities for the issuance of the registration certificate." The administrative costs of the action were considerable, and the Nazis cynically passed those costs along to the Jews themselves.

With the help of Dutch officials motivated by an unfortunate mix of conscientiousness, cowardice, ignorance, and—justified—fear, the Germans registered 160,820 people: 140,552 Jews, 14,549 "half Jews," and 5,719 "quarter Jews." Otto Frank once again went alone to register. It was better if Anne and Margot knew nothing of this, especially Anne, who would insist on an explanation.

On January 8, 1941, Jews had been forbidden access to movie theaters throughout the country. They were clearly distressed by this humiliating order, but they still didn't think themselves in any real danger. The order did, however, create a minor drama for Anne, who loved to go to movies and was fascinated by the glamorous world of Hollywood. She cut pictures of famous stars out of magazines, collected and traded autographed picture cards, and fantasized vividly about being a celebrated movie actress herself. Given her considerable gifts as a mimic and comedienne, it must have been hard for her not to be able to go to movies anymore. The Franks, like many other parents, soon found a solution. They rented projectors, screens, and films and held private screenings for their children in their apartments.

But the events of early February 1941 made it clear that the danger to Jews was mounting and could no longer be played down. Led by German soldiers, Nazi collaborators with members of the NSB terror group Weer Afdeling among them had raided the traditional Jewish quarter in Amsterdam first on February 9, then again two days later, meeting with resistance both from Jews and from their Dutch neighbors. A Dutch Nazi had plowed into a group of Jewish men with a truck and dragged one of them to his death. One Dutch Nazi terrorist had been killed, many young Jewish men had been arrested, and finally the entire Jewish quarter had been cordoned off.

A hundred thousand Dutchmen—barely 1.5 percent of the population but still a force to be reckoned with—proudly claimed membership in the NSB, the Dutch National Socialist Movement. Twenty to twenty-five thousand of them had volunteered for the "Germanic SS in the Netherlands," a division of the Waffen-SS, whose members swore oaths of loyalty to Adolf Hitler. Though most Dutch National Socialists had not been anti-Semitic up to this point and had even befriended individual Jews, there were many who let themselves be drawn into persecuting Jews by the hope of profiting not only economically but also socially. And more than a few regarded the opportunity the "Wehrmacht Travel Agency" gave them to escape the narrow confines of their village lives as a great blessing. Whatever the case, the Dutch Nazis no longer hesitated to make a show of their supposed power. They may have been a minority, but they set the tone. The time when Jews could feel safe in Holland was over. That was brought home to Otto and Edith Frank every day of their lives now.

Rioting had not yet broken out in South Amsterdam, where the Franks lived. But was that mere chance, and could Jewish residents there really assume they were not in danger? Fear, mistrust, and uncertainty were the adults' constant companions. As if to make the best of things, the Franks celebrated Margot's birthday on February 16 more lavishly than ever. "I haven't gotten as many gifts in years as I got this year," she wrote to her grandmother in Basel, "and that my birthday fell on a Sunday made it extra nice. . . . The table was far from empty." The gifts she particularly treasured were a copy of *Camera Obscura*—"That's a book one simply has to have here in Holland"—some visiting cards, and a suit. And of course there was Otto's traditional poem, lovingly dedicated, as always, to the birthday girl:

At fifteen you're a real teenager
And vastly more stylish, I would wager,
Than last year's birthday child,
But since you remain as shy and mild,
I've decided to come to your aid
With visiting cards, you tongue-tied maid.
If someone now your name should ask
You needn't cringe from the loathsome task
Of speaking your name in public aloud.
Instead, with mien haughty and proud,
You'll reach in your purse for a visiting card,

Which shouldn't prove impossibly hard.
But now, enough! Let's go and see
What gifts you have additionally.
Our dear Mutz, on this, your day,
We wish you happiness in every way.

So the family struggled to maintain a small island of harmony and normalcy as disorder and violence raged in the world outside. The rioting on February 9 and 11 marked the beginning of a series of brutal acts that prompted Paul de Groot's call for a general strike on the twenty-fifth. Three days after Margot's fifteenth birthday came an incident at an ice cream parlor called the Koco in South Amsterdam. Owned by two German immigrants named Kohn and Cahn, it had long provoked the anger and suspicions of the National Socialists. It was a favorite gathering place for Jewish refugees, who went there not only to drink coffee but also to talk politics. The German security police who stopped by Koco on the nineteenth no doubt assumed that still worse activities were taking place there, namely, that the patrons were plotting acts of resistance. Koco's regular customers, annoyed by the Nazis' frequent visits, had planned an unpleasant surprise for them. When the police came through the door, Koco's patrons sprayed them with ammonia. But the plan backfired. The patrons had expected Dutch Nazis, not German police. The police reacted violently, firing their handguns wildly into the room, arresting the owners and several patrons, and blowing the incident up in the press the next day, claiming that heavily armed Jews had attacked German policemen. Two weeks later Ernst Cahn was executed.

The so-called Koco affair played right into the hands of the occupation forces. At last they had an excuse for their actions. This "latest Jewish impertinence," as Hanns Albin Rauter, the SS commander for the Netherlands, called it, this brazen provocation, could not go unpunished. On the afternoon of February 22, a Saturday, a detachment of the "Green Police" (officially named the Civil Police) stormed the central square and randomly, senselessly, sadistically attacked every Jewish man they could get their hands on. They yanked people off their bicycles, separated couples, tore children from their parents' arms, knocked people down. They arrested and hauled off 427 Jewish men between the ages of twenty and thirty-five.

The National Socialists had put all scruples and inhibitions aside. Had they been able to, they would have robbed the Jews of anything they could. As it was, they had already begun systematically plundering Holland, sending Dutch foodstuffs to Germany and forcing the Dutch to work in German war industries; indeed, they were already planning to annex Holland. In the minds of many Dutch citizens, people who saw these things happening and refused to act were as good as accomplices. They had to fight the injustice; they had to resort to whatever means it took to force the release of the Jewish men arrested on February 22. And so the Communist Party, in outrage and fury, called for a general strike, and the greater part of the Dutch people followed that call.

But they had underestimated the violence the Nazis were willing to unleash on them. "Not only were small arms used, but several hand grenades were necessary as well," SS commander Rauter reported to his superiors after the strike had been quashed. "The Waffen-SS rapidly dispersed demonstrations and assemblies of any kind, with the result that by the late afternoon of the twenty-sixth all disturbances had been put down." In Amsterdam alone, seven strikers were killed and seventy-six wounded; countless numbers were arrested. The strike did not succeed in putting an end to anti-Jewish terror. On February 27 the 427 arrested Jewish men were deported, first to the Buchenwald concentration camp, then to Mauthausen, as it was later discovered. Only two of them lived to return to Holland.

The spring of 1941 passed uneventfully. Many Jews thought that with February's violence behind them the worst was over. Otto Frank would learn differently. On Friday, April 18, an unexpected visit interrupted his daily routine. A young man, escorted to Otto's office by an employee, introduced himself only after he had shut the door behind him and he and Otto were alone. "Tonny Ahlers . . . member of the NSB." He was twenty-three years old, a little taller than Otto, voluble, indeed downright garrulous; he had a slight limp. His correct and unostentatious appearance may well have made a favorable impression on Otto Frank.

"He said straight out that he worked as a courier between the Dutch Nazis and the Gestapo, and he asked me for twenty guilders," Otto Frank reported in the late 1950s in an interview intended for public release. "I gave him the money, and he gave me a letter. I opened it. It was a message from an acquaintance of mine to the Gestapo, saying I had expressed doubt about a German victory and had attempted to influence him."

Otto Frank had in fact a few weeks earlier happened to meet a former colleague, Joseph "Job" Jansen, of whom he said, "I didn't like him very much." In 1935 and 1936, Jansen had built Opekta stands for trade fairs. His wife, Jetje Bremer, had worked for Opekta during those years demonstrating the product, and one of her sons had been Otto Frank's warehouse man. When Jansen—two years older than Otto Frank and a devoted member of the NSB (membership number 29992)—accused his wife of having an affair with her boss, Otto Frank ended their business relationship. "In matters of business," he said in his usual reserved manner, "their behavior was unimpeachable."

Joseph Jansen was also a member of De Voortrekkers, a theater group with NSB leanings that had formed immediately after the Germans occupied Holland. The group was based in the Princess Theater in The Hague, which later became the German Theater, and it toured the country with propaganda plays presenting Germany in a favorable light. Jansen began his work with De Voortrekkers as a stage designer, then worked as a stage manager and actor. When the group was engaged to record radio plays for Radio Hilversum, Jansen was a member of the recording team. Jansen's wife ran a florist's shop in Amsterdam.

On that March day in 1941 Joseph Jansen and Otto Frank touched on the course the war was taking. "Mr. Jansen asked me, because I was a Jew, if I still received shipments from Germany, and I said yes," Otto Frank reported to the Dutch Office for National Security in August 1945. "Jansen said the war would soon be over, whereupon I replied that I was not convinced of that and that the Germans still had a lot of fighting ahead of them. Then we went our ways."

For Otto Frank this short conversation seemed initially of no consequence. But for the right-wing radical Job Jansen, whose marriage to a Jewish woman did not prevent him from being a notorious anti-Semite or from handing over to the Gestapo two of their sons, the meeting with Otto Frank was a welcome opportunity to attribute "statements hostile to Germany" to his rival and to do him intentional harm.

Otto Frank was well aware of what stood in store for him if he was reported to the Gestapo. It is therefore not surprising that he saw Tonny Ahlers not as an unscrupulous blackmailer but as a rescuer. Whether Ahlers and Jansen knew each other or if they were in cahoots is unclear. Otto Frank probably did not concern himself with these questions at the time. Nor did he have any idea what an unstable person Ahler was behind his friendly facade. A "difficult young man who gets in trouble wherever he turns up, who has an inflated idea of his own worth but never sticks with anything very long" was the assessment that a social worker for the city of Amsterdam had provided toward the end of 1938 when Ahlers was released from prison after serving time for crimes he had committed as a member of the Iron Guard. This anti-Semitic gang of thugs probably provided Ahlers with a sense of security and belonging. A year earlier, in a fit of lovesickness, he had tried to commit suicide by drowning himself.

Ahlers probably joined the NSB toward the end of 1940. The German occupation had, in a sense, legalized his depredations against the Jews. While many of Ahlers's friends from the Iron Guard had volunteered to serve on the eastern front, childhood polio had left him unfit for military or work service, and so he remained behind to stir up trouble in Amsterdam. Wherever a brawl between Nazis and Jews was in the offing, he was on hand. During the February strike of 1941, he reportedly lent support to the Weer Afdeling, and in order to document his fistfights photographically, he would intentionally provoke them. He sold the pictures to the SS, and he volunteered himself to the security service, as an informant.

A troublemaker and con man? Or a dangerous criminal? Whichever the case, the security service could make good use of zealots like him. In September 1941, five months after his first meeting with Otto Frank, Ahlers was enlisted as a permanent employee of the security service.

It is not clear whether Ahlers appeared at 263 Prinsengracht again—or perhaps regularly—after April 18 to relieve Otto Frank of money for "his cooperation" or to sound him out and blackmail him in some other way. (Ahlers's mother lived only five buildings away at 253 Prinsengracht. However, Ahlers's political leanings made him unwelcome there.) Otto Frank later recalled at the most only one further visit from Ahlers, on which occasion he gave Ahlers five or ten guilders. But Ahlers claimed he visited Otto often. Given Ahlers's record, it is unimaginable that his intention was to rescue Otto Frank from the Gestapo. It is also puzzling that in December 1942, more than a year and a half after his first meeting with Otto Frank, Ahlers registered a small business that, just like Opekta, dealt in unrefined sugar and sugar products. (To date, though, no solid proof of business dealings between Otto Frank or his colleagues and Ahlers has been found.)

In any case, in April 1941 it was not Tonny Ahlers but Joseph Jansen whom Otto Frank feared.

Otto Frank did not tell his wife about the meeting with Ahlers. Edith was, according to Otto, on the whole much more depressed than he was. He did give the letter to his employees to read, and they reacted with predictable dismay, but even they could not know how devastating this incident had been for him. For the first time, the persecution of the Jews had struck him personally. Otto Frank, the thoughtful man to whom others usually turned for advice, now sought the counsel of his lawyer, Antonius Dunselmann, who immediately destroyed the letter.

What if Joseph Jansen made further attempts to harm him? How could Otto Frank defend himself? And his family? And even if things went no further than this one attempt at denunciation, wasn't the arbitrary hand of those in power constantly striking down innocent men? And wasn't it already clear that they would tighten their regulations against the Jews and eventually impose a blanket prohibition on all Jewish businesses? How would he then be able to feed his family? Would he be able to rely on his Dutch friends and employees?

Although there is no documentation that his meeting with Tonny Ahlers motivated Otto Frank to once again pin his hopes on emigration, it seems highly likely that it would have. And, given political developments in Europe, the desired destination would surely have been America. "How long will it be that I may continue my work here? I am forced to look out for emigration and as far as I can see U.S.A. is the only country we could go to," Otto Frank wrote on April 30, 1941. "Who can tell if there is still a chance to leave Europe by the time this letter is going to arrive."

With every good wish
to a fine boss and a great
public servant.
Nathan Straus

Nathan "Charley" Straus

He noted hopefully that "one says that no special difficulties shall be made from the part of the German Authorities."

Before Otto Frank wrote these lines to his former university friend Charley Straus, he must have revealed his plans to his brothers-in-law Julius and Walter Holländer and asked for their aid. The two bachelors would do everything they could to help; on that Otto could depend. But they were having their own difficulties establishing themselves in America. Julius had arrived in New York on April 5, 1938, and traveled from there to Massachusetts. Walter was finally able to follow him in December. On the fourteenth, having of course first paid for his room and board, he was released from the internment camp. "Upon presentation of his passenger ticket and his visa for America, Walter Holländer is hereby discharged from the Jewish refugee camp Zeeburg in Amsterdam," his release document read. "He will depart on December 16, 1939 [according to the passenger list, the date was December 17], on the *Volendam* for America. He must notify the police registry for aliens of his departure."

The two businessmen, who upon graduation from the gymnasium had received "thorough private instruction in business" from a professor at the technical university, had not been able to find work until June 1940. In Aachen, they had not only conducted their business affairs but also served on the boards of various charitable organizations, held honorary posts in the Jewish community, and supported athletic groups like the Gymnastics Club 1906 and the Soccer Club Allemannia as well as the Reich Association of Jewish Combat Veterans. Now, for a weekly wage of twenty-eight dollars, Julius worked night shifts tending the furnaces of the Canton Japanning Company. Walter worked as a laborer for the E. F. Dodge Paper Box Corporation in Leominster, also for about twenty dollars a week. Living in tiny rented rooms near their places of work, the brothers worked hard and barely squeaked by.

The prospect of being able to bring their mother, their sister, and their sister's family to the United States lent purpose to their work. Their savings added up to $2,900. On May 10, 1941—coincidentally the day, one year earlier, on which the Germans had occupied Holland—they sent to Holland guarantees of support for Rosa Holländer and for Edith and Otto Frank. Walter's boss, Jacob Hiatt, signed the affidavit for Anne Frank. Harry Levine of the New England Novelty Company, an acquaintance of Hiatt's and, like him, an up-and-coming businessman, signed for Margot. In his native country of Lithuania, Jacob Hiatt had worked as a district court judge. He immigrated to the United States in 1935 and took over the direction of the carton factory in 1939. In a letter sent to his brothers-in-law after the war, Otto Frank wrote, "I will never forget that Walter's boss sent an affidavit."

To issue a visa, an American consul had to have the approval of the U.S. Department of State. The decision, however, was largely left to the consul's judgment. Would Otto Frank's application end up in the hands of one of the more humane officials? And would this official be convinced that Julius and Walter Holländer could support five people on their laborers' wages? Otto Frank was doubtful and went on the assumption that the consulate would demand a deposit of $5,000, a sum he could not raise and certainly not in foreign currency. He therefore had to swallow his pride and appeal to his old friend Charley in New York.

Charles Webster Straus was exactly one week younger than Otto Frank and had graduated from Princeton with a major in economics. According to *Time* magazine, he was a "serious, sardonic, rather shy" person. His father, Nathan, was born in the Rhine Palatinate and as a boy had emigrated with his parents and siblings to the United States. Together with several members of his family, he owned a number of businesses, among them Macy's. But his major interest was a process for pasteurizing milk that he wanted to establish in Germany. To this end, he set up the Nathan Straus

Pasteurized Milk Laboratories in Heidelberg's university district, proposing to run the business himself for a year. The plan was for his son, who was enrolled at Princeton, to study in Heidelberg, and in the fall of 1907 Charles accompanied his father and mother to Europe.

Charley and Otto Frank shared student quarters and became fast friends. They stayed in touch, even after Otto returned to Frankfurt from his internship in New York and Charley (named for one of the founders of Macy's) had completed his studies at Princeton. In July 1928 or thereabouts they vacationed together in Sils Maria. As early as the summer of 1910, Charley had changed his name to Nathan Straus Jr., both out of respect for his father and in the interests of his career. The name of Nathan Straus carried weight in the public eye and in the business world of New York.

Nathan Straus Jr. became a journalist, first as a reporter for the *New York Globe*, then as publisher of the satirical magazine *Puck*. Described by *Time* as a "liberal, almost Socialistic Democrat" and "pacifist," he held a seat in the New York State Senate from 1921 to 1926. He was also chairman of the board of the radio stations WMCA in New York and WBNY in Buffalo, and from 1937 to 1942, as chief administator of the federal Housing Authority, he managed an $800 million public housing program. He owned Nathan Straus & Sons, Inc., the largest producer of tableware in the United States, and counted Franklin and Eleanor Roosevelt among his friends. Nathan Straus Jr. was without doubt an influential man. "You are the only person I know that I can ask: Would it be possible for you to give a deposit in my favor?"

In his letter of April 30, 1941, Otto Frank tried to maintain a businesslike tone, but his desperation showed through. "I would not ask if conditions here would not force me to do all I can in time to be able to avoid worse. . . . It is for the sake of the children mainly that we have to care for." And of course he would not make use of the money himself: "I feel still young enough to work and I trust that I shall find means to get along." If possible, Otto would pay for the passage himself. A visa could not be had without proof of paid passage. "It is said that discussions were pending with the 'joint' in order to be able to pay them [the tickets] in Florins. . . . Should it be the case then I could manage to pay the amount myself." (In January 1942, Otto Frank declared his net worth to the Central office for Jewish Emigration as 10,029.51 guilders.)

On May 28, 1941, Helen Straus, Nathan's wife since 1915, passed Otto's letter on to the National Refugee Service, a private service, in New York. "We do want to help," she wrote in her accompanying letter. Despite their influence and their connections in the State Department, Nathan and Helen Straus still felt obliged to go through established channels, even for Nathan's "best friend during their university years—an extraordinarily fine man." They vouched for Otto's reputation without qualification. They were, however, initially hesitant about providing financial aid: "His request is hardly possible to fulfill and doesn't even seem to me to be what is needed."

Nathan and Helen Straus discussed with the Refugee Service the conditions and amounts that would guarantee support for Otto Frank and his family. They were advised to assure Otto Frank in writing of the following points: "That you are preparing affidavits of support on behalf of him and his family. That your affidavits will be accompanied by a covering letter from you to the American consul in Amsterdam stating the reasons for your interest in Mr. Frank and his family and your concern about their welfare. That you hope your affidavit and the accompanying documents will satisfy the American consul, so that no deposit of $5,000 will be necessary."

A race against time had begun. Formalities and bureaucratic process ate up weeks and months. In the spring of 1941, the chances for the Franks' emigration to the United States seemed significantly worse than when they applied for visas in 1938, and in the course of the year those chances grew slimmer still. "Many people have been waiting for months for permission to leave, and no one knows whether and when it will be granted. We don't know the requirements, and everyone hopes that despite all it will come through," Otto Frank wrote.

Since the beginning of the war, the already widespread fear in American official circles that refugees—fanatics, negative elements, Communists, spies—would endanger the country had grown. In June 1940, Breckenridge Long, undersecretary of state and chief of all U.S. consulates, had indicated to his colleagues in an internal memorandum that in the future as few refugees as possible should be allowed entry: "We can delay and effectively stop for a temporary period of indefinite length the number of immigrants into the United States. We could do this by simply advising our consuls to put every obstacle in the way and to require additional evidence and to resort to various administrative devices which would postpone and postpone and postpone the granting of the visas." The anti-Semitic Long had his way. The United States made the conditions for obtaining a visa harder to meet. "I found that he [President Roosevelt] was 100% in accord with my ideas," he recorded in his diary.

That someone as prominent in public life as Nathan Straus was pleading the Franks' case was helpful, but it would have been naïve to assume that his help would provide any guarantee.

Otto Frank was by no means naïve, and it was not in his character to sit back and just hope for rescue from the United States. As long as he and his family were stuck in Holland he was at least going to see to it that the National Socialists did not deprive him of his means of earning a living. "I was successful this past year. The business has grown," he wrote. Sales in spices, too, benefited from the opening of the German market and the temporary upswing under the German occupation. In 1941, Otto Frank's income increased threefold over that of the previous years. He did not, however, give himself up to illusions. Sooner or later, Jewish businesses in Holland would be completely Aryanized. Whatever he could do to rescue Pectacon and Opekta, he wanted to do, in spite of or, more accurately, on account of the bad news that kept arriving ever more frequently.

In June 1941, the National Socialists laid the groundwork for seizing control of Jewish capital assets. Jews were required to transfer their bank accounts to Lippmann, Rosenthal and Co. in Amsterdam, a Jewish banking house that the German occupation forces had placed under their supervision and made use of for their own purposes. Jews were also required to pay off their debts as soon as possible and to deposit all the cash and checks they received in Lippmann, Rosenthal. Every Jew was permitted to keep up to a thousand guilders in cash, but seen in the context of the 700 million guilders garnered by the Nazis, this concession seems more like a slap in the face.

Otto Frank no doubt realized that this move on the authorities' part amounted to a barrier against further emigration, which would now no longer be easy to finance.

At about the same time came another bit of bad news. The United States ordered the German consulates in the country to shut down for fear that they would spawn espionage cells. Germany retaliated, over the course of July expelling all American ambassadors and consuls from Germany and the countries it occupied. Diplomatic relations between the two countries were cut off. On July 10, the U.S. consulate in Amsterdam closed its doors. Who, if anyone, could issue visas to the Frank-Holländer family now?

Otto and Edith Frank kept their worries from their children as best they could, and Anne and Margot remained largely unburdened by their parents' cares. Even in moments of greatest uncertainty, Otto Frank still summoned thoughtful, warmhearted words and jokes when they were most needed. That was one of his strengths. But now the National Socialists had embarked on a focused campaign to exclude Jewish children and young people from daily life. Jewish children, like their parents, were to understand that they were pariahs.

On the last day of May, the Nazi lawmakers barred Jews not only from public beaches and swimming pools but also from parks, spas, and hotels. "We're not likely to get sunburned, because we can't go to the swimming pool," Anne complained, probably in mid-July, to her "dear Omi and all our other dear relatives" in Basel. "Too bad, but there's nothing to be done." Anne did not tell her grandmother that on the last day of school the Nazis had made

Anne Frank at the Jewish lyceum in Amsterdam, 1941.

their first move against Jewish children, requiring all pupils from Jewish families to register. Perhaps Anne just took this in stride and didn't think much about it, or perhaps she knew that information of that kind would not please the censors. She and the other Jewish pupils in her class had been given registration forms and been asked to fill them out and hand them in before the end of the school day. That was all there was to it. And then summer vacation began.

Anne's vacation started with a particularly exciting event. On July 16, Miep Santrouschitz and Jan Gies were married. After the wedding, Otto invited the small group of wedding guests to a reception in his office at 263 Prinsengracht. Anne, in a light-colored dress and white socks, gave Miep her family's wedding present, a silver tray, and served the assembled guests. A few days later, she traveled with Sanne and Sanne's parents to Beekbergen, near Apeldoom, about fifty miles from Amsterdam, where she visited Eva

Otto and Anne with friends, on the way to Miep Gies's wedding, July 16, 1941.

Kämpfer, a niece of Franz Ledermann, whom Anne called Uncle Frans. Because Eva had no longer felt safe living in The Hague, she had moved to Beekbergen with her family and found a delightfully situated summerhouse there. "I'm in Beekbergen now," Anne wrote her Omi in Basel on July 31. "It's very nice here, but it's a pity the weather is so bad. The house is very old-fashioned but still pleasant. Sanne and I have our own little room." Between the lines was an allusion to the nighttime air-raid alarms that had become routine in Amsterdam. "We sleep a lot better at night here than in Amsterdam. There's nothing at all to disturb us." The days, too, passed quietly and uneventfully. "I'm reading a lot. It's too bad we can't go outside." She sent the same message to her father, hinting gently at the same time that more books would be welcome: "I'm reading a lot and have read all my books and Sanne's books except for one."

Anne wrote several letters home, perhaps because she was homesick or because she was bored. Or perhaps she was already beginning to discover the pleasures of writing. Edith and Otto answered her in separate letters. "I haven't gotten a letter from Mother since Tuesday evening, and now it's Monday evening," she complained to her father. Edith Holländer was tending to her mother night and day. In June, Rosa Holländer had been taken to the hospital, where she underwent surgery. The diagnosis: cancer.

Letters and packages from her father pleased her all the more: "Thanks for your letter and the money. I can use it. I've already spent quite a bit, but none of it for unnecessary things. I had to have stamps for all the people I wanted to write to. Then I spent .25 guilders on citronella, .05 for envelopes, .10 for candy, .05 for a notebook, .73 for postcards, which comes to 3.20 guilders altogether." And on another occasion, after she had had to spend some time in bed: "Many thanks for the two film-star cards, which came right after the first ones. I didn't have either one. I was really happy to get your letter, and the sugar, jam, and rice, too. The rice is just what I need because I've got an upset stomach and have been eating a lot of rice. I got up for the first time today, and I feel better except that I still have a headache and a stomachache." She must have had time on her hands, for she even described the food: "This evening we had baked fish with potatoes and salad. I couldn't eat the salad or the bread. And afterwards we had a marvelous pudding with cherries and sauce." She was careful to say how much she liked pudding, but only with sauce. Surely Mother could make one, too, with raspberries, perhaps.

The harmony that Anne's letters portray does not seem to have prevailed at the summerhouse every day. Eva Kämpfer, whose one-and-a-half-year-old son, Raymond, Anne described as "basically nice but annoying sometimes," did not always find her an easy guest. While Sanne was content to be left alone, Anne was moody and complained often about boredom. Her spirits depended entirely on what activities were planned for the day.

Sanne and Anne probably got along as well as ever, though Sanne, who was prettier than Anne but who was nonetheless overshadowed by her, did not yet share Anne's awakening interest in the opposite sex. The adults observed, too, how much more developed Anne was than Sanne. All Anne's talk about boys seemed silly, Sanne told her older sister, Barbara. The fact is that, for all her seriousness, Sanne was still a child, while Anne seemed to be experiencing the first signs of puberty. Certainly they would account for the restlessness and flightiness Eva Kämpfer noticed in her, although the rebelliousness of this thoroughly spoiled child had, of course, always been quite pronounced.

Anne was probably already in Beekbergen when Nathan Straus's reply to Otto's April letter arrived. It gave no cause for hope. "I am afraid, however, the news is not good news. Unless you can get to a place where there is an American Consul, there does not seem to be any way of arranging for you to come over. I am informed that there are still American Consuls in Portugal, Spain, Free France, and Switzerland."

One of the conditions imposed by the State Department was that anyone wishing to emigrate had to appear in person at a U.S. consulate. But a trip to a consulate could be made only if one had an exit permit, which could be had only if one had a visa for the country one wanted to visit.

A catch-22. Was there no way out? Otto Frank was not ready to give up. "The only way to get to a neutral country are visas of others [*sic*] states such as Cuba . . . and many of my acquaintances got visas for Cuba." This was a realistic opportunity for anyone who had money: $2,000 per person had to be deposited as security in an American bank in Cuba as possible support for the newly arrived immigrant. The sum was "refundable if the alien does not arrive." The Cuban immigration service required $500 per person as a kind of debarkation fee. Another $150 had to be deposited for each adult's return trip and $75 for each child. And on top of that came $530 to issue visas for three adults and two children. "I know it is impossible for us all to leave even if most of the money is refundable, but Edith urges me to leave alone or with the children. I hate this idea but it has to be considered. There might be situations in which one tries everything."

Otto and Edith Frank both subscribed to the idea that the family must be kept together. That Otto nonetheless considered traveling ahead of the family if need be and leaving behind not only Edith with her seriously ill mother but also his children makes painfully clear how great the pressure on the Jewish population already was and how personally threatened Otto felt. And that Edith urged him to go with or without the children demonstrates her selflessness and her unbounded love for her closest relatives. Neither Otto nor Edith Frank could, of course, assess the actual severity of the threat. But they still had hope. If Otto succeeded in obtaining a visa for Cuba and an exit permit from the German authorities that would allow him to visit an American consulate in Spain or Portugal, then the U.S. State Department would accept Nathan Straus's affidavits for the Franks. The consul could approve direct entry into the United States, and the detour by way of Cuba would be unnecessary. In the ideal situation, the family could travel straight from Rotterdam to New York. Realistic observers were not so sanguine about Otto's prospects; "I am afraid that he is rather optimistic," someone who worked for the National Refugee service wrote to Helen Straus. By early September Otto Frank had learned that the cards were indeed stacked against him: "I was informed that nobody could enter the U.S.A. if he leaves family back in occupied countries."

That he was condemned to wait instead of taking the fate of his family into his own hands as he was accustomed to do no doubt weighed heavily on Otto Frank. He needed a break. Toward the middle of September he traveled to Arnhem, taking his younger daughter with him. Edith and Margot stayed in Amsterdam and cared for Oma Holländer, who was for the moment improving. "Your mother . . . appears to feel well, although she is skin and bones and weighs only one centner," Otto wrote to his brothers-in-law two months later to allay their worries. "She goes out regularly with the ladies and eats normally. The doctors are satisfied."

"Dearest Mother," Otto Frank wrote on a postcard on September 14, 1941, "Anne and I have traveled to this place for a few days." Despite the new regulations, they were staying in a hotel, the Groot Warnsborn, in the countryside. Perhaps the proprietor himself was a Jew or was someone who knew Otto. Or perhaps he was a decent human being who had decided to ignore the racial prejudice imposed by law.

"I wanted to have some peace again," Otto wrote in the postcard to his mother, "and not go all by myself. Anne is always good and dear company and she was easily able to get a few days off school." He did not indicate, however, that Anne was facing drastic changes as far as school was concerned. It had been officially announced on August 8 that from then on Jewish children would be required to attend separate schools apart from their Dutch classmates. On the last day of school before the summer holidays, as Anne later recalled, her beloved teacher, Hendrika Kuperus, had bid a tearful good-bye to Anne and her other Jewish students. In Anne's class alone half the children were Jewish.

It had orginally been planned that Anne would spend another year at the Montessori school. The previous year, she had been absent a lot because of her health. She was especially far behind in arithmetic. No one "stayed back" in the Montessori school. A teacher always taught three grades together in a single classroom; Anne would not have repeated the sixth year but would have simply added a seventh on. She had always been among the smallest and most delicate children in her class; now she would be one of the older ones.

But she could not stay after all. All schools had to report the names of their Jewish students. Like every other Jewish child, Anne had to change schools. "I have been tentatively accepted in the lyceum," she would recall a year later. And though there were some Jewish schools, they were far too few to accommodate all the children, so a whole new system had to be put together in just a few days. "For the time being," the state would assume the costs for these "Jewish institutions." The cynicism of that language was, of course, not evident to the Dutch people, who could not know that only a few days earlier SS commander Hanns Albin Rauter had mentioned in a letter to Reich Commissioner Arthur Seyss-Inquart the "imminent final solution to the Jewish question."

On February 13, 1941, the occupation had decreed the establishment of the Joodse Raad (Jewish Council) to maintain "order" in the Jewish population, and by early October, the council had in fact found premises for new elementary and secondary schools, hired Jewish teachers, and set up schedules and curricula. But until all that had been accomplished, the children had no school.

Otto Frank apparently thought it wise to provide some distraction for Anne by taking the trip to the country with her. Although he had surely long ago asked himself the questions that must have begun to preoccupy Anne—"Am I different from other people? What do they have against me?"—he was now obliged to find some satisfactory answers. But what explanation could parents offer their children for the mindless hatred directed against them? There simply was no explanation for the ever-increasing harassment.

While Otto and Anne were at the Hotel Groot Warnsborn, regulations went into force forbidding Jews to use any facilities or businesses open to the general public: libraries, theaters, museums, restaurants, coffeehouses, playing fields, the zoo; as if to rub it in, the prohibition barring Jews from hotels and parks was reiterated. Effective September 15, 1941, parks were closed to Jews. Signs reading "Forbidden to Jews" appeared on park benches and at the entrances to public buildings. No longer could parents play down or gloss over the things that were happening in their children's lives. Many children were shocked, others were ashamed and felt inferior. "You're scared to do anything," Anne heard her best friend say repeatedly, "because it may be forbidden." Their parents, who knew more than they, were even more afraid but still had to help them maintain their pride and self-respect as long as they had to remain in occupied Holland.

"Situations are changing daily," Otto Frank wrote to Nathan Straus, "and if nothing can be done for the moment there might be still possibilities developing." Just the contrary was the case. From October 1941 on, the Franks' situation became more critical still.

Information that Otto Frank received from various sources—among them, Gerard Oeverhaus, an official with the police department's division for aliens and an old friend and adviser of Otto's—indicated that young people over sixteen and capable of working, both boys and girls, might well be facing "work service" and whatever else that term might include. "But as Margot is going to be 16 in February I would not like to leave them here onder [*sic*] the present conditions, even if Edith would have to stay here with her mother." Did Otto know that Jews in Germany had to wear the Star of David and that Jews between the ages of eighteen and forty-five, which included Edith Frank, were no longer permitted to leave Germany or the occupied countries and, further, that deportations of Jews from Germany to temporary stays in ghettos like Lodz had already begun? Even if he was not aware of all these measures, his urgent words leave no doubt about the desperation he was feeling. "You can imagine that I am anxious to get your further news as I know that I shall never be able to leave without your help."

Numerous documents make clear that both Nathan Straus and Julius and Walter Holländer were in constant communication with the National Refugee Service and intent on finding a way out for the Franks. To that end, Julius Holländer acted as an utterly selfless petitioner to Nathan Straus: "My brother and I will pay for the boat ticket and Cuban visa for Mr. Frank. If you give the necessary deposit to the Cuban Government for Mr. Frank, I promise you that it will be returned to you untouched, as we will suport my brother-in-law while he remains in Cuba."

But for Nathan Straus the risk was still too great. "Mr. and Mrs. Straus are very much interested in helping Otto Frank and his family," someone at the National Refugee Service wrote, "but this is only one of many cases that the Strauses are interested in and they are not prepared to invest the large sum of money that is indicated in the matter of Cuban visas for the family. . . . Even after all this money has been deposited and invested there is still the question as to whether the family would succeed in obtaining the necessary exit permits and transit visas." Otto Frank was not aware of the contents of this letter, but he nonetheless understood that Nathan Straus could not fully appreciate his situation. "You are able," he wrote to his brother-in-law Julius, "to imagine how things are here in a way that Straus cannot." He closed by saying, "There is still plenty of business, so we have no reason to complain on that account."

And indeed there was no lack of orders, and sales continued to be satisfactory. Despite this, Otto Frank was being steadily driven into a corner. "In the meantime," he wrote to Nathan Straus on October 12, "I had order to liquidate my business and shall not be able to continue my work."

Six months earlier, at the time of the issuing of stock, he had transferred the directorship of Pectacon to Johannes Kleiman and reduced his personal share in the business to less than 25 percent. The latter especially was a prudent move and, according to the Bureau of Economic Investigation, legal. But it was not enough to satisfy the authorities.

This news distressed Otto Frank. "Father has rheumatism in his back," Anne wrote to her grandmother in Basel. But thanks to the trustee assigned to them, Johannes Kleiman and Otto Frank were able to save their business after all. Karel Wolters, an attorney in his early thirties, was the director of the law department of the Nederlandsche Bank. His loyalty to the Dutch and German National Socialists—he had joined the NSB in 1935 and since the occupation of the Netherlands had been active on behalf of the NSB's Economic Front—had earned him the favor not only of Meinoud M. Rost van Tonningen, his immediate superior at the bank, but also of SS Führer Hanns Albin Rauter. With their support he had become a trustee, or "administrator," in the Bureau of Economic Investigation. Nineteen cases are documented in which he expedited the liquidations of Jewish businesses. In September 1941, he had received instructions to liquidate Pectacon.

Wolters initially planned to let Pectacon continue operating as it had been. That was not at all to Kleiman and Otto Frank's liking as they assumed that he would sooner or later replace Kleiman with a director loyal to the regime. Kleiman objected and was given eight to ten days to liquidate the business himself. This allowed him to let Pectacon continue operating under a different name, an arrangement that could not, of course, be discussed openly.

Kleiman sold the machines and stock to a firm named Gies and Company, which had been established on the model of La Synthèse N.V. and behind which stood Jan Gies. (The name La Synthèse did not sound "Aryan" enough; hence the change to Gies and Company.) From the cash proceeds from the sale of Pectacon, the non-Jewish part owners Johannes Kleiman and Antonius Dunselman received their respective shares. A quarter of the remaining amount of about ten thousand guilders was paid to the Bureau of Economic Investigation to cover "the costs of liquidation." The rest was paid into an account at the Nederlandsche Bank. That was a highly unusual procedure and presumably an error, for according to regulations monies of this kind were to be transferred to Lippmann, Rosenthal and Co.

These irregularities were surely quite agreeable to Otto Frank despite the uncertainty inherent in them. As long as the money had not gone to Lippmann, Rosenthal, the bank would not intervene, and Gies and Company could continue doing business unimpeded. (Normally, once a liquidation had taken place, the Dutch Nazi Henneicke Column was dispatched, along with the shipping firm of Puls, to confiscate any items of value. Pectacon was never subjected to this plundering, and the money in the Nederlandsche Bank was astonishingly enough not transferred to Lippmann, Rosenthal until 1947, at which time it was immediately returned to Otto Frank.)

Are thanks due to Karel Wolters? He may have been a fanatic, but he was not a fanatical anti-Semite, and for whatever reasons and probably with the approval of his immediate superior, he made decisions beneficial to persecuted Jews or at least did not rule against them. Beneficiaries of his decisions confirmed this after the war. Then, too, Wolters was an extremely busy man who was probably pursuing other interests and had little time to give to his sideline at the Bureau of Economic Investigation. When, finally, the liquidation of Pectacon was officially concluded on May 7, 1943, almost two years after application for liquidation was made, Wolters, as a member of the Waffen SS, had already volunteered for the front. The Pectacon case was lost in the shuffle.

Wolters must have known in the fall of 1941 that Gies and Company and Otto Frank remained in contact. And so it is clear that he assured Otto Frank of at least a portion of his income. For it was still uncertain whether the Franks would be able to leave Holland.

Julius Holländer did not rest until he was certain about how best to help the Franks. And Nathan Straus changed his mind, possibly after personal (but unfortunately undocumented) consultations with high-ranking members of the State Department. "[Otto Frank's] letter is urgent," Helen Straus wrote. "Mr. and Mrs. Straus are prepared to arrange for the $2,000 bank deposits per adult and the $500 bond for each alien, which money is refundable," Julius Holländer was informed. In addition they are prepared to cover the cost of overseas transportation to the extent of about $1,500." We do not know whether this news ever reached Otto Frank, who, like all other German Jews in the occupied countries, had been stripped of his German citizenship. He did know that his chances of receiving an exit permit had become less likely. On November 27, he telegraphed Julius Holländer: "Please care only for obtaining a visa for Otto Frank for the time being to confine financial risk." Now he had to focus again on his business obligations.

Even more remarkable than the "self-Aryanization" of Pectacon was the eventual successful rescue of Opekta, which required Otto Frank and Johannes Kleiman to defend the business not only against the Bureau of Economic Investigation in Amsterdam but also against Opekta's parent company, the Pomosin-Werke in Frankfurt am Main. There, the question of Aryanization had been solved years earlier in a high-handed and outrageous manner. Otto Frank must have known about this.

After the premature death of Sandor Scheinberger, the Jewish founder of the firm, in December 1924, his Protestant wife, Emmy, had inherited the business, appointed Robert Feix, the son of Sandor Scheinberger's twin sister, Ida, as director, and transferred to him a half interest in the firm.

In 1936, Scheinberger's sons, Walther, Ernst, and Heinz, who in Nazi parlance were "half-Jewish" and who, until they attained majority, had remained silent partners in the business, initiated proceedings against their cousin Robert Feix to contest his share in the business. The legal battle ended in a compromise. In early 1937, Robert Feix was removed from the Pomosin-Werke. In exchange, Opekta in Cologne, which he had founded, was promised to him. As Feix's replacement, the Scheinberger brothers appointed Walter Fischer, a Nazi sympathizer who until then had been Pomosin's deputy director. Pomosin proudly claimed its role as a producer of goods "crucial to the war effort," and throughout the war Fischer headed the firm as the sole legally responsible trustee and a loyal front man for the Scheinbergers. The owners had thus conducted a self-Aryanization and one supported by Frankfurt's National Socialist police chief, Adolf Beckerle, a school friend of Walther Scheinberger's.

The Scheinbergers were still not satisfied. To gain control of Opekta in Cologne, they denounced Robert Feix as a "full Jew," a tactic that succeeded because Feix could not produce convincing evidence that his father was Aryan. As a consequence, he was repeatedly arrested and detained, first in Berlin, then in Dachau. The Rohstoff Verkehrs AG (Raw Materials Trade Company), or Rovag, together with its Opekta subsidiaries, was taken over by Pomosin.

On December 13, 1941, Otto Frank, who had the day before given up his directorship of Opekta Amsterdam, and Johannes Kleiman, the new director, met with two representatives from the Pomosin-Werke. These men had come to Holland to initiate "the measures necessary for the Aryanization of the stock company," and they had apparently received a warm welcome from the authorities. Among other inducements, they claimed they could prevent Opekta Amsterdam from being taken over by a competitor. Thus, they presented themselves as protectors of Opekta Amsterdam. At the same time, claiming they were the real owners of Opekta, they demanded that Otto Frank deposit his shares in the business into the account of the Pomosin-Werke at the Handelstrust West N.V., a branch of the Dresdner Bank. But Otto Frank refused. In the first place, he considered himself the legal owner of Opekta Amsterdam, and, second, if he felt himself obliged to anyone, it was to Robert Feix.

The Pomosin-Werke later made this same demand of Johannes Kleiman. In 1955, Kleiman stated that he had "shrewdly not complied with this request but simply kept the shares." Neither he nor Otto Frank ever acknowledged the Pomosin-Werke as the owner of Opekta Amsterdam, unlike the Bureau of Economic Investigation, which approved the Aryanization of the company on the assumption that Pomosin did own it. It would take until July 1, 1944, for the Bureau to acknowledge this step officially, but the "self-Aryanization" accomplished its purpose. Despite all the audit procedures Opekta was subject to, the company was able to carry on its business relatively undisturbed. Otto had not only rescued both his businesses but also—with the help of his front men Kleiman,

Kugler, and Gies—assured himself and his family of a regular income, minimal though it was, an income on which Otto Frank now built, for on the day before he officially gave up his participation in Opekta, he had had to abandon any hope of making a new beginning far from Holland. On December 11, 1941, the United States entered the war. Julius Holländer's application for Otto's Cuba visa was canceled that same day. The fresh hope that the Americans would quickly have the German army on the run gave the Franks and many of their friends heart, but encouraging as that prospect was, the Franks' personal situation was grave. They remained trapped in Holland.

How did Anne deal with this?

She was in the midst of a school year that made her and her schoolmates very happy. "After a lot of fuss, talk, and planning, things were finally fixed so that I could register at the lyceum and—without an entrance exam." This is the first sentence of a story Anne would write about two years later. In early October 1941, she was told to matriculate at the newly founded Jewish lyceum on Voormalige Stadstimmertuinen, a street named for the municipal woodworking plant that had operated there until 1906. Anne was worried: apart from Hanneli (called Lies Goosens in the story), she didn't know a single person in her class. "That situation," she wrote, "didn't strike me as very pleasant."

A week later classes began. Two years later, Anne's memories of her first day were still bitter. As soon as she arrived at school, she learned that she would be placed in a different class: "This meant that I would belong to a group in which I knew a few boys and girls, but Lies was to remain in 1 LI. When I was given the desk at the very back of the class, behind girls much bigger than myself, I felt lonely and forsaken."

Anne may still have been small and thin but she was never at a loss for words, and she was not about to take things lying down. "In the second hour I raised my hand and asked to be moved to another spot, as I could see very little unless I fairly hung into the aisle." She persisted with her requests until "Lies" was placed in the same classroom with her. "The third hour was gym, and the teacher seemed so nice that I asked her to try to have Lies transferred to my room. How the dear lady did it I will never know, but the next hour, in walked Lies and was given the desk beside mine."

Anne may have been true to the facts, but it's just as likely that Hanneli Goslar's version of the story is the more accurate one. She recalls that Anne was placed in her section, not the other way around, and that the change occurred later, because Anne's teacher could no longer put up with Anne's incessant talking in class. In any case, the two girls, who had lived rather free lives in the Montessori school and learned how to stand up for themselves, were soon sitting next to each other again, just as Anne wanted. "Now I was reconciled to the school," Anne concludes her story, "the school where I was to have so much fun and learn such a lot. Full of courage, I paid close attention to what the geography man was telling us."

Anne's feelings about her school reflected those of most of the other children. The 1941–42 school year turned out to be wonderful. For one thing, on Saturdays, as well as on Sundays and Jewish holidays, there were no classes. But that had been the rule for most of the pupils before; the previous winter, Anne's Montessori school had been closed on Saturdays to save heating costs. (Similar measures had been taken at Margot's school, where classes now started at nine-forty-five instead of at eight-thirty.)

What made the new school year wonderful was the teachers' special attentiveness to their pupils. Many of the teachers were among the best in the country (and some of the survivors became recognized scholars after the war). They worked more intensely with the children, their contact was warmer and more personal than under "normal" conditions, and the sense of community among the pupils was unusually strong, too. To preserve at least the illusion of normality, no one dwelled on the need for solidarity; it was simply a given: "We have something in common. We belong together." The children felt at home.

Even the quiet Margot blossomed. She had been attending the girls' lyceum for three years and been a model student who had coped well with the rigorous demands of the elite school. Now, at the Jewish lyceum, she discovered the pleasures of freedom. "There are only four girls in our class; but perhaps one more will join us," she wrote to Alice Stern Frank. "But there are twenty boys. I don't want to go back to the girls' lyceum. This evening our class club meets." She remained true to her reputation as a serious and modest girl and studied just as assiduously as she had before, but she had other interests, too. "Margot has plenty of company and is becoming livelier," Otto noted. "She's paying more attention to her clothes and hairdo now."

Barbara Ledermann had refused to go to the Jewish school and had switched to a private ballet school, so Margot now had a new best friend, Jetteke Frijda, who resembled Barbara in being a poor student. Both girls enjoyed the attention they received from the boys in their class, and they both had boyfriends, but it would never have occurred to either of them to allow a boy so much as a kiss.

"I'm still enjoying the lyceum. There are 12 girls and 18 boys in our class. At first we ran around with the boys a lot, but now we're not and it's a good thing, because they're getting too fresh." The tone of the letter Anne wrote to her grandmother in Basel shortly after Easter 1942 was happy and carefree. "Hanneli is in my class again at school. Her sister is very cute and can walk by herself now." Sanne was attending a different Jewish school, but the girls still saw each other often. "She's as crazy about Moortje as I am. That's our cat, whom we've had for six months now. Moortje's female, and I'm hoping she'll have children soon because she keeps meeting a lot of men."

Edith and Otto Frank had probably yielded to Anne's wish to have a pet at about the time she had to transfer to the Jewish school. Perhaps they thought having the cat might help her through this transitional period. For the stress of changing schools was intensified by confusing physical changes as she hovered on the threshold between childhood and youth. "[Anne] is experiencing a growth spurt, but she's doing fine and is very sweet," Otto wrote to Julius Holländer in November 1941. Strange new feelings were stirring in her and—because she had not found other ways to express them—took the form of effusiveness one minute, moodiness or a know-it-all disdain the next. "God knows everything," Ruth Goslar liked to joke, "and Anne knows everything better." Her parents didn't live up to her expectations anymore, nor did her old friends. She was looking for something new, something different. She could not—or did not want to—share her discoveries with Hanneli. Hanneli was a nice girl but, like Sanne, still a child. Jacqueline van Maarsen—who pronounced the *e* at the end of her nickname, Jacque, because her mother was French (her father was a Dutch Jew)—became Anne's new best friend. She had dark hair and huge, enviably blue eyes that Anne noticed immediately. Everybody, it seemed to her, admired Jacque's eyes.

With Jacque, Anne shared her secret thoughts, her dreams of Prince Charming rescuing her from her Cinderella existence and her doubts about her developing body—for example, the size of her breasts. Jacque, too, was small and slim but she was much farther along in her development. She didn't need to stuff cotton in her bra to impress the boys. Jacque was the only person with whom Anne could talk about sex. It was hard to broach the topic with Margot, but Jacque's sister had been more forthcoming with Jacque and had answered some of her questions.

The Jewish children saw very little of their former schoolmates. Anne lost touch with non-Jewish Dutch friends like Ietje Swillens, one of the best students in Anne's old class and her frequent companion on the way to and from school. Another friend had been Lucia van Dijk, whom she had sat across from only a few months earlier and with whom she had done homework and sung silly songs. In Lucia's autograph book Anne had signed herself "Your friend, Annelies Frank," and she had invited Lucia to her birthday parties. But Lucia's parents had joined the National Socialist Movement soon after its founding. Lucia's mother wore the triangular NSB pin on her lapel as if it were a precious brooch. Anne had heard about this, but Otto had told her that she mustn't automatically condemn the van Dijks. They could still be decent people even if their politics were wrongheaded. Otto employed two NSB members in his business, and they were hardworking, trustworthy men.

Now Lucia had joined the Jeugdstorm, or Youth Storm, the Dutch version of the Hitler Youth. At meetings, she wore the uniform—the black skirt, the light-blue blouse, and the unmistakable black-and-orange cap, symbols of allegiance. She was not altogether comfortable in this outfit. As long as you're wearing that cap, her beloved grandmother had told her, you had better stay out of my sight. Lucia was shaken. She wasn't sure what to think about the National Socialists. Her mother, after all, had told her that Adolf Hitler would create jobs for the Dutch just as he had for the Germans, and Lucia's father was out of work. When half her class disappeared overnight, no one told her why. The teachers said nothing, and the children, including Lucia, didn't ask questions. She wasn't indifferent, but she was afraid, just like the other children—and the teachers.

Although discrimination against Jews increased with every passing month, though they continued to be robbed of their dignity bit by bit, and though they were more and more frightened, they made the best of their situation. Because they were barred from cultural events open to the public, for example, they created their own cultural lives. Private concerts, which were by no means unusual in upper-middle-class families, now took place even more frequently. Depending on how many musicians could come and the instruments they played, the guests might hear Mozart piano quartets, movements from Beethoven trios, or other chamber music. Franz Ledermann was an accomplished violinist and violist, and he and his wife, Ilse, a pianist, performed every other Sunday. The Franks didn't play any instruments themselves, but they were often among the guests at these gatherings. When the whole family attended, the adults took the chairs, while Anne and Margot sat on the floor with the other children. Sometimes Edith went alone. She seems to have taken particular pleasure in these little musical occasions.

In conversations with other immigrant families, Otto Frank had hit on the idea of hiring a woman named Anneliese Schütz, a Berlin journalist who had not succeeded in finding work in Amsterdam, to introduce Margot and the other children in the Franks' circle to the classics of German literature. Every week a different family played host. With each of the young people taking a role, they read Goethe's *Egmont* and Schiller's *Don Carlos*, plays in which the theme of freedom was central. The children had to know their classics; education was half of life, their parents said. And they mustn't lose touch with the German language. After all, they had to think ahead to the end of the war.

Anne was too young to take part in the reading group, Otto told her, and her ties to the German language were tenuous at best. When the Germans had invaded Holland, her mother tongue had become an enemy tongue overnight. But anything that had to do with theater appealed to her, and when she heard that the children from about eleven to fourteen were going to put on a play, there was no holding her back. One of the girls, Hannelore Klein, or

Hansi, had talked the no-nonsense Anneliese Schütz into doing *The Princess with the Long Nose,* a Jewish children's play by Minna Blum set in the Near East. Hansi and Anneliese Schütz directed and, as best as Hansi can recall, she herself also played the queen. Anne had the lead role. Mrs. Kuperus of the Montessori school had done a lot of theater with the pupils and been struck by Anne's talent as a playwright. Her ideas were clever, and she could put them into lively, incisive language. As an actress, she had been admired for her spirited performances and her comic talents. She was the consummate show-off.

The Princess with the Long Nose was performed at Hanukkah in the apartment of the Kleins, who, like the Franks, were from Frankfurt. A heavy dark red curtain separated the dining room, which served as the stage, from the living room, where the audience sat. Parents, siblings, and friends packed the house.

Anne was evidently a convincing princess, tactless and demanding, just the character the play called for. A beautiful but arrogant ingrate, she ridiculed her courtiers and would not be satisfied with anything but the best. But when she started greedily gobbling the forbidden magic cake, she began to sprout a long, ugly nose, and only after she begged for forgiveness and drank the wine from the Promised Land ("Good I will be and sweet as a rose, / Good with, but better without, this wretched nose") did it shrink back to normal, clearing the way for the play's happy ending.

In the winter of 1941–42, the Franks treasured lighthearted moments like this one. In the course of December, Otto Frank received two notices to report to the emigration office of the Jewish Council. "We take this opportunity to notify you once again that you are obliged by order of the German authorities to apply through this office for an emigration permit." For eight long months Otto Frank had desperately tried—and failed—to emigrate legally. This summons to "emigrate voluntarily " that would obligate him to do what was now so obviously impossible must have struck him as bitter

Margot, Otto, Anne, and Edith Frank, Merwedeplein, 1941

mockery. And it must have frightened him. What purpose did the Germans mean to achieve by this? Were they contemplating organized deportation? And, if so, to where?

On January 20, 1942, after receiving these two warnings, Otto Frank finally turned in his family's applications to the Central Office for Jewish Emigration. The forms did not ask to which country the applicants wanted to emigrate because the applications had no bearing on any actual plan to emigrate. Otto had simply responded to a new decree ordering all Jews who were not Dutch citizens to register for "voluntary emigration." At considerable administrative expense—in terms of both cost and effort—a form was issued for every family member; all men and boys had Israel added to, or merely substituted for, their given names, women and girls Sara. So the Frank family's forms were headed: Frank, Israel. Frank, Sara. Frank, Sara. Frank, Sara. During the Enlightenment, Jews had been taught to give their children German forenames. Now those names were to be taken from them.

Otto Frank did not have to submit an emigration application for Oma Holländer, presumably because it was clear she would not live much longer. And in fact she died of cancer on January 29 and was buried in a Jewish cemetery called Gan Hasjalom recently founded by the Liberal community in Hoofddorp, a village near Amsterdam. This was Anne's first experience of death.

On April 29, 1942, SS Hauptsturmführer Ferdinand aus der Fünten gave the members of the Jewish Council 569,355 six-pointed patches of cloth about the size of a tea saucer, yellow stars on which the word *Jood* was printed in black letters meant to imitate Hebraic characters. Within the next three days, he told the Council, "all Jews over six years of age were to be identified by the Jewish star." His decree was accompanied by precise instructions as to how and where the star was to be worn. Were these directions not so intrinsically revolting and so fraught with dire consequences, the pedantic thoroughness of them might seem a laughable parody of German officiousness. The star was to be firmly stitched to outer garments, such as overcoats, suit coats, and dresses, and not just anywhere but breast-high on the left side and fully visible. Any Jew caught in public without a star—and "public" meant not only on streets and squares but also in front yards, in courtyards, or on balconies—would be subject to a heavy fine.

Everyone who had an identity card marked with a *J* received four stars, but not for free, of course. Each star cost four cents plus a coupon from the individual's textile rationing card, without which clothing could not be purchased. People would be proud to wear the Star of David, the Jewish Council was informed. It would protect them from evil spirits and other harm. But why, the council wanted to know, did the star have to be yellow, and not the golden yellow of the sun and stars that symbolized hope and security but a sickly, jaundiced yellow suggestive of envy and misery? Why this color of humiliation? "For clear visibility" was Hauptsturmführer aus der Fünten's curt answer—that and because it was the color of the star introduced in Germany the previous September. The color of ostracism.

The Germans were unprepared for the Dutch reaction. Some people now went out of their way to be particularly friendly toward their Jewish fellow citizens. Others, predominantly students, put yellow stars on their own clothes. The underground Socialist newspaper *De Vonk* printed and distributed thousands of leaflets that read, "There is no difference between Jews and non-Jews." But they also warned that the Nazi regime would come down hard on non-Jews who wore the yellow star. This was no empty warning. Adult Dutch citizens caught wearing a star were arrested and sent to the Amersfoort concentration camp for six weeks.

This show of solidarity gave the Jews courage, and the hope that the war would not last much longer consoled them. "In a month or two, the war will be over," a member of the Jewish Council said, "and then we will be free." Hitler's fantasy of invading England and bringing it to its knees had evaporated. The German incursion into Russia had been stalled for a long time, and the Soviet army was proving to be a determined opponent. Despite their political differences, the Soviets had convinced England and the United States—against whom Germany had declared war on December 11, 1941—to open a second front in the West as soon as possible. Anyone who listened to the BBC dreamed of the imminent Allied landing in France, Belgium, or Holland. Now, in May and June 1942, the nightly air-raid sirens that woke people was music to their ears. Increasingly, the planes over Holland were flying from west to east, launching major bombing raids on German cities, first Stuttgart, then Cologne and Essen. Germany would lose the war. There was no doubt about that in Otto Frank's mind or in the minds of most Dutch citizens. With his unfailing optimism, he tried to keep up not only his own and his wife's spirits but those of the whole neighborhood.

Hanneli Goslar was one of those who felt that the sun rose on her home when Otto Frank came to visit. She was especially impressed with the way he charmed her baby sister. Gabi didn't want to eat, and every day involved a battle to make her choke down her cereal. But when Otto took her on his lap, spoke softly to her, and placed one spoonful after another in her mouth, she swallowed without making the slightest fuss. Meanwhile, he chatted with Hans Goslar about politics and the war. Hanneli's father was convinced the Germans would win the war and kill all the Jews. But Otto was equally certain the Americans would come and put an end to the madness before it was too late.

7

INTO HIDING

"On Friday, June 12th, I woke up at six o'clock, and no wonder; it was my birthday." Anne could hardly wait to get up, wake her parents, and open her presents. She knew that Otto and Edith had prepared the table with her gifts the night before, after she had gone to bed. That was the tradition in their family. Finally, it was a quarter to seven. Anne was nearly bursting with excitement and curiosity, even though she already knew she would get the gift she most wanted. And there it was, among the flowers and other presents, many more than she had expected. A squarish notebook bound in rough red-and-light-green checkered cloth. Attached to the back cover was a cloth strap with a narrow metal tongue that snapped into a small lock on the front of the book. The lock could easily be opened by pulling a tiny lever on the side. This was the same notebook she had pointed out to her father a few days earlier, possibly in the window of Blankevoort, the bookstore on the corner of Waalstraat, or at Perry, a department store on Kalverstraat. It was really an autograph book, but it was perfectly suitable as a diary. Anne had already done a lot of writing, although she was mysterious about it with her friends. Now, finally, she had a real diary. On June 14, 1942, two days after her thirteenth birthday, she wrote that there had been a number of presents, but "the first to greet me was *you*, possibly the nicest of all." Two years later she added on a loose sheet of thin pink office paper what a strange and utterly new experience it was for her to write in a diary. It would never have occurred to her to buy a notebook and fill it with her thoughts if she had a close friend to confide in, she wrote. As it was, no one would be interested in her silly ideas, but since she had the notebook, she would make sure that in a month it would not be lying forgotten in a corner.

Birthdays and other family celebrations were always important events at the Franks'. They were prepared for with love and care, and the birthday child was lavishly feted and showered with presents. In the dark time they were enduring now, this celebration took on special importance. It proved to Anne—without anyone's spelling it out—how much she could rely on her family. It gave her a sense of security, of being protected from the world outside. It provided the assurance of normality and continuity that Anne—still delicate and given to extremes of mood—needed so as to remain carefree. It created no illusions, yet it bolstered her trust and her hope.

Her parents could not have felt like celebrating. Daily existence was becoming increasingly difficult, the necessities of life more and more expensive, and the laws imposed on the Jewish population ever more outrageous and malevolent. Many adults, Otto and Edith Frank among them, found wearing the yellow star the most humiliating imposition yet. Children took it in stride, however, and many of them even wore the star proudly. But it was demoralizing to always have to worry that one might be unknowingly doing something forbidden—and would be punished. "Every kind of sport—including rowing, swimming, tennis, soccer, fishing, etc.—is prohibited to the Jews," the official Jewish weekly, *Het Joodse Weekblad*, announced on the day of Anne's birthday. Another absurd torment the regime had come up with—and just in time for the summer holidays.

The same issue called attention to two other forms of harassment—the ban on bicycling and the evening curfew. Regulation 58/1942 of May 21 had informed all Jews that they would have to register their bicycles. The purpose was clear: if the Nazis decided to confiscate all bicycles, they wanted to be able to determine quickly who was disobeying the order. Now, on June 12, 1942, the occupation forces announced that the forms for registering bicycles were available for purchase and should be filled out and returned by June 30 at the latest. Reich Commissioner Arthur Seyss-Inquart gave the press his personal promise that the bicycles would not be confiscated.

The fact that the general commissioner for public safety, SS commander Hanns Albin Rauter, issued his own decree a few days later only went to show how little a promise from the Germans was worth. On June 22, Rauter decreed that all Jews outside Amsterdam were to hand over their bicycles within forty-eight hours. (A similar order for Jews living in Amsterdam would follow on July 20.) All bicycles were to be in perfect condition and supplied with spare tires.

We do not know how many bicycles were actually registered or turned in. The Franks, in any case, did not obey the registration order. As long as the bicycles were not used, no one knew they existed. The Germans were once again relying on intimidation. They assumed that many of the Jews living in Holland had bicycles, but only registration could prove that. "Daddy has given Mummy's to some Christian acquaintances for safekeeping," Anne noted in her diary entry of June 24 (ver. B). She herself had been managing without wheels since Easter vacation, when the bicycle her mother had given her for her twelfth birthday was stolen. The theft occurred on April 13, 1942, between the hours of noon and 2:00 p.m. About an hour after she noticed the bicycle was missing, Anne reported the theft to the police station on Pieter Aertsstraat. "Stolen . . .

from in front of the residence. Value: 45 guilders. Identity of thief: unknown," the officer on duty recorded in the day's police log. The family decided to hold on to Margot's bicycle. Of course, they no longer dared use it but kept it in reserve for an emergency.

The curfew was hard on both adults and young people. Otto and Edith Frank, in their concern for their daughters, had taken precautions earlier. "I'm not permitted to go out on the street alone in the evening. Everything is a lot easier where you are," Margot had complained to her grandmother in Basel back in April 1942. The regulations became ever more confining, and eventually Jews would even be forbidden to go out into their gardens and onto their balconies during those hours. For the children, these restrictions were painful experiences of isolation, humiliation, and rejection, a noose that was pulled tighter each day, leaving them less and less room to breathe. "I hope that you will be a great support and comfort to me," Anne wrote in the flyleaf of her diary on the evening of her birthday.

Hanneli picked Anne up that Friday morning for their walk to school. A few days earlier, Jews had been forbidden to use public transportation. The streetcar the girls ordinarily took to the Jewish lyceum now belonged to another world, a forbidden world. The weather was unseasonably cold, and it looked like it would rain any minute, so they hurried along, Anne describing her presents and proudly enumerating all the people who had remembered her birthday—Aunt Leni, Sanne's mother, Jacqueline's father, Peter van Pels, Hello Silberberg (Anne's latest admirer), and the girlfriend of the dentist Fritz Pfeffer, Charlotte Kaletta, whose beauty Anne admired. Even her birthday letter from her Omi in Basel had arrived on precisely the right day. Anne was going to treat her classmates and teachers to birthday cookies she had baked, and she was making plans for her birthday party that Sunday. She had invited various boys and girls from her class, her neighborhood friends, and, of course, the members of her Ping-Pong club—

Hanneli, Sanne, Jacque, and Ilse Wagner, whose family had the Ping-Pong table. Hello, too, would be there, and Margot had been allowed to invite Jetteke and others of her friends. Neither Anne nor Hanneli brought up the fact that this year, for the first time, only Jewish children would attend.

Anne took seriously the question of who would be allowed to come to her party, as if she were dispensing a great honor to her friends. And many children seemed to regard the invitation that way. Anne's birthday parties had the reputation for being exceptionally entertaining and exciting. Her mother served the best cakes, Pim helped with the games, and every guest received a small party favor. This year, the high point would be the showing of a Rin Tin Tin film. Anne and Jacque had made and distributed invitations to it.

This would be the last big party the Franks would host. For the next three weeks Anne and Margot had to buckle down and study: the school year was ending and report cards were coming up. Margot would no doubt get excellent marks as always and be among the top students in her class. It was less clear how Anne would fare. Her marks in math were far from stellar. Besides, she had many other interests and was easily distracted from schoolwork.

Although Anne was becoming increasingly interested in boys, she still had a passion for reading. From the time she was twelve until she turned fourteen, one of her favorite authors was Cissy van Marxveldt, a Dutch writer who had written a number of highly successful books for adolescents in the 1920s. Anne may well have read *Een Zomerzotheid* ("A Summer Folly") more than once. But her favorite was *Joop ter Heul,* a serial novel in four volumes. Anne identified with Joop, the heroine with a boy's name, who develops into a young woman in the course of the story. Joop, just like Anne, was plucky and adventurous and, like Anne, she had lots of girlfriends. There were Pop, Pien, Noor, and Conny, but her best friend was Kitty. Joop had pen pals, too, but when her father forbade her to write any more letters, she began to keep a diary. . . .

Anne and Jacque spent hours lost in the world of Joop ter Heul, reading passages out loud to each other and enacting favorite scenes. If Anne could have, she would have spent all her time with Jacque. She did not like to be alone. She was always suggesting overnights at each other's houses, and when she had to go for tutoring in math—which happened regularly in the weeks just before grades were to be given at school—she asked Jacque, who had no trouble with math, to come along. Because they were forbidden to ride bicycles or use public transportation, getting to the math lesson took almost as much time as the lesson itself. Jacque waited outside while Anne was tutored, then the two girls walked home together, talking the whole way. Sometimes, though, Jacque found Anne's possessiveness overwhelming. Much as she appreciated Anne's enthusiasm and much as Anne's affection flattered her, she felt herself literally besieged.

Hello Silberberg, on the other hand, was charmed by Anne's intensity. His cousin Wilma had introduced her to him, and they had run into each other again at the bicycle shed behind the skyscraper, probably a few days before Anne's birthday, because on June 24 she wrote, "He came shyly towards me and . . . asked if I would allow him to accompany me to school." Anne was delighted: Hello was already sixteen. "He was waiting for me again this morning and I expect he will from now on" (ver. B).

In late June Anne developed a slight fever. She had to take it easy and stay in bed, but she was allowed to have friends over. Hanneli and Sanne came, of course, as did Jacque, bringing homework assignments as well as the most recent gossip from school.

Anne was particularly surprised by a visit from her childhood friend Kitty Egyedi, who had found out about her illness only by chance. The two girls had grown apart during their last two years at the Montessori school. Before that, Kitty had admired much about Anne, including the ease with which she composed stories. Kitty herself was good at drawing, and she had illustrated several of them. But it seemed to Kitty that Anne changed around the time she turned ten. She became shrill and loud, always needing to take center stage. Kitty disliked her flightiness and her new fascination with movie stars. Anne tended to judge people by their looks, liking them, Kitty felt, exclusively for their pretty faces, wavy hair, and expensive clothes. She also found Anne's way of telling people to their faces how she felt about them undiplomatic and cruel. After Kitty's family moved from Merwedeplein to the outskirts of the River Quarter and the girls no longer walked to school together, they hardly saw each other outside of class. And when they stopped going to the same school, they lost touch almost completely. Kitty, a serious, pensive, somewhat introverted child, had refused to change to the Jewish lyceum. Seeing no point in forcing her, her parents had sent her to study with a teacher named Henri van Praag, who gave private lessons to a small group of Jewish children.

The afternoon Kitty came to visit, she changed her mind about Anne. Instead of carrying on about who was going with whom, who was in whose favor or disfavor, and which movie star was the greatest, Anne talked seriously. She was thinking about life, about the war and the future, just as Kitty was. Like Kitty, she said she was unafraid. That afternoon a delicate bond was formed. Perhaps they would see each other again more often.

Unlike their children, Otto and Edith Frank hardly ever had guests anymore. ("There'll be no more entertaining," Otto Frank had written as early as November 1941 in the last of his letters to the United States that have been preserved.) Their non-Jewish friends were not allowed to visit Jews, and Jews had to stay at home from eight o'clock on. Fear and anxiety dominated everyday life.

For some time, there had been rumors that Jews were no longer being merely threatened but were actually being picked up from their homes or on the street and taken away, with or without warning. At first people thought that these roundups were limited to unmarried and "unemployed" young men, who were to be sent to work in Germany. Because of the enforced "Aryanization" of the workplace, the number of unemployed Jews had risen dramatically, and Otto Frank was officially among them. But in late June 1942 word spread that the Germans were planning to systematically deport all the Jews living in Holland. Nobody knew where they were to be sent or for what purpose. To Germany or somewhere else? To Poland, as the BBC had reported? The only certain thing was that no one was safe.

Adolf Eichmann and Franz Rademacher, the head of Section D III for "Jewish affairs" of the Foreign Office in Berlin, did in fact have a secret telephone conversation on June 20, 1942, in which they decided to send 40,000 Jews from France, 40,000 from Holland, and another 10,000 from Belgium to Auschwitz for "labor service." The Foreign Office, whose function within the ministerial bureaucracy was to maintain an appearance of respectability and continuity, suggested they begin with the deportation of stateless Jews, which meant primarily those Jews who had emigrated from Germany and Austria to Holland. The Foreign Office assumed that if no Dutch citizens were affected, the Dutch people would not be particularly concerned. The removal of German Jews could even be represented to the public as "repatriation."

But the Amsterdam Central Office for Jewish Emigration was under pressure to meet quotas, and it therefore ignored the recommendation. Its chief administrator, SS Hauptsturmführer Ferdinand aus der Fünten, summoned the Jewish Council to a special meeting at ten at night on Friday, June 26. Naturally, aus der Fünten had deliberately chosen the odd hour because it coincided with the beginning of the Jewish Sabbath, and he insisted that the meeting could not be postponed. He had important news to announce, he said. All Jews between the ages of sixteen and forty were to be sent in "contingents supervised by police" to work in Germany, effective immediately. No need to get excited—it was merely a matter of labor service. The labor camps were of course on German soil, and the inmates' religious practices would of course be allowed. After all, the Germans had never interfered with the practices of any religious community.

The Jewish Council was given one day to report how many people it would be able to "assemble," process, and send on the daily transport trains. It complied, reporting that 350 to 375 would be feasible.

There the haggling over human lives began. Aus der Fünten insisted on 600. Impossible, the Jewish Council replied. The registration procedure was too complicated.

Then, came the reply, the registration procedure would be simplified.

Still impossible. The council could manage only 350.

The Nazis agreed to a compromise, holding the number to 350 for the first eight days. After that the quota would be raised no matter what. As far as the procedure was concerned, anyone who received a personal notification was to report to the Jewish Council. And if the rumor that the council was interfering with the smooth functioning of the transports turned out to be true, the consequences would be severe.

"My dear loved ones," Otto wrote to his family in Basel on July 4, 1942. "All is still well with us, but otherwise things are getting worse from day to day, as you probably know. But don't worry, even if you don't hear much from us." He was not allowed to go to work, but he had a great deal to do and to think through, and "one often has to make decisions one would rather not make." The children were on vacation now, Otto went on. Their grades were excellent, Anne's much better than expected. "We are not forgetting about you, and we know that you always think of us, but there is nothing you can do to change things, and you must see to it that you are safe yourselves. With much love as always, your O."

Anne had passed all her subjects, though in algebra she had just squeaked by, despite the tutoring she had received. Hanneli had failed geometry altogether. Both girls were promoted, but they would have to take a test at the beginning of the school year to prove they had not forgotten the little they knew.

Although her summer would not be entirely free of schoolwork, Anne was in high spirits. She wanted to enjoy the lovely summer weather and sunbathe during the day on the balcony. It was true that the Germans had forbidden her and her friends to go to the swimming pool, to drive to the shore, to take a bicycle tour; one false step and a person was in enemy territory. All you had to do was set foot in a store that was off limits to Jews and you could be arrested and put in prison—even children. All you had to do was sit on the wrong park bench. Anne was clearly aware of the danger, and she obviously thought about it, but Pim kept saying the Germans were going to lose the war and then the nightmare would be over. That was what Anne told Jacque to try to console her.

Anne's positive attitude was contagious. Around other people, she was like a whirlwind, drawing them into her cheerfulness. Her exuberance could, of course, be tiresome, too, and not everyone appreciated her insistence on being the center of attention. When she went for ice cream with her girlfriends, she was always in especially high spirits. The café Delphi and the ice cream parlor Oase were the only nearby eating places where Jews were still allowed, and one was likely to see familiar faces there. Anne always found it flattering when, inevitably, an admirer materialized and insisted on paying for her ice cream. She seemed convinced that God and the world adored her.

Hello Silberberg was someone who really did adore her. Anne was not as pretty as her sister or Ursula, the blond girl he had had a crush on before he met her, and she was only thirteen, much too young, according to his friends and his grandmother. But her vivacity, her wit, and her cleverness fascinated him, and he liked her self-confidence. He had never had such a good time talking to a girl, especially one who was so young. He and Anne agreed that her girlfriends were terribly childish. Hello didn't want to have anything to do with them, but he enjoyed listening to Anne and answering her questions.

The two of them went for walks, although just around the block, and Anne invited him home. Her parents liked him, too. He was always polite, considerate, not shy but pleasantly reserved. They treated him with special hospitality and made him feel truly welcome. Otto Frank seemed to take him seriously. Only Margot laughed in a strange way when he appeared. It wasn't clear if she disliked him, liked him, or simply found it amusing to see her little sister sitting in their living room drinking lemonade with an admirer. When Anne and Hello talked to each other, they spoke Dutch, never German.

In Amsterdam, in those days, one heard many stories like Hello's. He had been living with his grandparents since 1938, when his parents had sent him from Germany for safety. The men's clothing store his father, Leo, had run in Gelsenkirchen had been ransacked by the Nazis in the early morning hours of *Kristallnacht* (a ridiculous euphemism, Anne and Hello agreed—as if crystal and windows were the only things destroyed that night). It was then that Hello's parents finally realized that they had to leave Germany. Hello was to escape first and go to his grandparents in Amsterdam; his parents would follow. It was the obvious solution, as he knew the city, having spent summer vacations with his grandparents in Holland from the time he was six, and was fluent in Dutch. The name Hello had been given him by his grandfather, who disliked his real name, Helmuth.

Anne had heard practically nothing from her parents about the

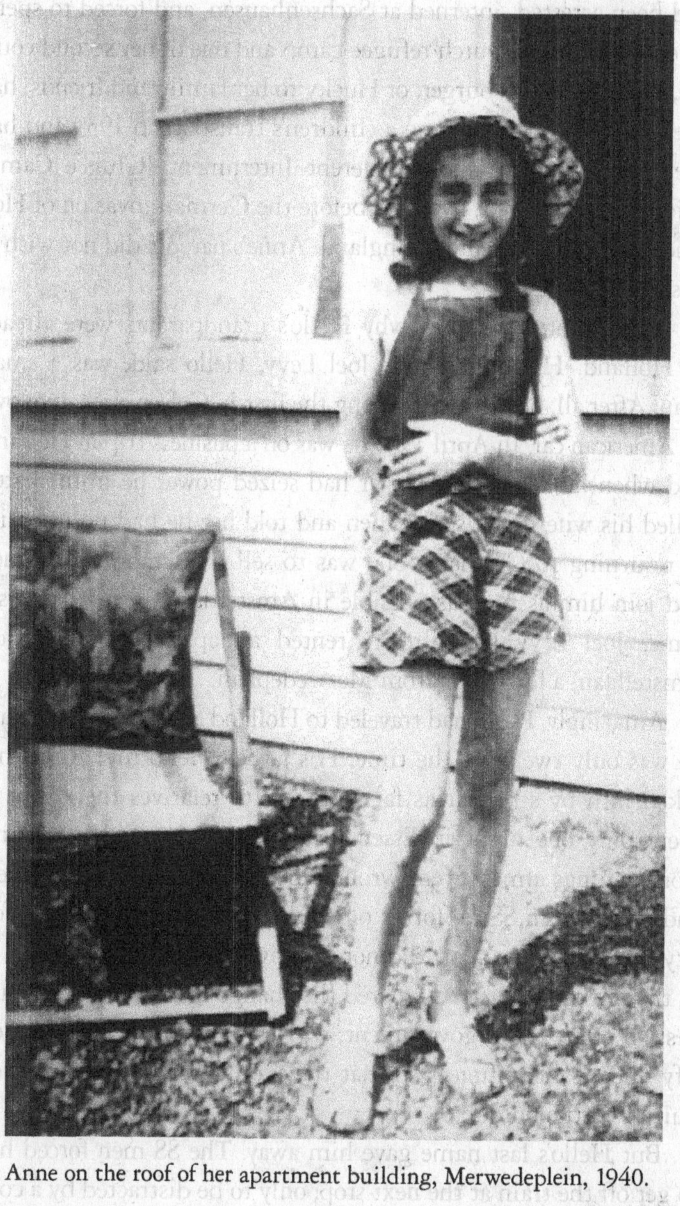

Anne on the roof of her apartment building, Merwedeplein, 1940.

horrors of the November pogrom, even though her uncle Walter had been arrested, interned at Sachsenhausen, and forced to spend an entire year in a Dutch refugee camp and one of her second cousins, Dorothee Würzburger, or Hucky to her family and friends, had been sent to Amsterdam on a children's transport in 1939 and had spent over a year in four different Internment Refugee Camps before being allowed, five days before the German invasion of Holland, to join her parents in England. Anne's parents did not wish to upset her.

Anne wanted to know why Hello's grandparents were already in Holland. His grandfather Joel Levy, Hello said, was a smart man. After all, he had been among the first in Gelsenkirchen to own an American car. In April 1933 he was on a business trip in Holland, and when he heard that Hitler had seized power he immediately called his wife in Gelsenkirchen and told her he had no intention of returning to Germany. She was to sell his scrap-iron business and join him as soon as possible in Amsterdam. By the time she came, Joel Levy had already rented an apartment on Zuider Amstellaan, a few yards from Merwedeplein.

Amazingly, Hello had traveled to Holland all by himself though he was only twelve at the time. His father, Hello told Anne, had taken him by streetcar as far as Essen, to relatives there. But he spent only one night in Essen before continuing on his journey alone. Things almost went wrong when he ran into a police check and two men in SS uniforms ordered him to show them his identity papers. His passport did not yet have the telltale *J* stamped on it, though the Nazis had ordered the change in October at the suggestion of the Swiss government, which wanted to be able to identify undesirable refugees so that they could be turned back more quickly at the border.

But Hello's last name gave him away. The SS men forced him to get off the train at the next stop, only to be distracted by a commotion at the other end of the platform. When they ran off in that direction, Hello did the only reasonable thing and quickly slipped back aboard the train bound for Amsterdam. His grandparents were surprised to see him. News of the pogrom reached Holland only a few days later.

Anne was horrified. It was four years since Hello had last seen his parents. They had been unlucky and were too late to get an entry visa for Holland. Hello knew that his father had escaped through the forest to Belgium. As for his mother, she had paid a truck driver to take her and some other refugees across the Belgian border. Instead of doing as he promised, he took them straight to the Gestapo, and Hello's mother had spent ten days in a prison in Cologne. Immediately after her release, she tried to escape again. This time she had better luck, finding a truck to smuggle her across the border. All she had with her was ten marks and a small suitcase.

Hello could not join his parents in Belgium, even before the war, because they were illegal immigrants. They were not allowed to work in Belgium and could not legally earn money. His grandparents were in a better position to take care of him. He did not wish them to know, however, that he attended meetings of a Zionist youth group, something they did not approve of. He got letters from his parents every so often, and he had talked to them on the telephone a few times in the four years since their separation, although not since the German invasion of Holland. His grandfather did not want them to call anymore; it was too dangerous. People were saying that the SD was about to tap the telephone lines of Jews. That was also why Hello could call Anne only in an emergency.

Hello's story made Anne realize how lucky she was. Her parents were always there for her, spoiling her and cheering her up when she was sad. No matter what happened, Pim had assured her repeatedly, the family would always stay together.

Sunday, July 5, was a gorgeous, bright summer day, the kind rarely seen in Amsterdam. Anne had a date with Hello before lunch. They had planned to go for a walk, but it was too hot, so instead they lounged on the balcony. Hello enjoyed watching Anne—the way she ran her hand through her hair, twisting strands into curls and then releasing them, the way she looked straight at him, coquettishly but with great naturalness. Too shy even to take Anne's hand, Hello amused her by telling stories. He told her about a teacher at the Jewish school in Gelsenkirchen who tried to talk the students into attending synagogue. Hello had no desire to go and pretended to have a headache, but later, out roller skating on the street, he ran into his teacher. And then there was the story about his bar mitzvah in the Orthodox synagogue on Lekstraat. For the first time in his life he was wearing knickers instead of short pants. He wore a top hat, too, but it was too large for him, so his grandmother had wadded some newspaper and stuck it under the rim. Hello had to stand very straight so that the elegant hat would not slip sideways. At the same time he had to think about the text he had to recite, a particularly long passage from the Torah. To his surprise, he managed to get through it quite well in spite of his poor Hebrew. When he finished and the rabbi put his hand on Hello's head—or rather on his hat—to bless him, the hat slipped so far down over his face that he could no longer see. His friends in the first row burst out laughing.

"Hello . . . can tell all kinds of amusing stories," Anne wrote in her diary (June 24, 1942; ver. B). Perhaps he would become a really good friend. She was sure she was not in love with him, though. It was Lutz Peter Schiff she loved. He went by Peter and was three months younger than Hello.

He had fled to Holland only in 1939, presumably with his mother. Before that he had lived in Berlin. His schoolmates at the Holdheim School, a private gymnasium of the Jewish Reform congregation, remembered him as a cheerful, imaginative boy, an outstanding student, and an occasional class clown whose bright ideas never failed to astonish them. Everyone wanted to be friends with someone like him. He was gregarious and charming—and he had a secret: his parents' marriage had broken up in the early 1930s, and his mother had remarried in March 1936. Even his closest friends were not to know this. Peter revealed very little about his personal life, and his friends never set eyes on either his mother or father. In times like those, they simply accepted that without asking any questions. Before they left their native country—each to go in a different direction—they had sworn eternal friendship to one another and exchanged photos.

Peter's stepfather, a graphic artist in advertising, had already gone to Amsterdam in mid-April of 1937. When Anne got to know Peter, he was living with his stepfather and mother on Deltastraat, a kind of extension of the Merwedeplein and in the same row of apartment buildings as the Franks'.

Peter attended the HBS, the Hoogere Burgerschool (higher public school), located across the street from Anne's school. For a while, Anne recalled later, they were inseparable and walked "hand in hand." "I like Peter so much, more than I've ever liked anyone before," Anne raved about him. Then the boy with the "velvet brown eyes" moved to the Zuider Amstellaan, behind the Merwedeplein. He found a new friend in Rolf Winterberger, a neighbor three years older than Anne, and from then on took no further notice of Anne.

"I keep telling myself that it's only to hide his feelings for me that Peter goes round with all those girls" she wrote (July 1, 1942, ver. C). She suffered from unrequited love and jealousy, and she found it hard to keep her feelings to herself. Hello took her mind off her troubles. He was good-looking, with friendly blue eyes and full lips. And he knew how to drive; indeed, he had been driving since he was eleven. A friend of the family had taught him, and before the war his grandfather had sometimes let him drive the car. In any case, right now it was more fun talking with him than with Jacqueline.

The morning passed in no time. Hello went home for lunch but announced he would be back in the afternoon. The Franks, too, sat down to eat. After the meal Otto set out for Weesperstraat, as he often did on Sunday afternoons, to visit Albert Anton Dreher, a friend in his seventies from Frankfurt, or to cheer up some lonely older friends in the Joodse Invalide, the Jewish old people's home. Edith was busy in the kitchen, and Anne, the sun worshiper, withdrew to the balcony with a book. Margot preferred the cool indoors.

Shortly before three o'clock the doorbell rang. It seemed too early for Hello to be returning, but Edith opened the door. An employee of the post office was there, asking for her signature and handing her a registered letter. Edith stared at the sender's address: Central Office for Jewish Emigration, 1 Adama van Scheltemaplein. What they had always feared was about to happen—the Germans were coming for Otto. Up until now there had always been warnings when roundups were likely, and Otto had always been able to leave the house in time and spend the night at a friend's. Even one of his salesmen had taken him occasionally. So now the Nazis had devised a new method, summoning people with written notices delivered to their homes.

When Edith opened the letter she was stunned. The summons to labor service was addressed not to Otto but to Margot. Margot was ordered to report to the Central Office; from there a train would take her to the transit camp at Westerbork. She was to bring two blankets, sheets, food for three days, a towel and toilet articles, a plate, a cup, and a spoon. She was also allowed to take a suitcase or backpack with one pair of solid winter shoes, two pairs of socks, two pairs of underpants, two undershirts, and one pair of overalls. The suitcase had to have first and last name, date of birth, and the word *Holland* written on it. This was important because it would be sent by separate train. Those called up were to take with them and have ready at hand all their ration cards and their identity papers. How could the Germans do this! Hadn't they promised not to split up families?

Edith forced herself to stay calm. Thinking quickly, she decided to tell Margot it was Otto who had been called up. There was no need to worry, though. Under no circumstances would he obey the summons; they had long since made plans for just such an emergency. Edith told Margot she had to run over to the van Pelses on Zuider Amstellaan to discuss something with them. In the meantime Margot should break the news to Anne gently. And she was not to open the door if the bell rang, no matter what.

The afternoon crept by at an unbearably slow pace. Margot had to tell her younger sister the bad news. Unsurprisingly, Anne's reaction was emotional, but she let herself be comforted. Her father would not go under any circumstances. Anne sat motionless, passive, as though in shock. Then her mother came back, accompanied by Hermann van Pels. The two grown-ups were deliberating about what to do, but the girls were not allowed to listen. They would not be told of the plan until the last minute. Meanwhile they all waited impatiently for Otto to return. When the doorbell rang, they jumped: Don't open it.

Hello didn't know what to think. Why wasn't anyone opening the door? Hadn't they agreed he would come back? He had so looked forward to the afternoon. Annoyed and disappointed, he went home. What could have happened? Why hadn't Anne told him before lunch that she was going to be out?

In the apartment Hermann van Pels and Edith were making plans. The Franks had to disappear the next morning, whether their hiding place was ready or not. The van Pelses would follow one week later. The hiding place was so obvious it would never occur to anybody to look for the two families there. They had originally planned to go into hiding on July 16, even if there was no immediate threat to their safety. By then, they would have completed their preparations. But now the Nazis had forced their hand, and ready or not, they had to go into hiding ten days ahead of schedule.

Otto finally returned home around five o'clock. It is not hard to imagine the greeting he received from Edith and the girls. Otto responded in his usual placid manner. Of course they were going to go into hiding—immediately, tomorrow morning, twelve hours from now. No need to panic; everything had been prepared long ago. Their tenant, Werner Goldschmidt, and all their friends and neighbors would assume that they had managed to escape to Switzerland, as many others before them had.

But no, they would not take Goldschmidt into their confidence. They had known him too short a time for that. They didn't trust him enough. Anne would describe this thirty-seven-year-old Berliner later in her story "Roomers or Renters": "He was a tall man, . . . with glasses and a very unpleasant face." In Berlin, he had worked in his father's business in central heating, sanitary installations, and sewage systems. He left Berlin at the end of August 1936. In the spring of 1938, the firm of Felix Goldschmidt was Aryanized. Goldschmidt lived in The Hague and in the neighborhood of Huizen and Naarden, but a marriage having failed, he moved into the Franks' "big room" in March or April 1942. His expertise as a heating engineer was in demand, and as an employee of the Joodse Raad, he worked as the heating supervisor in the Joodse Invalide, the Jewish hospital.

The Franks would leave behind, as though inadvertently, an address scribbled on a scrap of paper that would confirm the assumption that they had fled to Switzerland. Victor Kugler later reported that for quite a while Otto and Edith Frank had spread the notion to certain friends and acquaintances that they were seriously considering escaping to their relatives in Basel, and they had even gone so far as to say good-bye to those people.

Before Anne and Margot went to bed they were to pack their schoolbags with whatever personal belongings they wanted to take along; there would be no time for that in the morning. Probably they would all have to hide for several weeks, perhaps for several months, until the war was over and they could reemerge. The cat, unfortunately, would have to be left behind. An animal in their luggage would not do. The neighbors would take Moortje in. Anne had often practiced handstands and played hopscotch with Toosje Kupers. They had always gotten along well together. Toosje would take good care of Moortje.

Anne wanted to know where they were going to hide but Otto would say only that it was in a safe place and that the family would stay together, as he had promised. She would find out where in the morning. "In a town or the country, in a house or a cottage, when, how, where? . . . These were many questions I could not ask but I couldn't get them out of my mind," Anne would write in her diary on July 8 (ver. B).

It was hard for Otto to keep calm. Some plausible fiction had to be invented for their tenant, and Otto's employees, Johannes Kleiman and Victor Kugler, had to be told. After all, it had been Kleiman, as early as the summer of 1941, who had suggested to Otto that the empty rooms in the annex behind the office at 263 Prinsengracht would make a comfortable hiding place.

Though Otto Frank had still nurtured the hope of rescuing his family by emigrating to the United States with Nathan Straus's help, he had also planned an alternative means of escape. Without the aid of his loyal employees, this carefully thought-out plan would not, of course, have been possible. Otto Frank had informed Victor Kugler of his intentions when he realized that once Jews in Germany had been forced to wear the Star of David the Jews of Holland would soon be compelled to follow suit. "Mr. Frank . . . had often said he would not comply. When things did come to that point, Mr. Frank and his family . . . immediately expressed the wish to ready the annex as a hiding place," Kugler would later say.

Over the course of several months, Kleiman's brother, who ran a cleaning business and whom Otto Frank had taken into his confidence, had been picking up furniture a piece or two at a time from the Franks' apartment, transporting it in his truck to Kleiman's apartment on Biesboschstraat and storing it there temporarily. As Jews, the Franks and the van Pelses were not permitted to take furniture out of their apartments. While Anne and Margot were given to believe that the furniture was being refurbished, it eventually made its way to the annex along with dishes, bedding, clothing, and large amounts of foodstuffs. A washstand was installed and the toilet already in place was repaired and made serviceable. "Since electricity, water, and gas were already installed," Victor Kugler said, "these rooms, which incidentally had only one entrance, seemed ideal for a hiding place." In good time, Otto had taken some of the family's silver to his friend Joop Hofhuis's house in Hilversum. There the tableware and candlesticks continued to be used throughout the remaining war years. This was the most unobtrusive way to store these valuable items.

When all the arrangements for the next morning had been made, Hermann van Pels took his leave. He had to go quickly because he could not be seen on the street after eight, and he still had to let Jan and Miep Gies know what was happening. Otto had revealed his plan to Miep—and to Bep Voskuijl as well—weeks before. "Are you prepared to take responsibility for us when we are in hiding?" he had asked her. Taking responsibility meant first of all shopping, finding food in an economy where food was in short supply. It meant always being on call for her friends in hiding and never ever breathing a word to anyone. Taking responsibility meant keeping a secret that was a matter of life and death. Miep responded without a moment's hesitation, as if Otto had asked her to take care of some routine matter in the office. Yes, of course, she told her employer without asking a single question. She respected Otto Frank; he was her friend, and not only her friend but also her employer, the most fair-minded employer she could imagine. He was a man to whom anyone would be loyal. It never occurred to her to say no.

When Hermann van Pels told Jan and Miep what had happened that afternoon, they didn't hesitate. As soon as it was dark, they would pick up clothes, shoes, towels, and other necessities at the Franks' and store them temporarily at their place. (Neither the van Pelses nor the Franks could do this, of course, because they could not leave their apartments after 8:00 p.m.) Then, over the course of the next few days, they could take these items to the hiding place on Prinsengracht.

Naturally, Jan and Miep were terribly nervous. They knew what would happen if the police caught them. Although they wanted to run from their apartment on Hunzestraat to Merwedeplein, they walked normally so as not to attract too much attention. They had had enough presence of mind to put on their raincoats, unusual garments for a warm summer evening but ones in which they could conceal all sorts of bulky items. They would have been conspicuous marching through the streets with suitcases in hand.

Late that evening Otto wrote a short letter to his sister, Helene, in Basel, wording it carefully so that it would get by the German censors without giving anything away. Miep would mail it the following day. "Dearest Lunni, because we will not be able to write later, we are sending you our birthday wishes now so that they will be sure to reach you in good time." Helene's birthday was not until September 8. "We wish you all the best. We are well and together; that is the main thing." The Franks' relatives in Basel were to understand that Otto, Edith, and the children were going into hiding but would under no circumstances be separated. Edith could not get word to her brothers in America. Since Hitler's declaration of war against the United States in December 1941, mail service to the States had been cut off. But Alice Stern Frank passed news from her daughter-in-law on to Julius and Walter Holländer. And certainly she passed on Otto's coded message: "Everything is difficult for us these days, but we have to take things as they come. I hope peace will come this year and that we will be able to see one another again." The letter also contained a brief note for Otto's mother: "I regret that we're unable to continue to correspond with I. and her family, but there's nothing we can do. I'm sure she will understand. Once again, our warmest greetings. Your O." Anne was allowed to add one short sentence: "I won't be able to write you a holiday letter now."

When Hanneli Goslar rang the Franks' doorbell the next afternoon, Mr. Goldschmidt answered. Hanne asked shyly for Anne's mother and explained that she had come to pick up a kitchen scale Mrs. Frank had borrowed. Her mother was about to make jam and needed it. The tenant hesitated to let the girl in. Didn't she know the Franks weren't there anymore?

The news spread quickly among the Franks' friends and acquaintances. Hanneli told Jacque immediately: Anne has gone to Switzerland. But Jacqueline had had a long phone conversation with Anne the previous afternoon, and Anne hadn't mentioned leaving. The Franks had fled to Switzerland, the Goslars whispered behind their hands to the Ledermanns. The word was that they had left in such a terrible hurry that they didn't even straighten up their apartment; the beds were unmade, the dishes left unwashed in the sink. People seemed to know that Margot had been called up for service, but no one had seen the Franks leave. Rumor had it that a German officer—one of the few decent ones, an old comrade-in-arms apparently—had helped Otto. After all, Otto had been an officer himself and been awarded the Iron Cross, at that.

Hello, too, heard all kinds of rumors about a hasty flight

abroad. He knew that such things happened. Back in Germany he had seen one of his schoolmates disappear overnight, and now Hello suddenly thought about him again. On October 27, 1938, the police had forced the boy and his parents to leave the country precipitously because they were Polish Jews. The Germans drove out seventeen thousand people, allegedly to preempt a move on the part of the Polish government to refuse reentry to all Poles abroad who had not renewed their passports by October 29. Back then Hello had had simply to accept what had happened and not ask questions. And now he didn't inquire into Anne's disappearance either.

Hanneli and Jacque worked up the courage to go back to the Franks' apartment in search of some mementos of Anne, perhaps her new diary. Jetteke, too, looked to see if her best friend, Margot, had left her a hidden message; she took from Margot's bookshelf a little volume of poetry called *Nieuwste Dichtkunst, De Uilenreeks Nr. 1*, intending to return it when the war was over. But Hello never went back. He was sixteen and likely to be called up himself. Life had to go on.

Starting on July 5, 350 Jews per day were being called up for labor service in Germany. On July 15, a total of 4,000 were to be sent to Westerbork. Some of them dutifully reported as instructed, either out of fear of endangering their families if they didn't or in the naïve belief that things would not be all that bad. Most of them, terrified by the order, sought a way out. Some, like the Franks, went into hiding. A few actually managed to escape German-occupied territories. Others fought desperately for a temporary postponement. Anyone who worked for the Jewish Council or could prove that his work was essential to the day-to-day functioning of the Jewish community was spared for the time being.

Anyone who had a passport from a neutral foreign country—in

South America, for example—was temporarily safe, too. Such a passport could be bought in Switzerland for a great deal of money. The Goslars were fortunate enough to have an uncle who provided them with Paraguayan passports. Also temporarily safe were German Jews who had close relatives—children, parents, or siblings—in Palestine; they could have their names put on the so-called Palestine lists. The SS had, of course, an ulterior motive for compiling these lists. The Germans thought they might at some point be able to use these Jews to trade with the English: German Jews for German prisoners of war.

Although the Goslars had no relatives in Palestine, Hans Goslar was nonetheless regarded as a "veteran," that is, he was a well-known Zionist who had worked all his life to establish a state of Israel. And so his family found a place on the second of the Palestine lists. The Ledermanns, too, ultimately managed to get on one of the subsequent Palestine lists, of which there were eventually forty.

There was no straw so thin that someone didn't attempt to grasp it. Supervisors wrote letters claiming that this or that employee was utterly indispensable. Doctors certified innumerable illnesses. Hordes of people stormed the Jewish Council hoping to get at least a week's postponement.

But the German security police were under pressure. The quotas Berlin had set for the first three trainloads had still not been met; the police would have to resort to drastic measures. To intimidate the Jews and bring them into line, SS chief Rauter ordered a special "action" to round up seven hundred Jews from the streets and hold them hostage. Throughout the entire city, German Nazis and Dutch police hunted down Jews even more brutally than they had during the raids on the Jewish quarter in February 1941. They arrested men arbitrarily, even men accompanied by women and children, and forced them onto a streetcar provided specifically for the purpose. Men who tried to run away were chased down and dragged back. A few were able to escape by hiding in shops or doorways. Women and children ran screaming after the departing streetcar, crying for their husbands and fathers. Dutch pedestrians were horrified and disgusted by the savage spectacle but did not dare to interfere.

"About 700 Jews were arrested in Amsterdam today," the *Jewish Weekly* wrote in a special edition. This announcement was followed by a threat from the German security service: if the four thousand Jews called up for labor service in Germany did not report within the week, the seven hundred prisoners would be sent to a German concentration camp.

Rauter had good reason to be pleased with himself. He had managed to frighten the Jewish population. Many Jews gave themselves up. They had to draw their strength from a tiny spark of hope: perhaps they would still be saved. The Communists would certainly help them . . . the Allied invasion would surely begin soon . . . the English would destroy the main railroad station . . . the railroad workers would go on strike. But none of these things happened.

In its underground paper, *De Vonk*, the Socialist Internationale published a manifesto that it sent to workers and intellectuals, calling for demonstrations, open letters, and boycotts to protest the deportations. The Dutch had to stand up and defend themselves, it declared. Only that kind of resistance would make the German occupation forces take notice. Passivity amounted to complicity, and as for blind obedience, it was as bad as murder: the secretaries who typed up lists of Jews, the policemen who came for Jews in their homes, the railroad workers who put together the trains and set up the schedules—they were all guilty.

But this manifesto from the opponents of the regime accomplished no more than previous appeals. People did nothing. Their fear of Nazi reprisals was just too great. Two special trains carrying about seven hundred Jews each left Amsterdam on the nights of July 15, 16, and 17. Family members were not allowed to see their relatives off at the train station. On July 17, General Consul Otto Bene, the representative of the Foreign Office to the Reich commissioner for the occupied territories in The Hague, reported that the first train had left the Westerbork camp for Auschwitz without any untoward occurrences. Westerbork had been provided with a new siding for the express purpose of accommodating the arriving and departing cars.

A few days later telephone service to Jewish customers was cut off: one more step toward total isolation.

On July 31 Otto Bene could report his successes to Berlin: "Re: Deportation of Jews. With the trains leaving today included, 6,000 Dutch Jews will have been removed from the Netherlands to date. These trains have been dispatched without incident, and we do not at this time anticipate any difficulties or disturbances with the trains scheduled to depart in the coming weeks." The machinery was up and running.

8

THE SECRET ANNEX

"It's not really all that bad here, for we can cook for ourselves, and downstairs in Daddy's office we can listen to the radio." Anne had been in hiding less than three days when she again opened her red-and-light-green checkered diary. "I can write all the names and everything openly in my diary now. Mr. Kleiman and Miep and also Bep Voskuijl have helped us so much, we have already had rhubarb, strawberries and cherries, and I don't think we'll be bored here just yet" (July 8, 1942; ver. A). The first days in hiding seemed like a holiday adventure to Anne, even more so than the camping trips she had taken in past summers, like the one in Bussum in 1938.

Clearly, she was in shock. Just a few days earlier she had been sunbathing; now she was in danger if she went near a window. She had been able to laugh out loud at Hello Silberberg's funny stories; now she had to whisper, control her emotions, watch every move. She had talked with Jacque on the telephone; now her friend had no idea where Anne was. No one knew where she was. But unlike Edith and Margot, Anne was not paralyzed by despair and helplessness. Indeed, she seems to have adapted to her new life with a light heart and as a matter of course, a sign that she had not the faintest idea what a life in hiding would really mean for her.

Monday, July 6, 1942. It had been raining steadily since early morning, a warm but heavy early-summer rain that the Franks welcomed. As agreed, Miep knocked on the door at Merwedeplein at seven-thirty to pick Margot up. There were fewer people than usual on the streets—anyone who could was staying inside. No German soldier or Dutch policeman was eager to get himself drenched.

Margot and Miep had the streets pretty much to themselves. Like two young Dutch women on their way to work, they pedaled from the south of Amsterdam toward the center of town. Margot, riding the bicycle she had not registered in violation of the Nazi order, stayed close behind Miep, apparently calm but inwardly terrified. She had no idea where she was going. The mere fact that she was not wearing her yellow star was a serious crime, enough to get her arrested.

Soaked to the skin and trembling with fear, she reached Prinsengracht, and Miep hurried her into the annex. Her only consolation was that she would not have long to wait alone before her parents' and Anne arrived. The three of them had left the apartment shortly after Margot and set off for the Old City on foot. They had left in such haste that Anne didn't even look back. And why should she have? After the war, she would return to Merwedeplein, perhaps in a few weeks, perhaps in a few months. The only thing she regretted was leaving her cat behind. But the neighbors would take care of Moortje.

"We left the house by a quarter to eight. I had a 'combination' [a kind of slip] on then two vests and two pairs of pants then a dress and a skirt then a wool cardigan and a coat"—with the Jewish star sewn on the left side—"it was pouring and so I put on a headscarf, and Mummy and I each carried a satchel under our arm" (July 8, 1942; ver. A). Luggage would have aroused suspicion: for some time Jews had been forbidden to change residences.

They walked through the rain for almost an hour, at first along the modern streets of the River Quarter, then along the canals and narrow streets of Amsterdam's Old City, crossing one bridge after another. Despite the rain and despite their nervousness, they struggled to walk normally. Jews in a hurry could have been regarded as Jews attempting an escape, and they might have been stopped.

By the time they reached 263 Prinsengracht, the rain had stopped, and throughout the rest of the day the sun kept breaking through the clouds. But the Franks hardly noticed. Once Miep had shut the door to the annex behind them, the world outside disappeared, reduced to a memory. Their world had shrunk to a little less than fifty square meters. On the second floor of the annex were two small rooms, stuffy and damp, one no more than three meters wide and five long, with massive ceiling beams that seemed to press down on the little room and squeeze the air out of it. It would be Otto and Edith Frank's living room and bedroom. The other room was considerably narrower, only as wide as its window. It would have to do for Anne and Margot. The bathroom, accessible both from Anne and Margot's room and from the hallway, was spartan but at least included a washbasin with running water—only cold, unfortunately—and a separate toilet, which could not be flushed during business hours. The water and sewer pipes ran down inside a wall adjacent to one of the storerooms on the first floor. The flushing of the toilet could be heard by anyone below.

A dizzyingly steep staircase led to the annex's largest room, which contained kitchen cabinets, a stove, and a sink and had originally served as a kind of laboratory for Pectacon. Apo Lewinsohn, Otto's pharmacist acquaintance, also used it, frequently conducting experiments there. Off this room was a tiny one with a window opening onto the interior courtyard. This cramped space was no

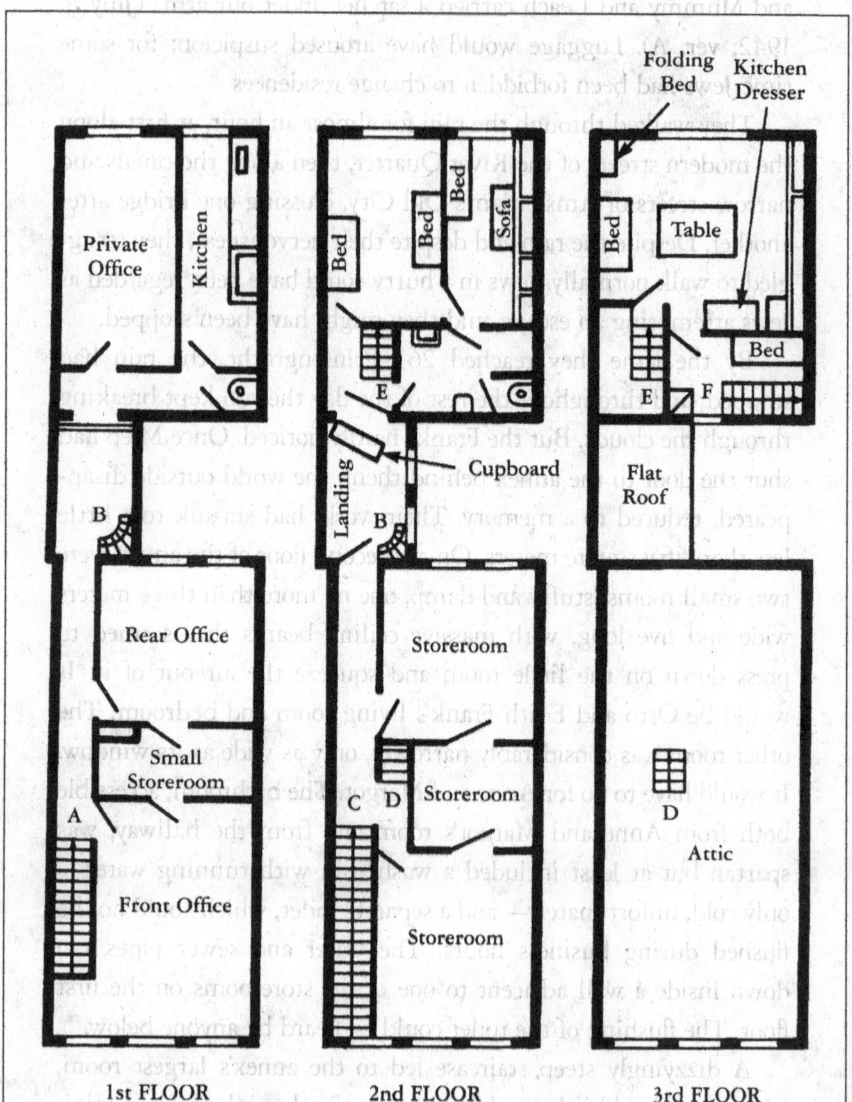

263 Prinsengracht. The office spaces on the first floor and the storerooms on the second floor are connected with the annex on both floors.

more than a little vestibule or passageway; the stairs leading to the attic left barely enough room for a narrow bed and a very small table. This cubbyhole would be a bedroom for Peter van Pels, who with his parents and his cat, Mouchi, would join the Franks in the annex a week later, on July 13. During the day, the large room would be available to everyone in the annex as a kind of common room; at night it would be the van Pelses' bedroom.

Four adults, three near adults, and Peter's black cat that he had brought along despite a prior agreement that he would not—seven people and a cat in rooms as small as prison cells, in fifty square meters that were hot and stuffy in the summer because the windows always had to stay closed and bone-chillingly cold in the winter because the coal stove often failed to supply enough heat. Under no circumstances would Anne and the others be able to go outdoors. Their only "outings" would be to the attic, where, standing back at a safe distance from a large closed window, they could look out into the backyards of neighboring buildings and onto the crown of a huge chestnut tree that let them watch the seasons change. Through a skylight they could catch a glimpse of the Westerkerk's tower, whose black and gold clock, once illuminated at night, was now often dark. More important, the window permitted them an occasional breath of fresh air. In the evening, as soon as the warehouse workers had gone home and Miep or one of their other helpers had given them the all-clear signal, they could venture into the front part of the building. They could work in the "small, stuffy, dark director's office," as Anne described Kugler's office (July 9, 1942; ver. B). Or, if they went into the "showroom of the whole building, the private office," with its "dark, dignified furniture linoleum and carpets on the floor, radio, smart lamp, everything first-class," they could play the radio softly. They could wander through the warehouse areas, breathe the air of freedom. Anne described the large main office that Miep, Bep, and Johannes Kleiman shared and that looked out onto Prinsengracht as "very big, very light, and very full," but the annex residents didn't dare enter it. Through the outsized windows, which reached nearly from floor to ceiling, they would have been as visible to passersby as actors on a stage.

After their arrival in the annex, Edith and Margot collapsed into utter helplessness, too disoriented to make themselves useful. But Otto and Anne went straight to work. Otto hoped to quell his anxiety with well-organized activity; Anne was simply following his lead. There was, of course, plenty enough to do.

Their first chore was to cover the windows. From the chaos of boxes, bags, and furniture, they dug out what rags and scraps they could find, hastily stitched them together into patchwork curtains, and hung them over the windows with thumbtacks. These masterpieces of improvisation were sufficient during the daytime, but in the evening heavy blackout cardboard had to be mounted on the windows to prevent any glimmer of light from escaping. That had to be done from inside, of course, because any changes visible from outside could betray the hiding place.

Otto and Anne worked for hours organizing the jumble of boxes and crates, shoving furniture into place, scrubbing the floors and rolling out the carpets, unpacking cartons and bags, stowing pots, pans, china, tablecloths, sheets, clothes, canned goods, and books in cabinets and on shelves—in short, making their claustrophobic place of exile as comfortable as possible. Anne was surprised to see again those pieces of furniture that had disappeared from the apartment on Merwedeplein weeks and even months earlier.

When Otto finally dug out of the confusion of trunks and boxes a carton containing Anne's collection of movie stars and royal princes and princesses, Anne was ecstatic. He realized that by providing these little reminders of a normal life, these sentimental knickknacks, he could help his family get through this state of emergency. Nothing seemed more important to him than lending an appearance of normality to life in hiding, and so he suggested to Anne that she paste her favorite pictures on the wall next to her bed. Mixed in with photos of Heinz Rühmann, Greta Garbo, Ginger Rogers, and Ray Milland were innumerable pert, pudgy-cheeked offspring of European royal houses—the future Queen Elizabeth and her sister, Margaret Rose, for example—as well as the Dutch royal family exiled in Canada. Later, she pasted new pictures over some of the old ones: now she preferred to look at Michelangelo's *Pieta* instead of the Hollywood actresses Rosemary and Priscilla Lane. A postcard from her childhood gave way to a self-portrait by Leonardo da Vinci. That painting—along with Rembrandt's *Portrait of an Old Man*—and a picture of a statue of Hermes attest to Anne's increasing interest in art history and in Greek and Roman mythology.

Because creating a sense of normal life was Otto Frank's top priority in these first days, he quickly established a daily routine. It was not, however, primarily his love of order and sense of decorum—characteristics that would earn him the nickname of the "Prussian officer"—that prompted him to institute a regular schedule. He recognized the danger of falling into idleness, of wallowing in self-pity, or of simply giving up. Anyone who fell apart would be not only a burden but a real liability to them all.

And so no one was exempt from the routine in the secret annex. On weekdays everyone had to be up by seven at the latest. The blackout cardboards came down first thing to let in the morning light and help everyone wake from an unrestful sleep. Nights rarely went by without some sort of disturbance. Frequent air-raid alarms interrupted the sleep of the highly sensitized *onderduiker* (undergrounders), as the Dutch had dubbed people in hiding. Even at rest they were always on the alert, and in the quiet of the night, every sound seemed doubly loud and ominous. Even harmless sounds like a housemate's cough or the yowling of a cat in the backyard,

The Annex. Anne's room was located behind the left window on the second floor.

not to mention the rustlings of a rat helping itself to the stores of food in the attic, were enough to terrify them. With daybreak came new hope.

The order in which the annex residents used the bathroom was quickly established and remained unwritten law from then on.

Only strict adherence to this rule ensured that by eight-thirty they would all have completed their morning toilet, dressed, and stowed their bedding to give them as much living space as the little rooms could provide. Then they could move about only on tiptoe, for downstairs the warehouse workers had begun their morning shift. The warehouse foreman, Bep Voskuijl's father, had been let in on the secret, but his workers, who were often temporary, could not be given the slightest cause for suspicion.

Everyone waited expectantly for Miep, and faces brightened visibly when she managed at some point early in the morning to sneak out of her office to pick up the daily shopping list for groceries, toilet articles, and other necessities and to offer a few hastily whispered snippets of news. Only with the appearance of Miep, their guardian angel, did they finally feel released from the uncertainties of the night. Among all their helpers—Johannes Kleiman, Victor Kugler, Bep Voskuijl, and Miep's husband, Jan Gies, who worked in the Amsterdam Bureau of Social Work and stopped by her office every day at noon—Miep was their vital link with the outside world. But this young woman, who maintained the appearance of composure and good cheer, even when she was under the greatest strain, could spare only a few minutes in the morning. Before hurrying back to work, she would console Anne and the others with a promise to return either at noon or in the afternoon.

Until twelve-thirty, Anne, Margot, and Peter did schoolwork—languages, mathematics, geography, history—so as not to fall behind their classmates. Anne called her lessons her "daily time killers" (March 27, 1943; ver. A). The adults read, sewed, knitted, did kitchen duty, cleaning vegetables, if any fresh vegetables were available, and peeling potatoes, every day peeling potatoes. All the residents of the "orphanage"—as they called their hiding place, with grim black humor—had to take turns at that task. Potatoes, stored in large barrels in the attic, were their primary staple.

Anything that made noise was forbidden. In the absolute quiet, broken only by the bells of the nearby Westerkerk and the muffled sounds rising from the warehouse, the four morning hours seemed an eternity. Too much time, too little space. The ringing of the tower bells echoed through the annex, reminding its residents that they had been shut out of the world and that their lives—despite their program of activities—had been reduced to waiting and hoping. Only Anne liked the tolling of the bells, perhaps because each tone assured her that a life of freedom was nearby, audible, and therefore not altogether lost. And when in August 1943 the bells stopped ringing temporarily, probably because of a power failure, she noticed their absence at once, and it made her anxious.

The historic carillon played every fifteen minutes, day and night, and its thirty-seven bells gave each quarter hour its unique musical identity. A brief tune announced the end of the first quarter hour, and a similar but noticeably different one the end of the third quarter. A longer melody sounded at the half hour, and, at the full hour, the carillon played its longest and most elaborate tune. As if that were not enough, one of the large tower bells struck the half hour, and after the melodies had ended, the deep, rich tones of the Westerkerk's oldest bell marked the hour. The tower bells were operated back then, just as today, by an electrical device. But on Saturdays—and sometimes once again during the week—the master bell ringer climbed into the tower and played familiar songs, some of which Anne must have recognized from school.

If the adults minded the bells most of the time, they greeted the one at twelve-thirty like children set free at the end of a school day. At last, the midday break. The workers would be out of the building for an hour and a half, a precious hour and a half in which the fugitives could make some noise and even use the toilet instead of the communal bucket. And there were visitors.

"Twelve forty-five: One by one they trickle in," Anne wrote in a story she titled "Lunch Break." One after another, the shy Bep,

Jan Gies, and sometimes Miep came up to the common room. Victor Kugler or Johannes Kleiman—whichever of them had the time; more often it was Kleiman—brought up the rear. They passed their copies of the *Telegraaf* and *Het Volk* on to Otto Frank and Hermann van Pels, although both newspapers were rigorously censored by the Germans and the information they contained about the war had to be taken with a grain of salt. Kugler and Kleiman would have business matters to discuss, as both Pectacon—now officially under Kugler's direction and known as Gies and Company—and Opekta, now managed by Kleiman, had to continue operation. Neither Kugler nor Kleiman took a step without Otto's advice and approval.

Confronted with the expectant faces of their charges, with the total dependence those faces expressed, the helpers and protectors were embarrassed and ashamed. For them, Otto Frank was still their boss, even if the roles were reversed now. "Quarter past one. The great share-out. Everyone from below gets a cup of soup, and if there is ever a pudding some of that as well," Anne wrote in her story. But the food hardly mattered. What was important to the fugitives was that at least one or another of their protectors joined them at the table. They hungered most of all for news and were grateful for every bit of information. What had happened since yesterday? In the office? In the neighborhood? How were their Jewish friends? Was Werner Goldschmidt still living in the Franks' apartment? Had he gotten married? And what had the subtenant done with the dishes and clothing that Miep and Jan had wanted to pick up from Merwedeplein? Had he made off with them as the Franks feared? Had there been more roundups? Had anyone obeyed the summons to labor service? Were there new anti-Jewish regulations? Any new rumors? What about Hitler's Russian campaign? Weren't people certain that the Allies would land soon and liberate Holland?

The Franks and van Pelses had lots of questions, but they tried not to ask too many of them at once. They realized the pressure their helpers were under and didn't want to make themselves more of a burden than they already were. But Anne was sometimes unable to control her curiosity and pestered Bep and Miep for news. What did they know about Jacqueline van Maarsen? After all, Miep lived right across the street from her. Hadn't Jacque asked about her? And how were the Goslars? And Moortje? Was Toosje really taking care of her? Eager as Anne was for information from her former life, she didn't dare interrogate Kleiman or Kugler.

The "guests" stayed for an hour, Anne wrote, but at a quarter to two they went back to their offices before the warehouse workers returned. And in the annex, four more hours would have to pass before the workday ended. There would be a nap, more writing, reading, studying, hushed conversation. Only upstairs in the common room could the families speak without whispering. But the Franks usually went to their room on the floor below. They couldn't remain at the same table with the van Pelses all day long.

Finally, at five-thirty, one of the helpers came upstairs, often Bep or Miep, "to give us our nightly freedom," as Anne aptly put it. "Things get going right away." The entire population of the annex headed downstairs for the radio in Otto's office, "a big Philips" (June 15, 1943; ver. B) on which they tuned in anti-German stations, the BBC in particular. They listened eagerly to the news in English and then to Radio Oranje, whose broadcast was introduced by a rendition of the Dutch national anthem in appropriately somber, pious, and tragic tones.

Otto Frank and Hermann van Pels looked through file folders, curious to see what the day had brought in the way of correspondence and orders. Peter van Pels busied himself in the warehouse and even took the cat along with him. Anne and Margot, to make up for their lack of physical activity during the day, went through their daily routine of dance steps and mild calisthenics; Anne's problematic joints still would not tolerate any sudden or extreme contortions. Afterward, they often sat at one of the desks to do some simple office tasks Miep had designated for them. No doubt her motive had much less to do with reducing her own workload than with satisfying a need in the girls: she realized how much good it did them to feel they were making themselves useful.

By nine o'clock the annex residents started converting their living quarters into halfway comfortable bedrooms and getting ready for the night. Because there was only cold water in the annex, its residents usually limited themselves to a quick wash in the morning; but in the evening, with the hot water of the office kitchen available, they allowed themselves the luxury of real baths. Each person developed a special ritual and reserved one day or another for a long soak. The bather took the wooden washtub that served as a bathtub to some quiet corner and filled it with hot water. The washtub was just large enough for one person to squeeze into. "Peter uses the kitchen in spite of its glass door," Anne wrote in her diary. "When he is going to have a bath he goes to each one of us in turn and tells us that we must not walk past the kitchen for half an hour." Hermann van Pels hauled the tub into the annex and upstairs to the common room: "To him it is worth the bother of carrying hot water all that way, so as to have the seclusion of his own room." Otto Frank retired to his former office to bathe; Edith preferred the kitchen, where she cautiously hid "behind a fire guard" (Sept. 29, 1942; ver. B).

It took a while for Anne to find her favorite spot. At first, she and Margot chose the "front office" as their spacious bathroom. "The curtains there are drawn on Saturday afternoons, so we wash ourselves in the semi-darkness while the one awaiting her turn peers out of the window through a chink in the curtain and gazes in wonder at all the funny people outside." But Anne soon tired of carrying the hot water that far and having to ask for help in emptying the washtub, so she established a new routine, which she described in detail: "First I carry a small washtub downstairs to the large W.C., then I take it to the water heater, run hot water into the tub in the office kitchen, and then I go and put my feet in it, meanwhile sitting on the W.C. and start to wash myself. . . . At home I would never have believed that one day I'd be taking a bath in a W.C., but it isn't all that bad, for it could still happen that I might have to live in a W.C. one day, then I'd have a little bookshelf made and a little table and use the toilet as a chair" (Sept. 27, 1942; ver. A).

About ten o'clock everyone went to bed, hoping for a night without incidents that would rob them of sleep. For oppressive as the days in the annex could be, the nights were worse. Still, whenever the annex residents felt miserable and hopeless, it helped them to realize how comparatively well off they were—how much more fortunate than many Jews in Holland: "If I just think of how we live here, I usually come to the conclusion that it is a paradise compared with how other Jews who are not in hiding must be living" (May 2, 1943; ver. A).

The Franks' decision to go into hiding was not, however, an unusual one. Of the Jews living in Holland between 1942 and 1943, twenty thousand and perhaps as many as thirty thousand—the estimates vary widely—saw going into hiding as their only alternative to deportation. "We are quite used to the idea of people in hiding, or 'underground,' as in bygone days one was used to Daddy's bedroom slippers warming in front of the fire," Anne noted (Jan. 28, 1944; vers. B/C). But the way the Franks went into hiding was by no means typical. Most families separated, with the parents entrusting their children to the care of organized resistance groups. They drummed new family names into the children's heads, names that didn't sound Jewish, and arranged for them to live with people who—at least to the children—were utter strangers. The adults sought out other refuges. Most married couples had to separate. Very few of those who went into hiding could rely on the kind of loyal, well-organized team of helpers the Franks had, selfless people whom they had known for years and who not only provided them with essentials but also stood by them as friends, even bringing them gifts on their birthdays and on holidays.

Many Jews had to entrust themselves to strangers, and not all their choices were fortunate ones. Some people who offered to help suddenly lost their nerve or unintentionally betrayed a hiding place with careless talk. The German occupation forces had threatened to shoot any Dutch citizens who dared to help Jews. In reality, it turned out that, with some exceptions, people convicted of resistance drew only light sentences—at most, four months in a Dutch labor camp like Amersfoort—but people couldn't be sure that the Germans would not act on their dire threat. Then, too, there were isolated instances of Dutch citizens exploiting the Jews' situation, masquerading as helpers but in fact fleecing their persecuted charges of exorbitant amounts of money for room and board. Those unfortunate enough to run out of money or valuables either had to sign promissory notes or find some other hiding place. And most hiding places were small, wretched quarters hardly fit for human habitation, damp cellars and drafty attics that would hold no more than a few pieces of clothing and perhaps a few books and photographs—certainly not places one could call home. A hiding place as comfortable as the Franks'—which, for all its disadvantages, the residents had managed to convert into a reasonably cozy refuge—was an exception.

Separation from their children—painful as it was—still seemed to most parents the only sensible solution. For one thing, it was safer. If one hiding place happened to be discovered, family members in another would still be safe. There were practical and logistical reasons as well. The more people there were in one location, the greater the risk of their betraying themselves through carelessness. Provisioning was more difficult, too. The longer the war lasted, the more imagination and ingenuity it took to scrape together enough food for several people every day. People in hiding could not, of course, legally obtain rationing coupons, and no coupons meant no food.

Acting selflessly and so secretly that at first he didn't even tell his wife what he was doing, Jan Gies solved the problem of obtaining rationing coupons for the Franks and van Pelses. Jan was a member of the Landelijke Organisatie voor Hulp aan Onderduikers (LO), the nationwide organization formed to help people in hiding and the most effective of all the Dutch resistance groups. Opponents of the German occupation were slow to organize after the German takeover, and in the meantime a decentralized network of various splinter groups became active, supported by a foundation established by the Dutch exile government in London. From late 1942 on, the LO located hiding places for the persecuted, Jews and non-Jews alike, and provided them with fake identity papers, ration coupons, and money.

Jan's job in the social services required him to make house calls on needy citizens officially registered with the social services. Because this work allowed him to move about freely in Amsterdam without arousing suspicion, he was able to aid the needy in hiding as well. When Jan presented the LO with counterfeit identity cards and others marked with the black *J* to prove how many hidden Jews he was supplying with food, the organization would in turn supply him with ration cards and coupons, some of which went to the Franks.

"Thousands and thousands of identity and ration cards are being provided," Anne knew, "sometimes for nothing and sometimes for money. Goodness knows how many false identity cards are in circulation. Jewish acquaintances are going about under ordinary Christian names and there are certainly not many people in hiding like ourselves who have no identity cards and never go out" (Jan. 28, 1944; ver. A).

Equipped with the coupons Jan supplied her, Miep Gies set out on her daily shopping trips. "Miep is just like a pack mule," Anne wrote admiringly, "she fetches and carries so much" (July 11, 1943; ver. B). Miep had quickly learned where she could shop without risk. Shortly before Hermann van Pels had gone into hiding, he had made an arrangement with a butcher on the Rozengracht who was a friend of his. When Miep came to the butcher's shop and handed him, without comment, the annex shopping list, the butcher wrapped up whichever of the requested items he had on hand. From Henk von Hoeve, the greengrocer located on the Leliegracht just a five-minute walk from 263 Prinsengracht, Miep bought all the fresh fruit and vegetables he could give her. He quickly understood her situation without ever asking about it, and put aside for her anything he had to spare. Also, during the mid-day break, between twelve-forty-five and one-forty-five, he personally delivered heavy sacks of potatoes to 263 Prinsengracht. Miep then hid them in a cupboard for Peter van Pels to pick up in the evening.

Bep Voskuijl smuggled milk into the annex. As was customary in Holland, the milkman brought the order to the office door every morning. Bep then had to take it to the annex during the midday break without getting caught by one of the warehouse workers. Johannes Kleiman was in charge of bread for the annex. The owner of the W. J. Siemons Bakery on the Elandsgracht was a friend of Kleiman's and had agreed, without asking for an explanation, to include in his regular deliveries to the office enough fresh bread for seven people, significantly more than the office workers' official bread coupons entitled them to. It was also agreed that Kleiman would pay for the extra bread after the war, but that debt for four hundred coupons was one Kleiman never had to pay because Jan Siemons forgave it.

As long as there was still enough food in the shops, the provisioning of the annex went smoothly. "In the three months I have been here I have gained 17 pounds, an enormous amount isn't it!" Anne wrote on October 18, 1942 (ver. A). But the weight gain hadn't made her any plumper. In the first year alone she grew four inches.

But the longer the war lasted, the harder it became to buy food. "The whole globe is waging war and although it is going better for the Allies, the end is not yet in sight," Anne wrote on January 13, 1943 (ver. B). The occupation forces had allowed everyone with a ration card to have an additional portion of real butter for Christmas in 1942, but there were noticeable shortages by the spring of 1943. Anne took the deprivation in stride and was able to laugh about it: "Our food is miserably poor. Dry bread and coffee substitute for breakfast. Dinner spinach or lettuce for 14 days on end. Potatoes twenty centimeters long and tasting sweet and rotten. Whoever wants to slim should stay in the 'Secret Annex'" (April 27, 1943; ver. B). Fruit had become prohibitively expensive, fats a rarity. The vegetables were so bad that sometimes Anne could not suppress her disgust: "It's incredible how kale that is probably a few years old can stink! The smell is a mixture of W.C., bad plums, preservatives + 10 rotten eggs. Ugh! the mere thought of eating that muck makes me feel sick" (March 14, 1944; ver. A). It was a good thing that Otto Frank and Hermann van Pels had laid in a considerable supply of nonperishable food. Now, if food ran short in the shops or none at all could be had, the annex could fall back on canned vegetables, canned fruit, canned fish, canned milk and dry milk, rice, oatmeal, and salami that the master butcher Hermann van Pels had made out of black-market meat. "With the help of our business connections, we laid in enough condensed milk to last us through the whole war. In addition, we had several hundred kilos of wheat starch that made an excellent pudding. We were richly endowed with sugar as well. Every month throughout the entire war, our firm got 150 kg of sugar, not all of which was used for the business purposes it was meant to serve," Victor Kugler related. For legumes, of which they had all kinds in abundance, the annex residents had developed a special preparation technique: "Bean rubbing is making moldy beans decent again" (Nov. 11, 1943; ver. B).

Months passed, and hopes of a quick end to the war faded. In April 1944 it was almost impossible to buy fresh greens anymore, and when they were available, it was only on the black market and at prohibitively high prices. But Miep Gies offered her charges some consolation: they weren't the only ones who had to get by without the vitamins in fresh vegetables. Everyone else had to do without them, too. "We don't get any greens at all," Anne wrote on April 3, 1944. "We eat potatoes at every meal, beginning with breakfast, because of the bread shortage" (ver. A). Edith Frank, who before the family had gone into hiding had fortified Anne with snacks of heavily buttered bread between meals, worried constantly about her frail daughter's health and tried to maintain it with dextrose, cod-liver oil, yeast tablets, and calcium. But Anne didn't trouble herself much about food. Her priorities lay elsewhere: "Quite honestly, the food wouldn't matter so much to me if only things were more pleasant otherwise. Here's the rub precisely, this boring life is beginning to make us all boring" (March 14, 1944; ver. A).

However quickly Anne adjusted to her new environment, however exciting and uncomplicated those first days in hiding seemed, when she wrote on July 11, 1942 (ver. B), that it was "more like being on vacation in a very peculiar boardinghouse," the sad awakening came soon enough. Without warning she had been locked up, "feeling like a songbird who has had his wings clipped and who is hurling himself in utter darkness against the bars of his cage" (Oct. 29, 1943; ver. B). Having just set out to see the world, she now had to make herself invisible in it. Hemmed in though she had been by the cynical chicanery of the German occupiers, this restless explorer, hungry for life, had just begun to dance at parties, to flirt innocently, and lead a "divine life," as she put it. Anne needed an audience. Being alone, sitting still, keeping quiet—all that went against her nature. She had been able to give in to her mood swings whenever she felt like it and to deal with the by no means trivial day-to-day problems of a thirteen-year-old girl who was free to conduct her own affairs: her awakening sexuality, her first inklings of an instinct previously unknown to her, a vague romantic yearning for love that swept earlier interests aside and wakened new desires. She desperately wished she had a close girlfriend with whom she could share her feelings, someone as engaged with the outside world as she was, someone she could model herself after and tell her desires and worries to day by day.

Curious, bold, Anne had bid childhood farewell and set out to explore this exciting unknown territory between childhood and adulthood. But now the possibility of choice had been taken from her.

In her cage, each day was like the next, and although she had time enough to indulge her feelings, there was no space for them. She couldn't scream, sing, or cry when she wanted. She had to learn to express her feelings only at certain times, an ability even adults acquire only with difficulty. When the bathroom was unoccupied, she would hide there and weep from loneliness. "I can't refrain from telling you that lately I have begun to feel deserted, I am surrounded by too great a void," Anne wrote in her diary on November 20, 1942, three and a half months after she had gone into hiding. "I never used to feel like this, my fun and amusements, my girlfriends, completely filled my thoughts. Now I either think about unhappy things, or about myself" (ver. B).

The diary had been the first thing Anne packed in her schoolbag on the hectic last evening at home, as if she already knew what an important role it would play in her life. Two months would pass in the annex, however, before Anne began to write in it regularly. Until then, she had managed to record something only every few weeks; her new situation claimed all her attention. But toward the end of September 1942 she had the idea of treating her entries as letters: "I would just love to correspond with somebody, so that is what I intend to do in the future with my diary. I shall write it from now on in letter form, which actually comes to the same thing" (Sept. 21; ver. A). Anne wrote this entry with her fountain pen, a gift she had received on her ninth birthday from her grandmother in Aachen (her fingers, friends recalled, seemed always to be stained a grayish blue thereafter). Unlike her later entries, which she wrote in a fluent, confident cursive, this one is printed in the rounded letters of a child's hand.

From then on, Anne wrote in her diary almost every day. Holding her pen in her own particular fashion between her index and middle fingers, she wrote to Jettje or Emmy, to Pop or Marianne, to Pien, Conny, or Kitty. For these imaginary friends, she chronicled everyday life in the secret annex in long letters. With them, she could laugh, cry, forget her isolation. Here and there she pasted photos of herself and her family in among her letters, adding captions that were critical but always humorous.

Anne's correspondents may have been imaginary, but Anne had not made up their names. All these girls—Anne never once wrote to a boy—were characters from Cissy van Marxveldt's *Joop ter Heul* series, part of which Anne had read before going into hiding and part apparently in September 1942. Anne did not write to Joop—who also kept a diary—probably because she felt *she* was the protagonist of the series. Then, too, it was probably through Joop that she conceived the idea of diary letters. Jacqueline van Maarsen, who had shared Anne's enthusiasm for these books, hit upon this connection many years later; only then did it occur to her why, when Anne mentioned her in revisions of the diary, she called her Jopie instead of Jacque. Jopie, too, was a character in the book.

Jacque, as it happens, was the only real person to whom Anne addressed any of her diary letters. "This is the promised farewell

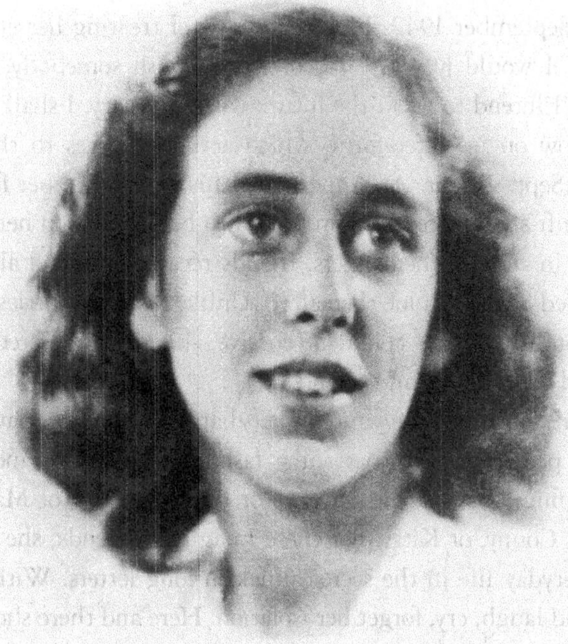

Jacqueline van Maarsen

letter," she wrote at the top of her entry for September 25, 1942 (ver. A), in which she asked Jacque to keep up a secret correspondence with her, as if she now understood how grim life without a friend was and wanted to make up for ever having doubted Jacque's friendship.

Anne and Jacque had known each other for a little less than nine months, but short as their relationship was, it had not lacked in intensity or, for that matter, in conflict and jealousy, for Anne did not suffer rivals gladly. The two girls were very different. It may have seemed that Anne was the leader, but actually she deferred to the more reserved Jacque. Anne hoped that Jacque could tell her something about sexuality, for example. When Anne—betraying both her naïveté and her lack of inhibition—asked if she could touch Jacque's breasts as "a sign of friendship," Jacque had refused. Disappointed, Anne was mollified only when Jacque had allowed her a kiss on the cheek.

The same day as her "farewell letter," Anne wrote Jacque a second. She fantasized that her friend had already answered her earlier letter. "I think of you so often," wrote Anne, who worried a lot about the fates of her friends. Some months later, she would learn from Miep Gies that Jacque and her family had been saved from deportation. Jacque's Catholic mother had been able to convince an official of the security service that her husband, a Jewish antique dealer, had registered their children in the Jewish congregation against her will. After a number of exchanges and much nerve-racking correspondence, not only were Jacque and her sister struck from the Nazis' list but their father was as well. He had managed to acquire a false medical certification that he had been sterilized. Such certification saved Jews in mixed marriages from deportation.

Jacque took off her Jewish star and switched from the Jewish lyceum to the highly regarded girls' lyceum, the school in which she should have been enrolled two years earlier but to which, as a Jew, she had not been admitted. Now a stamp in her identity papers had radically changed her life.

Jacque may have been safe, but she was uprooted, a commuter between two worlds. In the morning, she went to school with "Aryan" pupils and saw how little they knew about the suffering of the Jews and how they never spoke about it. In the afternoon, she met with her Jewish friends, the members of her Ping-Pong club, for example—Hanneli Goslar, Sanne Ledermann, and Ilse Wagner—or her former lyceum friend Nanette "Nanny" Blitz. Anne and Nanny were probably too much alike to be good friends. Of this pretty girl from a well-to-do family, Anne had written that her "dreadful tittle-tattle is beyond a joke. When she asks you something she's always fingering your hair or fiddling with your buttons" (June 15, 1942; ver. A). Nanette's father had been the director of the Amsterdam Bank, but when all the bank's Jewish staff were laid off, he, as a senior executive, was forced to retire.

After Anne's disappearance, Jacque's friendship with Nanny grew closer, but it was a friendship that would soon end. Month by month Jacque's circle of Jewish friends grew smaller. One friend after another was arrested and deported, and Jacque often learned only much later what had happened to them. Ilse Wagner was the first, in January 1943; then, in a large roundup on June 20, 1943, Hanneli and Sanne; finally, in September—"at daybreak there was a fateful, unforgettable pounding on our door"—Nanny Blitz was one of the last. The last major roundup in Amsterdam took place on September 28, the eve of Rosh Hashanah, the Jewish New Year. With this action the Jewish Council was dissolved, as its leaders and elders were among the two thousand Jews deported to Westerbork.

All this was yet to come when, on September 25, 1942, Anne closed her second letter to Jacqueline von Maarsen with "be seeing you and a little kiss from Anne."

In the following weeks, Anne continued her correspondence with her circle of fictitious friends but did not write to Jacque again. At some point, she began to write only to Kitty, perhaps because Kitty's family name, Francken, was close to her own. Exactly when Anne decided to write exclusively to Kitty cannot be determined because the final entry in her red-and-light-green checkered diary is dated December 5, 1942; the last page of that volume was full. The next entry we have is dated December 22, 1943, but Anne surely did not stop writing that long. "Perhaps I'll ask Bep if she can go and see sometime if Perrij's [Anne no doubt meant the Perry department store on Kalverstraat] still sells diaries, or else I'll have to use an exercise book," Anne wrote on October 20, 1942, "because my diary is getting full, what a pity" (ver. A). A few days later, Otto Frank asked Johannes Kleiman to find a new diary for

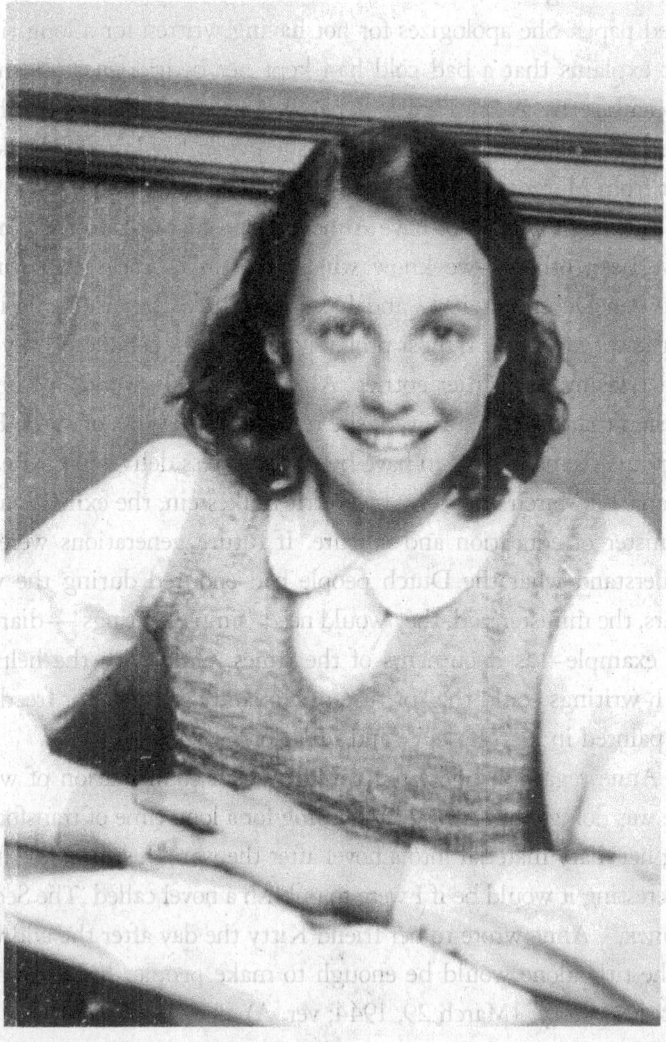

Nanette Blitz

her. The notebook Kleiman got her has been lost, but Anne's next two volumes have been preserved. On December 22, 1943, she began writing in a thick school notebook with a black binding and lined paper. She apologizes for not having written for a long time but explains that a bad cold had kept her bedridden since mid-December. By April 17, 1944, barely four months later, she had filled this book, too, and that day she began her last notebook, a gift from Margot.

Although we do not have Anne's second diary—and there may have been others—we know what went on in the secret annex between December 1942 and December 1943 because sometime in the spring of 1944, most probably in May, she set about copying and revising her earlier entries. Almost certainly working from a version that has not survived, she recorded the events of 1943. Her impetus seems in part to have been an address delivered on Radio Oranje on March 28, 1944, by Gerrit Bolkestein, the exiled Dutch minister of education and culture. If future generations were to understand what the Dutch people had endured during the war years, the minister said, they would need "simple writings"—diaries, for example—as documents of the times. Only with the help of such writings could the "picture of Holland's struggle for freedom be painted in its full depth and full glory."

Anne regarded Bolkestein's address as a confirmation of what she was doing. She had been dreaming for a long time of transforming her diary material into a novel after the war. "Just imagine how interesting it would be if I were to publish a novel called 'The Secret Annex,'" Anne wrote to her friend Kitty the day after the address. "The title alone would be enough to make people think it was a detective story" (March 29, 1944; ver. A).

That Anne had the talent and persistence to write a novel was clear from the twenty months in which she wrote uninterruptedly in her diary. The pleasure Anne took in writing was evident even in her first entries. Her writing was detailed but never tiresome, perhaps a bit rough at times but humorous and never insipid. Each month, her choice of words became more colorful, her style more sure and elegant, her descriptions and interpretations more subtle and sophisticated. She was idealistic but not naïve. Her style improved rapidly, with astonishing speed considering her age. She experimented with language but didn't indulge in any of those strained literary contortions that apprentice writers often twist themselves into; she wrote instead in a precise, confident, economical style stunning in its honesty and occasional mercilessness. Although very little was happening in Anne's life—or perhaps because of that—she always had something new to report. The more she wrote, the sharper her observations became and the clearer her expression of those observations; the keener, too, her understanding of others and—as if she could step outside herself and look back in—of herself as well. What she had begun in adolescent dreaminess ultimately achieved, in many passages, a maturity that was as convincing as it was astonishing.

But Anne wasn't satisfied with writing only in her diary, and along with her chronicle of daily life, she began writing stories. At first, toward the end of 1942 and in mid-1943, these were primarily autobiographical pieces in which she related, with considerable wit, incidents from her school years or from her life in hiding. "A few weeks ago I started to write a story," she noted on August 7, 1943, though, "something that was completely made up and that gave me such pleasure that my pen-children are now piling up" (ver. B). Later, from about December 1943, she wrote melancholy fairy tales and parables in which she dreamed of freedom and justice and sketched out the rudiments of her philosophy. She revised each story extensively before she copied it into her "story book," a big ledger that one of the helpers had brought her. And though she kept her diary entries strictly to herself, she read her stories aloud to her housemates, studying their reactions, and dreaming of publishing her tales. More than once she begged Johannes Kleiman and Bep

Voskuijl as well to send at least one of them to a newspaper under the name of Kleiman's daughter Jopie. Perhaps it would be published! But that never came to pass. Both Bep and Kleiman thought the risk too great.

Finally, Anne threw herself into revising her earlier diary entries while continuing to write new ones every day. On sheets of thin blue and pale-pink office paper, paper so thin that the slightest mishandling would tear it, she rewrote her diary from the first entry on. Anne knew that paper was scarce, and she treasured the paper that Miep and Bep put aside for her from the office supply. She completely filled each sheet, both front and back, and then carefully put it away in a folder.

If she didn't like the original text anymore, she went at it like a stage director, changing sequences of events and reformulating entire passages. She replaced all the earlier addressees with Kitty and cut sections that, in retrospect, she found too immature, personal, or simply embarrassing. "When I look over my diary today, 1½ years on, I cannot believe that I was ever such an innocent young thing," Anne noted with amazement on January 22, 1944. "I still understand those moods, those remarks about Margot, Mummy and Daddy so well that I might have written them yesterday, but I no longer understand how I could write so freely about other things" (ver. A). She also added to entries that seemed unclear or dull in their original versions, and she made up a list of pseudonyms. Her helpers Johannes Kleiman and Victor Kugler became Simon Koophuis and Harry Kraler. Bep Voskuijl became Elly Kuilmans; Miep and Jan Gies, Anna and Henk van Santen. The van Pelses were transformed into the Family van Daan. Hermann was Hans; Auguste, Petronella; their son, Peter, Alfred. Anne considered new names for her own family, too. At first, she thought she would use the family name of Aulis, but she finally decided on Robin. Edith Frank would be Nora Robin; Otto, Frederick; and Margot, Betty. Only Anne would remain Anne—Anne Robin.

Although she didn't actually use the pseudonyms, many of the changes she made in the diary, both in style and content, suggest that in the course of her revisions she was thinking about her future readers, that she meant after the war to use entire passages from her diary in her novel. Or she may even have planned to retain the diary format, just as Cissy van Marxveldt had let Joop ter Heul tell her own story in diary form.

She would take care, however, that only she would have access to her diary; sometime between May and the end of July 1944, she wrote on a pink sheet of paper that she laid on top of her stack of written pages that "no one else should lay hands on it." She was composing what would prove the last of several different versions of an "introduction" to her diary, and this unambiguous and undated sentence appears in the last of them.

Was the purpose of that sentence to increase suspense for her reader? Or did parts of her fictional conversations with Kitty in fact seem too personal to publish? Or was she—by adding that her diary and the secrets she was sharing with her friend were no one else's business and most certainly not "Father's, Mother's or Margot's"—simply issuing a warning to the annex's other residents not to invade the private world of her diary? There is plenty of room for speculation here, speculation that Otto Frank chose not to indulge in. When he finally granted his permission, in 1947, for the publication of *Het Achterhuis* ("The House Behind"), which became in English *Anne Frank: The Diary of a Young Girl*, he omitted this passage, kept the pink sheet of paper separate from the rest of Anne's diary papers, and did not include it in his literary estate.

The fact that in writing her diary Anne developed literary talents that are all the more impressive considering her age—thirteen to fifteen—should not blind us to the main reason she kept her diary and conducted such intense conversations with her imaginary friend Kitty. At the very point in her life when she might, like other young people, have begun to shed her ties to her parents, Anne was confined in close quarters with them. Just when her childish obedience to parental authority was fading and she was entering a period of negation, rebellion, and opposition, she was obliged, for the sake of survival, to be more adaptable and cooperative than ever before. She had to keep her emotions in check, had to be reasonable and disciplined instead of indulging in the normal mood swings of adolescence. At a time when a young person is recalcitrant and restless, defiant and temperamental, full of questions and searching for answers, baffled, helpless, and often irritable, Anne had no outlets for her feelings, no way to let off steam. She couldn't talk with friends who were going through the same things; there was no possibility of running away and no place to run to. Anne herself described the period from 1942 until well into 1943 as a difficult time. In the long days of loneliness and despair and of conflict not only with her housemates but also and primarily with herself, Kitty and the diary became her closest confidants.

Anne saw herself as an adult, or at least as grown up enough to have an equal voice in running the annex. But in the small circle of her adult companions, she was a child, and she was keenly aware of being treated as one. Anne felt the adults bossed her around and—even more annoyingly—did not take her seriously. She had the same duties and obligations as they did but not the same rights. It was Anne's perception of this inequality that caused her problems with the adults, primarily with her mother, and with Fritz Pfeffer, Miep Gies's dentist, who had been living in the annex since November 16, 1942.

A man of Otto Frank's age, Pfeffer, who had been practicing without a work permit, had turned to Miep in a desperate search for a safe hiding place, and she had asked her charges to take him in. The Franks had no objections. Introduced by a friend from Otto's youth, they had known Pfeffer since 1940, and he and his partner, Martha Charlotte Kaletta, had been among the regular guests at their Saturday-afternoon teas before the anti-Jewish laws had been passed. Born in the Hessian city of Giessen, Friedrich Pfeffer, who went by "Fritz," had fled by train on December 8, 1938, from Berlin to Amsterdam a few weeks after the pogroms of November 1938 because his original plan of emigrating to London had fallen through. He had had to leave his money and possessions behind, and no sooner was he gone than an "Aryan" dentist took over his flourishing practice.

According to records of the immigration police, Charlotte Kaletta followed him "as a political refugee" on December 29, 1938, though by her own recollection she left Germany in March of 1939. Both of them were divorced; each had a child from their former marriages. The racial laws in Germany had forced them to keep their love secret. Kaletta was not a Jew. They had hoped to marry in Holland or Belgium, but the Nazis had caught up with them. The authorities there forbade their marriage and also prevented them from leaving the country for Australia, as they had planned. Because Pfeffer had intended "to emigrate as soon as possible," he had only a short-term visa and, consequently, no work permit. Now, like so many others, he was stuck in Holland.

The problem of who would sleep where had been solved before Pfeffer's arrival. Margot would move her bed into her parents' room, and Anne would share her little room with Pfeffer. Otto and Edith's decision to put Pfeffer in the same room with Anne instead of with the sixteen-year-old Peter van Pels corroborates Anne's complaint that she was in fact regarded as a child. Not only Otto but Edith Frank as well disregarded her growing need for privacy and obviously ignored their adolescent daughter's sense of modesty, which was of course becoming all the more acute as she matured sexually. Had they been aware of her feelings, it is hard to imagine that they would not have found a solution that would have spared her the discomfort of sharing such close quarters with a grown man.

Fritz Pfeffer and Charlotte Kaletta, ca. 1939

It did not take long for conflicts to arise between Anne and Fritz Pfeffer. Barely two weeks after his arrival in the annex, Anne was describing her roommate as "a stodgy, old-fashioned disciplinarian and preacher of long, drawn-out sermons on manners" (Nov. 28, 1942; ver. B). As time passed, the harsher her judgments became. At night his snoring disturbed her, and during the day she was irritated by his reserve, which she interpreted as stiffness and rigidity. "After a while," Victor Kugler reported later, "Anne could imitate Mr. Pfeffer to a T. She captured his slow way of speaking, his gestures, and so on perfectly. These performances took place of course only when neither Mr. nor Mrs. Frank nor any of the other adults was present."

"A person of 54 who is still so pedantic and small-minded must have been made like that by nature, and will never improve," Anne wrote on July 11, 1943 (ver. A). When she revised her diary, the pseudonym she settled on for him was Albert Dussel, that is, Albert Dope.

Anne's antipathy for the old-fashioned dentist was understandable; in matters of child rearing he was—unlike Otto Frank—of the old school and had little tolerance for the silliness of a thirteen-year-old. But Pfeffer was surely not as dreadful as Anne thought him. Indeed, he must have been a man of sensitivity and charm, qualities evident in the farewell letter he wrote to his "dearly beloved Charlotte" the day before he went into hiding. "I find it very difficult to write to you because we are accustomed to discussing things together every day," he wrote. "And yet my heart prompts me to write because it is so full of pride in you, my dearly beloved. I have always admired the brave, calm dignity and nobility with which you have faced these indescribably difficult times. My pride consists in my total devotion to you, in my attempt in everything I do to prove worthy of your love. This break—very short, I hope—in our eternal bond will prove of little consequence. Keep up your marvelous courage. Your trust in God and your love will strengthen us both and give us courage. I embrace you and kiss you warmly. Your Fritz."

It is understandable that Anne, at her age, did not give much thought to Pfeffer's inner life. All the other annex residents had their closest relatives with them—and often got on one another's nerves—but Pfeffer had no one.

"He keeps me up until half past 9 with stories about his wife and children," Anne complained once (April 15, 1944; ver. A). Preoccupied as she was with her own problems, she was unable to empathize with Pfeffer. But the fact is he had his share of burdens to shoulder. He hadn't had any contact with his only son, Werner, since the beginning of the war. After his divorce from Vera Henriette Bynthiner in January 1933, custody of the six-year-old boy was awarded to him, the father, as was customary at the time. To ensure that Werner was properly looked after and no longer exposed to the kind of anti-Semitic hostility he had already experienced, Pfeffer enrolled him in the private Forest School, located in the exclusive Dahlem district of Berlin and under the direction of the progressive educator Lotte Kaliski. From 1934 on, only Jewish children attended this school, with their numbers shrinking every year. Everyone who could leave had left Germany by 1938 at the latest. Kaliski herself had emigrated to the United States in the summer of that year, and the school had had to close in 1939. On December 1, 1938, Werner fled Germany, too. A children's transport took him to Fritz Pfeffer's brother in London. Two days later, the "ban on Jews" was declared in Berlin. Jews were no longer allowed to move about in the city and were "evacuated" from the better residential districts, but Fritz Pfeffer could know that his then eleven-year-old son was for the time being safe in London.

While Anne could both depend on her parents' love and also be at odds with them, Werner lacked this kind of emotional security. He was often obliged to change schools and eventually wound up in a boarding school in the west of England. Could Pfeffer have known how unhappy his son was?

Along with his anxiety about Werner came worries about Charlotte Kaletta's son, Gustav, who was barely a year older than Anne and had been left behind in Berlin. Like Werner, he lived with his father after his parents' divorce. Kaletta seems to have had hardly any contact with him, but every bit of bad news that reached her in Amsterdam about the harassment that Jews in Berlin were enduring increased her fears for her son. She tried to bring him to Amsterdam or, with the help of Pfeffer's contacts, to arrange a safe haven for him in London. "I pray to God," Kaletta said, "that my child together with his father will soon be quit of that country of thieves." But the necessary money was lacking. Her divorced husband, Ludwig Löwenstein, whom the Nazis kept sending from one hard-labor detail to the next, had preferred to remain with his son and apply to emigrate with him to the United States. But as he knew, the waiting lists were long and the demands of the authorities impossible to meet.

When postal service between Holland and Germany was cut off, Gustav and Ludwig Löwenstein were stuck in Berlin. What Fritz Pfeffer and Charlotte Kaletta could not know was that father and son were soon taken in one of the eastbound transports directly to Raasiku in Estonia and probably shot and buried in a mass grave immediately after their arrival on September 30, 1942.

Miep Gies felt great sympathy and concern for Pfeffer (who she thought bore a remarkable resemblance to Maurice Chevalier) and for his fiancée, Charlotte, who was nineteen years younger than he. She volunteered to carry letters back and forth between them, despite Otto Frank's disapproval of the arrangement.

During the entire time the Franks were in hiding, not a single word they wrote ever left the annex. Nonetheless, thanks to Johannes Kleiman, their relatives in Basel knew how things were going, though not in detail, of course. Kleiman maintained contact with

Otto's brother-in-law Erich Elias by means of postcards that ostensibly dealt with business matters but also contained tidbits of encoded news. Elias responded in kind. In this way, Anne learned that her uncle Herbert had escaped from France to Switzerland and that her cousin Bernd had realized his dream of becoming an actor and had played the role of the innkeeper in Lessing's *Minna von Barnhelm.*

The consoling love letters that Miep carried between Fritz Pfeffer and Charlotte Kaletta could not, of course, reveal where Pfeffer was hiding. Such hints would have endangered the lives of everyone involved. Miep also brought Pfeffer packages of food from Charlotte, although she had to struggle herself to survive. Left without any regular income after Pfeffer went into hiding, Charlotte was barely able to provide for her own needs and—as she later testified—she lived in a rented room to escape the attention of the occupation authorities.

If we can believe Anne's disparaging reports, Pfeffer hoarded these food packages in his cupboard and secretly consumed their contents alone at night instead of sharing them with his housemates. It would have been asking a lot of Anne for her to forgive him that.

The letters and packages from Charlotte provided Pfeffer only temporary relief from his loneliness. When arguments arose between the Franks and the van Pelses, Pfeffer was caught in the middle, and as the two families became increasingly estranged—even to the point of temporarily communicating only in writing—Pfeffer responded by retreating more and more from communal life. In the evening, he would often retire to the bathroom, where he could read in peace. During the day, he wanted to sit undisturbed at the little table in Anne's and his room, where he wrote and studied Spanish. After the war, he planned to marry Charlotte and emigrate with her to South America. Like Anne, he took refuge in dreams of a promising future.

That little table proved a bone of contention between Anne and

Pfeffer. She needed it for studying and, more important, for writing in her diary. Pfeffer, for his part, could not understand why he should indulge a child's whims. Only after Otto Frank tactfully intervened and worked out a schedule acceptable to both of them did peace on that point prevail.

The two of them never became friends. Pfeffer demanded respect from young people, and for him respect meant no back talk. The stubborn Anne was not disrespectful to adults, but she always spoke her mind whether or not her opinions were solicited, and she vehemently objected and complained when she believed she was right. But that didn't mean she was basically negative. On the contrary, the periodic rebellions that irritated her housemates and that repeatedly obliged Otto Frank to summon his diplomatic skills were signs of inner strength. It would not have been unusual for someone in her circumstances to have simply given up. But instead she fought against her periodic frustration—with the sensitive support of her parents, of course, and the encouraging example of her sister—by reflecting more intensively than ever on her own behavior and by continuing her studies.

Anne pursued her schoolwork with astonishing diligence, particularly considering that she had no exams to take or schoolmates to compete with. What motivated both Anne and Margot was hope, an optimistic belief that the war would soon be over and they could go back to school. Neither girl wanted to risk falling behind her class.

Margot's ambition surely helped to inspire Anne, though Anne would never have admitted it. Unlike Anne, the industrious seventeen-year-old was the soul of patience even in hiding; she suffered silently and only rarely lost her self-control. She had always enjoyed studying, but now her hunger for knowledge became insatiable. Studying helped her keep loneliness—and fear—at bay.

It was thanks to Otto Frank that Anne and Margot were capable of independent study at such an early age. Never a star student himself, he regarded education as the most valuable thing parents could give their children, and it attests to his liberal views that he continued to think so even when his children turned out to be girls. He impressed on his daughters early on that learning demanded more than just doing what was expected, more than just reciting what one had been told, more than just memorizing for an exam and forgetting afterward. He succeeded in awakening their curiosity and inspiring them to think for themselves and to search out underlying connections and causes.

The girls had taken some of their schoolbooks into hiding with them. The helpers provided others. Anne and Margot studied, among other things, French and English grammar, history, geography, and religious history. Margot was also learning Latin. Otto Frank had registered for a correspondence course at the LOI (Leidsche Onderwijs Instellingen), taught by the well-known Latin teacher Arie Cornelis Nielson. Bep Voskuijl sent in Margot's Latin exercises under her name, and no one in the annex was surprised when they came back with high grades. Both of the girls also took a course in stenography, and practiced writing shorthand in different languages; Anne thought it "very important to learn a secret script like this."

Anne did not like all the subjects in her schedule. While Margot enjoyed math, physics, and chemistry—she had originally planned to study chemistry but had changed her mind and now wanted to emigrate to Palestine and become a midwife—Anne, like Otto, had no gift for the logical structures of algebra and geometry or for science. Sympathy for Anne's plight did not, however, move Otto to excuse her from her painful math lessons. It seems he occasionally even applied gentle coercion to steer her toward her math book. "Daddy is grumbling again, and threatens to take my diary away, oh insuperable horror. I'm going to have to hide it in future" (Oct. 4, 1942; ver. A). And a year and a half later: "He has warned me that if I don't do any algebra, I mustn't count on getting extra lessons later" (March 20, 1944; ver. A).

Otto had awakened Anne's interest in history, and she needed no prodding from him in that subject. Whenever his Annelein, as he sometimes called her, had come to him with a question about history, he had always responded by saying, "Well, let's see what we can find." When Anne had been asked to give a report to her class in the Jewish lyceum on the Roman Empire under Nero but had found the sparse information in her schoolbook uninteresting, Otto had helped her research the topic in various reference works and history texts. Her report had drawn enthusiastic applause from the class.

The "Well, let's see what we can find" attitude she had acquired from Otto proved a great asset to Anne in hiding, for there—along with her parents and Margot but more so than any of them—she found books were her teachers and her best friends, her antidote to the agonizing silence in the annex, her treasure trove of ideas and fantasies. "Ordinary people," Anne wrote, "simply don't know what books mean to us shut up here" (July 11, 1943; ver. B).

Before she went into hiding Anne had been touched by several light novels. "*Daisy's Mountain Holiday* is really a very beautiful book," she wrote about three weeks before moving into the annex. "I was deeply moved by the story" (June 20, 1942; ver. A). Now she immersed herself in fictional worlds to escape her real-life confinement, to experience a sense of freedom despite her imprisonment. "Mad on books and reading" is how she summed up her passion (April 6, 1944; ver. A). "If I read a book that impresses me I have to take myself firmly in hand before I mix with other people; otherwise they would think my mind rather queer" (Nov. 8, 1943; ver. A).

In her first months in hiding, Anne read primarily books for young people, including one called *Eva's Jeugd* ("Eva's Youth"), a romantic story by a Dutch writer named Nico van Suchtelen that related the heroine's development into a woman. The descriptions of Eva's physical maturing and her experience of menstruation increased Anne's longing to be sexually mature herself. It was a longing she wrote about again and again.

The boxes of books Otto Frank had brought to the annex beforehand couldn't begin to satisfy the occupants' demand for reading material, but the supply line for books functioned flawlessly. Along with many other books Johannes Kleiman brought for Anne was *Het Boek voor de Jeugd,* a collection that contained fairy tales, short stories, and poems by authors like Hans Christian Andersen, Jack London, and Jules Verne. And Victor Kugler could be depended on to bring Anne her favorite magazine, for her interest in movies and the stage continued unabated. "I am awfully pleased whenever Mr. Kugler brings the *Cinema & Theater* with him on Mondays, although this little gift is often called a waste of money by the less worldly members of the household" (Jan. 28, 1944; ver. B). Kugler, however, enjoyed providing Anne with this keenly desired reading matter, and he made a habit of hiding it in the inside pocket of his jacket so that he could "savor her questioning look for a while" before he handed it over.

Jan Gies went to the library for books the Franks requested, and these Miep would smuggle into the annex each Saturday: "We always long for Saturdays when our books come, just like little children receiving a present" (July 11, 1943; ver. B). As soon as one member of the household finished a book, he or she passed it on to someone else. This system ensured that everyone had enough to read and also that by the end of the week, when several people had read the same books, they would be able to discuss what they had read.

Anne's literary discrimination kept pace with her intellectual development. The more she read, the less interest she had in so-called girls' or young adult literature. "I'm mad about Mythology and especially the Gods of Greece and Rome," she announced on March 27, 1943 (ver. B), and as the months passed, her interest in history intensified. Individual lives were what captured her imagination and roused her curiosity, so she turned to biography, devouring books about Marie Antoinette, the Holy Roman Emperor

Charles V, Rubens, Rembrandt, and Liszt. These books provided her with both entertainment and instruction. "I have made great progress with a lot of them," she wrote on April 6, 1944 (ver. A), "as, for a long time now, I've been taking down notes from all the biographies and history books that I read; I even copy out many passages of history." Inspired by these readings, she also worked up genealogies of her heroes.

Anne kept a kind of card file of the books she read and she wrote down sentences she liked in a special notebook. She mentions twenty-six books in her diary, but she obviously read many more, books that expanded her horizons, nourished her imagination, and, last but not least, helped develop her writing style. In July 1944, a book called *Hoe Vindt U het Moderne Jonge Meisje?* ("What Do You Think of the Modern Young Girl?") prompted her to write one of her most detailed and mature letters to her imaginary friend Kitty. The judgment of the author, Helene Haluschka, that "today's youth" was not doing all it could to make a better world prompted Anne to write a fascinating defense. She does not respond to Haluschka's criticism with an indignant defense of her generation but provides instead a moving analysis of her own fate and that of youth in general in time of war. "It's twice as hard for us young ones to hold our ground, and maintain our opinions, in a time when all ideals are being shattered and destroyed, when people are showing their worst side, and do not know whether to believe in truth and right and in God." These are the words of a girl just turned fifteen, a realistic girl who, after two full years in hiding, was still not ready to abandon hope, even though she could "see the world gradually being turned into a wasteland" and could "hear the ever approaching thunder, which will destroy us too." She managed to hold to her "ideals, dreams and cherished hopes" in the face of "the horrible truth." Anne had freed herself from her parents in the course of those two years, and whether her ideals struck others as being "absurd and impossible to carry out" did not matter to her. With her irrepressible will to live and her determination to rise above the shortcomings of the adult world, she wrote the sentence that remains the one most often quoted from her diary, though frequently out of context: "I keep them [her hopes], because in spite of everything I still believe that people are really good at heart" (July 15, 1944; ver. A). This conviction made Anne a symbol of hope throughout the world, hope that would, however, be taken from her only a few months later.

Hardly a book came into the annex that did not arouse Anne's curiosity, especially if it was meant for someone else. "Every book I read must be inspected," she complained but admitted that her parents were not strict and that she was allowed to read nearly everything (March 17, 1944; ver. A). It was understood that the annex curriculum would include the German classics; they were, after all, an essential part of Anne's cultural heritage, and Otto was not going to allow the National Socialists to deprive her of it. "Daddy wants me to read Hebbel now as well as other books by other well-known German writers," she wrote on October 18, 1942 (ver. A). He allowed her romantic, sentimental entertainment like *Gone with the Wind*, too, of course, but he was happier to have her reading Goethe or Schiller. After the war, he recalled reading some of Schiller's poems with Anne, then *Wilhelm Tell*, *The Maid of Orleans*, and *Maria Stuart.* Otto doubtless had his reasons for including Lessing's *Nathan the Wise*, which relates how the Jew Nathan, having lost his wife and seven sons in a pogrom, raises a Christian girl and struggles with the question of religious tolerance.

In his youth, Otto Frank had been a great admirer of Heinrich Heine and must have believed in the character-building qualities of literature. In 1917, when his sister, Helene, was embroiled in an unhappy love affair, he had recommended the Romantic poet Mörike to her. "You have to be reasonable and understand what you are doing," he wrote her from the front. "Mörike will be very good reading for you. I have his complete works on my shelves. If you read them, please don't get them dirty, for they are bound in white, and keep them in order."

In hiding, Otto seems to have found consolation in Dickens, whom he read in the original. One reason for reading Dickens was to improve his English, but the far more important one was that Dickens's novels of social criticism were a great source of support to Otto, on whose shoulders so much responsibility rested. Dickens's interest in marginal groups, his understanding of human weakness, his strong sense of justice—Otto took strength from all these qualities, and on top of that, Dickens's sense of humor cheered him up.

Edith Holländer, ca. 1916

We don't know whether Otto concerned himself with what Edith read, and the only comment Anne made on her mother's habits was to say that she read "everything except detective stories" (May 16, 1944; ver. A). Nor do we know whether literature was as important to her as to her daughters and husband. We do know that she took a copy of Spinoza's *Ethics* into the annex with her, but we can only speculate as to whether it was simply a memento from her library or something she studied seriously. Did she ask herself Spinoza's fundamental question of how happiness and freedom can be attained in a strictly deterministic world? Did she have any interest in philosophy? The answers to these questions would tell us a great deal about Edith's inner life.

Edith Frank's state of mind grew increasingly desperate during her years in hiding. She gradually lost all hope that Hitler and his armies would soon be defeated, that she and her family would soon be saved. But she kept her worries to herself. She was certainly not given to hysterical outbursts, unlike the quick-tempered Auguste van Pels, who railed against her fate and threatened suicide—she would hang herself, she would shoot herself in the head. Edith guarded her emotions carefully; that, she must have thought, was what others expected of her. But although she kept outwardly calm and stoically maintained that complaining didn't make things better, she was inwardly on the verge of collapse. She did not want to, or could not, reveal her feelings to anyone in her family. Instead, she turned to Miep Gies for comfort and consolation. Once, when Miep was getting ready to leave after one of her visits to the annex, Edith detained her in the entryway and poured out her fears. She could not see the light at the end of the tunnel, she told Miep. She was at the limits of her strength. She feared for her children's lives. She spoke in a rushed whisper and without tears, but her despair was unmistakable. Miep—taken by surprise, distressed, but unable to help—listened in silence. What could she tell her employer's wife? Nothing she might have said could bring Edith Frank out of her deep sorrow. But Edith had at least been able to open her heart to someone.

Along with the justified fear of being discovered and deported, she suffered from personal disappointments as well. From their first day in hiding, she and Anne were in conflict. They had never been on easy terms even before, since it had always been Edith's role to discipline her high-spirited daughter. But the tension between them had more to do with the vast differences in their natures. Anne was the uninhibited performer, thoroughly charming if she wanted to be, tearful and hot-tempered if things did not go her way. Edith was an introverted woman, serious and basically shy; people who knew her only superficially were likely to think her dull. While Anne demanded attention, Edith stayed in the background and mostly went unnoticed by strangers. Her occasional displays of good humor and combativeness consequently came as a surprise but did allow a fleeting glance into her true nature.

In the extreme confinement of the annex, it was inevitable that these two opposite personalities would clash more often than before. Edith didn't understand her, Anne thought. Sometimes Edith mothered her too little, sometimes too much. If Edith seemed to show undue concern, Anne repulsed her. "Mummy always treats me just like a baby, which I can't bear," she wrote on August 14, 1942 (ver. A). But if Edith then pulled back and left her alone, Anne didn't like that either. She played the offended princess if Edith criticized her, and she felt humiliated if Edith did not take her tantrums seriously enough. Then Anne would accuse her mother of being insensitive, sarcastic, cold. Nothing Edith did could please Anne. But one of the sources of Anne's confidence must have been the knowledge that her mother would stand by her no matter what. In the annex, when the others complained about Anne's outspokenness and demanding personality, it was invariably Edith who came to her defense.

In short, Anne was going through the normal adolescent process of separating from her parents, but in the confinement of the annex, the simple physical withdrawal that would have eased some of the friction was impossible. At the same time, she had no girlfriends to whom she could complain about her mother. So it is understandable that she ranted against her mother in her diary, understandable, too, that her comments were sometimes extremely harsh. "I simply can't stand Mummy, and I have to force myself not to snap at her all the time and to stay calm with her," Anne wrote in the original version of her diary. "I could easily slap her in the face, I don't know how it is that I have taken such a terrible dislike to her." Later she would tone this passage down (Oct. 3, 1942; ver. A).

The more Anne rejected her mother, the more she idealized her father and the more intently she tried to win his friendship and love. "Finally I told Daddy that I'm much more fond of 'him' than Mummy, to which he replied that I'd get over that. But I don't believe it," she wrote in the October 3 entry. It was an unpleasant situation for Otto Frank, whose role as peacemaker between his wife and his daughter required considerable strength and empathy. In a talk he gave in 1968, he described the strain of mediating between the two: "On the one hand, I did not want to hurt my wife's feelings, but at the same time it was often not easy to discipline Anne when she was fresh and rude to her mother." After an argument, Otto ordinarily let some time pass before he took Anne aside and talked to her "like an adult"—such, at any rate, was his perception. Anne's view of these conversations was quite different: "Daddy tried the wrong methods, he always talked to me as a child who was going through difficult phases," she wrote on July 15, 1944. "It sounds crazy, because Daddy's the only one who has always taken me into his confidence, and no one but Daddy has given me the feeling that I'm sensible. But there's one thing he's omitted, you see, he hasn't realized that for me the fight to get on top was more important than everything else."

"To get on top"—what that meant for Anne was finally to be taken seriously. Intelligent as she was, she was also at an age when one is at odds with oneself and one's emotions, unsure of oneself and lacking in self-irony. Consequently, she misinterpreted many things Edith probably said with the best of intentions. "It is hard to speak the truth, and yet it is the truth: she herself has pushed me away, her tactless remarks and her crude jokes, which I don't find at all funny, have now made me insensitive to any love from her side" (April 2, 1943; ver. B).

Even after a year and a half in hiding, when Anne had already developed a degree of objectivity and tolerance astounding for her age, she was still not ready to give her mother the benefit of the doubt. Indeed, at a certain stage she even blamed Edith for the constant quarrels that erupted between the Franks and the van Pelses: "If Mummy wasn't so impossible during every discussion, so severe, so disapproving and so unfeminine, then all our quarrels could easily have been avoided" (Jan. 22, 1944; ver. A).

On the other hand, Anne was ready to glorify her father even when she felt he failed her. After a disagreement they had in early May of 1944, Anne explained her position to him in a letter to which Otto—who was only human, too—reacted with hurt feelings and reproaches and demonstrated once again that he continued to see Anne as an immature girl. "At a crucial moment," the author Ernst Schnabel wrote in the 1950s, "he failed his daughter miserably. He hadn't understood a word she had written him and only complained that this was 'the most hateful letter' he had received in his life." Schnabel's harsh judgment fails to take into account that, although Otto had deeply offended his daughter, they later made peace with each other. In a heart-to-heart talk, Otto spoke more openly with her than he probably ever had before, and she was deeply moved to hear of his worries and the moments of despair in his life. He once again proved himself to be the model Anne still urgently needed after almost two years in hiding. "I will take Daddy as my example," she wrote as the final sentence in her diary entry for that day, "and I *will* improve" (May 7, 1944; ver. A).

Anne remained hard and unyielding in keeping her mother at a distance. One reason for this was Anne's jealousy of Margot. Edith and Margot had similar personalities and therefore got along well. "It's obvious that Mummy would stick up for Margot; she and Margot always do back each other up. I'm so used to that that I'm utterly indifferent to both Mummy's jawing and Margot's moods. I love them; but only because they are Mummy and Margot, as human beings they can both go hang," Anne wrote on a sheet of thin blue paper sometime in the spring of 1944 when she was revising her original entry of November 7, 1942 (ver. B). Back then, she had been furious with Margot: "Margot is more catty than ever. . . . I can only describe Margot as a little wretch who gets on my nerves horribly day and night." Why exactly, Anne does not say.

The sisters had never been particularly close. When Anne was little, she had had to hear constantly about Margot's exemplary behavior. Margot was regarded as prettier and better behaved, and she got better grades in school. And indeed Anne never once saw her parents scold Margot, or so Otto Frank later recalled. Anne, on the other hand, was often reprimanded. Yet it is striking that, in photographs taken before Anne's birth, Margot appears much more self-confident than in those that show her together with her little sister. The good-natured Margot was always very affectionate with Anne, but the more temperamental Anne became, the quieter and more retiring Margot grew. That is evident in later photographs that show the sisters together. Anyone who—like Margot—is steady and always does the right thing runs the risk of getting less attention.

In the annex, where both girls were without their friends, it became acutely apparent how little they had in common. True, they would occasionally crawl under a blanket together, read out of the same book, tell each other stories, or try to laugh away their constant fear; but they didn't really become closer until after their second winter in hiding. In March 1944, Anne was finally able to elicit criticism of their parents from the much more reticent Margot. "Here everything is still all right! Except that Margot and I are getting a bit tired of our parents. Don't misunderstand me, I still love Daddy just as much as ever and Margot loves Daddy and Mummy, but when you are as old as we are, you do want to decide just a few little things for yourself. . . . Also, Margot [and I] realize for the first time that you can talk more freely about yourself to your girlfriends than to your parents." Anne added emphasis to her unusual use of "we" with this statement: "It is a great blow to us both, suddenly to realize how little remains of the comfort and harmony that we used to have at home" (March 17, 1944; ver. A).

The prime mover behind the sisters' new intimacy was Otto Frank. Anne desperately needed someone she could confide in, he had told Margot; it would be a great help to the family's little rebel if she could share a secret with her sister, something they would not reveal to either of their parents. After that, Margot and Anne talked to each other more and started writing each other letters that dealt mostly with their growing need for love but not the kind of love that parents could supply. At any rate, Margot and Anne had a closer relationship from this point on, and the struggle to win their parents' favor, which Anne had engaged in actively and Margot within herself, faded into the background. Not only did Margot treat Anne as an equal now—"Margot . . . isn't nearly so catty these days and is becoming a real friend. Nor does she any longer regard me as a little kid who counts for nothing"—but she even expressed a certain admiration for Anne's cheerfulness and strength (Jan. 12, 1944; ver. B), qualities Anne could always draw on to pull herself out of any hole.

There were still moments when Anne thought her parents were more loving toward Margot, and if she suspected Otto of favoring Margot, she was especially enraged. "If he holds Margot up as an example, approves of what she does, praises and caresses her, then something gnaws at me inside," Anne admitted in her revised entry of November 7, 1942 (ver. B), "because I adore Daddy, he is the one I look up to. I don't love anyone in the world but him. He doesn't notice that he treats Margot differently from me: now Margot is just the prettiest, sweetest, most beautiful girl in the world. . . . I'm not jealous of Margot, never have been. I don't envy her her good looks or her beauty. It is only that I long for Daddy's real love."

What jealousy Anne felt was unfounded. "I got on better with Anne than with Margot, who was more attached to her mother," Otto confirmed many years later. "The reason for that may have been that Margot rarely showed her feelings and didn't need as much support because she didn't suffer from mood swings as much as Anne did." Still, Otto was not always ready to listen to Anne when she wanted to complain about Edith. "My wife suffered from this situation more than Anne did," he explained. Moreover, he admired Edith's maternal understanding and her patience despite Anne's rejection. Anne's attitude toward her was to be expected in a girl going through puberty, Edith told Otto; eventually it would pass. In the meantime she was glad Anne at least had him.

But Anne would need considerably more time before she could accept Otto's loyalty to Edith. "Daddy doesn't understand that I need to give vent to my feelings over Mummy sometimes. He doesn't want to talk about it; he simply avoids anything which might lead to remarks about Mummy's failings. . . . We are exact opposites in everything; so naturally we are bound to run up against each other," Anne complained. Her harsh conclusion: "I

Edith Holländer, ca. 1920

only look at her as a mother, and she doesn't succeed in being that to me; I have to be my own mother" (Nov. 7, 1942; ver. B).

Anne gradually began to temper her anger and even began to feel ashamed of it. When she revised her diary, she asked herself, "'Anne, is it really you who mentioned hate, oh, Anne, how could you?'" and for the first time she admitted her share of responsibility for the strained relationship with her mother: "It's true that she doesn't understand me, but I don't understand her either" (Jan. 2, 1944; ver. B). In the coming weeks, it would become clear to Anne how much suffering her antagonism caused her mother, and she would develop some sympathy for Edith. But Anne still had a long road to travel from this incipient and rather remote awareness of her mother's feelings to the first stirrings of tolerance and respect and finally to a genuine understanding of Edith's behavior. The fact is that Anne would never become truly close to her mother while they were in hiding.

As Anne herself admitted, she never tried to learn more about her mother than what she picked up in their daily life together, but every last detail of her father's history fascinated her. She wanted to know what his life had been like before she was born, what his youthful dreams and ambitions had been, what passions had moved him.

Anne probably tried repeatedly to probe Otto's past. The more pronounced the need for love became in her and the more she began to long for the warmth and tenderness of a love relationship, the more urgent her questions for her father became and the more closely she observed her parents' relationship.

Otto and Anne were very open with each other, and it is evident from Anne's diary that subjects like love and sexuality were not taboo. We do not know what details of his private life Otto revealed to her, but a December 24, 1943, entry contains some hints. Anne was clearly alluding to an early, unfulfilled love Otto experienced before he was married when she wrote, "I don't think Margot has any idea of what Pim has had to go through. Poor Pim, he can't make me think that he has forgotten her. He will never forget" (ver. A). When Anne's diary was published, Otto insisted that "he has forgotten *her*" be changed to the much more innocuous "he has forgotten *it.*" He no doubt felt that the history of his personal relationships was irrelevant to a reader's understanding of the diary and that he did not want to give rise to any speculation. The latter reason probably also explains why he cut the second part of Anne's next sentence: "He has become very tolerant, for he too sees Mummy's faults." It is hard to understand what motivated Otto Frank, when publishing the first edition of the diary, to include several passages unfavorable to Edith that Anne herself had cut in her second version (e.g., Oct. 3, 1942; Dec. 24, 1943; Jan. 5, 1944; March 2, 1944).

There is nothing surprising about Otto's having known other women intimately before he married Edith; after all, he married relatively late, at thirty-six. But nothing suggests that he was a womanizer in his bachelor days. "You know how I get along with girls," he wrote to his sister, Leni, from the front, "well, but not too well." If this sentence suggests that he was not yet ready to settle down, he began to think more about marriage as the war went on. "A man alone is an incomplete half-being," he wrote her on June 16, 1918. After almost three years on the Western front—his last post was with an artillery reconnaissance unit in northern France—he longed for safety and security. On June 27, the twenty-nine-year-old Otto once again confided in Leni: "You can't know the feelings that our loneliness and isolation from culture and women waken in us out here. We think of a thousand old, treasured things and are only too happy to lose ourselves in our dreams," he wrote, yielding briefly to emotion, only to return in the next few lines to his usual dispassionate tone. "We all have it so good at home that we aren't especially eager to have homes of our own, strong as the impulse to do so may be in us. Yet we do realize that we can't wait too long after the war if we want to be young for the children we hope to have." Much as Otto wanted to have children, he seemed to have few illusions about marriage—a perspective that was altogether in keeping with the times and with his social class. Marriage was primarily a practical arrangement; passion between a man and a woman—if it entered into the picture at all—was secondary. "For children are, after all, the be-all and end-all of a healthy marriage." He went on in this vein, writing abstractly and in the third person, as if he were an uninvolved observer: "It is not just immediate happiness but the future that one's thoughts return to time and again, and the moments when one does not think of the future are few indeed."

Seven more years would pass before Otto would marry—the last of the Frank siblings to do so. Otto and Edith were introduced to each other in March 1925 in San Remo. They celebrated their engagement on April 5, and the wedding took place a month later, on May 12, in the Aachen synagogue, with a reception afterwards in the Great Monarch Hotel. Family members recall that Otto's mother, Alice, was overjoyed that her son had finally put his bachelor days behind him.

After the war, Otto hardly discussed his marriage. Anne's comments on it, he decided, were none of the public's business. Forthcoming as he otherwise was, he remained tight-lipped where his reputation was concerned. Ernst Schnabel's judgment: "In matters of 'publicity,' he tends to manipulate things to his liking."

His relationship with Edith was not, he believed, a matter of concern to posterity. But for Anne that relationship was very relevant indeed; had it not been, she would not have reflected on it so extensively. On February 8, 1944, she wrote her assessment of her parents' marriage. Her analysis was prompted by what appears in retrospect to be a very minor family crisis. Edith had sewn a patch on Margot's blanket and accidentally left a pin in the blanket. When Margot rolled up in the blanket that night, she stuck herself on the pin. Otto, usually eager to play the mediator and peacemaker, took sides against his wife on this occasion, however, and speaking in the condescending tone supposedly well-meaning fathers adopt in disciplining their children, he reproached Edith for her carelessness. Anne found this incident so upsetting that for the first time in her diary she showed sympathy and understanding for her mother, commenting shrewdly on her mother's position in the marriage.

About three months later, she reworked her original text into an analysis seventy-four lines long and covering three sides of a folded sheet torn in two, a work so carefully and sensitively written that its authorship by a girl not yet fifteen years old seems extremely unusual. Significantly, she omitted the needle incident altogether, focusing only on her parents' relationship.

Her parents' marriage, Anne complained, had always been portrayed to her as the ideal marriage—a marriage unmarred by quarrels or differences of opinion, a marriage of constant harmony. But she had long realized that it was a marriage of convenience. "His ideals were gone and his youth was a thing of the past." Otto may well have found Edith an altogether suitable partner, but he was not in love with her. "She loved him above all others, and it is hard to see this love remain unrequited." Anne was right. Otto had swept Edith off her feet well before their marriage, and—as her relatives confirmed—her love for him was genuine. Anne did not doubt that Otto valued and respected his wife, but his feelings for her had nothing to do with real love. Wherever Anne looked, she saw clear signs that love and passion were absent in her parents' marriage: that Otto kissed Edith the way he kissed his children, that he looked at her in a "teasing and mocking way but never a loving way," that he hardly ever argued with her but preferred instead—for the sake of appearances—to hold his tongue and avoid disagreement, all these things indicated to Anne a lack of love and passion in the marriage. "Daddy appreciates Mummy and likes her, but not with the kind of love that a marriage as I imagine it should have."

When Otto Frank decided to publish Anne's diary, he withheld these seventy-four lines from it. As we know, he took this same liberty with others of his daughter's thoughts. But this entry of February 8, 1944, seems to have hit him particularly hard. The public, he decided, would not have access to it. Otto saw to that easily enough. He put the loose sheets into an envelope, along with Anne's last draft of the "introduction" to her diary, and kept them separate from the rest of Anne's diary pages. At some point, all the loose sheets, both the pink and the light-blue ones, were paginated sequentially in pencil—all, that is, except the folded, torn sheet dated February 8, 1944, and the introduction. So now readers of the loose sheets would find an unbroken sequence of page numbers and never suspect that anything was missing.

This strategy of Otto's did not rid the world of Anne's critical reflections on her parents' relationship, for there was still Anne's similar passage, in version A, in a bound volume. How could Otto make these lines disappear? He couldn't simply tear a page out of the diary.

But Otto came up with an argument he found altogether acceptable for withholding the passage from public scrutiny: the published diary, he had already decided, was to be based on version B, which contained Anne's revisions. In reworking her text, she herself had often found—several months after writing her original entries—that her views of things had changed, and she therefore either omitted or revised various passages in version A. Thus, Otto could simply claim that Anne had come to see her parents' marriage differently three months later.

But was Anne's view the product of an immature teenager's fantasy, as Otto suggested? Or was she right when she claimed that Otto did not truly love and desire his wife to the degree a man and a woman are capable of loving and desiring each other?

It is absolutely clear that Otto was not head over heels in love with this twenty-five-year-old woman from a well-to-do Aachen family. As was still customary in this couple's social circles, their marriage was arranged. Whether this was done by a family member or a professional matchmaker can no longer be determined. That was not relevant then. Conventional wisdom held that love—quite apart from being in love—was less important than reason to the kind of "healthy married life" Otto wanted. Then, too, the substantial amount of money included in Edith's dowry helped Otto Frank solve his family's financial problems and must have influenced his decision.

Otto was certainly a good husband. He respected Edith, was

attentive to her needs, and praised—as one might praise a friend's virtues—her "strength of character" and the "harmony between us." On Sundays, the Franks' friends knew, he even served her breakfast in bed; no one would have expected that from a businessman who had been spoiled by his mother and the family servants in his youth.

Otto's brother Herbert liked to tell a story that illustrated Otto's absolute dependability and loyalty. When the armistice was declared in November 1918, every soldier wanted only one thing, to get home as soon as possible—every soldier but Otto. He still had something he had to attend to. On its way to the Western front, his regiment had commandeered two horses from a farmer in Pomerania for the duration of the war. They were the only two the farmer owned, and Otto was determined to return them. When the young reserve officer led the horses into the farmer's barnyard, the man could not believe his eyes.

Otto's mother, who had thought her son lost, was just as amazed when he turned up on her doorstep three weeks after his two brothers had returned home. The letter Otto had sent to tell her he would be delayed had gotten lost in the postwar chaos. In celebration of Otto's return, Alice Stern Frank assembled the clan, and from the coffee beans she had guarded through the war, she brewed a pot of real coffee. When Otto finally told her why he had come back so late, his mother could not contain her rage and threw the full coffee pot across the room.

Otto kept his promises and could be relied on. His feelings were tenacious, too: he did not shrug them off lightly. Anne's observations were correct. Before Otto Frank went to America for his internship in business, he was engaged to a girl from Frankfurt whom he loved deeply and wanted to marry. She came from a wealthy upper-class family, and her parents opposed the marriage, probably because they were aware of the difficulties of the Michael Frank Bank and thought Otto's financial prospects uncertain. By the time he returned from the United States, the girl had married another man.

Even after his marriage Otto did not forget that his great love had given in to her parents' demands. When he told his secretary, Miep Gies, about this personal disappointment—either in 1937 or 1938—he still appeared so despondent about it that Miep felt great sympathy for him. Anne shared that feeling. "Poor Pim," she wrote in December 1943 (ver. A). "I hope I shall grow a bit like him, without having to go through that as well."

Had Otto—as Anne intimates—also told the retiring Edith that he had lost his heart to someone else before he met her? "It can't be easy for a woman in love to know that she will never hold the first place in her husband's heart," Anne wrote on that day in February 1944. Edith had resigned herself without complaint, and if she felt jealousy, she had never shown it. Not surprisingly, Anne reasoned, this painful situation had hardened Edith's heart and made her somewhat defensive and unapproachable. And these qualities—Anne said, always able to see things from her father's perspective—would not make her any more attractive to her husband.

Did Edith have grounds for jealousy? Had word gotten back to her, for instance, that Job Jansen, who tried to denounce Otto in March 1941 (see chapter 6), suspected his wife, Jetje, and Otto of having an affair and acted out of jealousy and a desire for revenge? Did Edith know how close Isa Cauvern and Otto were and how much his employee had confided in her considerate and obliging boss? Did it bother her—or did she enjoy—the fact that Otto was so much more gregarious than she and, with his amiable ways, won over not just women but men as well? Anne's reflections did not take her this far.

But for all the empathy Anne felt for her father and her sense of closeness to him, her curiosity about his earlier life and love was primarily motivated by her own needs. She was aching for a kind of fulfillment, recognition, and tenderness that Otto could not give her: "At long last I have made the discovery that Daddy, although he's such a darling, still cannot take the place of my entire world of bygone days" (Nov. 20, 1942; ver. B). Anne was longing to find love herself.

"Once when we spoke about sex, Daddy told me that I couldn't possibly understand the longing, yet I always knew that I did understand it and now I understand it fully," Anne wrote on January 6, 1944 (ver. A). The night before, she had dreamed about Peter Schiff, the boy who had rejected her when she was twelve. "I adored him so that I didn't want to face it. I tried to hold on to him until I realized that if I went on running after him I should soon get the name of being boy-mad." In her dream, she had looked into his "fine velvet brown eyes" and felt his cheek against hers. After that, she could no longer suppress her desire for someone who would reciprocate her exuberant feelings: "I love Peter with all my heart."

The day after Anne's dream, and from then on with new regularity, she visited Peter van Pels—the other Peter—in his little room on the floor above hers. "My longing to talk to someone became so intense that somehow or other I decided to speak to Peter," she confessed in her diary. "And I can tell you that it gave me such a queer feeling each time I looked into his deep blue eyes."

As if fate had chosen to underscore the notion that teenage girls are in love with being in love and are therefore not particularly discriminating in choosing the objects of their affections, it had now provided Anne with a real flesh-and-blood Peter to replace the Peter of her school days, who was present now only in her dream world. Anne had a vague feeling that the Peter of her dreams had been deported to Westerbork because he, like Margot, had not obeyed the Nazis' summons to report for work service. And indeed, Peter Schiff had been held in Barrack 67 in Westerbork for the past three and a half months when Anne wrote in her diary on

October 14, 1942 (ver. B), more than a year before her dream: "Perhaps the poor boy is already dead in Poland."

That Peter van Pels had been locked up with Anne for a year and a half and that both of them had been robbed of their youth as well as their freedom—these circumstances made Anne's coming together with him more than an episode of self-indulgent teenage infatuation. It was instead a powerful attempt to maintain hope and an interest in life. "Because my life now has some object and I have something to look forward to," she wrote on February 18, 1944 (ver. A), "everything has become more pleasant."

Anne had lived that year and a half with Peter van Pels without paying much attention to him, and when she did have something to say about him, it was not particularly flattering. She found him "frightfully touchy and lazy," a "rather soft, shy, gawky youth," despite his being three years older than she. "Can't expect much from his company" was her terse analysis (Sept. 2, 1942; Aug. 14, 1942; ver. B). His attempts to be friendly—a touch on the cheek or a joke in passing—only irritated her. While Anne threw herself into reading and studying, Peter preferred to busy himself with all kinds of repairs and tinkering, activities that bored Anne.

Peter seems to have been of only average intelligence, but he was good-natured and willing to learn. He had not had the advantage Anne and Margot had enjoyed—parents who made every effort to instill a love of learning in their children. Hermann and Auguste van Pels had not even bothered to teach Peter something as ordinary as swimming, much less encouraged him to study. Otto Frank was able, however, to waken Peter's interest in English, French, and stenography.

Instead of resolving difficulties with quiet discussion, as the Franks did, the van Pelses were short-tempered and unable to keep their feelings under control. He was restless and pugnacious; she was domineering, moody, and flirtatious. If they were annoyed with Peter, they banished him to the attic or hit him. But even though they argued often and uninhibitedly, unembarrassed to fight in the presence of others, their battles were followed by effusive reconciliations, which gave way in turn to considerable billing and cooing and sometimes to great bouts of laughter. The Franks no doubt found these displays excessive. Such carrying-on was not their style, and they withdrew from the van Pelses more and more. The van Pelses, for their part, must have found the Franks' unfailing composure hard to take.

His parents' erratic natures contributed to Peter's insecurity. That he could not rely on their support surely accounted for some of his feelings of inferiority. It was easy to make him nervous and start him blushing and stuttering. But Anne no longer found his shyness and nervousness ridiculous, as she had earlier. Rather, she found them touching, even attractive. She began to seek Peter out. She was no longer content to admire someone from afar without declaring her feelings. She wanted not just to love but also to be loved. She needed to be acknowledged, as all people need to be, and adolescents in particular.

Anne had always been vain, but in hiding she had had to learn to do without pretty clothes. Because she had worn out or outgrown the few clothes she had brought with her, she had had to make do with hand-me-downs from Miep and Bep. But even in the annex Anne was fastidious about her appearance. Her hopes for straight teeth, however, had to be postponed for the time being. She does not seem to have taken along the braces she had worn for the first six months of 1942. "I have a kind of machine and metal bow in my mouth now," she had written to her Basel relatives a few months before she went into hiding, "and I have to go to the dentist every week, but the next day after each visit the braces fall out again." How could Anne have known that she would spend the next two years of her life practically closeted with a dentist. Fritz Pfeffer could have made the necessary regular adjustments to her braces.

To compensate for the lack of stylish new clothes, she gave all

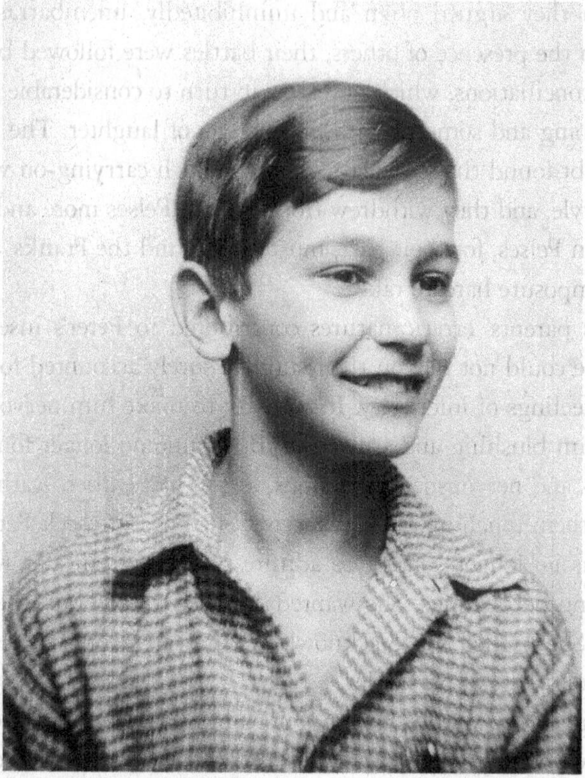

"I need no photo of him, I can see him so, so well." Anne Frank (January 6, 1944) on Lutz Peter Schiff, photo ca. 1938/1939.

the more attention to small cosmetic rituals. She manicured her nails, tried to bleach her moustache with peroxide, and curled her hair. It is not a coincidence that just at the end of January 1944 she started reporting in her diary that she was experimenting with new hairstyles. She wanted to look nice, first and foremost for Peter van Pels. "Oh, the boy has such warmth in his eyes; I believe I'm pretty near to being in love with him" (March 2, 1944; ver. A).

With great single-mindedness, she conquered the awkward Peter, suffering at the same time all the ups and downs of being in

Dit is een foto, zoals
ik me zou wensen,
altijd zo te zijn.
Dan had ik nog wel
een kans om naar
Holywood te komen.
Annefrank.
10 Oct. 1942
(translation)
"This is a photo as I would wish
myself to look all the time. Then
I would maybe have a chance to
come to Hollywood."
Anne Frank, 10 Oct. 1942

"This is a photograph of me as I wish I looked all the time. Then I might still have a chance of getting to Hollywood." Anne Frank, October 10, 1942.

love: fear of being ignored, jealousy of a potential rival in Margot, longing to be embraced. She approached Peter cautiously at first, but finally tender words were not enough for her anymore. "Give me a kiss or send me out of the room, but like this I'll do something desperate," she wrote (March 12, 1944; ver. A).

Then, on April 16, 1944 (ver. A), "Remember yesterday's date, for it is a very important day in my life. Surely it is a great day for every girl when she receives her first kiss?" That first shy kiss on the mouth was followed by ardent embraces that stirred them profoundly. "Peter has touched my emotions more deeply than anyone has ever done before—except in my dreams. Peter has taken possession of me and turned me inside out," she reflected on April 28, 1944 (ver. A).

Anne had had an experience that, she assumed, "almost no one at my age has had." But at the same time, as if she wanted to prevent herself from getting too close to Peter, she appraised him critically: "Peter hasn't enough character yet, not enough willpower, too little courage and strength. He is still a child in his heart of hearts, he is no older than I am." Anne continued to spend a lot of time with Peter, but their tentative sexual exploration did not progress further. Anne's moral upbringing precluded that, as did the many things Anne objected to in Peter's personality.

Once her visits to Peter began, Anne had to battle her parents and their fears that their daughter might see her relationship with him in "unnaturally" serious terms and that what Otto disrespectfully called their "smooching" might go too far. But she was fighting not so much for the sake of her relationship with Peter as for her independence, for the freedom to make her own decisions and to accept responsibility for them. Her brief, stormy interest in Peter was an important station on her way to inner maturity. Anne had to learn much too early in life that in situations of loneliness, fear, and despair, people may well take temporary comfort and consolation from others, but ultimately they have to rely on themselves. "I have been given a lot, a happy nature, a great deal of cheerfulness and strength. Every day I feel that I am developing inwardly," Anne wrote. "Why, then, should I be in despair?" (May 3, 1944; ver. A).

9

LIVING IN FEAR

"Again and again I ask myself, would it not have been better for us all if we had not gone into hiding, and if we were dead now and not going through all this misery, especially as we should be sparing the others," Anne confided to her diary on May 26, 1944 (ver. A). It was not hopelessness that drove her to this statement, "for we still love life; we haven't yet forgotten the voice of nature, we still hope, hope about everything." It was instead the debilitating "pressure from expectation and hope but also from fear" (May 2, 1943; ver. A) that moved her to write: "Let the end come, even if it is hard; then at least we shall know whether we are finally going to win through or go under" (May 26, 1944; ver. A).

Fear constantly haunted the eight residents of the secret annex. "You might really ask us does a day go by without some excitement" (July 26, 1943; ver. A). For a few hours here and there, it could be overcome; for example, during a birthday party, when thoughtful little gifts were presented and comic poems read, or during a Hanukkah or St. Nicholas's Day celebration that the annex residents enjoyed together with their helpers. But fear always found a thousand ways to make itself felt again. If promising radio reports renewed hopes for a rapid end to the war, those hopes were always dashed and, with each disappointment, fear returned.

The Franks had expected to be in hiding for only a few weeks or at the most a few months. But each time Anne thought the Allied invasion was about to take place—she mentions it a total of twelve times in her diary—she waited in vain for it to begin. When Miep Gies finally came into the annex in high spirits on the morning of June 6, 1944, exactly twenty-three months after the Franks had gone into hiding, and told her friends that the British and Americans had at last landed in Normandy, the eight annex residents hugged one another and wept. But salvation was still far off. They still had to be patient, for the liberation of Europe had just begun, and it would take almost another year before the German occupation forces would leave Holland.

As they settled into a daily routine, the annex residents were better able to cope with their fears, but they and their helpers knew they were sitting on a volcano. Any number of forces could precipitate an eruption, and they themselves had as good as no influence over those forces. Well equipped as the annex was in comparison with other hiding places—despite the obvious dilapidation of the building—and however unselfishly and reliably the helpers saw to the needs of their charges, the annex was hardly self-sufficient.

Along with fear for their lives—the fear that they would be betrayed or that they might betray themselves through some small act of carelessness—minor emergencies and ordinary, everyday worries also contributed to tension in the annex, worries that loom large for people living in freedom, too, but that periodically overwhelmed the fugitives. A short circuit, for example, was enough to throw everyone in the annex into a panic: "suddenly ping the light went out," Anne wrote of this emergency on October 28, 1942 (ver. A). "We got a terrible fright of course."

"Anne didn't write every day," Otto Frank said after the war, "but mostly when something particularly upset her and she was able to find relief in writing." And he had a different view of daily life: "She therefore made no mention of the many days and weeks that passed in normal family life—we did not live in constant tension."

Although Anne may have sometimes embellished occurrences in the annex, she did not exaggerate. While she was able to unburden herself by writing, Otto Frank had to find other means to keep his fears hidden from the others. That could not have been easy for him. He had several nerve-racking months behind him. All his attempts at emigration had failed, and he had invested considerable effort in saving his business from the Nazis, a struggle that was ongoing. Someone had denounced him to the German security service, and he found himself left with no alternative but to hide; fleeing was not a possibility. Yet he felt personally responsible for the fate of everyone in the annex, and he realized what awaited them if they were discovered and deported.

As early as the fall of 1942, less than four months after they had gone into hiding, Anne, too, knew that Dutch Jews were not being sent to Germany, as the Nazis claimed they were. They went first to the Westerbork concentration camp, which had originally been built as a refugee camp, and from there to Poland. She also knew that not only able-bodied men were being shipped off but all Jews, the old and the weak as well as children and pregnant women. "Miep told us about a man who escaped from Westerbork; things are terrible there, and if it's so bad there what can it be like in Poland?" (Oct. 26, 1942; ver. A).

Anne answered that question herself when she revised this entry in the spring of 1944. "These people are treated by the Gestapo without a shred of decency, being loaded into cattle trucks and sent to Westerbork, the big Jewish camp in Drente. Westerbork sounds terrible. . . . If it is as bad as this in Holland, whatever will it be like in the distant and barbarous regions they are sent to?

We assume that most of them are murdered. The English radio speaks of their being gassed; perhaps that is the quickest way to die" (Oct. 9, 1942; ver. B).

Anne had learned that week by week more and more of her friends and acquaintances had been taken away, until the River Quarter in South Amsterdam was "cleansed of Jews." She knew that the only way a Jew could escape deportation was to go into hiding. And she knew that in Holland, too, there were people who would betray hidden Jews to the police for the bounty offered. "It seems like the slave hunts of olden times," she observed (Nov. 19, 1942; ver. B). At first the Nazis paid 7.50 guilders—about the equivalent of 45 euros today—and twice that amount for any Jew who had violated a regulation. Later, they raised the amount to 25 guilders for denunciation of any Jew who had gone into hiding. Some officers of the Amsterdam police force, on the one hand, and those employees of the Central Office for Jewish Emigration who were members of the so-called Henneicke Column founded by the auto mechanic and radical NSB member Wim Henneicke, on the other, acted as willing informants. The authorities were pleased to see that the competition between these two groups spurred them on to ever greater efforts, and their example prompted the authorities to offer bounties to civilian informants as well. Now even the man on the street could make some money by persecuting the Jews.

Anne's diary makes it clear she was fully aware that the Nazis were committing mass murder against the Jews. "Nobody is spared, old people, children, babies, expectant mothers, the sick each and all join in the march of death" (Nov. 19, 1942; ver. B). "You could cry when you think of your fellow creatures," she added on December 29, 1943 (ver. A). "We can only pray that God will perform a miracle and save some of them."

However much she may have heard, either on the radio or from the annex's helpers, the idea of millions of victims must have remained incomprehensible and abstract. The BBC remained the most important source of information in the annex even after a law enacted in May 1943 obliged all Dutch citizens to turn their radios in to the German occupation forces, a desperate attempt—and a vain one—to put an end to the enemy's radio propaganda. When Victor Kugler dutifully handed over the big Philips set from Otto Frank's private office, Johannes Kleiman smuggled a small portable radio—Anne called it the "baby" radio—into the annex that not even the other helpers knew about.

Little by little, new details about atrocities committed against Jews kept making their way into the annex. Some were doubted, others confirmed, but they still did not provide a coherent picture. On the last day of March 1944 Anne wrote again about the atrocities Jews had to fear. In concise, detached language she reports the unimaginable extent of the National Socialist madness. "Hungary is occupied by German troops. There are still 1 million Jews there, so they too will have had it now!" (March 31, 1944; ver. C). Within two months, Adolf Eichmann had half a million Hungarian Jews deported to Auschwitz. Almost all of them died in the gas chambers.

So little opportunity to act, so much time to worry. What, for instance, if someone became seriously ill? "Think of it, we can't even call in a doctor!" Anne anguished when Otto Frank, just three months after the family went into hiding, took to his bed with a high fever and thinking he might have measles (Oct. 29, 1942; ver. B). It was sheer luck that in their twenty-five months of hiding not one of the eight people in the annex was taken so seriously ill as to need to leave their hiding place. But there were still causes enough for anxiety—a high fever, a rheumatism attack, bumps, bruises, minor cuts, Mrs. van Pels's bruised rib, and then a horrendous flea infestation that Peter's cat, Mouchi, brought down on the house and that a yellow powder Johannes Kleiman found was only moderately successful in quelling. Margot's chronic bronchitis was doubly alarming, raising worries both about the health of her lungs and about everyone else's safety, as her fits of coughing echoed in the night, and nocturnal coughing inside an office building was bound to make the neighbors suspicious.

Anne, whose constitution was far from robust, was constantly battling colds and bouts of fever. But her eyesight presented a more serious problem. She had strained her eyes by reading and writing in her dimly lit annex room. She was suffering from headaches, and only glasses would help. But to be fitted for glasses, she would have had to go with Miep to an optometrist. The family council met and voted no. Impossible. To go out onto the street would be to court death. Anne would simply have to read less and practice her shorthand less.

Her excessive psychosomatic reactions were cause for worry, too. If she was frightened, her body responded dramatically. "This evening . . . there was a long, loud penetrating ring at the door," she related on November 8, 1943. "I turned white at once, got a tummy-ache and heart palpitations, all from being scared" (ver. B). These responses hardly imply that Anne was hysterical; along with frightening rumors, there were sound enough reasons for her to be afraid.

The danger often announced itself from afar and was accompanied by the howling of sirens as it drew nearer. Every air-raid alarm unnerved Anne, and she could calm down again only in her father's arms: "We don't have a single quiet night. I've got dark rings under my eyes from lack of sleep" (April 27, 1943; ver. B).

Then, too, danger often came quite close to the annex, sometimes in the form of thick clouds of smoke from nearby buildings. What if the annex were to catch fire? A little less than four months before the Franks went into hiding, there had been a fire at 263 Prinsengracht. Packing material in the warehouse had caught fire, and the fire department and police had to be called in. While the office staff left the building and waited out on the street, the firemen carefully inspected not only the warehouse but also the annex and its attic and were particularly critical of the lack of fire extinguishers. The neighborhood had also been hit frequently by incendiary bombs.

Then there were the frightening rumors, one of which spread quickly in February 1944. What if the Germans flooded the entire region to deny the Allies access? Where, as illegal Jews, could the annex residents flee? Although they had no answer to that question, they made all manner of preparations. They had their backpacks ready for departure at a moment's notice, and they considered sewing little cloth bags they could carry around their necks and hidden under their clothing for concealing their money.

And there was the problem of money, which kept melting away as the months passed. What were they to live on? What would they eat once their shrinking financial reserves were depleted? The Franks and the van Pelses managed their money separately, and while Otto Frank as the owner of Opekta and Gies and Company could apparently count on a modest income, even in hiding, the van Pelses were nearly at the end of their resources by October 1943. On top of that, Hermann van Pels lost his last hundred guilders from his jacket pocket one evening when he was downstairs in the warehouse. Worse still, the money was in his wallet. The next morning the warehouse foreman, who had been with Gies and Company only a short time, brought the wallet, minus its contents, to Victor Kugler and insisted on finding out to whom it belonged. Not only had van Pels lost his money, but the suspicion of the new foreman, Willem Gerard van Maaren, had been aroused.

The residents of the annex tried to play down the incident, but it was precisely one of those tiny blunders that could cost them their lives. It had been tragic enough when Auguste van Pels had been forced to sell her fur coat. Miep Gies was eventually able to find a buyer for it on the black market, but the price she got was so paltry it wouldn't have been enough even to furnish Hermann van Pels, a chain smoker, with his daily supply of cigarettes, and the fewer he had to smoke, the worse his mood became.

The Franks' financial reserves also began to dwindle, and they, too, had to part with some valuables. "We can see the bottom of our black chest; what are we going to live on next month?" Anne wondered on June 5, 1944 (ver. A). "When we started running low on money, Miep Gies and Johannes Kleiman sold some of our jewelry," Otto Frank recalled in 1971. "Mr. Kugler had sold some spices without booking the income from them so that he could cover some of our expenses with that money. Along with food, we needed many other things as well, of course: toilet articles, medicine, . . . books, and other things to keep us busy."

And danger sometimes came to the very threshold of the annex itself, sometimes right to the hinged bookcase that hid the doorway. Danger came with everybody who entered the building or merely observed it but was not privy to the secret of the annex. Any people who knew the secret, even if they harbored no evil intentions, could endanger the annex's residents. Avoiding unnecessary noise and making themselves not only invisible but also inaudible both in the front part of 263 Prinsengracht and in the neighborhood was the one small thing the annex residents could do to protect their security. But unthinking carelessness if not downright recklessness crept into their routine as the months went by. "That's how every careless act begins and ends. 'No one will see, no one can hear, no one pays any attention,' is easily said, but is it the real truth?" Anne asked on November 3, 1943 (ver. B), as alarmed as she was perceptive.

Much of what she describes gave cause for alarm. The annex residents made loud scraping, rumbling, and thumping noises every evening when they shoved tables and chairs out of the way to push the beds together and prepare for the night. What if someone heard those noises from the annex? What if someone determined to find out who was responsible for the sound of the vacuum cleaner? What if the blows from Peter van Pels's wood splitting could be heard outside the open window and startled someone there? And mustn't someone have noticed long since that one or another of the annex's windows was sometimes open just a crack? And that smoke continued to pour from the chimney of 263 Prinsengracht even if no one was present in the front part of the building?

Today, the area called Jordaan, between Nassaukade and the north end of Prinsengracht, is one of the most desirable sections of Amsterdam. Back then, it was the city's slum. Most of its residents lived on the brink of poverty, and whoever could afford to left the area at the end of the workday. The dilapidated buildings along the canal dated from the seventeenth century and served primarily as warehouses and workshops or as low-rent housing. In warm weather, the canals gave off foul, dank odors. This was a foreign world for Anne, who was accustomed to the fashionable new quarter around the Merwedeplein and had rarely visited her father's office. "The people in this neighborhood don't look so very attractive now. The children especially are so dirty you wouldn't want to touch them with a barge pole, real slum kids with running noses; I can hardly understand a word they say," Anne wrote (Dec. 12, 1942; ver. B). Did the neighbors perk up their ears when they heard strange noises? Or were they too concerned, in the midst of war, about their own survival to care? How many of them worried whether or not hundreds of people—or perhaps many more—were hiding out in the nooks and crannies of the neighborhood?

Otto Frank learned after the war that most of the neighbors began to have their suspicions sooner or later. Some had heard the flushing of a toilet; others had heard voices; still others had seen a beam of light or a shadow hurrying by in the half dark. Some, it came out later, even believed they knew who had lived behind those walls for two years. It was certain, in any case, that whisperings circulated through the neighborhood.

"This morning," Anne wrote on September 30, 1942 (ver. A), "we were glad that the plumber didn't come. . . . Mr. Lewinsohn came instead. . . . It wasn't very pleasant, because this person, just like the plumber, knows the whole house, so we had to be as quiet as mice." On one occasion, an unannounced carpenter had the annex in a paroxysm of fear. "Downstairs they are such geniuses that they didn't warn us. . . . The result was that we weren't making any attempt to be silent until I heard hammering on the landing opposite our cupboard door," Anne wrote (Oct. 15, 1942; ver. B). "I was horribly frightened and thought our last hour had come" (ver. A).

The annex residents were on edge whenever Arthur Lewinsohn was in the building. Victor Kugler employed him to conduct research and experiments in Opekta's test kitchen. "We are always afraid that he'll take it into his head to have a peep in the old laboratory" (Oct. 1, 1942; ver. B).

It is unlikely, however, that Arthur Lewinsohn represented any real danger. True, he got around a lot and talked with a lot of people, but he was in danger himself. Although he had made himself indispensable to the Joodse Raad as an expert in the industry for food substitutes, he had discovered how quickly such so-called exemptions could become worthless. On the night of August 8, 1942, he was taken from his apartment and sent to the collection point Joodsche Schouwburg. "With the help of a Berlin police officer who happened to be on duty I was able to escape," Arthur Lewinsohn stated in the 1950s. "Later, through personal connections, I was granted legal status and was not harassed anymore except for a few nighttime attempts at arrest that I was able to foil by showing records of the military honors I had earned. But then on May 21, 1943, I received a summons to the Westerburg [*sic*] camp."

In early 1943 the sale of 263 Prinsengracht caused no little anxiety in the annex. The former owner, Frederik Johannes Pieron, a blacksmith, had lived in the annex from 1901 until sometime in the 1930s and used the front of the building for his workshop. Then he began renting the building, with Opekta as the most recent tenant. His desire to sell came as a surprise to his tenants Kleiman and Kugler and occasioned still another crisis, for the time being at least.

Would the annex residents be able to remain at all? What did they know about the new owner, the twenty-nine-year-old Maurits "Max" Alexander Wessels? His descendants described him as an erratic and hotheaded gambler type with a sizeable ego. But he was also a shrewd businessman, had a commercial license, had dealt first in scrap iron, then in sugar, spices, and ersatz foodstuffs, had a share in his grandfather's confectionery factory, and on top of all that had established a dealership in wastepaper. And he was a Jew.

"Luckily, Mr. Kleiman was present and showed the gentleman everything except our little 'Secret Annex'; he professed to have forgotten the key to the communicating door" (Feb. 27, 1943; ver. B), Anne wrote after the new owner and his architect showed up at the building.

There is no record of what was discussed during this inspection. Did Johannes Kleiman and Otto Frank already know Mr. Wessels because—as one of his descendants believed—they had had business dealings with the Wessels confectionery factory? Did they know that Wessels, like his mother, had managed to acquire by whatever means possible proof that he was "Aryan"? Did they know that Wessels had presumably gotten that proof with the aid of Hans Georg Calmeyer, who, as an attorney and director of the department for "internal administration" in the Reich Commissariat for the Occupied Dutch Territories, had saved several thousand Jews from deportation by classifying them as "half Jews" or "quarter Jews" or "dubious cases"? Had they therefore assumed

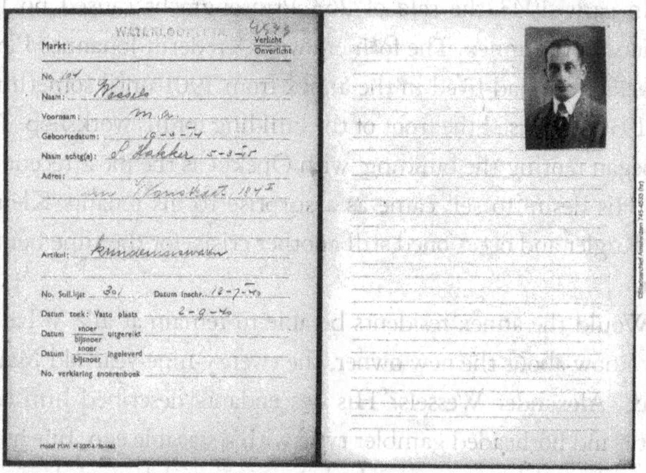
Markt:
Verlicht
Onverlicht
No.
Naam: Wessels
Voornaam:
Geboortedatum:
Naam echtg(e):
Adres:
Artikel:
No. Soll.lijst 301 Datum inschr. 12-7-40
Datum toek: Vaste plaats 2-9-40
Datum snoer/bijsnoer uitgereikt
Datum snoer/bijsnoer ingeleverd
No. verklaring snoerenboek

Maurits Alexander Wessels

that the well-connected Wessels was protected from expropriation and deportation—or knew how to protect himself?

Wessels had presumably purchased 263 Prinsengracht as a base for his wastepaper business that was close to his competitors. The collection of wastepaper was deemed "essential to the war effort"; the paper was used as building material and in other ways as well. Was it a lucky coincidence or the result of an agreement that Wessels finally located his business ten minutes away on the Groenburgwal and never occupied 263 Prinsengracht at all?

Answers to these questions could clarify whether the annex residents were threatened or not by this change in the building's ownership. That Anne never mentioned Max Wessels again after his visit in February 1943 does not necessarily mean that the danger had been averted. The uncertainty may have loomed so large that Otto Frank and the helpers decided to keep it secret from the other residents and in any case from Anne.

Perhaps Wessels was among those who were intentionally told

about the secret annex or who learned about it by other means. And who else would find out about it in the course of time?

Burglars who rummaged through the warehouse for spices to sell on the black market also caused repeated panics in the annex. After more than three years of war, burglaries had become common all over Holland; dire circumstances drove people to steal. "You can't leave your home unoccupied, for in the five minutes you are away your things are gone too," Anne wrote on March 29, 1944 (ver. A).

In July 1943, after several failed attempts, burglars succeeded in breaching the front door with a chisel, breaking open the warehouse door, and taking sugar, food coupons, and money. The helpers did not, of course, take the usual step of notifying the police. The annex residents feared the police much more than the thieves, who were sometimes harmless boys testing their mettle and eager to get away with their booty as quickly as they could. One of these young thieves from the neighborhood, Hans Wijnberg from 251 Prinsengracht, stated later that one evening as he was climbing over the wall to the rear courtyard of 263 he had seen a girl through the window of Otto Frank's office. After the fact, it became clear to him that it was Anne Frank.

At least two more times thieves broke into the warehouse at 263 Prinsengracht. On the night of April 9, 1944, the night watchman, Martinus Slegers, noticed a board missing in the front door and—following instructions—called in a policeman. Slegers and Cornelis den Boef combed through the building, coming as far as the hinged cupboard that hid the entrance to the annex and even rattling it. "None of us has ever been in such danger as that night," Anne wrote of her "most terrifying moments." "God truly protected us, just think of it—the police at our secret cupboard, the light on right in front of it, and still we remained undiscovered" (April 9 and 11, 1944; ver. A).

The next day, Jan Gies engaged the night watchman to check

on Opekta's office building from then on, as he did for many other buildings in the neighborhood. Did the helpers and the annex residents assume that Slegers would carry out that duty without asking any further questions? Or were they taking the bull by the horns by hiring him, hoping to allay any suspicions he might have?

Files accessible to us now do not implicate Slegers. But the question remains as to why he called on Cornelis den Boef to help him. Did he have no other choice because den Boef was the officer on duty that night? Was this just one more coincidence? Or did Slegers know him and even know that he was showing through the building an active NSB member and thereby posing great danger to regime opponents and people in hiding?

And what did Gezinus Gringhuis want of Slegers when he wrote the night watchman's name down in his notebook in January 1944? Gringhuis was one of the Amsterdam policemen who assisted Department IV B4 of the security service, the Jewish Division modeled on Adolf Eichmann's department in Berlin. He regularly arrested Jews in the neighborhood and had no qualms about accepting bounties for them. All these questions—and the larger one they raise of whether Gringhuis and Slegers played any role in the fate of the annex residents—will have to remain unanswered.

"Every day our living space gets smaller," Anne wrote (March 29, 1944; ver. A), but despite her constant fear of being discovered, deported, and killed, she took courage from her plans for the future and formulated over and over again her hope of being saved. She was distressed toward the end of May 1944 when she heard a rumor "that the German Jews who emigrated to Holland and who are now in Poland will not be allowed to return here; they once had the right of asylum in Holland but when Hitler is gone they will have to go back to Germany again" (May 22, 1944; ver. A).

Anne assumed that such a ruling would apply to her, too, because she had remained in Holland illegally. She was appalled by this, for she considered herself Dutch and was determined to apply for Dutch citizenship after the war. "And if I have to write to the queen myself, I will not give up until I have reached my goal" (April 11, 1944; ver. A).

Anne detested the Germans, and given her dire situation, she can surely be forgiven her refusal to differentiate among them. "There is no greater enmity than that between the Germans and the Jews," she wrote categorically (Oct. 9, 1942; ver. B), and by "Germans" she meant not only the entire population of Germany but also that of Austria. She could listen to reason when Otto Frank warned her against prejudice and reminded her of German friends like Gertrud Naumann or his former secretary, Emeline Schneider, who had helped his cousin escape to Luxembourg. And he reminded her, too, that their loyal helpers Victor Kugler and Miep Gies had both been born in Austria.

But Anne felt divided about her German heritage. On the one hand, she often listened to German radio programs and read German books; German culture was part of her. On the other hand, she rejected the German identity she had been born with. And ultimately she settled on total rejection: the Germans were barbarians and German was a barbaric language. For the time being, she wanted as little as possible to do with either one. And she spoke Dutch with Miep and Mr. Kugler, anyway.

"Miep often says she envies us for possessing such tranquillity here," Anne wrote on November 8, 1943 (ver. B). The responsibility that the helpers had assumed weighed heavily on them. Although the selfless care they gave to their charges eventually began to seem almost routine, they were under constant pressure and could never relax their vigilance.

We know very little about what the helpers were feeling. They never liked to talk about themselves. They did not want to portray themselves as heroes; they did what they did simply because they were who they were and could not do differently and because they knew the lives of their charges were at stake. And they had learned to keep silent. The war and the German occupation in particular had put an end to idle talk. It was not wise to talk, with anyone, about which side you were on. Informants like Job Jansen, who reported his former boss Otto Frank for supposed anti-German statements, were everywhere. The helpers were wary of taking anyone into their confidence, much less sharing their worries about the annex residents. A single word could be a word too many. The helpers didn't even talk among themselves about their charges any more than was absolutely necessary.

Victor Kugler, for example, who had taken over Otto Frank's place in the office and therefore felt he was the one primarily responsible for the fate of the annex residents, found this burden increasingly difficult to carry. "Kugler never told his wife about the annex," Otto wrote, "and kept his fears to himself those two years. He is a nervous person and suffered from this strain." Anne found more drastic words to describe Kugler's distress: "The enormous responsibility for the 8 of us is sometimes so much for him that he can hardly talk from pent-up nerves and strain" (May 26, 1944; ver. A).

In the early 1920s Kugler had met Laura Maria Buntenbach, a Dutch woman five years older than he. A machine fitter by trade, he had just turned twenty himself and had come to Holland on short-term loan from his employer, the Deutsche Maschinenfabrik AG (Demag), to do some assembly work in Utrecht. But out of love he wound up staying in Holland and married Laura in 1928. They settled in Hilversum and had no children. Mrs. Kugler's health was delicate. We know nothing about her political convictions.

When the annex residents learned that they might lose Victor Kugler as one of their helpers, Anne was troubled. "This morning I really didn't know what lay in store for us," she wrote on the afternoon of March 23, 1944 (ver. A). "Kugler has had a call-up notice from the employment office." Although he was able initially to get a medical release exempting him from the call-up, in mid-June he received a second summons.

Kugler felt himself sufficiently threatened that he had acquired a fake identity card early in the year. Whether he actually used this card in the name of Johannes Kuinders remains unclear. What is clear is that the NSB mayor of Hilversum, "a fanatic," had his eye on all the able-bodied men in Hilversum, Kugler included, and that the NSDAP office in Hilversum expressed interest in him and summoned him for an interview.

That Kugler—a Dutch citizen only since the end of May 1938—was expected to report "to the German home" (or Deutsches Heim, a kind of NSDAP community center) in Hilversum on the same day there was "a long, loud, penetrating ring at the door" of 263 Prinsengracht may be coincidence (Nov. 8, 1943; ver. B). But perhaps someone was intent on chasing down this man who kept evading work service.

The incident prompted Anne to report in her diary a recurring nightmare: "At night, when I'm in bed, I see myself alone in a dungeon, without Mummy and Daddy. Sometimes I wander by the roadside, or our Secret Annex is on fire, or they come and take us away at night and I go and lie down under my bed in despair." She wrote these lines with the sense that "it could all happen to you very soon!"

That one of the helpers could temporarily or permanently drop out hung in the air as a constant threat. It was impressed on the annex residents time and again how dependent they were not only on the helpers' strong nerves but also on their helpers' good health.

When diphtheria struck her home, Bep could have no contact

with the annex residents for six long weeks (Nov. 17, 1943; ver. B). This hit Anne particularly hard. She felt a strong tie of friendship with Bep, the youngest of the helpers, whom Ernst Schnabel described as a person who "lived purely in the realm of feeling," a bit shy and easily moved but of a fundamentally cheerful nature. "It makes it very awkward over food and shopping," Anne complained, "not to mention missing her companionship."

Absent at this same time was Johannes Kleiman, whom Anne called "the one who always cheers us up" (April 1, 1943; ver. B). Kleiman had stomach trouble and sometimes had to stay in bed for several weeks and, as he felt, to abandon his charges. Unlike Kugler, he was able to share his fears and worries with his wife, Joke, and on rare occasions she even accompanied him on visits to the annex. His brother, too, was let in on the secret. The family was Social Democratic through and through. A cousin, Dirk, served in the resistance as a printer. He died in captivity in Germany.

But with his daughter, Kleiman played the cheerful, carefree father. Jopie, who was Anne's age and played field hockey in the same club as Anne's friend Jacque van Maarsen, was not to be troubled with his secret; it was burden enough for him. Being ill in bed and prevented from doing his part for the annex only added to his stress and made his stomach problems worse. He spent almost all of April 1943 bedridden and consequently missed a planned visit of representatives from the Frankfurt Pomosin-Werke. Otto Frank had gone to great lengths to prepare his trusted friend for this meeting, and now at the last minute he had to prep Victor Kugler for the negotiations. What was at stake was not only the pectin deliveries but also the independence of Dutch Opekta, not to mention the financial support and security of the annex residents.

Even though Kugler succeeded in putting the gentlemen from Frankfurt off again, he was constantly beset by new worries. Anne noted repeatedly in her diary the increasing irritation Kugler felt the following year about the annex residents' occasional carelessness. Despite the danger involved, they did not want to give up having the run of the entire building once the workday was over. Kugler considered this, quite correctly, much too heedless.

In April 1944, he had once again to demonstrate the steadiness of his nerves. On this particular day, the window in Anne and Fritz Pfeffer's room was open just a crack, as was often the case. It caught the eye of the "manager of Keg's," the old established company next door, that traded in coffee and tea, who fetched a ladder from a neighboring house so he could take a closer look. "Kugler was only able to stop him in time," Anne wrote, "because the ladder was fortunately too short" (April 17, 1944; ver. A). That this near intruder gave up his interest in the annex is unlikely. And it is all the more understandable that Kugler had trouble keeping a cool head. He also had to look after Johannes Kleiman. In mid-September 1943, after suffering recurring hemorrhages, Kleiman underwent surgery. Once again he was absent, this time for four weeks, and even afterwards his complaints continued. Anticipating that he might eventually be unable to come back to work, either for reasons of health or because he had been arrested, Kleiman had put aside money to pay the employees' salaries.

The annex residents felt the effects of breaks in the supply chain when, as in January 1944, Miep and Jan Gies were out of commission with stomach problems. The provision of fresh food depended on Miep much more than on the other helpers. What might have appeared to the casual glance as routine actually presented Miep with a new challenge every day. What if someone began to wonder for whom she was carrying such large amounts of meat and vegetables into the office building? What if someone denounced her? If she were hard pressed, she would of course say that she was shopping and cooking for the employees of Opekta and Pectacon. But would anyone believe her?

That their greengrocer, Henk van Hoeve, "guessed a lot" (April

11, 1944; ver. A), as he told Jan Gies after one of the break-ins at the Prinsengracht warehouse, didn't particularly trouble the annex residents at first. Van Hoeve and his wife were hiding two Jews themselves. As Mrs. Hoeve later said, "Being tight-lipped didn't help. Someone ratted on us." At the end of May 1944, four state security men surprised the grocer and arrested not only the two Jews he was hiding but him, too. "We're to be hungry," Anne worried, "but nothing is worse than being discovered" (May 25, 1944; ver. A).

Would the security service make van Hoeve talk? Would they offer him a light sentence if he gave them some hint or even some names? Names of other resistance members, tips on other Jews in hiding?

Miep and Jan Gies acted sensibly when they decided to tell their charges little about their resistance activities apart from the annex. Otto Frank grumbled about Miep's carrying letters between Fritz Pfeffer and his fiancée, Charlotte Kaletta. Miep did not underestimate the risk, but her sympathy for the lonely dentist proved stronger than her fears. In August 1943, when she had a "forbidden book" for Pfeffer with her, an SS motorcycle ran into her on her bicycle. This time her usual self-control failed her. "She lost her nerve, shouted, 'Miserable wretches,' and rode on," Anne wrote (Aug. 10, 1943; ver. B). But Miep did not let incidents like this interfere with her resistance work.

Along with the Franks, the van Pels family, and Fritz Pfeffer, Miep and Jan were helping friends and acquaintances in Hilversum. They were in touch with the former Opekta employee Isa Cauvern and her husband, Ab, who had gone into hiding at different addresses, Isa with her three-year-old daughter, Ruth, whose birth in September 1941 had meant enough to Anne that she later glued the birth announcement into her diary. Through their connections with Otto Frank, Miep and Jan were subletting the apartment on Hunzestraat of a woman named Hendrina Saartje Stoppelman, who had gone into hiding. At her request, they visited her when they had time.

Going by the name Antje, Mrs. Stoppelman had taken refuge with an acquaintance, Catharina van der Horst, in Hilversum (and not, as Anne had assumed in her diary in October 1942, in Bussum). But she found the isolation of living in hiding difficult, and she permitted herself occasional long walks in the neighborhood, endangering both herself and her helpers. What would she say if the police asked for her identity card? She knew, too, that Miep and Jan were sheltering Mrs. van der Horst's son, Kuno, in Amsterdam in return for Mrs. van der Horst's hospitality to her. Like so many other Dutchmen, Kuno, a student at the time, had gone into hiding to avoid conscription into labor service in Germany. But like Mrs. Stoppelman, he tolerated confinement to his room poorly and had to be called to his senses when he left his hiding place without telling anyone, usually to pursue his passion for horse races. In his case, too, it was not only his own safety that was at stake but that of his helpers and of all the other people dependent on their reliability.

It was Kuno's good fortune that in addition to Jan and Miep Gies his fiancée and future wife, Henny, tended to his needs. She worked for an Amsterdam insurance company and commuted from Hilversum to Amsterdam during the week. She gathered up vegetables and other foodstuffs from farmers in the Hilversum area and passed them on to Miep during her lunch break, often several times a week. The two young women had agreed that not all of this food would go to Kuno but that it would be shared with the annex residents. Henny was just about in on the secret of the annex, though not in any great detail.

Who else knew about the eight annex residents? As long as they could rely on Bep's father, they felt reasonably well protected. As the longtime warehouse foreman at Prinsengracht, Mr. Voskuijl discreetly guarded the annex. He himself stayed away from it and took care that the men working under him adhered strictly to working hours and never so much as thought about snooping around behind the storage rooms. Also, on Victor Kugler's suggestion, he built the swinging bookcase that hid the entrance to the annex. "Mr. Voskuijl . . . can't do enough to help," Anne said of him (Aug. 21, 1942; ver. B). The annex residents were fully appreciative of the friend they had in Johannes Hendrik Voskuijl. He apparently shared the secret of the annex only with Bep. None of his other family members—Bep was the eldest of her siblings—were to be burdened with it. Only after the war did Wilhelmina, who was a little less than three years younger than Bep, learn how close to Bep Anne Frank had been. Consequently she had no idea to whom the dietary supplements and medications Bep regularly ordered from her were going. "Wil" worked as an invoice clerk for the pharmaceutical company Gist-Brocades. She filled the orders and didn't ask any questions.

The Voskuijls probably guarded their secret so well because one of the siblings was strongly partial to the German occupiers. As early as November 1941, the then seventeen-year-old Hendrika Petronella, who went by Nellie, was picked up by the police in the company of a German noncommissioned officer in a harbor bar. The police held her for about nine hours; late that evening her father was able to arrange her release.

Finally—no doubt wanting to escape from the modest, crowded conditions at home and lacking a political conscience—she volunteered to work for the Germans. From about the end of 1942 on, she worked at a Nazi military airport near Laon in northern France. In May 1944, afraid of the Allied advance, she applied for a leave of absence, returned to Holland, and lived, like Bep, at home, when she was not visiting her German friend, stationed in Eindhoven. By law, she was still a minor.

Did Nellie show any interest in conversations between Bep and her father? Did she pick up anything from them? Bep would surely have been careful about what she let reach her sister's ear. Bep disliked the path Nellie had taken, but that did not keep her from talking about it in the annex. More and more often family members of different persuasions were obliged to live together or at least close to one another. Bep's openness explains at any rate why Anne could write at length about Nellie and come to the conclusion: "They are sure here that [she] is not one hundred percent right in the head" (May 11, 1944; ver. A).

In mid-1943, Johannes Hendrik Voskuijl fell ill and had to have an operation. The annex residents, who by now had been dependent on their helpers for a year, had to abandon hope that he would soon be able to return to work. The doctors had found stomach cancer. "It is a disaster for us that good old Voskuijl won't be able to keep us in touch with all that goes on, and all he hears in the warehouse," Anne wrote. "He was our best helper and security adviser; we miss him very much indeed" (June 15, 1943; ver. B). For the eight annex residents a new phase of heightened danger was beginning.

Every new warehouse worker and every new cleaning woman Victor Kugler hired made the annex residents uneasy. "We've always been frightened of the warehousemen," Anne noted. Willem Gerard van Maaren succeeded Mr. Voskuijl as warehouse foreman. Van Maaren was in desperate need of money because a laundry delivery business he had run had failed. He was a good worker and went about his duties with a will, but even so he soon lost his employer's trust. Instead of simply doing his work, he snooped about. The office workers' "sneaking around," as he later described it, had piqued his curiosity, and he was determined to find out what was going on in the narrow annex behind the warehouse. Victor Kugler had had the windows of the main building that looked out over a small courtyard toward the annex painted over, but van Maaren had scratched some of the paint away. "When I caught him looking up through an opening scratched in the blue paint on the window pane," Victor Kugler wrote years later to Otto Frank, "he asked me what was upstairs there and said he'd never been there." And when Kugler tried to throw him off, van Maaren dug his heels in all the more. There was a door up there, he insisted. It had to lead to the annex.

"Of course anyone with any brains at all must have noticed that Miep keeps saying she's off to the laboratory, Bep to look at the records, Kleiman to the Opekta storeroom, while Kugler makes out that the 'Secret Annex' is not part of our premises but belongs to the neighbor's building," Anne wrote of van Maaren's increasing suspiciousness. "We really wouldn't mind what Mr. v. Maaren thought of the situation if he wasn't known to be so unreliable and if he wasn't so exceptionally inquisitive, so difficult to fob off" (Sept. 16, 1943; ver. B).

Van Maaren had noticed that the office and storerooms were used at night, and he concluded that whoever was poking around there in the dark must be hiding in the annex during the day. Like a detective in pursuit of a criminal, he set little traps. "He often placed a small stick of wood on the packing table with its end sticking out over the edge," Victor Kugler recalled in his letter to Otto Frank. "Because the space between the table and the containers on the other side was not very wide, it was very likely that someone passing through there would displace the stick." Van Maaren also spread flour to pick up footprints and placed pencils in locations where anyone moving about at night would be likely to knock them over.

Every time his suspicions seemed to be confirmed, he would question Kugler again: "Were you in the warehouse last night?" Kugler's answers did not satisfy van Maaren, who kept pestering Kugler with his questions. "Didn't a certain Mr. Frank work in this office at one time?" he eventually asked one day. And when he found a wallet in the milling room one morning—the wallet that had slipped out of Hermann van Pels's jacket pocket when he took the jacket off to weigh himself on the scale—van Maaren was certain he had finally gotten to the bottom of the mystery.

Why was van Maaren so intent on solving it? Van Maaren was neither a Nazi nor an anti-Semite. But he himself was sheltering a fugitive at home—not a Jew but his own son, who, like Kuno van der Horst, was evading the German occupiers' order to report for military or labor service and for whose safety he was naturally concerned.

But what was of greatest concern to van Maaren was his own personal advantage, and he may have continued pursuing his game of cat and mouse with the helpers to protect it.

Kugler and Kleiman quickly realized that van Maaren was stealing from the warehouse on a regular basis. One of the warehouse workers, Johannes Jacobus de Kok, who worked at 263 Prinsengracht for a while in the second half of 1943, helped van Maaren sell the stolen goods on the black market. And it is highly likely that the two men continued their "business relationship" after de Kok left the employ of Pectacon (Gies and Company) and Opekta. (De Kok had proven ties to Nazi circles and was later arrested at least twice for theft and fencing stolen goods.)

Did van Maaren share his observations about the annex with de Kok? And did this accomplice know, too, that the warehouse foreman was able to keep his employer in checkmate with his suppositions and increasingly concrete suspicions about the annex? For the sake of his charges, Victor Kugler could not afford to fire van Maaren. Not a bad setup for a brazen thief.

Was van Maaren acting out of pure ruthless self-interest? Or was readiness to help himself to others' property born of his own duress, and was his curiosity the curiosity of a man with morality and a heart? The truth may lie somewhere in between, as it so often does.

For many months the helpers feared more than ever that they would be exposed. What was van Maaren up to? Was he really capable of betraying the Jews? "For us [the suspense] has never lifted for a moment, not for two years now," Anne wrote. How long will it keep bearing down in us with its almost unbearable, ever more oppressive hand?" (May 26, 1944; ver. A).

And weren't there yet other people who knew the building and talked to one another, still other leaks to be feared?

With whom, for instance, did Johan Marie Joseph Broks and his wife, Anna Sophia (Ans, for short), speak? Both had worked for Otto Frank, Johan as a salesman, Ans as a product demonstrator. Before he went into hiding, Otto had told them about his supposed plan to escape to Belgium and perhaps from there to Switzerland, and he had given them, as he had his business associate and friend Joop Hofhuis in Hilversum and Miep and Jan Gies, some of his things, including furniture and clothing. He had even rented a room in the Broks' apartment to store his family's property. It came as a surprise that Johan Broks did not believe Otto's escape plan. Johannes Kleiman did his best to convince Broks otherwise, apparently without success.

It is possible that Broks, whom Anne considered among the "dangerous people" (Oct. 1, 1942; ver. A), was in touch with Job Jansen, who had occasionally helped prepare Opekta displays at trade fairs and had denounced Otto Frank for alleged treason. Jansen and Broks had lived in the same building in The Hague about two years earlier, before Broks's marriage to Ans, so it seems likely the two men knew each other.

Did Broks make the mistake of speculating about the Franks with Job Jansen? Did he even have the opportunity to do so? Anne was wary of the Brokses despite their friendship. In May 1944, Ans Broks was made president—pro forma, presumably—of Gies and

Company. Her announcement that she would from now on spend every midday in the office on Prinsengracht precipitated in the annex a panic that subsided only after "the Ans Broks danger" had been warded off by Kleiman's talking her out of her plan (May 19, 1944; ver. A).

In this context of intertwined threatening relationships we cannot ignore Tonny Ahlers, who had not simply disappeared after he wormed his way into Otto Frank's life by rescuing him from the consequences of Jansen's denunciation letter. Even after the Franks had gone into hiding, Ahlers kept turning up as a troublemaker, instigating arguments and brawls, ingratiating himself with the occupying forces—and with their bounty hunters as well—and cheating his way through life. A confidential report of the Dutch state criminal police of February 1964 says of Ahlers: "During the German occupation . . . he was an informant for the German detective Kurt Döring, who worked for the so-called Amsterdam branch of the German security police and the SD. . . . [Ahlers] has on his record convictions for theft, public violence, and malicious property damage. . . . His behavior during the war bordered on punishable fraud." He was also regarded as "politically very unreliable."

Along with occasional odd jobs as a press photographer, Ahlers started up in the winter of 1943–44 a business dealing in goods including ersatz foodstuffs "without special sales requirements," that is, goods sold without food coupons and therefore suitable for the black market. The very nature of the business, plus the fact that it offered its services to the German armed forces as a purchasing agent, gave cause for further speculation.

Did Ahlers mean to buy goods from Pectacon (or Gies and Company)? Did he remain in contact with 263 Prinsengracht even after the Franks had gone into hiding? Did he know about the hiding place in the annex? There is no way to answer these questions conclusively. What is clear is that this business, which never amounted to more than a minor enterprise run primarily by Ahlers's wife out of their living room, had to declare bankruptcy in August 1944. Was the business a mere sideline for the wheeling-and-dealing Ahlers, who was always on the lookout for sources of income, or was its failure a bitter defeat for him that produced unfortunate consequences?

In keeping with his urge to insert himself into the middle of things, Ahlers sent a letter to the Austrian Ministry of the Interior in Vienna in the winter of 1963–64. The Austrian authorities were initiating proceedings against Karl Josef Silberbauer, and Ahlers meant to come to Silberbauer's aid with his letter. "From April 18, 1941, on [the day Otto Frank purchased Jansen's letter of denunciation from Ahlers], I had to visit Otto Frank repeatedly at his address at 263 Prinsengracht to persuade him to go into hiding," claimed Ahlers, who identified himself as a journalist for "Private Information and Discreet Inquiries at Home and Abroad." "In those days, every Jew who received a warning went into hiding instantly, but not Otto Frank."

It could be that Ahlers made this claim up. Or it could be that there's a grain of truth in it. (If the latter, then after the war Otto Frank—either on purpose or accidentally—did not speak the truth. He claimed to have had only two meetings with Ahlers.) In any case, the Austrian authorities looked into Ahlers's background and characterized him as a "person given to fantasies and unclear about the distinction between truth and fantasy." The Austrian inquest had no further consequences either at that time or later. No one interviewed van Maaren, Victor Kugler, or Miep Gies about Ahlers. (Johannes Kleiman had died in 1959.) Even the Netherlands State Institute for War Documentation, which had the files of the Austrian inquest available when it was working on the critical edition of Anne's diary, ignored them, and it has continued to ignore them to the present day.

Still another instance illustrates how talkative Willem van Maaren was and what a chain reaction his talk could set off. He told Lammert Hartog, his assistant in the warehouse, that ever since he had started working at 263 Prinsengracht he had seen unusually large amounts of bread and milk delivered to the building, and he'd noticed other odd things, too. There was no doubt in his mind: the office workers were hiding Jews. Hartog had been working illegally in the warehouse since the spring of 1944—illegally because he, too, had not obeyed a summons to labor service. He could not go into hiding, because he had nothing to live on. He had to earn money and consequently lived in fear that the Germans would catch up with him.

We know that his wife, Lena, learned about the hidden Jews as well. Lena van Bladeren Hartog worked for the cleaning firm Cimex, which was owned by Johannes Kleiman's brother. At Lena's request, the manager of Cimex, Petrus Josephus Genot, had put her husband in touch with Johannes Kleiman, who had then hired Lammert Hartog as a warehouseman. Lena did cleaning work in a number of buildings, among others in the Genot home and at 263 Prinsengracht.

Sometime in July 1944, Lena, whose twenty-three-year-old son, Klaas, had been conscripted for labor service in Germany and was stationed somewhere near Berlin, asked Anna Genot if she knew there were Jews hiding at 263 Prinsengracht. Anna was upset: how could Lena ask such a thing? In times like these, she shouldn't be spreading such gossip. The next day, Petrus Genot told Johannes Kleiman about the conversation.

One of Bep Voskuijl's office tasks was to pay Lena for her cleaning work, and at some point in July 1944 Lena asked Bep the same question. Didn't she know there were Jews hiding in the building? Bep went to Victor Kugler immediately. Should they regard Lena's questions as a serious warning? Did she realize how dangerous her gossip could be?

"About a week before the police raid Mr. Kleiman came to me one morning and said his worker . . . had told him that his wife had heard we had people hidden in the building," Victor Kugler recalled later in a letter to Otto Frank. "We discussed whether we should find new quarters for you and the others because anything you hear on the street will soon be known all over town. The situation was becoming critical, and in the days that followed we talked about it often."

Weren't the Franks and van Pelses sitting in a trap just waiting to snap shut? Shouldn't Margot and Anne at least have been taken to a new hiding place? But how could even one of the eight have been smuggled out of the house without being noticed? It was July, after all, and bright as day until ten in the evening.

Victor Kugler and his coworkers alternately hoped and despaired. Allied victory over the German forces could be only a few weeks away. They would just have to hang on for a few more weeks. For just a few more weeks they would have to keep their charges' courage up. "Now I'm getting really hopeful, now things are going well at last. Yes, really, they're going well! Super news! An attempt has been made on Hitler's life," Anne wrote on July 21, 1944 (ver. A). "I can't help it; in anticipation of sitting on school benches next October I feel far too cheerful to be logical!"

On the morning of August 4, 1944, Karl Josef Silberbauer, a "specialist" in the Gestapo's Department IV B4, the Jewish Division, on Euterpestraat, and his Dutch henchmen staged their surprise raid on the office staff at 263 Prinsengracht. Silberbauer testified twenty years later that the raid had been preceded by a telephone call to his immediate superior, Detective Julius Dettmann. Silberbauer claimed he never knew who had made that call to Dettmann.

"If Silberbauer's report is correct that an action was carried out on the very same day a telephone tip was received, then my sense is that the informant was known to be reliable and that his reports in the past had always been factually correct." This was the judgment of Willy Lages, the former director of the Amsterdam security service, on Department IV B4's unusually rapid response to the call.

Had the gossip about the annex in fact reached one of the bounty hunters who, like Gezinus Gringhuis, were on the security service's payroll and had often struck in the past? It is just as likely that the authorities had had their eye on 263 Prinsengracht for a long time and moved in now to search the building for resistance fighters and possible weapons caches. As the war progressed, Department IV B4's primary focus had shifted to tracking down those involved in the resistance.

"You have Jews hidden in this building. Where are they?" Was this just a routine question? Or a trick question?

10

THE LAST TRAIN

For Anne, life in Westerbork seems to have brought a sense of relief. After twenty-five months of being cooped up in the confines of the annex, she enjoyed meeting strangers, seeing familiar faces, breathing fresh air, feeling the sun on her skin. These new—or old—freedoms distracted her from the frightening reality that she was in a transit camp, on her way to Auschwitz. Otto Frank later recalled that Anne seemed relaxed, even cheerful, in Westerbork.

After they were arrested, the annex residents and their protectors were taken directly from Prinsengracht to the headquarters of the security service, a former school building on Euterpestraat in South Amsterdam. The policemen had taken their money and valuables, briefly interrogated the men—Otto Frank, Fritz Pfeffer, and Hermann van Pels, as well as Victor Kugler and Johannes Kleiman—and then locked everyone up in cells. The SD men quickly realized that hours of interrogation would be useless with prisoners who had spent the last two years completely cut off from the outside world. What could they possibly know about other Jews in hiding? Also, time had worked in favor of the captives. The Nazis had other things on their minds besides torturing Jews.

When American forces had taken Avranches on July 31, they had broken through the Germans' defensive line, and now they were pressing on with the liberation of France. All German occupation troops, including those in the Jewish Division, had only one mission, the defense of Holland. The ten new prisoners were merely an annoying routine case at this point. The eight Jews had to be shipped off to Westerbork as quickly as possible, Johannes Kleiman and Victor Kugler to Amersfoort, the penal camp for enemies of the regime. After a few days at Amersfoort, they were to be sent to Germany, but (as Kugler later commented) "fortunately for us the Americans bombed the railroad station."

After a night at SD headquarters and three more in the Weteringschans prison, the Franks, the van Pelses, and Fritz Pfeffer were taken, on the morning of August 8, 1944, to Amsterdam's main rail station and put on a passenger train to Westerbork. Anyone who saw its third-class cars with their normal windows and wooden benches might have supposed that the Germans were actually treating the Jews as human beings.

On the train trip, the adults suffered bitter self-reproach for having endangered the lives of their protectors and dread of what awaited them. Weren't "fugitive" or "criminal" Jews, as they had been classified by the German security police, automatically deported to Polish concentration camps? But now that the war was almost over, might they not remain in Holland? Hadn't the Red Army already advanced into Poland? The prisoners kept offering one another grounds for hope.

Anne, however, seems to have temporarily repressed her fear of the future. As her father recalled later, she stayed glued to the window the whole trip. "I wonder if it's because I haven't been able to poke my nose outdoors for so long that I've grown so crazy about everything to do with nature?" Anne had asked herself less than two months earlier (June 13, 1944; ver. A). Hungry for visual impressions, she stared raptly at the landscape flitting by outside the train windows—pastures and fields, grazing cows and sheep, the colors of summer. At last, more green than just the green of the chestnut tree in the backyard. At last, the endless expanse of the sky and not just that little patch of it she could see through the skylight, although on August 8, 1944, the sky was clouded over.

Before she had gone into hiding, Anne had had little interest in nature. She took its gifts for granted, and like most other children, she found country outings boring. The city was where the excitement was. But the longer she was confined in the annex, the more intense her longing for nature became. "When the birds sing outside and you see the trees changing to green, the sun invites one to be out in the open air, when the sky is so blue, then—oh, then I wish for so much!" Just thinking about nature in all its variety had given her courage and strength. "And the best remedy for those who are afraid, lonely or unhappy is to go outside, somewhere where they can be quite alone with the heavens, nature, and God" (April 14, 1944; Feb. 23, 1944; ver. A).

Westerbork was hardly such a place. It was a barren no-man's-land located in the extreme northeastern corner of the country, as if its builders would have preferred to push it out of Holland altogether. Bleak and gray even in summer, it remained damp and windy all year long. If the slightest breeze came up, everything was immediately coated with dust. A few drops of rain, and Westerbork became a sea of mud. In July 1942, this Central Camp for Jewish Refugees was designated a "police transit camp," and a barbed-wire fence was built around it. A German officer assumed command of the camp, but a Jewish administrative body, similar to the Jewish Council in Amsterdam, was retained. Since then, about 100,000 Jews had passed through Westerbork. The camp had barrack buildings for every purpose: a school, an orphanage, an infirmary, an old-people's home, a theater, a cabaret. The camp even issued its own currency. It had housed as many as 16,000 people at a time, many too many for the available facilities, and the overcrowding made it impossible to maintain hygiene at a level fit for human beings. The infirmary's 1,800 beds were constantly occupied. Some prisoners stayed at Westerbork only a few days, others a few weeks. A chosen few were spared deportation for several months, but eventually they, too, were sent on. A small number who, like the Goslars or the Blitz family, were on the Red Cross's so-called Palestine lists or who had foreign passports, were sent to the exchange camp of Bergen-Belsen, the section reserved for Jews who could be used as "trade goods" in exchange for German prisoners of war. Baptized Jews went to Theresienstadt. But the great majority of Westerbork's inmates were shipped off to the death camps of Sobibor and Auschwitz in Poland. The camp command had quotas to meet and dispatched a transport train every week, usually on Tuesdays. Adolf Eichmann's office determined the schedules and destinations of the trains, as well as the number of passengers. Who, specifically, would be sent was determined by the Jewish administration in the camp. Carefully maintained lists aided the selection process. On the evening before the train's departure, the names of those selected were called out.

But because hope is stronger than experience, the prisoners maintained a semblance of normality. They worked hard because the accepted wisdom was that if you made yourself indispensable you might be able to stay at Westerbork. And they tried to maintain ties with their former lives. Sanne's father, Franz Ledermann, for example, had requested in July 1943 that his daily newspaper be sent to him in Westerbork instead of to his old address in South Amsterdam. "That is some comfort," he wrote on lined camp stationery to his elder daughter, Barbara. Before the major roundup of June 20, 1943, in which more than 5,500 Jews were arrested, this blond-haired school friend of Margot's had left home and gone underground in Amsterdam with a false identity card in the name of Barbara Waarts. Franz Ledermann sustained himself by reading his newspaper, studying Hebrew, and playing the viola. During the day—following the directive to make oneself indispensable—he sorted beans.

The children in Westerbork were organized into youth groups and attended school. Before they were sent off on the transport trains, four hundred of them a week, each child was given a report card and earnestly instructed not to lose it and to give it to the teacher in the next camp.

Ironic as it may sound in the light of her eventual fate, Anne was far from unhappy in Westerbork. She had patiently endured the long, tiresome registration process and the humiliation of having to strip naked, stand in line, and submit to a head check for lice and a general physical exam. Like all other "criminal Jews," she had to give up her own clothes and shoes and put on a dark-blue prison coverall with red patches on it. For shoes, she was given rough wooden clogs. If they fit, it was only by chance. In most cases, the clogs were too large or too small, and that was probably the camp command's intent. Standing for hours at a time in formations for roll call was an especially trying torment the prisoners had to endure. A high fence kept "criminals" like the Franks apart from the rest of the camp. "Criminal" families were not allowed to live in barracks designated for families but were separated by sex. Anne, Edith, and Margot were assigned places in one of the women's penal barracks, where three hundred women slept in one large hall and where even the idea of private space was inconceivable. Otto had to go to a men's barracks, but in the late afternoon and in the evening, he could be with his family. Anne also saw Peter van Pels at these times.

The workday began at five. Otto Frank had tried to get his daughters jobs in the camp kitchen, but he had not succeeded. As a rule, Jews who had been in hiding were ineligible for the easier jobs. Anne, Margot, and Edith were assigned the work of taking batteries apart, forced labor in the service of the German war effort. The worker first broke the battery open with a small chisel or a screwdriver, then removed its metal cover and took out the little carbon rods, scraped the tarlike ammonium chloride paste out of the casing, and put the different parts in separate boxes. The work was dirty. The brown paste from the batteries got on the workers' hands, their faces, their hair, and their clothes; there was hardly any soap and almost nowhere to wash up. The work was also unhealthy because ammonium chloride is mildly toxic; its fumes irritate the bronchial tubes. The women coughed and coughed, but still they worked hard. Make yourself indispensable, they thought; work faster, get a "release," and maybe you won't be shipped off. And unpleasant as the work in the battery section was, the women were glad they could sit together at the long tables and talk to one another. They didn't talk about their troubles: they might be overheard, and complaints were useless, anyway. Instead they tried to steer their conversations to the pleasant things of life, to find something to laugh about, and, most of all, to imagine life after the war. As long as they could remain in Holland, everything would be fine. Even Edith Frank proved to have a talkative side. One of her fellow prisoners later wrote of the "warm, loving human being" she discovered in Anne's mother. "She told us a lot; we had the feeling that now she had a chance to get things off her chest."

And what about Anne herself? She was particularly friendly and sociable. Her pale face and big eyes glowed with confidence. One day she happened to be seated next to the mother of her friend Kitty Egyedi, with whom she had gone to the Montessori school. Kitty had been assigned better tasks in the camp. She worked as a courier for the camp doctors and did some work on the sewing machines. In the evenings, she rejoined her mother. When Kitty learned from her mother that Anne was in the camp, she was eager to see her friend, whom she had believed long since safe in Switzerland. But the two of them never did get together again. Anne fell ill and spent the next several days in the infirmary.

Despite the camp command's blockade on any kind of information, news made its way into the camp and spread quickly. Rumors could raise the inmates' spirits to levels of near euphoria and knock them back down again to the depths of despair. The Franks had been in Westerbork for two and a half weeks when American troops took Paris on August 25, 1944. A few days later, after four years of German occupation, large areas of France were liberated. Now the Allies were advancing toward Belgium. Then, coming from the south, they would take Holland as well.

A general letdown followed this brief moment of elation. Rumor had it that there would be no more deportations, not to Germany, Bohemia, or Poland. But then word spread that Westerbork would be evacuated and another transport train would indeed be leaving for Germany soon. Or would it go to Theresienstadt? Or Auschwitz? An empty train had been standing on the tracks for several days. Would it leave after all?

We don't know how much the sensitive Anne was affected by the intense emotions rampant in the camp. But we know from her diary that in the years in hiding she had followed the war closely and that every Allied success had given her new courage. We also know that her faith in God had helped her overcome her anxiety. "God has never deserted our people," she felt certain (April 11, 1944; ver. A).

Anne is reported to have visited often with an ill twelve-year-old boy in Westerbork. He was from an Orthodox family, and according to Rosa de Winter, a woman who became friends with Edith Frank in Westerbork, he and Anne talked about God together. Though Anne had shown little interest in religion before she went into hiding, it occupied her more and more in the course of those twenty-five months. As a young child she had recited an evening prayer, as Edith had taught her to do. But her parents had left it up to her to choose whether she would attend synagogue or not. Like Otto, she had gone only rarely. There was no tradition of religious observation in Otto's family; indeed, the only time his grandmother Cornelia Elisabeth had been in a synagogue was for her wedding. Otto had never been bar mitzvahed and, unlike Edith, never learned Hebrew. Even on Yom Kippur, the Day of Atonement and the most important of Jewish holidays, Edith and Margot had always gone to synagogue without Anne and Otto. Edith no doubt remembered the example of her grandfather Benjamin, who was known for his devoutness, standing in the back of the synagogue all day, praying. Anne and her father spent the day at home and prepared the holiday meal for the whole family.

In hiding, Edith Frank had tried, with little success, to give her younger daughter some religious instruction. "Today I have to read things in the prayer book," Anne complained on October 3, 1942 (ver. A). "I have no idea why Mummy wants to force me to do that." The world of religious tradition was her mother's world, and at the time she wanted to keep her distance from that. "Why does she force me to be pious?" she grumbled again on October 29, 1942 (ver. B). And when her mother—accompanied by Fritz Pfeffer—prayed on the Sabbath eve, Anne would sometimes be present, but it was Otto's impression that she felt no involvement.

If Anne had doubts about the existence of God, she never expressed them in the conversations she conducted with her diary. After more than a year in hiding, she wrote, "The second half of 1943, I became a young woman, an adult in body and my mind underwent a great, a very great change, I came to know God" (March 7, 1944; ver. A). Anne had been searching not for a God to whom she could submit her requests but rather for one she could trust, not with a blind, childish faith but out of her need for a bit of security in her very insecure life.

Whatever doubts she had were not about God but about herself in relation to him. "Why do I constantly dream and think about the worst things and just want to scream for fear? Because I still don't have faith enough in God," she had written. "He has given me so much that I certainly haven't deserved, yet every day I do so much wrong" (Dec. 29, 1943; ver. A). As she developed a clearer world view and a sense of her place in the world, her trust in God grew. Air raids had always been very upsetting to her, but one evening in January 1944 when "lots of German airplanes were about," she wrote, "I realized that I was a-person-to-myself. . . . "My fear vanished, I looked up at the sky and trusted in God" (Jan. 30, 1944; ver. A). Despite her situation, she never questioned God's motives, at least not in her diary. "Who has inflicted this upon us? Who has made us Jews different from all other people? Who has allowed us to suffer so terribly up till now? It is God that has made us as we are, but it will be God, too, who will raise us up again" (April 11, 1944; ver. A), a God to whom she could turn not just when she was in need of him but one who was constantly present and inseparable from what was good in human beings and beautiful in nature. Anne's God was not one who bound her to him with commandments and prohibitions, not one who insisted she be, literally, God-fearing. She took a pantheistic view of God and the world, attributing a divine dignity to nature or, perhaps more accurately, seeing God and nature as one and the same source of strength. "When I looked outside right into the depth of Nature and God, then I was happy, really happy" (Feb. 23, 1944; ver. A).

Although Anne developed a very personal view of God untethered to any specific religion, her Jewish identity was never in question nor, of course, was it something she could cast aside. "If we bear all this suffering and if there are still Jews left, when it is over, then Jews, instead of being doomed, will be held up as an example," Anne wrote as she reflected on the persecution of her people. "Who knows, it might even be our religion from which the world and all peoples learn good, and for that reason and that reason only do we have to suffer now. We can never become just Netherlanders or just English or any nation for that matter, we will always remain Jews, we must remain Jews, but we want to, too" (April 11, 1944; ver. A).

In spiritual matters Anne seems in at least some ways to have followed Otto's lead. Like him she wanted to be cremated (as traditional Jews are not). "My fountain pen has been cremated," she wrote after her pen accidentally landed in the stove, "just what I want later!" (Nov. 8, 1943; ver. A). In hiding in 1943, she and the others celebrated a secular Christmas: "For the first time in my life I received something for Christmas" (Dec. 27, 1943; ver. A). And for Hanukkah, Otto wanted to give her a children's Bible "so that I could find out something about the New Testament at last" (Nov. 3, 1943; ver. A). Throughout his life Otto had advocated tolerance and understanding between Christians and Jews, and after the war he carried with him until his death not only a few lines from a Jewish prayer but also a prayer by Saint Francis of Assisi: "Lord, make me the instrument of your peace." But because Margot was "perturbed" at the idea of the New Testament as a Hanukkah gift, Otto retreated a bit and gave Anne the children's Bible as a gift for St. Nicholas's Day.

In a 1979 interview, Otto Frank said of his own relationship to Judaism: "I was raised in a very liberal milieu, but because of the persecution I experienced, I, like many others who suffered a similar fate, have come back to Judaism." He never, however, became religiously devout. "All that must lie in our natures," he explained to his sister, "and if it doesn't, our feelings are not the less strong for that lack." In hiding, Anne had become proud of her religion. "Let us remain aware of our task and not grumble, a solution will come," she asked of herself and of her people (April 11, 1944; ver. A). She was therefore all the more disappointed when she discovered how indifferent her friend Peter van Pels was to every aspect—ethnic, religious, and cultural—of Judaism. Peter's indifference to religion prompted her to reflect again about the power of faith: "Although I'm not orthodox either, it still hurts every time I see how deserted, how scornful and how poor he really is. People who have a religion should be glad, for not everyone has the gift of believing in heavenly things. You don't necessarily even have to be afraid of punishment after death; purgatory, hell and heaven are things that a lot of people can't accept, but still a religion, it doesn't matter which, keeps a person on the right path" (July 6, 1944; ver. A). Believing in God, Anne was convinced, did not mean being afraid of him and his punitive wrath but feeling obliged to be honest and straightforward. The most important thing her faith in God did for her was to help her have faith in herself and not lose hope.

"Without God I should long ago have collapsed," she wrote on March 12, 1944 (ver. A). "I know I am not safe, I am afraid of prison cells and concentration camps, but I feel I've grown more courageous and that I am in God's hands!" On the afternoon of September 2, 1944, after barely four weeks in Westerbork, this faith and confidence would be shattered.

Fall in for roll call. The announcement was swift and direct that Saturday, September 2, 1944: a transport train would be leaving Westerbork the following morning. Such things were routine for the administrative personnel. Since mid-July 1942 they had prepared a hundred trains and kept precise records on them: sixty-seven to Auschwitz, nineteen to Sobibor, six to Theresienstadt, and eight to Bergen-Belsen. In the Reich's railroad jargon, these were called "special trains." The administrative staff read off, in alphabetical order, the names of those to be sent on the next day's train: 498 men, 442 women, 79 children—1,019 names in all.

The Franks soon learned that they would be on that train. When the sixth letter of the alphabet came up, they heard Frank, Otto, Edith, Margot, and Anne. Was there no chance of getting a release or at least a postponement? Rescue could come any day now; the Allies were almost at the door. Under the letter *P* came Hermann, Auguste, and Peter van Pels and right after them Fritz

Pfeffer as well. They were not told their destination but only that they could take with them the things they had had to give up when they arrived at Westerbork. The Franks consoled themselves with the thought that they would at least remain together, and they agreed that if they should at some point become separated on the trip, they would try to reestablish contact through Alice Frank, 11 Herbstgasse, Basel.

The prisoners packed their suitcases and rucksacks with the clothing and blankets they still possessed and any food they could get hold of. Edith Frank supposedly smuggled her coverall into her luggage, having first removed the red patches on it. Wherever she thought she might wear it again, she did not want to be recognized as a "criminal."

At dawn on September 3, the guards roused the 1,019 people from their barracks and marched them to the train tracks under the supervision of armed SS troops with attack dogs. The prisoners were horrified to see that they would travel not in passenger cars but in cattle cars. There were no windows, only two ridiculously small barred openings for ventilation. There were no seats, only a cold floor with a little straw scattered on it. Through cracks in the floor, the passengers could see the ties fly by beneath their feet. In one corner of the car was an empty bucket; next to it, another filled with water. As one of the women guards recalled later, there was no protest, no resistance. Most of the prisoners were calm and composed as they handed up their luggage and climbed up onto the loading platform, the men helping the women, the children, and the elderly.

Sixty, seventy, or more people, along with their luggage, were packed into each car, crowded to the point of near suffocation. A person who was lucky or aggressive enough to be among the first to enter a car and could secure a place in a corner or next to a wall could at least crouch or lean against something—a great luxury, for it was impossible to sit, much less lie down, in the cars. Those who weren't alone were fortunate; they could lean against a spouse, a parent, a friend. In fully loaded transport trains, the space allowed each person was less than a quarter of a square meter.

The instant the car was full, the guards shoved the metal door shut and secured it from the outside with a heavy metal rod. It was pitch black inside. The glimmer of light that came in through the vents was useless. And after a few minutes, the air was so foul that people could hardly breathe. Perhaps, they hoped, the trip would not take long.

The loading of the train took at least an hour; then it finally pulled out of the station. It was the 101st of a total of 103 trains that would leave Westerbork. The next day, September 4, a transport train was dispatched to Theresienstadt. On it were Kitty, her little brother, and her parents, as well as the Franks' former lodger, Werner Goldschmidt; and on September 13 still another train departed for Bergen-Belsen. The train with the Franks on it was the last train to leave Holland for Auschwitz. They had a premonition about their destination, but they tried to dispel it with halfhearted optimism: maybe they would wind up in a German work camp after all. Or maybe the Allies would stop the train; they couldn't be far off now. Maybe the tracks would be bombed . . .

They realized that they were leaving Holland, but as the train crept along at thirty or thirty-five miles an hour and as they huddled in the dark, squeezed together, they gradually lost all sense of time and distance. Occasionally the train would stop at a provincial station, often for several hours. Sometimes the door would open and water would be passed in, so little, though, that it could only have seemed a cruel joke to the thirsty prisoners inside. Usually there was no water and only a harsh German voice demanding the prisoners' valuables, their rings, their watches, their gold coins. And most of the time the door remained closed, and the only purpose of the stops seemed to be to prolong this agonizing journey, to let the disoriented passengers stay hungry and thirsty and rob them of their energy and will. When the train was standing still and there was no breeze through the cracks in the cars, the air became intolerably close and muggy, and the stench from the buckets and from the wretched people who had been unable to reach the buckets was unbearable. The Nazis understood how to strip people of their sense of self-worth. They knew how to bring people to the point at which they would just give up.

While Anne spent the night of September 3 huddled in a cattle car somewhere in central Germany and tried to snatch a little sleep leaning on her father's shoulder, her former admirer Hello Silberberg was celebrating his liberation in a small village near Brussels, only about 125 miles from Westerbork. After he had seen Anne on July 5, 1942, for what would be the last time, his life, too, had changed drastically.

Hello was sixteen; his summons to labor service seemed imminent. One evening in early August 1942, he was caught in a roundup as he was on his way home from visiting a friend. It was a few minutes past eight, and the curfew for Jews began at eight. Hello was arrested and loaded onto a truck with other Jews, but as soon as the truck started to move, he jumped off and ran. That evening, he tore the yellow star off his jacket in a rage and never wore it again.

The next roundup came only a few days later. German soldiers blocked off the streets in the neighborhood of Zuider Amstellan and systematically searched each building for young Jewish men, reinforcements for labor service. When they knocked on Hello's grandparents' door, Hello hid behind a wardrobe. It was a miracle that the police didn't find him—and an unmistakable sign to him that he had to either go into hiding or leave the country.

In a few weeks everything was arranged. He had found a young journalist who would take him to his parents in Belgium. To quell any possible suspicion that his grandparents had been involved

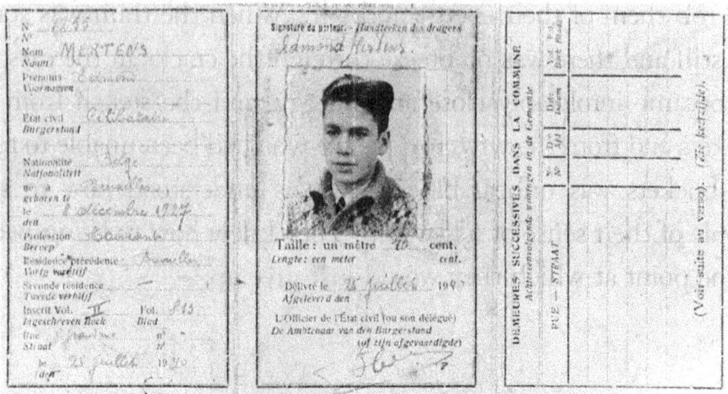

Hello Silberberg's false identity card, 1942

with their grandson's disappearance, they themselves reported to the police that Hello was missing.

Hello took a train to Roermond with three other refugees. In a coffeehouse near the border, they waited until the border police changed shifts. Then, on bicycles, they crossed into Belgium. Riding either trains or bicycles was forbidden for Jews, and Hello considered his flight abroad a wild adventure. Having fooled the Germans gave him the feeling that he was no longer defenseless.

In Brussels, Hello's guide took him to the street where his parents lived, and just by coincidence, he soon saw his father coming toward him. Leo Silberberg had not seen his son for four years and surely would have walked past him if Hello had not whistled the musical password his father and grandfather had always used, a bar from Beethoven's Eighth Symphony.

But even in Brussels, daily life had become too dangerous for Jews, so the Silberbergs, too, decided to go into hiding. They took refuge in a house not far from Brussels, but unlike the Franks, Hello got hold of a fake identity card. Silberberg became Mertens, and because the French-speaking Belgians could not produce an *h,* Helmuth was transformed into Edmond.

Like Anne and her family, the Silberbergs remained in hiding for twenty-five months. Twenty-five months of wondering whether they would be betrayed or not, but Hello had a much better life than his former friend. He could go outdoors. Just a few steps across the street and he was in a forest. Not far from the house were potato fields and vegetable gardens where he could help himself with impunity. If things began to look dangerous, he and the others could hide in a cave in the woods. He could also find shelter in a nearby cloister. In an emergency, he could climb over the cloister wall and into the cloister gardens, where the nuns would feed him.

On the day Anne was herded onto the train for the Auschwitz death camp, Hello climbed up onto the roof of his hiding place, as he often did, to scout out the nearby streets. Off in the distance, he could see white stars on the approaching armored vehicles. The Allies! The war was over, he and his family were rescued, fear and misery were forgotten. And less than 150 miles away, Anne was entering a whole new universe of suffering.

After two days, two nights, and a third day, most of the passengers had made some accommodation to conditions in the cars. Their weary anger had given way to a dazed lethargy. On the third night, the train stopped once again. No one could say how many times it had stopped already. But this time the doors opened, and now everybody had to hurry.

"Move, move!" German voices bellowed. "Everybody out! Leave your luggage—everything—rucksack, handbags, the works! Get moving!" The prisoners were overwhelmed. Their eyes—blinded by the harsh floodlights—searched in vain for some orientation point in this melee of SS troops with machine guns and of prisoners with their shaved heads and striped uniforms. Their ears struggled to separate out the yelping from the loudspeakers and that of the attack dogs. A sickly sweet, penetrating odor assailed their nostrils, an odor that the new arrivals could not identify. They were in Auschwitz-Birkenau.

Yelling directions and wielding leather dog whips, the SS men drove the new arrivals out of the cattle cars and to the end of the ramp. Commands from the loudspeaker instructed children, the ill, and anyone feeling too weak to walk to take a seat on the trucks provided for them. "Don't get on!" the old hands whispered to the newcomers. "Don't say you're sick! You're healthy, understand? You want to work, understand?" Then the fully loaded trucks pulled away. Driven by the whips, which were tipped with thin leather thorns, the arrivals left behind were forced into rows of five. Hastily the men were separated from the women and children, and that was the last Otto Frank saw of his wife and daughters.

Everything proceeded at a frantic pace. The so-called physical examination lasted perhaps two or three seconds. An SS doctor wearing white gloves—maybe Josef Mengele, maybe Johann Kremer, maybe someone else was on duty that night—signaled a prisoner to step toward him. A quick look, perhaps a question—How old are you? Any chronic illnesses?—perhaps no questions at all, then the examining doctor nodded to the left or right or had an SS man point the way with his whip. Older, gray-haired people and children under fifteen or sixteen were normally sent to the left. Strong young adults went to the right. But there was no way to predict for sure. Who knew what criteria or whims moved the doctor at any given moment? In any case, the group on the left was always the larger one.

This game of chance was called the "selection." Anyone sent to the left and anyone who had climbed onto the trucks earlier would be killed that same day or used as a guinea pig in medical experiments. Dr. Kremer, who regularly sent new arrivals to the gas chambers, wrote in his diary in October 1942, "Compared with this, Dante's inferno seems almost a comedy to me. Auschwitz is not called a death camp for nothing." Prisoners who wound up to the doctor's right-hand side would work as unpaid laborers for as long as they could stand. That was called "annihilation by work."

Of the 1,019 Jews who arrived from Westerbork on September 5, 258 men and 212 women survived the selection process. The remaining 549 people, among them all the children, were killed immediately after their arrival in the gas chambers of Birkenau and their bodies burned in the neighboring crematoria. All eight residents of 263 Prinsengracht survived the first round. Anne, at fifteen years and three months, was among the youngest.

To arrive in the death camp was to become a plaything of the camp command. Otto Frank, Hermann and Peter van Pels, and the other men were forced to march hastily to the main camp, Auschwitz I, about two miles away. The women went to quarters in Birkenau. But first, both men and women had to undergo "disinfection" in a so-called sauna, then stay in a quarantine block.

Each prisoner had a number tattooed on his or her left forearm. Edith, Margot, and Anne were branded with numbers between A-25060 and A-25271. Exact records have not been preserved. Human identity in Auschwitz was reduced to a number, and the higher the number, the more difficult it was to hold one's own against the long-term inmates and the kapos, the prisoners—often Polish criminals—appointed by the SS to supervise the work details. A particularly high number assigned its bearer to the bottom of the camp pecking order, a hell of mistrust and aggression.

Next came step-by-step degradation. Disinfection involved stripping naked, giving up one's clothes, having all one's hair shaved off, first the underarm and pubic hair, then the head hair. Allegedly, this was to prevent lice infestations. The real reason was to humiliate the women and make a mockery of their modesty. For Anne, her hair had always been an important means of expressing her personality. And that was precisely the point for the Nazis: to deprive the Jews of their personalities.

Prisoners in Auschwitz-Birkenau

Some of the women had their head hair and pubic hair shaved by other women and were spared the worst of the humiliation. Others were shaved by men, among whom the Nazis instigated a cynical bargaining system: the senior man in a barracks or block of barracks, that is, a privileged prisoner in charge of a group of fellow prisoners, could earn himself a slice of bread or a few cigarettes by assigning certain prisoners to shave the women and so get some relief from hard labor. And the camp command profited as well. The hair, sold by the SS to German textile firms for fifty pfennigs per kilo, was used in blankets, pipe insulation, and other textiles that were marketed as horsehair products.

After disinfection and shaving, the naked, bald, thirsty, and totally demoralized women were sent into a large shower room but supplied with neither soap nor towels. They huddled together, shivering, until water suddenly poured down on them, sometimes scalding hot, sometimes cold. Don't drink it, they were warned. The word had already gotten around that they should never drink water from faucets; if they did, they would get typhus or dysentery.

The flow of water stopped as suddenly and arbitrarily as it had begun, and the guards made use of the omnipresent dog whips to prod the soaking wet women outdoors. Sometimes the guards sprayed them with a delousing powder. Then the women could finally put on some ragged, worn sacklike dresses, much too thin for the climate, and stand in formation for roll call. This shower routine was repeated every week of the year, not just in the summer but also in the pouring rains of fall and in the cold of winter.

Roll call was held not just after showers, but every day. The twelve-hour workday began with a roll call, usually brief, but then in the evening there was another, which lasted at least an hour but could go on much longer as punishment for alleged transgressions. The prisoners were repeatedly roused in the middle of the night and driven outside to stand in formations of five rows, maintaining the required distance of at least an arm's length from their neighbors so that they could not lean on one another for support. Then they would be counted, and heaven help them all if anyone was missing. It was crucial to stand stiffly at attention and create an impression of health and strength. Stumbling or any other sign of physical weakness could send a prisoner to his or her death. "Selection" was a constant, ongoing process.

Once prisoners had gotten past the initial shock of arrival at Auschwitz, they had to adapt quickly to the "norms of the abnormal" if they were going to survive. They had to give up their conventional values, practice theft as a means of survival, harden themselves against all manner of injuries and humiliations. They had to learn to regard their bodies as machines that had to be kept going; they had to learn to ignore hunger and cold and to support one another against the terror. They had to learn to treasure and guard their soup bowls and spoons, for without them the prisoners could not get even the little bit of soup they were entitled to. And above all they had to learn to be constantly on the alert. The guards could find an infinite number of reasons to mete out punishments:

a prisoner went to the bathroom at the wrong time, was caught eating potato peelings behind the kitchens, was working too slowly, or happened to look in a direction a guard deemed wrong. And the severity of the punishment depended on the whim of the guard.

We have little information about Anne's time in Auschwitz-Birkenau. Women who knew her there recall that she was quiet and introverted, that she had great difficulty coping with the horrors she had to witness, and that she wept when she saw children being led to the gas chambers. At the same time, other prisoners reported, she was strong and courageous, and with her winning, friendly, and confident ways even managed to obtain extra rations of bread for Margot, her mother, and herself. One version does not necessarily negate the other. In any case, Anne, Edith, and Margot were an inseparable trio once they were moved from the quarantine block into Women's Block 29. Now there was no sign of the differences that divided them in the past. Edith, who had been so depressed in the months before Auschwitz, now appeared keenly alert, a mother whose one role on earth was to save her children's lives. She exchanged her shoes for a promise of extra rations for Margot and Anne. The promise was broken, however—an everyday occurrence in the camp—and Edith had to go barefoot from then on.

During the day, Anne had to work, probably—like most of the other Dutch women from her transport train—hauling stones or digging up rolls of sod. Every night brought another test of the women's patience and resilience. More than a thousand women slept in a barrack that had originally been designed as a barn for fifty-two horses. The beds were bunks three tiers high and without mattresses. The more fortunate prisoners had thin blankets to wrap themselves in. In "beds" like these about ten women had to lie side by side, as still as possible. If one of them wanted to turn, the others had to turn, too. All the prisoners, without exception, suffered from lice, against which the weekly dousings with insecticide powder were useless; they also had to battle mites and bedbugs. These parasites bored into their weakened victims and left itchy bumps that turned into painful abscesses and open wounds if they were scratched with dirty fingers.

It was not long before Anne's body began to rebel. After a few weeks her skin was so badly inflamed and her entire body so covered with sores that she was sent to what was called the scabies block. As Rosa de Winter, who had gotten to know the Franks in Westerbork, wrote in 1945, this was a particularly dreadful block. Surrounded by a high wall, it was completely isolated from the rest of the camp. It was unlit, and the prisoners had to grope around in the dark to find their sleeping places. Mice and rats ran over the women, who screamed and wept and could not even think about sleeping under these intolerable conditions. Anne was not alone. Margot went with her into this frightful infirmary; perhaps Edith did, too. The survivors' recollections vary on this point. Edith may have remained in a different barrack and passed her own bread ration in to her daughters through a hole she dug under the surrounding wall. As long as she could be near her children, Edith went without food herself.

Providing one another with mutual support, Anne, Edith, and Margot Frank had survived about eight weeks in Birkenau when, toward the end of October 1944, a new rumor spread through the camp. The Russian army was only sixty miles from Auschwitz. Once again, the prisoners experienced the extremes of hope and fear. Would the Russians arrive in time to liberate the camp? Would they bomb Auschwitz? Would the Allies, who up to now had undertaken no action against Auschwitz, show the slightest concern for the prisoners? Or would the Nazis, seeking to eliminate all trace of their crimes, send everyone to the gas chambers? The RSHA, or Reichssicherheitshauptamt, the headquarters of the German security service in Berlin, ordered the camp commander to begin evacuation of this, the largest and most efficient of all the work and death camps—and there were well over a thousand of them, 22 main camps and 1,202 satellite camps.

More selections took place. On October 28, 1944, an evacuation train carrying 1,308 Jewish women left Birkenau for Bergen-Belsen in north Germany. Anne and Margot were probably among them and perhaps Auguste van Pels as well, either on the same day or a few days later. In any case, all three of them numbered among the 8,000 or so women who were transferred in late October and early November from Auschwitz-Birkenau to Bergen-Belsen, about one hour north of Hannover, women the Dutch Red Cross would later describe as "ill but potentially capable of recovering." The two Frank girls and Mrs. van Pels would remain in touch.

The Nazis were building up a reserve force of workers. They no doubt thought these women might still prove useful in their war industries. That Edith Frank was left behind in Auschwitz is another illustration of the capriciousness of the system. But then there may have been a different reason why the mother and her daughters were separated. Anne apparently told a fellow prisoner in Bergen-Belsen that an SS man had attacked Margot and that Edith had intervened. After that, Anne never saw her mother again.

Anne and Margot knew what to expect in the cattle cars. This time, however, the prisoners were all women and were apparently even given some minimal amounts of bread, cheese, margarine, and water for the trip. But the cold and dampness penetrated the cars and the prisoners' weakened bodies. Their thin, ragged clothing provided little protection, and the trip lasted at least five days and five nights because the train had to make detours or simply stop and wait to avoid bombings. When Anne and Margot arrived at their destination weak and frozen to the bone and for the first time in their lives without the protection of their parents, they were marched about four miles from the tracks to the part of the camp designated for their group. For healthy people, this trek would have taken at least an hour and a half. But the march was just the beginning of a series of unimaginable torments.

Chaos reigned in Bergen-Belsen. There was no room for the influx of new prisoners. In July 1943, the Nazis had converted portions of this camp, originally designed as an army and POW camp, into various auxiliary concentration camps, one of which was the "SS transit camp" for the privileged "exchange Jews." Most of the prisoners in this so-called star camp had been sent there from Westerbork between January and September 1944, 3,670 people in all, among them Anne's lyceum friend Nanette Blitz and her elementary-school friend Hanneli Goslar, along with Hanneli's father and little sister, Gabi.

To alleviate the crowding, the Nazis put up tents in August 1944 to serve as temporary quarters for women from other concentration camps. Anne and Margot were quartered in one of these tents after their march but provided with neither food nor an opportunity to clean up. Several hundred women were crowded into this huge cloth shed and left to cower together with only a little straw between them and the damp clay soil. There were no toilets, no washstands, no beds, no light. "The four of us crawled in together under our blankets," Rebekka Brilleslijper (who would become an artist known as Lin Jaldati) reported later. She and her sister Jannie had gotten to know the Frank girls in Westerbork. At their reunion in Bergen-Belsen, they fell "into each other's arms and cried." The tent provided them only minimal shelter against the wind and rain.

Four days after their transport's arrival, a violent storm swept through the camp and tore out the guy wires of several of the tents. The one Anne, Margot, Jannie, and Lin were in was among those that toppled. Until the star camp was reorganized and new quarters could be provided, the women were left to huddle under their collapsed tent. Some survivors say for a few hours, others say for a few days. Margot and Anne were probably among those who took shelter in a shed while many others wandered about in the icy rain searching in vain for something to eat. "Why do they want us to live like animals?" Anne is said to have asked her fellow sufferers.

To provide quarters for the prisoners from the destroyed tents, the two-story bunks in the barracks of the star camp were removed and replaced with even narrower three-tiered bunks that were more like wooden shelves than beds. The former tent inhabitants were crammed into the vacated barracks, two and sometimes three to each sleeping place. Every day food was dispensed more sporadically and scantily, scraps of bread or a thin soup with chunks of fodder beet swimming in it. Drinking water was scarce, and prisoners scuffled over the few available blankets. The authorities had long since abandoned even rudimentary hygiene in the camp. Anne and Margot, "like all sisters, of course, had their little quarrels," Lin recalled. But they maintained their sense of responsibility to each other, for they had little hope that their parents were

A barrack in Bergen-Belsen

still alive. Sometime that winter Anne discovered her schoolmate Nanette Blitz. First they merely caught a glimpse of each other through a barbed-wire fence. Then Nanny, as she later said, found out that the fence between Camps 7 and 8 had been taken down, and she set out to find Anne.

In February 1944 she had been taken with her family from Westerbork to Bergen-Belsen. That the Blitzes' names were on one of the Palestine lists gave her some hope, but in the meantime Nanny had to learn to fend for herself. On November 24, 1944, her father died "from starvation and self-recrimination for not having had the foresight to spare us the concentration camps," as she later put it. His wife and children were consequently no longer protected. On December 4 and 5, Nanny's seventeen-year-old brother, Bernhard, and her mother were sent off on separate transports, and she was transferred to another section of the camp. Why was she kept back in Bergen-Belsen? A whim of the camp administration.

Nanny had not been among Anne's closest friends in the Jewish lyceum, although she had been invited to Anne's birthday party in June 1942. Now the two girls were ecstatic at seeing each other again. Memories of their earlier life, however remote and unreal, provided some diversion, and for a few moments they could think of something other than the gloomy present.

Despite prohibitions on meeting, the girls still managed to get together several times. Nanny Blitz—horrified at Anne's physical condition, her bald head, her sunken cheeks, her inflamed skin—told Anne about the fates of some of their friends, relating, for example, how Jacque van Maarsen had been saved by acquiring an "Aryan" identity card. Anne described her life in hiding and made plans for the future: after the war, she wanted to write a book based on her diary.

But Anne was most preoccupied with her parents' fate. Her mother, she told Nanny, had not been with her on the transport to Bergen-Belsen, which surely meant that she had been murdered by the Nazis. And her father, at fifty-five and with his thinning gray hair, must have seemed an old man in the eyes of the SS guards. If what she had heard in Auschwitz was true, then he had surely been sent to the gas chambers soon after his arrival.

Anne could not know that Edith Frank, weakened and in despair over the loss of her daughters, nonetheless continued to fight for her life. Rosa de Winter had become a real friend, and the two women did all they could to help each other. For instance, when the two of them were sent to the scabies block, they clung to each other and crept in together under a blanket with a woman they did not know. Shortly after the war Rosa recounted that they had been dead tired but had found it impossible to sleep. The next morning, several women, Rosa and Edith among them, were ordered outdoors for roll call. All outside! On the double! A Greek woman had grabbed hold of Rosa and Edith and dragged them bodily into the yard for roll call. What at first seemed like just one more torment saved their lives. They watched from a distance as the scabies block was emptied of every last patient and trucks carried more than three hundred women off to their deaths. Edith and Rosa were taken to the "rehabilitation block" for prisoners no longer able to work.

Weeks passed. Killings in the gas chambers ceased. At the orders of Heinrich Himmler, the dismantling of the gas chambers began; Crematoria I and II were torn down. Between December 1, 1944, and mid-January 1945, more than half a million people were evacuated from Auschwitz. Along with a group of dentists, engineers, and electricians, Fritz Pfeffer was sent to the Neuengamme camp, a former brick factory near Hamburg, supposedly to do work important to the war effort. Compared with figures from other camps in Germany, the death rate in Neuengamme was extremely high. "Prisoner 64971" died there on December 20, 1944. Official cause of death: inflammation of the large intestine.

The Nazis kept Edith Frank in Auschwitz, where conditions grew worse day by day. Rosa de Winter recalled how thirsty she and Edith were: there was no water. In the morning, they washed themselves as best they could with snow. The lice drove them nearly mad, and lice are also carriers of typhus and other illnesses. Edith's constitution could not hold up long against these assaults. She had a fever of 104 when Rosa took her to the infirmary. Edith resisted, fearing the selections that took place regularly among the ill. Edith did not want to die. But at least the infirmary barracks were heated.

Sometime in January 1945, Anne and Margot were transferred to a rehabilitation block in Bergen-Belsen. Nanny Blitz never saw them again after that. But another girl, from Holland, Margot Rosenthal, who had just been shipped to Bergen-Belsen from Auschwitz in 40-degree-below-zero weather, brought Anne and Margot word of their mother. She told the girls that she had seen Edith Frank before she left Auschwitz.

But shortly after that, Edith Frank's health declined rapidly. By the time she was transferred to the barrack where Rosa de Winter had regained her strength, Edith was, as her friend said, only "a shadow of herself." Edith didn't eat anymore but hoarded the bread that was given her under her blanket, for her daughters and her husband, she indicated. Toward the end, she didn't speak or respond if spoken to, and on January 6, 1945, she died.

It seems that Anne, even after she had spoken with Margot Rosenthal, could not really believe that her mother was still alive. Weeping, she whispered to Hanneli Goslar through the barbed-wire fence that she no longer had a mother. Like Nanette Blitz, Anne's childhood friend Hanneli had been in Bergen-Belsen since February 1944, but she had had no contact with Nanette.

Hanneli had heard from an acquaintance of Auguste van Pels's that there was a group of Dutch women in the other part of the camp and that Anne Frank was among them. Every day the Dutch women dragged themselves to the barbed-wire fence tightly packed with straw that had been built to separate the great mass of the prisoners from exchange Jews like Hanneli and Nanette. They were in fact strictly forbidden to approach the fence, beyond which the exchange Jews received considerably better care. The exchange Jews were also allowed to receive packages, and often they shared their food with those on the other side of the fence.

One evening Hanneli went to the fence and quietly called Anne's name. She could not afford to be caught doing so. Auguste van Pels heard Hanneli's voice and brought Anne, already seriously ill, out to meet Hanneli. Margot was too weak to accompany Anne. This must have been on February 5, 1945, at the latest, because the next day Auguste van Pels was put on a transport to Raguhn in Saxony-Anhalt, a satellite camp of Buchenwald. The prisoners in Raguhn worked at forced labor for a Junker airplane and motor vehicle factory. She was to be sent from Raguhn to Theresienstadt in Czechoslovakia but presumably did not live to make it there.

Anne was overjoyed to hear her friend's voice. At 263 Prinsengracht, Anne had often dreamed of Hanneli and felt ashamed that in her preadolescent self-centeredness she had often neglected her childhood friend in the months before she had gone into hiding. "It was horrid the way I treated her, and now she looked at me, oh so helplessly, with her pale face and imploring eyes," Anne wrote in her diary on November 27, 1943 (ver. B). She knew at the time that Hanneli and her family had been deported in June, and she assumed they were in Poland or perhaps already dead. "I am not more virtuous than she; she, too, wanted what was right, why should I be chosen to live and she probably to die? . . . Hanneli, Hanneli, if only I could take you away." Now it turned out that things had gone much better for Hanneli than for Anne. Hanneli had been in Bergen-Belsen for a year. She, her sister Gabi, her father, and her grandmother had been allowed to stay in Westerbork for six months, an unusually long time. Their names were on the second of the forty Palestine lists, which saved them from deportation to Poland. Then on February 15, 1944, they had been sent to Bergen-Belsen. Hanneli's grandfather, Alfred Klee, had died of a heart attack in Westerbork. As for Hanneli's mother, Anne had heard in hiding that the Goslars' third child had been stillborn, but to avoid upsetting her unnecessarily, her parents had not told her that Ruth Goslar had died in childbirth. Hanneli had come down with jaundice two days after her arrival in Bergen-Belsen, but she had been well cared for in the camp infirmary, as she was an exchange Jew. Of course, the promised exchange of Jews for German prisoners of war never came to pass.

The two friends had found each other again under tragic circumstances. They couldn't see each other through the straw-packed fence but they could at least speak through it. In Auschwitz, Anne said, they had shaved her head and taken everything from her, including her clothes. She was freezing and couldn't bear the lice any longer. Anne's voice was barely recognizable, and her words were despairing. She had suffered too much already. Her father was dead, and, she told Hanneli, she did not want to live any longer.

In fact, Otto Frank had been liberated from Auschwitz only a few days earlier, on January 27, 1945.

After the selection on their arrival in Auschwitz, Otto Frank, Hermann and Peter van Pels, and Fritz Pfeffer had all been sent to Block 2 in the main camp, Auschwitz I. They were lucky. One of the senior men in that block was Max Stoppelman, whose mother's apartment in South Amsterdam Jan and Miep Gies were renting part of. Otto Frank had placed the classified ad that had led Miep to Mrs. Stoppelman, and he had gotten to know Max on that occasion. With the help of Jan Gies, Max and his wife, Stella, had gone into hiding with a Dutch family in Laren in the fall of 1943, but six months later they had been betrayed and arrested.

Peter van Pels, too, became friends with Max Stoppelman, a

short man of about thirty with the shoulders of a wrestler. Peter was able to assure Max that Saartje, his mother, was still alive; Miep had paid Mrs. Stoppelman several visits at her hiding place in Hilversum. Max, who had been in Auschwitz since May 1944 and was thoroughly familiar with the rules of survival in the camp, took Peter under his wing. All Peter had to do, Max told him, was stick close to him and not even consider giving up.

Peter seems to have worked in the camp post office, and he held up well. His father, however, like Otto Frank and Fritz Pfeffer, was assigned an outdoor job. When Hermann injured his finger digging, probably in early October, he asked his kapo to assign him to a barracks detail for the next three days, even though he must have known how dangerous it was for anyone to show weakness. And indeed on one of those days, the SS made a clean sweep of the barracks. Hermann van Pels died in the gas chamber that same day.

By November 1944, Otto, too, had reached the limit of his endurance. Already weakened by hard work and hunger, he was beaten by his kapo. After that, he no longer had the will to get up. What happened to him next he described in a letter of July 1945 to his mother: through the intercession of a Dutch doctor he was admitted to the hospital and remained there until the camp was liberated by the Russians on January 27. There was no treatment provided in this "hospital," but at least people were not beaten.

Otto, who stood almost six feet tall, weighed a mere 114 pounds at this point, but ever since their arrival in Auschwitz, Peter van Pels had attended to Otto's needs with a touching loyalty. Max Stoppelman's protection and tutelage had obviously benefited Peter, who seemed surprisingly well nourished. Peter came to the infirmary to see Otto for the last time in mid-January 1945. The camp was being forcibly evacuated, Peter told Otto. Both he and Otto had to leave. Max assured Peter that if Peter stuck with him on the journey he would come through fine. Otto tried unsuccessfully to convince Peter to stay. On the night of January 17–18, the eighteen-year-old young man, in thin prison clothes and without provisions, set off on foot with thousands of other prisoners, most of them Jews, for Wodzislaw, about sixty-five miles away. They were en route for several days with nothing but snow to eat, and on this trek to Wodzislaw, Peter lost contact with his protector when Max Stoppelman was diverted to a different column. After several detours, Peter wound up in the Mauthausen concentration camp on January 25, 1945, and was registered as prisoner number 119162. Four days later, he was transferred to Melk, a satellite camp of Mauthausen. In the official camp records, his date of death is listed as May 5, 1945, the day the Americans liberated the camp. When he actually died remains unclear.

Back in Auschwitz, Otto, prisoner B-9174, barely escaped death. "On the 26th, the SS took us outside to murder us, but they were ordered away before they could do so—we were saved by a miracle," he wrote to his mother. The SS had fled from the Red Army troops that arrived in Auschwitz on January 27. The Russian soldiers found 7,650 prisoners still alive: 1,200 in Auschwitz I, 5,800 in Auschwitz II Birkenau, and 650 in Auschwitz III Buna Monowitz.

The survivors remained in the camp for the few weeks it took the Russians to decide what to do with them. There was plenty of food because the Nazis had laid in huge amounts of supplies for themselves while they let their prisoners starve. Drinking water, though, continued to be a problem and had to be obtained by cutting blocks of ice out of nearby lakes and melting them down.

Of the 1,019 prisoners sent on the last train from Westerbork to Auschwitz, Otto Frank was one of forty-five men and eighty-two women who survived. On Friday evenings, Otto joined a group of liberated prisoners in celebrating the coming of the Sabbath. None of these men was religious. But after all the times he had attended the Friday-evening ceremony at the Goslars' apartment in Amsterdam, Otto could still hear the Hebrew of the Sabbath blessing in his ear, and now he spoke it aloud in the presence of the assembled company.

"I have no news of Edith and the children. They were probably deported to Germany," Otto wrote to his mother on March 15, 1945, from Kattowitz, where he was waiting for transportation to Holland. "Will we be reunited again in good health?"

Like all other Auschwitz prisoners, Otto assumed that life in the German concentration camps was better than in the Polish ones. He knew nothing of the conditions that prevailed in Bergen-Belsen in the winter of 1944–45. "Auschwitz was organized hell," Rebekka Brilleslijper wrote. "Bergen Belsen was now hell without mercy, pure chaos." No executions took place in the hopelessly overcrowded camp, but ten of thousands died anyway. Weakened by hunger and thirst, they died slow, agonizing deaths from infectious diseases—dysentery, diphtheria, tuberculosis, and typhus. Describing after the war the part of the camp where Anne and Margot had been held, a British army captain, Andrew Pares, wrote of the horrendous conditions, of six hundred people crowded into barracks for sixty, of corpses, human excrement, and filth strewn everywhere. The prisoners, in rags crawling with lice, had been beaten down to the level of animals.

Hanneli Goslar had met her friend Anne three or four more times, always with the barbed wire between them. Anne had cast off her lice-ridden clothes and now clutched only a blanket around her shoulders. Twice Hanneli had thrown a small packet containing a cookie, a stocking, or a glove over the fence. The first time, a woman Anne didn't know had caught the package and run off with it. Anne was able to catch the second one.

Hans Goslar died on February 25, 1945, and Hanneli stayed in her barrack for several days mourning her father. When, suffering from typhus herself, she managed to drag herself to the fence, she could not find her friend. Apparently Anne and Margot, along with all the other inhabitants of their barrack, had been moved to another part of the camp.

Well over 17,000 people died in Bergen-Belsen in March 1945 alone, most of them too weak and listless to struggle against death. Morning after morning they were found dead in their barracks and were buried in mass graves. The camp administration had long since stopped keeping death records.

The typhus epidemic struck Anne and Margot, too. Against the advice of their friends Jannie and Lin, they let themselves be admitted to the infirmary barrack. Their strength finally failed them only a few weeks before April 15, 1945, the day British troops arrived at Bergen-Belsen, the first of the concentration camps on German soil to be liberated from the Nazis. Sometime between the end of February and mid-March 1945, Margot died, followed a few days later by Anne.

11

LONGING

"The sun is shining, the sky is deep blue, there is a lovely breeze and I'm longing—so longing—for everything. . . . To talk, for freedom, for friends, to be alone. And I do so long . . . to cry!" Anne had been cooped up for a year and a half when she attempted to understand the vague but powerful emotion she was feeling. "I believe that it's spring within me, I feel that spring is awakening, I feel it in my whole body and soul." Chaotic emotions—loneliness and expectation, suffering and desire, deprivation and craving—had left her restless and unsettled. "I feel completely confused, I don't know what to read, what to write, what to do, I only know that I am longing" (Feb. 12, 1944; ver. A).

Like anyone else her age, Anne felt an inchoate yearning and an urgency without any real sense of what exactly was so urgent. Her yearning was partly a consequence of her dissatisfaction with herself and her surroundings—and partly an effort to overcome her stubborn loneliness. This loneliness in turn resulted from her fear that she was misunderstood by her parents and by the people she loved most. All adolescents experience a similar isolation, which would have troubled Anne even had she been free. Ordinary life provides most young people some distraction from their loneliness, but Anne's existence in hiding was no ordinary life. She was denied what others her age, living in freedom, could take for granted, those diversions that ease the pain associated with growing up: "To have lots of fun myself for once, and to laugh until my tummy ached. . . . Cycling again, dancing, flirting and what-have-you, how I would love that" (Dec. 24, 1943; ver. A). There was no escape; she had to confront her loneliness constantly: "I desperately want to be alone" (Jan. 30, 1944; ver. A). What she perceived as a vague desire to be alone was accompanied by the longing for someone with whom she could share her loneliness and who could understand her, by the longing for a first kiss and the tenderness that would prove to her that someone else appreciated her, cared for her, and desired her.

But there was more to Anne's yearning than a defiant need for escape or an unsatisfied need for love. Her ambitions for herself, her sense of intellectual independence led her on the path toward self-discovery. Instead of turning to melancholy fantasizing as a means of escaping her tiny world, she struggled through months of debate with herself until she could even accept as a challenge the limitations she faced. "Everything grew much worse at this point," Anne wrote, referring back to a period before the family had gone into hiding. But now, she wrote, probably sometime in the early summer of 1944, as she was revising her diary, "I've reached the stage that I . . . think 'what do I care about the lot of them,' and make plans for the future" (Jan. 12, 1944; ver. B).

The Nazis had taken from Anne her freedom to make decisions and choices in so many routine matters of life. But until a few months before her death in Bergen-Belsen, her interest in life, the hope that interest gave her, and her will to live did not desert her. Under the pressure of persecution, she created for herself—much earlier than young people normally do—her own place in life and insisted on setting specific goals for herself and working toward their realization.

Anne was no prodigy. Her family called her "a little bundle of contradictions" (July 21, 1944; ver. A). She herself felt that two souls coexisted inside her, two contradictory Annes who were at odds with each other. There was the extroverted, cheerful Anne and the introverted Anne, who was thoughtful, "deeper," and "purer" (Aug. 1, 1944; ver. A), the Anne who tackled questions for which there were no simple answers—problems of growing up, of love and sexuality, of relationships between parents and children—and also issues of religiosity, faith, and personal freedom. Apart from herself, she thought, no one knew this inner Anne. And indeed Otto Frank had to confess when he read the diary after the war that he had scarcely known the "quiet" Anne, that he had underestimated the depth and range of her thinking, and that—close to each other as they had been—she had kept most of her thoughts to herself. "Her outstanding traits," he wrote to his cousin, "were: her self-criticism, her faith, social feeling, love of nature, her courage and optimism."

Anne was too intelligent to accept herself as she was. Her life was not comfortable, and she was a discomfort to herself. She was a keen observer and merciless critic, but her harsh judgments fell not only on those around her but also on herself. "I have one outstanding trait in my character, . . . and that is my self-knowledge," Anne wrote, correctly, in her diary on July 15, 1944 (ver. A). She watched herself in everything she did, as if she were standing outside herself. "There are so many things about myself that I condemn," she continued in the same vein in her entry of August 1, 1944 (ver. A). "If I'm to be quite honest, then I must admit . . . that I try terribly hard to change myself, but that I'm always fighting against a more powerful enemy . . . and [I] keep on trying to find a way of becoming what I would so like to be and what I could be, if . . . there weren't any other people living in the world." Anne could not know of course that this would be her last diary entry, and because it is the last, it obliges us to contemplate the full horror and tragedy of the brutal way in which Anne's dialogue with herself was interrupted.

Much as Anne still had to struggle to define her character, she nonetheless already had her life's goals firmly in mind. Although she wanted to marry and have children, she also knew very clearly before she was even fifteen that she could never be satisfied with a traditional female role. "I have made up my mind now," she wrote, "to lead a different life from other girls and, later on, different from ordinary housewives" (May 3, 1944; ver. A). She wanted to be famous and make a place for herself in history. This gifted young autobiographer had let the world know that repeatedly even as a ten- and twelve-year-old. But over time this idea born of a childish and innocent egotism developed into a concrete goal. "Oh yes, I don't want to have lived for nothing like most people. I want to be useful or give pleasure to the people around me yet who don't really know me," she wrote on March 25, 1944 (ver. A). "And therefore I am grateful to God for giving me this gift, this possibility of developing myself and of writing."

Writing would be her means of holding on to everything—her thoughts, her ideals, and her fantasies. And the more intently she devoted herself to her diary, the more clearly she perceived her calling as a writer: "I can shake off everything if I write, my sorrows disappear, my courage is reborn" (April 5, 1944; ver. A). Difficulties that might easily have made other people unproductive seemed only to have spurred Anne on. As if possessed, she threw herself into her work, pressing on. "You've known for a long time that my greatest wish is to become a journalist someday and later on a famous writer," she wrote on May 11, 1944. "In any case, I want to publish a book entitled *Het Achterhuis* after the war." Her diary would provide the basis for this book. She had a clear sense of her talent.

The Nazi regime stole Anne's youth and forced her and her generation to grow up quickly. But instead of yielding to defeat, she lived a life of singular intensity. She even occasionally succeeded in overcoming her fear of death and her fear for her life; paradoxical as it may seem, she experienced moments of great happiness. "I long for freedom and fresh air, but I believe that we have ample compensation for our privations. . . . When I sat in front of the window this morning I suddenly realized that we have had a great, great many compensations. I mean inward compensation," Anne wrote (Feb. 23, 1944; ver. A). Otto Frank often told his family that after the Allied victory, when they were all safe again, they would look back with gratitude on the time they had spent in hiding. His words of hope gave them all the strength to go on.

But the murderous hatred of the Nazis, their will to destroy, was apparently stronger; too many people, moreover, stood silently by and watched the Nazi machine grind on. "The little man is just as guilty, otherwise the peoples of the world would have risen in revolt long ago!" Anne realized. "There's in people simply an urge to destroy, an urge to kill, to murder and rage" (May 3, 1944; ver. A).

The Nazis and their silent helpers could take Anne's life from her but not her voice. "I know what I want, I have a goal, have an opinion, have a religion and love. . . . If God lets me live, I shall attain more than Mummy ever has done, I shall not remain insignificant, I shall work in the world for mankind" (April 11, 1944; ver. A). In the end, the Nazi terror could not silence Anne's voice, which still rings out for all of us, whom she had hoped so ardently to serve.

EPILOGUE

After serving a prison term in 1939, **ANTOON CHRISTIAAN "TONNY" AHLERS** was incarcerated several times again after the war. He was in jail repeatedly, first in 1945, then from 1946 to 1949, and again in the early 1960s. Like hundreds of others, he took advantage of the chaotic conditions in the internment camps in 1946 to escape four times.

Investigations to determine whether he was an informant for the security service and had, as research by the Dutch police claimed, betrayed people to the security service were inconclusive and no charges were brought against Ahlers. For ten years, he was subject to the restrictions usually applied to a collaborator: confiscation of his property—did he even have any property?—limitation on the right to vote, withdrawal of the right to work in public service or for the military.

A few weeks after his return from Auschwitz, Otto Frank went in search of the man whom he still considered to be his rescuer. When he learned that Ahlers was in prison and that direct contact with him was not possible, Otto sent to the Dutch Office for National Security a letter of support for Ahlers dated August 21,

1945. On November 25, 1945—Ahlers was now no longer in prison—Otto Frank wrote another letter exonerating Ahlers and gave it to him and his wife, Martha, to use as they saw fit. Otto had his eye on Job Jansen at this point and may have hoped Ahlers could provide him with further information about this former employee. It had still not occurred to Otto that Ahlers could have been in league with his denouncer and, indeed, might even have had a hand in betraying him. But he supposedly heard two weeks later—as he later reported to Ernst Schnabel—that "he was the only one Ahlers had saved. All the others Ahlers had betrayed."

Ahler's wife, Martha, divorced him in the 1980s. But before that she remained loyal to him for decades despite his escapades and supported him in his dubious dealings. He was too unstable to hold a steady job. In November 1946, he reregistered his Petoma company, which had gone bankrupt in 1944. Petoma remained in business until December 1980 but seems to have functioned only sporadically and in various fields of endeavor, including, in the 1970s, door-to-door sales of kitty litter. In the early 1950s, Ahlers went off to exotic regions like Southeast Asia and Australia as a seaman and photographer, and he turned up as a freelance photographer again later, working for *De Telegraaf*.

In the winter of 1963–64, he tried to insinuate himself into the investigation of Karl Josef Silberbauer. He attacked Otto Frank sharply in his letters to the Austrian authorities, who did a brief background check on Ahlers and concluded he was a "fantasist" and not to be taken seriously. In 1948, the Dutch police's Department for Political Research had labeled him "a nonstop talker, very stupid and capable of saying and doing just about anything." Ahlers died on August 4, 2000; his wife, Martha, on October 3, 2012.

NANETTE BLITZ survived the Bergen-Belsen concentration camp, where her father died in November 1944. After her return to Holland in June or July 1945, Nanny—whom Anne referred to as "E.S." in her diary—spent several years in a Santpoort sanatorium recovering from a severe case of tuberculosis. While there, she learned that her mother and brother had died after they were sent away from Bergen-Belsen in early December 1944. Immediately on his arrival in the Oranienburg concentration camp, the seventeen-year-old Bernhard was shot. Nanny's mother, Helena, was sent to the Beendorf camp near Magdeburg, where she was forced to work in a factory that produced airplane parts and was located about 1,500 feet underground in a former salt mine. The date of her death is given as April 10, 1945, the day the camp was evacuated.

From Santpoort, Nanny began corresponding with Otto Frank in late October 1945. Hanneli Goslar had put him in contact with Nanny, and she was able to tell him about the last months of his daughters' lives. In the early 1950s, she moved to England to live with relatives. There she met John Konig, a Hungarian Jew who had spent the war in London. An orphan like Nanny (both his parents had died of cancer), he fell in love at first sight, a love that only grew stronger despite years of separation when John emigrated to Brazil to establish a means of support for Nanny and himself. For the next two years, the couple stayed in regular contact by mail. Then, as John's wife, Nanny too moved to São Paulo, where they are still living today. They have three children, six grandchildren, and a growing number of great-grandchildren. Nanette frequently gives talks about her personal history, most recently to the Argentinian Senate.

ISA AND ABRAHAM CAUVERN divorced in 1943 as a means of protecting themselves from the Nazis and then survived the war in separate hiding places. Otto's former secretary and her daughter, Ruth, went into hiding in Laren in the home of her brother-in-law, the well-known Dutch graphic artist Theo Kurpershoek. For quite a while, Ab went under the name of Albert Cauvern with a fake identity card fabricated at the Kurpershoek studio, and he continued to work for the Hilversum radio station, which had been taken over by the German occupation. But then he too went into hiding.

As soon as Otto Frank returned from Auschwitz, he reestablished contact with the Cauverns, who helped him prepare Anne's diaries for print. "Tomorrow," he wrote to his mother on December 12, 1945, "I'm going to Laren to take Anne's diary to Ab and Isa for them to correct and copy." Ab had in the meantime returned as a dramaturge to the VARA Radio Association, which is what this socialistically oriented radio station had been called before the Nazis took it over. Ab checked the texts Otto Frank had chosen for Germanisms, corrected grammatical errors, and wrote the sentence that remained the closing line of the published diary through many editions: "Anne's diary ends here. On August 4, 1944, the Green Police raided the Secret Annex." Beyond that, he also took liberties with Anne's writing style. As an article of April 1950 in the German magazine *Der Spiegel* noted, "he felt no compunction about occasionally flattening Anne Frank's fresh, youthful style if an expression struck him as too forceful or overly emotional. . . . Passages with different dates in the notebooks Cauvern pulled together under a single date."

Isa typed a clean copy of the corrected version, and this manuscript is known as typescript 1. (Notes that Ab entered onto this copy later added to doubts about the authenticity of the diary and led to numerous deliberations by the courts.) Isa's relatives feel that the intense work on Anne's diaries brought on a serious psychological crisis; she was clearly unable to get over her wartime experiences, and after months of psychiatric treatment and a brief stay in the Santpoort psychiatric hospital, she committed suicide on June 27, 1946, by jumping from a window of her Amsterdam apartment. Her daughter, Ruth, was not yet five.

Ab Cauvern, who shared an apartment with Otto Frank and

the Gies family from 1946 to 1950, remarried in 1961. He lived in Hilversum until his death on June 15, 1986. His daughter, Ruth, decided to live in South Africa, where she worked as a teacher until her retirement.

JULIUS DETTMANN, who presumably received the telephone call of the betrayer or his middleman on August 4, 1944, could not be interrogated about his role in the Amsterdam headquarters of the security service. On July 25, 1945, he hanged himself in his prison cell.

The **DIARIES** waited in Miep's drawer almost a year for Anne's return. On the same day that Otto Frank learned of his daughters' deaths, Miep Gies gave him Anne's red-and-light-green checkered diary, her notebooks, and 327 loose sheets of onionskin paper. "I had it in my hands but I couldn't read it yet," Otto wrote to his cousin Milly at the end of August 1945. "Perhaps I shall have the force to do so later."

In the next few months, Otto gradually acquainted himself with his daughter's work and tried to put the papers in some kind of order. He reread Anne's writings again and again, translated some passages into German, and sent them to his relatives in Basel. "I can't stay away from Anne's diaries; they are so unbelievably exciting," he wrote, adding: "I can't let the diaries out of my hands. There is too much in them meant for no one else."

By October 1945 he had typed a final copy of the diaries and made an extensive selection of the entries that he considered "essential" to a document of World War II. He altered several of Anne's tirades about her mother and Fritz Pfeffer and omitted for the most part references to her sexual awakening. In this process, he relied primarily on Anne's own revisions, which she had recorded on the loose sheets, and added only a few supplementary passages from her original version as well as excerpts from her book of stories. For the period from March 29, 1944, until the diary was broken off on August 1, he had to draw entirely on Anne's first draft. She had not been able to go back over this material.

After Ab Cauvern had edited the text and his wife, Isa, had typed a clean copy of it, Otto gave this copy to several friends and relatives to read. One of them, Kurt Baschwitz, a professor of public relations and mass psychology, urged Otto to publish the diary. It was, he said, "the most moving document about that time I know, and a literary masterpiece as well." Otto hesitated at first. For one thing, he thought the letters of an adolescent girl too personal to publish. Also, though Anne had made it plain that she wanted to become a famous writer, she had also made it clear that she wanted to keep her diary to herself. But finally he decided that publication was what Anne would have wanted.

Finding a publisher proved more difficult than he had anticipated. Only after a well-known Dutch historian, Jan Romein, had praised the diary in a brief article on the front page of the Dutch daily newspaper *Het Parool* on April 3, 1946, did publishers begin to show an interest. The Contact publishing house got the contract, and in March 1947 the first Dutch edition appeared with the title *Het Achterhuis* ("The House Behind") that Anne had originally planned to use for her novel. German and French translations followed in 1950, and the first American edition appeared in 1952 under the title *Anne Frank: The Diary of a Young Girl.* The diary became a best seller when it was adapted for the stage and performed throughout the world. From the start, critics expressed reservations about the play's tendency to sentimentalize and to banalize the sufferings of the Holocaust's victims.

The first dramatization, written by the American author Meyer Levin, did not find a producer. Otto Frank, too, had his reservations about Levin's work and was supported in this by the judgment of his New York friend Nathan Straus Jr.: "The theme of Anne's diary seems to me a universal one," Straus wrote. "The fact that it was written by a Jewish girl is a very fine thing for any Jew. But so far as the world is concerned, it would seem to me a distinct advantage if the play were written by a non-Jew. In the first place that would emphasize the universality of the theme. In the second place, there is, to my mind, little doubt but that the play would be much more readily accepted on its merits if it were written by a non-Jew."

Otto was not much happier at first with the second dramatization, written by Frances Goodrich and Albert Hackett. Only after the couple's reworking of the script had dragged on for two years did Otto give it his approval. The play premiered in New York on October 5, 1955, and soon garnered a Pulitzer Prize. Otto Frank did not see any of the performances.

In late August 1956, the European premiere took place in Göteborg, and the play toured in German-speaking countries later that year. Next came a film version directed by George Stevens and starring Millie Perkins and Joseph Schildkraut.

In the following decades, as the commercial success of Anne's story continued to grow, doubts about the authenticity of the text began to crop up. Deniers of the Holocaust were particularly ready to declare the text a fake. (It had still not become public knowledge that there were several diaries and two versions derived from them.) In the late fifties, for instance, a Lübeck secondary-school teacher named Lothar Stielau voiced his doubts. In 1975, the historian David Irving claimed the diary was not genuine, and from 1978 on a literature professor, Robert Faurisson, attacked both the work and Otto Frank, who did not hesitate to sue him for libel. Although dissemination of Faurisson's work is against the law, attacks on the diary continue to this day; they are investigated now as incitement to hate crimes.

In 1980, the state court of Hamburg commissioned the federal criminal police office (*Bundeskriminalamt*) in Wiesbaden to confirm the authenticity of the diaries and refute the accusations of a group of neo-Nazis. In support of this effort, Otto Frank was to turn over all the documents in Anne's handwriting that he had. Cooperative as the now elderly Otto Frank had otherwise shown himself to be, he was still not ready to share with the public Anne's as yet unpublished entry of February 8, 1944, in which she reflected on her parents' marital relationship and which she retained in the diary revisions she wrote on blue onionskin paper, thus emphasizing the importance of this passage to her.

Otto Frank could not make this passage from the original version A of the diary disappear, because it was written on bound pages. But he did make the presumably final text of the passage disappear from version B. Destroying it would have been a simple and permanent solution to his problem, but for whatever reasons, doing that was out of the question for him. Along with several versions of the introduction to the diary, Otto gave these pages for safekeeping to Cor Suijk, who was the financial director of the Anne Frank Foundation in Amsterdam at the time. Otto then seems to have assured the federal criminal police office that he did not have any further documents in Anne's hand in his possession.

The federal criminal police office confirmed the authenticity of the diaries but made various ambiguous statements that gave rise to a myth about diary entries made with a ballpoint pen, a myth that the newspaper *Der Spiegel* unfortunately spread further. Rumors about these alleged ballpoint entries circulate to this day. Because a ballpoint pen could have been used only after the war—so the rumors maintain—the diary must therefore be a fake. These claims are untrue, misleading, and easy to disprove. The ballpoint writing that the police office mentioned in its statements was not in Anne's diary, but on two separate sheets of paper found inside it—and these pages were notes made by the Hamburg graphologist Dorothea Ockelmann in 1959–60, when she had examined the diary as an expert witness for an earlier legal case that centered on the diary's authenticity. Ockelmann's son, also a handwriting expert, confirmed this again in 1987.

Scholars at the Netherlands Institute for War Documentation

(NIOD) in Amsterdam did a comparative study of versions A, B, and C to trace the changes that had gone into the published version of the diary and to provide further evidence for the authenticity of Anne's texts. Version C is the text that Otto and Ab Cauvern had jointly edited. The results of the study were first published in 1986 as the "complete, critical, annotated edition" of the diaries. When the publishers wanted to include in this edition the entry of February 8, 1944, as it appears in version A, Otto's living relatives—his second wife, Fritzi, and his nephew Buddy Elias—protested. Anne's commentary on her parents' marriage was not only unkind but also untrue. Furthermore, they claimed, following Otto's line of argument, that Anne had realized this herself three months later. That explained why the passage did not appear in version B. Unaware that this passage did exist in a B version, the NIOD scholars acceded to the relatives' wishes and explained in a footnote to version A that "in the 47 lines [actually 74 lines] omitted here Anne Frank gave an extremely unkind and partly unfair picture of her parents' marriage. "At the request of the Frank family this passage has been deleted."

In 1997 Cor Suijk decided to let me see the pages that had been kept secret until then. Suijk regarded himself as their owner and claimed to be acting on Otto Frank's instructions to release them only when he and his second wife, Fritzi, could no longer be confronted with them.

I informed the Anne Frank Fonds (Fund) in Basel of the existence of the five pages and requested its cooperation in publishing them. The Fonds declined, claiming that Suijk's statements were not credible: Otto Frank had not left any of his daughter's original pages even to his closest relatives. The Fonds worried, too, that news of previously unknown pages of the diary could encourage Holocaust deniers to again question the authenticity of Anne's work. In 2001, the Fonds itself finally published the lines worldwide in new editions of the diary.

The overly negative picture of the mother-daughter relationship that had been in circulation for years was finally set aright, for Anne's entry is not only a portrait of a marriage of convenience but also a first step in a daughter's growing understanding for her mother. There is no doubt that at the time of this diary entry the relationship between Anne and Edith was at a turning point. It was beginning to develop and become deeper.

In the meantime, Cor Suijk came to an understanding with NIOD, which laid claim to the original pages on the basis of Otto Frank's will. Suijk gave up the pages, and in return the Dutch Ministry for Education, Culture, and Scholarship contributed $300,000 to Suijk's American "Contemporary Holocaust Education Foundation."

The 2001 edition of the diary is based on the so-called final edition of 1991 that Otto's beneficiary, the Anne Frank Fonds in Basel, commissioned the writer and translator Mirjam Pressler to prepare. Pressler knows the various versions of Anne's diaries well. In the 1980s, she translated the complete critical, annotated edition into German. For the 1991 edition, she added to Otto's 1947 version many passages from Anne's first version that Otto had omitted. What the Anne Frank Fonds had in mind was an easily accessible text for a wide audience of young readers. The Fonds's response to critics of this edition was that the additions made to the content were appropriate for contemporary readers and made no scholarly demands of them. The literary scholar Laureen Nussbaum is one of those critics. She regretted, for instance, that the Pressler edition, "without any commentary to that effect, mixed together passages from Anne's carefully revised version B with spontaneous, less considered entries from version A." This conflation, Nussbaum thought, might well satisfy readers' appetites for the sensational but ran counter to Anne's true literary concept. David Barnouw, a historian and a coeditor of the critical edition of the diaries, complained about this commercialization of the diary and the failed effort to extend the copyright to Anne's work. The Fonds's version has been translated into about seventy languages and remains a best seller in many countries.

Annual royalties up to 80,000 Swiss francs, Otto stipulated, were to be shared by his immediate relatives during their lifetimes. Any income exceeding that amount was to go to the Anne Frank Fonds to give to causes it deemed most appropriate. "We are a charitable organization," the Fonds emphasizes. It does not spell out in detail how much it donates annually but refers to the strict regulations imposed by Swiss law governing charitable donations. The largest portion of the royalty income and the yield from the Fonds's assets goes to projects dedicated to fighting racism and anti-Semitism, assisting children, and fostering international understanding. Regular support also goes to research projects, and the Fonds is increasingly intent not simply on supporting projects financially but also on enlisting them in cooperative enterprises. Project Aladdin is a successful example of this approach: one of its initiatives, made possible with financial aid from the Fonds, is the diary's translation into Arabic, Persian, and Turkish editions available for free on the Internet.

The Anne Frank Fonds is, then, in the process of redefining itself. Protecting Anne Frank and her work from excessive commercialization, in accordance with Otto Frank's wishes, is now more than ever central to its mission. Consequently, the Fonds decided in 2012 to join with the Jewish Museum in Frankfurt to found—as a counterweight to the Anne Frank House in Amsterdam—the Frank Family Center with a permanent exhibit, archives, and a pedagogical center. A further concern for the Fonds is that, assuming that current copyright law does not change, Anne Frank's writings, which UNESCO in 2009 included in its Memory of the World Register of documents of "outstanding universal value," will pass into the public domain in most European countries on January 1, 2016.

LUCIA VAN DIJK, under the influence of her grandmother, an adamant opponent of the Nazi regime, resigned from the Jeugdstorm toward the end of 1942. Her father had already quit the party by August of that year. He died in 1944. But Lucia's mother remained true to the NSB to the bitter end. When a neighbor, a party member herself, advised Lucia's mother in September 1944 to flee to Austria, as many other Dutch Nazi sympathizers had, she refused. She proudly declared that her conscience was clear. She had never applied for supplementary ration coupons, which were routinely given to NSB members, nor had she tried to benefit in any other way from her party membership. So she assumed she had nothing to fear, and in fact, unlike the great majority of Dutch Nazis, she was not arrested or punished after the war.

Lucia van Dijk completed her secondary schooling by attending night school in the late 1940s and worked first as a stenographer, then as an executive secretary for a major printing firm. This friend of Anne's from the Montessori school married in 1955 and had two sons. She lived in Amsterdam, widowed, until her death in January 2000.

BERND "BUDDY" ELIAS, Anne's cousin, four years older than she, was drawn to the theater even during the war years, and he studied acting in Basel and Zurich. Although he performed on the legitimate stage in Zurich and elsewhere, his agility and limberness made him a great success as a clown on skates. From 1947 on, he appeared first in an English ice revue, then in a Danish one. In 1949, he was discovered by Holiday on Ice and toured the world for some eleven years before returning to the legitimate theater in 1961. During a 1963 engagement at the state theater in Tübingen, he met his future wife, an Austrian actress named Gerti Wiedner. He appeared in Basel, Zurich, Bremen, and Mannheim before becoming a member of the Berlin-based Freie Volksbühne company in 1974. He later made guest appearances at various theaters and played often in movies and on television.

Buddy's mother, Helene, died in October 1986. A few months before her death, Buddy and his wife returned to Basel, and they have been living in his childhood home at 11 Herbstgasse ever since. Until 2001, Gerti continued to run the antique business that Helene Elias started during the war. When Otto Frank established the Anne Frank Fonds, he asked Buddy Elias to be a member of its board, and in 1996, Buddy became chairman of the foundation while continuing to work in the theater. Since 2007, he has awarded annually, on Margot Frank's birthday and in the name of the foundation, a grant for research on subjects related to Anne Frank, the so-called Margot Frank Stipendium. In 2012, he received an honorary award from the city of Frankfurt. Buddy and Gerti Elias have two sons, Patrick and Oliver, both of whom are actors.

KÄTHE "KITTY" EGYEDI, along with her parents and her brother, numbered among the relatively few people who survived Theresienstadt. Of the 140,000 Jews who were deported to the ghettolike camp in northern Czechoslovakia, 118,000 died. Back in Amsterdam, the psychic wounds the sixteen-year-old had suffered were given little attention; she had to adapt quickly to a "normal" life. Anne's friend left public school and studied with private tutors to take the exams that qualified her to study at university. Kitty went to dental school and then, like her father, practiced dentistry.

Otto Frank remained in touch with Kitty after the war. He assumed—mistakenly, as we now know—that Anne had had Kitty in mind when she named her fictitious correspondent "Kitty" in her diary. Concerned that she would find herself in the public eye, this disciple of Spinoza decided to remain anonymous. In no way did she, a survivor, want to bask in the worldwide fame of her dead friend Anne. But through new media, her full name and residence have in the meantime become public knowledge. She is married, has two children, and lives in Bloemendaal.

After Otto Frank went into hiding, his mother, **ALICE STERN FRANK,** continued to receive encoded reports about him through Johannes Kleiman. Kleiman's letters and cards let her know that Otto and his family were well. But the last note she received came in May 1944: "We lack nothing of importance." Almost a year later, shortly after the end of the war in Europe, Alice Frank tried to resume contact with Kleiman. "We understand that it is possible now for us to be in touch again," she wrote to him on May 20, 1945, "and if you are able to do so, please let my children know how terribly worried about them I am."

Until the end of May 1945, the branch of the Frank family in Basel had no idea what had happened to Otto and his family. The numerous letters Otto had written after his liberation in January took five months to reach Basel. The first sign of life from him to reach his relatives was a short telegram he sent from Marseilles on May 27—ARRIVÉ BONNE SANTÉ MARSEILLE PARTONS PARIS. BAISER. OTTO FRANK—a message that proved subject to misinterpretation.

"We completely misunderstood your first telegram and read *partons* to mean that you would all be leaving for Paris together, when in reality *partons* was just a reference to the train you would take. What a dreadful mistake!" Alice Frank wrote to Otto on June 19 after she had finally received a letter he had written in March telling her of Edith's death. "To know that you are alone in your mourning for Edith and still without news of your beloved children is the most terrible experience I have had to bear in a life that has often been very hard," she wrote, stunned by the death of her daughter-in-law, "who was always such a staunch support for you through thick and thin and for the children a devoted mother and the best of friends." At this point, she still hoped that Anne and Margot might return from the concentration camp. "We have requested the International Red Cross in Geneva and the local consulate to initiate a search." But in July 1945 she learned from Otto that her granddaughters, too, had died. "The facts are so dreadful, and no words are capable of expressing what I feel," she wrote to Otto on August 4, 1945, offering what little consolation she could. "Perhaps I can ask later what I would like to know about Edith. That is all I can hope and wish for now that all else would be in vain and you seem to be holding up bravely. If only I could be with you, but I doubt that I could find any way to express my great anguish. All I could do is lean my head on your shoulder and cry."

In the following years, Otto Frank visited his mother often, and in 1952 he finally settled permanently in Basel. Alice Frank died there on March 20, 1953, at the age of eighty-seven.

Reports from refugees about the persecution of homosexuals and Jews prompted **JEAN-MICHEL FRANK** to leave Paris in 1940. By way of Lisbon, he emigrated to Buenos Aires, where this furniture designer with a worldwide reputation remained only briefly, even though—thanks to the connections of Ignacio Pirovano, director of the Museum of Decorative Arts—he quickly found a circle of affluent clients. Once he received an entry permit to the United States, he immediately moved to New York, where he taught at the School of Fine and Applied Arts and found ready access to society. On March 8, 1941, like his father, he committed suicide.

After his liberation from Auschwitz, **OTTO HEINRICH FRANK** was sent first to Kattowitz, where Adam and Zofia Kukulski took him into their home. "I have never forgotten the two of you," Otto wrote later in one of his many letters to this Polish couple, "and I've always recalled with gratitude how you spoke to me on the street and welcomed me into your home at a time when no one had much to spare." They became friends Otto would stay in close touch with for many decades.

From Kattowitz he was taken to Odessa by way of Czernowitz and then traveled by ship through the Dardanelles and on to France. He arrived in Marseilles toward the end of May and finally reached Amsterdam on June 3, 1945. At the end of March, he had run into Rosa de Winter, whom he had first met in Westerbork, and she told him of Edith's death. "I am in good health and am holding up well despite the sad news of my wife's death," Otto wrote to his relatives in Basel on March 31, 1945. "If only I can get my children back!"

Weeks of anxiety followed. "There is never news from Russian-occupied territory," Otto complained to his sister, Leni, and his brother-in-law Erich on June 21, 1945, "and that is why I cannot get any news about the children in case they are in Germany. Up to now I was convinced I would see them return but now I begin to doubt." Otto went to his office every day, and the little problems he had to deal with there provided him with at least some temporary distraction from his worries. "I can't think how I can go on without the children, having also lost Edith."

But on July 18 or 19, 1945, Otto finally discovered that his daughters had died in Bergen-Belsen. "The only consolation is the short years of happiness you gave to each other," Robert Frank wrote to his brother. Robert had spent the war years in London. "They don't suffer anymore, but your lot is to carry on in life and not to despair and to cherish the remembrance of your dear ones. We admire you greatly for the way you can think and act without a word of bitterness or hatred after all you have been through."

Otto opened his heart to his cousin Milly: "Of course I know that I shall never get over it and miss the children far more than Edith. It was the hope and the future and that counts more than the present life," he wrote in English.

Otto slowly learned to live with his grief. "There is no point in wasting away in mourning, no point in brooding," he wrote. "We have to go on living, go on building. We don't want to forget, but we mustn't let our memories lead us into negativism." And, nine months later: "I . . . don't brood, don't give myself over to living in the past. If we are to live, we have to keep looking to the future," Otto wrote, occasionally noting, to his astonishment, how well he was holding up. "I behave surprisingly calm. There is so much misery around me that I try to help where I can. I feel no bitterness, because I saw so much misery, lived in wretchedness and meet all over the same situation. So I cannot say: Why me? Out of the more than 100,000 Jews who were deported about 2,000 returned as yet."

One source of support for Otto was the Amsterdam Reform congregation that he helped found after the war and of which he remained a member until his death, even though he was never observant.

He received support, too, from relatives and friends all over the world. He returned to Amsterdam with nothing but the clothes on his back. "I lost all I ever had," he wrote to America. "There is nothing to buy and I lack of everything," he wrote to his brother. "I borrowed most of what I wear."

Unlike many other survivors, Otto got help—material and otherwise—from many sides. After his return he lived rent-free with Jan and Miep Gies, at first at 120 Hunzerstraat, later at 65 Jekerstraat. Julius and Walter Holländer sent him money and packages from the United States; his brother Robert and the family of his cousin Milly Stanfield sent him aid from London. In October 1945, Nathan Straus, his friend from his university years, whom he still called Charley, sent him five hundred dollars. Otto used some of the money for himself but gave the rest to other survivors, especially orphaned children like Hannah and Gabi Goslar. "Everything is scarce here and of bad quality," he wrote in English to Julius and Walter on August 20, 1945. "Underwear I received from London now. Of course I would like to help my people here who have no relations. We don't get any meat except the tins 'meat and vegetables' and very little butter. Tea and coffee still is 'surrogate,' milk we get, but not enough, so if there is milk powder it is welcome."

Otto immediately attempted to reestablish himself professionally. "We are trying to work, but it is difficult because we have hardly any raw materials to work with," he wrote to his sister and brother-in-law in June 1945. The business took in so little money over several months that Otto fell behind with salaries and had to ask his employees like Miep to be patient. In the following years, he struggled to find new sources of income. "I'm trying to develop some import-export business, but just about everything I attempt runs aground on currency regulations and other problems in various countries," he wrote to his friend Joseph Süttendorf in June 1947, when he was still stateless. "I don't have much experience in textiles and work more in foodstuffs and chemicals. . . . I have talked with a friend about importing suspenders and other such clothing accessories." Otto did not receive Dutch citizenship until November 22, 1949.

Otto Frank (center) with the helpers Miep Gies, Johannes Kleiman, Victor Kugler, and Bep Voskuijl, postwar photo

On November 10, 1953, Otto Frank married Elfriede "Fritzi" Markovits Geiringer, a native of Vienna whom he had met on his way back from Auschwitz to Holland. Her husband, Erich, died on January 31, 1945, in Mauthausen. Her son, Heinz, presumably died on a death march from Mauthausen back to Germany. The date of his death is recorded as May 10, 1945.

Before the Geiringers were deported, they, too, had lived on Amsterdam's Merwedeplein. The Franks and Geiringers had never met. Their children probably knew one another by sight but had not become close friends. In any case, it was said to have been Fritzi's daughter, Eva, who recognized Otto Frank on the train to Odessa and introduced him to her mother.

Otto and his second wife lived at 11 Herbstgasse with Otto's relatives for seven years before settling in Birsfelden on the outskirts of Basel. They often spent their summer months in Beckenried on Lake Lucerne. From both residences, they spread the message of Otto's daughter Anne. They had made it a principle to reply to every letter they received from readers of the diary, and thousands of letters came. Anne's diaries provided them with a fulfilled "second life." On January 24, 1963, Otto and Fritzi Frank set up the Anne Frank Fonds (AFF), a charitable foundation with offices in Basel. Otto named the foundation his sole beneficiary.

On the occasion of Otto's ninetieth birthday, Queen Beatrix awarded him the Order of Orange-Nassau. Otto had not been feeling well for quite a while. "I'm not really ill physically but 'always tired,' inactive, and listless. And all food is repugnant to me," he wrote to his cousin Milly. "Not a pleasant situation, and hard for Fritzi, too." He died at ninety-one on August 19, 1980.

After Otto's death, the copyright in Anne's diaries and all the royalties from the book, the play, the film, and any radio or television presentations devolved on the Anne Frank Fonds. Otto willed the original diaries to the Netherlands Institute for War Documentation (NIOD). To each of his closest relatives, he left bequests amounting to six figures in Swiss francs. Among all the other individuals and organizations named in his will—the liberal Jewish congregation in Amsterdam, the Pestalozzi village in Trogen, the friends of the Swiss children's village Kiriath Yearim, the Hadassah National Youth Aliya Committee in New York, Jan and Miep Gies, and Bep Voskuijl—he divided a total of about 30,000 francs.

Annual royalties up to the amount of 80,000 francs, Otto had stipulated, were to be shared by his immediate relatives for their lifetimes. Any income above that amount was to go to the Anne Frank Fonds to give to causes it deemed most appropriate.

In the summer of 1942, only a few weeks after her best friend Margot Frank had been summoned for labor service, **JETTEKE FRIJDA** received a similar summons. Obeying the summons was out of the question. She went into hiding and survived the war.

"The child is left here almost all alone," Otto Frank wrote to his mother at the end of 1945. Her mother had managed to escape to Switzerland shortly after the Germans occupied Holland. Her father, Herman Frijda, a respected professor of economics who had been one of the few opponents of the Jewish Council since its inception, was deported and murdered in Auschwitz on October 3, 1944. Jetteke learned from the newspapers that her older brother Leo Herman, a medical student and dedicated resistance fighter, had been executed by the Nazis. In Amsterdam, where she lives now, a street has been named after him.

Jetteke became a librarian, then a nurse specializing in social work and home care. Now, though of retirement age, she continues to teach and to care for the elderly.

After their friends were arrested, **JAN AND MIEP GIES** made every effort to rescue them. On Monday, August 7, 1944, Miep found the courage to go to Euterpestraat and confront SS Oberscharführer Karl Josef Silberbauer. She discreetly offered him money, which a representative of Opekta was willing to provide, if he would arrange for the release of the prisoners, but he rejected her offer and sent her on to his boss. Miep entered his office to find him listening to an enemy radio station, and she quickly fled.

A few days later the secret annex was "pulsed." "To puls" was a verb the Dutch had coined because moving vans from the firm of Abraham Puls were customarily sent to strip the homes of deported Jews of their furnishings. In the employ of the Nazi occupation forces, the furniture movers took everything that seemed of value to them. The goods were then sent to Germany, where they were passed on to German citizens—party members first and foremost—whose homes had been bombed out.

Shortly before the movers came, Miep had sent the warehouse foreman, Willem van Maaren, up to the annex once more to pick up and bring to her all the loose diary pages still on the floor. She put them in her desk drawer along with Anne's other writings. If Miep had read the diaries, she said later, she would have had to destroy them. There was too much in them that would have incriminated her and the other helpers in the Nazis' eyes.

In the winter of 1944–45, living conditions in Amsterdam became even more difficult. There were shortages of basic necessities: food staples, fuel, clothing, bath and laundry soaps. Warm water was a luxury; power plants were no longer generating electricity. Anything that could be burned went into heater stoves. Like many other city dwellers, Miep went out into the country to find food. Starving people gave their last savings or their heirloom jewelry for a handful of food. Their hopes that the war would soon end were frustrated. The Canadian Army did not enter Amsterdam until after the German surrender on May 8, 1945, and even after the war was over, it took a long time for things to return to normal in Holland. In August 1945, for example, cooking gas was still available for only an hour a day, and the streetcars ran only from seven to nine in the morning and from four to six in the afternoon.

Miep took charge of Opekta and Pectacon until Kleiman's release in September 1944. But in May 1947 she resigned from her job. She had three men to look after now, and that was work enough. She cooked, washed, and ironed not only for her husband but also for Otto Frank, who had been living with Jan and her in their Hunzestraat apartment since his return from Auschwitz. "I never eat at a restaurant, she [Miep] does the laundry as there are no laundryshops working. I am cared for in every respect," Otto wrote to his relatives. And from November 1946 on, she also cared for Otto's old friend Ab Cauvern. Jan, Miep, and Otto moved into his apartment at 65 Jekerstraat about four months after the death of Ab's wife, Isa.

In mid-1950—shortly after Ab moved to Hilversum—Miep had still another person to care for: on July 13, at age forty-one, she gave birth to a son, Paul. The family had to make do with Jan's modest civil-service salary, although Otto Frank paid a fourth of the food budget. "All these people who helped us so unselfishly despite all the dangers are still a great support to me," Otto wrote to his relatives in Basel.

In both 1948 and 1963–64, Miep Gies was one of the most important witnesses in the investigation into the question of who betrayed the Franks. Van Maaren had tried to discredit her to the Dutch police with all sorts of outrageous accusations, claiming that she had been having an affair not only with her employer but also with a German officer. He said that she had even flirted with SS Oberscharführer Karl Silberbauer. Jan's reaction: Miep, how did you find the time for all that! Otto Frank's response was that if Miep's name was on the list of suspects, then the police should add his own name to it. There was no one in whom he placed greater trust than Jan and Miep. After Otto moved to Switzerland in 1952–53, the Gies family visited him regularly, saving up all year long to be able to make these trips.

A few years before his death, Otto promised Miep that he

would leave her son, Paul, a "significant" amount of money. Anne's diary had become a worldwide best seller, and Otto's assets amounted to several million Swiss francs. In his will he ended up giving the woman who had saved the diary 10,000 guilders, or the equivalent of about 6,000 dollars today.

In the mid-1980s, an American writer, Alison Leslie Gold, persuaded Miep to collaborate on a book that proved a great success. *Anne Frank Remembered* appeared in the United States in 1987, then shortly afterward in Holland and Germany. It was reissued in 2009 on the occasion of Miep's hundredth birthday. The book also pays homage to Jan Gies, who always preferred to stay in the background. He didn't even tell his son about the war and his role in the resistance. Jan Gies died on January 26, 1993, in Amsterdam.

In the years since, Miep has been frequently honored for the help she gave the Franks. On November 3, 1994, the German ambassador in The Hague awarded her the Order of Merit of the Federal Republic of Germany. On March 17, 1995, Queen Beatrix of the Netherlands appointed her a knight of the Order of Orange-Nassau, and in that same year, she received the highest honor granted by the Commission for the Righteous of the Yad Vashem memorial in Jerusalem. In addition, she was honored with the Raoul Wallenberg Award and the Cross of Honor for her service to the Republic of Austria.

In the spring of 1996, Miep and the South African filmmaker Jon Blair jointly accepted an Academy Award for the documentary film *Anne Frank Remembered.* In her final years, she lived unassisted and mentally alert in her apartment in Hoorn, about an hour from Amsterdam. In early January 2010, she fell and injured her neck. She died a few days later, on January 11.

WERNER GOLDSCHMIDT, the Franks' tenant, remained registered at the Merwedeplein apartment until mid-December 1942.

On August 5 he had married his second wife, Eva Schwarzschild, a seamstress from Cologne. The couple moved often after that, and because Goldschmidt took furnishings with him whenever he moved from one sublet room to the next, his relatives started calling him "the Pulser" after the moving firm of Abraham Puls that cleared out the homes of deported Jews. So Anne Frank was right in her diary when she suspected Goldschmidt of having profited from the Franks' possessions.

Goldschmidt worked for the Jewish old people's home, his wife, Eva, for the Jewish Council (Joodse Raad). For a while, their employment kept them from being deported. "When he [Goldschmidt] was about to be arrested in the spring of 1943," Eva Schwarzschild reported later, "he went into hiding, just as I had done. I didn't see my husband during my time in hiding. I was sent to Bergen-Belsen in November 1943 when my hiding place was discovered." Werner Goldschmidt, too, was arrested—apparently a little less than three weeks after the Franks—and taken to Westerbork on August 21, 1944. It remains unclear why he was not treated as a so-called criminal Jew, like the Franks, and, like them, deported to Auschwitz. Instead he was deported to Theresienstadt on September 4, 1944. At the end of September he was sent to Bergen-Belsen, where he died on February 5, 1945. He had not seen his wife again. She belonged to that favored minority of exchange Jews who were allowed to emigrate to Israel in June 1944.

HANNELI GOSLAR survived fourteen months in Bergen-Belsen. When British troops were nearing the camp, the camp command decided to assemble three trains to transfer 6,800 prisoners, all of them so-called exchange Jews, to Theresienstadt, perhaps intending to use them as hostages later. On the night of April 10–11, 1945, five days before the camp was liberated, the last of these trains departed, carrying 2,400 prisoners. On it were Hannah and her four-and-a-half-year-old sister, Gabi, who had been suffering from a serious ear infection for many months.

The train proceeded through central Germany for nearly two weeks, often attacked by low-flying aircraft. Sheets and other white cloths were tied onto the cars in hopes of warding off further attacks. More than 550 prisoners died, victims of starvation, malnutrition, and the catastrophically inadequate hygienic conditions.

On April 23, advancing Red Army troops near the Brandenburg village of Tröbitz came upon the "lost train," as it has come to be called. Hannah Goslar was so weak and ill that she slept through the capture of the train's SS guards. When she woke up, the doors of the car were standing open. Anyone who had been able to walk had already left the train.

For weeks the two sisters, the sole survivors of their immediate family, sat stuck in the Tröbitz area until the Americans took them to Maastricht by way of Leipzig on June 15, 1945. But their sufferings were still not over. Seriously ill with tuberculosis, Hanneli could not return to Amsterdam but had to remain in a Maastricht clinic for several months. Otto Frank visited her there, probably in August 1945. From that day on, he cared for the Goslar sisters like a father; their official residence was temporarily registered as the Hunzestraat apartment of the Gies family.

Hanneli received several more weeks of treatment in an Amsterdam hospital before Otto Frank sent her and Gabi to Zurich by plane on December 5, 1945. The girls had an uncle living there, and in Switzerland Hanneli was initially placed in a sanatorium. Finally, though, she and Gabi were taken in by a Dutch family with seven children living in Basel. Anne's friend, who had missed three years of school by now, finished her schooling in Basel, always with a concrete goal in mind: "I hope to go to Palestine and study pediatric nursing," this religious young woman wrote to her school friend Iet Swillens on August 4, 1946. In 1947, she and Gabi emigrated to Jerusalem. Hanneli became a nurse, married the publisher Walter Pick, and had three children. Hannah Goslar Pick still lives in Jerusalem. She has ten grandchildren and, at present, eight great-grandchildren.

GEZINUS GRINGHUIS, NSB member 105036, was employed by the Amsterdam Bureau for Jewish Affairs, an arm of the German security service that worked with Jewish SD informants. He was arrested on May 8, 1945, and less than two years later condemned to death by a special court in The Hague. Witnesses confirmed, among other things, that Gringhuis had mistreated his victims and made considerable amounts of money stealing Jewish property. Six months later, his death sentence was

Gezinus Gringhuis

commuted to life in prison. In October 1953, he submitted his first appeal for pardon. In July 1957, his sentence was reduced to twenty years, and in October 1957, in view of his increasingly confused mental condition, he was transferred from prison to a minimum-security facility. Finally, in September 1958, he was released.

The 263 Prinsengracht case was one of his last actions against hidden Jews. In September 1944, he was temporarily assigned to the security police in Groningen. His final post until the end of the war was in the SD department for economic crime. Gringuis died on November 5, 1975, in Windschoten.

WILLEM GROOTENDORST, NSB member 155414, was arrested, like Gringuis, on May 8, 1945. At his trial two years later, he was sentenced to life in prison. In 1952, his sentence was reduced to eighteen years, and on May 6, 1955, the tenth anniversary of Holland's liberation, he was pardoned. A year later, he was released from prison.

In his defense, this trained police officer and father of two daughters had argued that he could no more refuse the party than he could his assignment to the Bureau for Jewish Affairs. He worked there from March 1943 until the summer of 1944 as a police investigator and—like Gringuis—regularly collected bounties for turning in Jews.

In September 1944, Grootendorst was assigned to espionage duties against resistance fighters in Zundern and then in Apeldoorn. Shortly before the end of the war, he was called back to Amsterdam.

In January 1964, Grootendorst, who had an office job at the time, was called as a witness in the interrogation of Karl Josef Silberbauer. He claimed he could recall neither his irrefutably documented work with Silberbauer nor the raid of August 4, 1944, on 263 Prinsengracht. He spent his last years in a Utrecht old people's home and died there on July 2, 1973.

Willem Grootendorst

LAMMERT HARTOG, employed, according to his own statements, "from about the spring of 1944 to August of that same year" as a warehouse worker for Opekta, was interrogated on March 20, 1948, in connection with the betrayal of the eight Jews hidden at 263 Prinsengracht. It had not escaped his attention, he said, that a baker delivered large quantities of bread to the building and that a greengrocer brought a lot of vegetables, but he never suspected the presence of fugitives there "until van Maaren . . . told me about fourteen days before the Jews were taken away that Jews were hidden in the building." Regarding the actual arrest he said, "I was struck by the fact that the investigators did not search for the hidden Jews but were fully informed about the situation."

This statement should have alerted the interrogators, for Johannes Kleiman had stated that when the police arrived on the morning of August 4, 1944, Hartog disappeared at the first opportunity. He should have been pressed to explain how he could nonetheless have known how the police had proceeded. But by the time the police reopened the investigation in 1963, Lammert Hartog could no longer be questioned. He had died on March 6, 1959.

On March 18, 1948, Hartog's wife, **LENA VAN BLADEREN HARTOG,** appeared before the Political Investigation Branch of the Amsterdam police in connection with the investigation into the betrayal of the eight hidden Jews and the interrogation of the main suspect, Willem van Maaren. At that time Lena and Lammert's son Klaas was reported as missing. He had voluntarily worked for the German navy since August 22, 1944. His death from a shot to the head in early May 1945 was not confirmed until 1952.

"It must have been sometime in August 1944 that my husband came home upset and told me that about eight Jews had been arrested in that building," the then fifty-year-old woman stated. "Before that, my husband had mentioned that a baker was delivering large quantities of bread to the building." Lena Hartog apparently wanted to create the impression that she had known nothing about the hidden Jews until they were arrested. "Whether the bread was intended for hidden Jews or not, we did not know. My husband and I never talked about that," she claimed.

During this interrogation, she withheld from the uniformed police the fact that before the arrest she had worked regularly at 263 Prinsengracht as a cleaning woman. And of course she also failed to mention that neither she nor her husband ever set foot in 263 Prinsengracht again after August 4, 1944. Nor did she mention that a few weeks before the arrest she had raised the subject of the hidden Jews with Bep Voskuijl. Bep, who might have been able to help clear up the case, was not questioned in 1948.

Although Anna van Wijk Genot, whose husband, Petrus Genot, worked for Johannes Kleiman's brother, distinctly recalled that Lena Hartog spoke to her about the hidden Jews several weeks before the arrest, probably in June 1944 (Anna Genot also stated this to the police on March 10, 1948), Lena Hartog claimed that the conversation did not take place until after August 4, 1944. "I remember very well that I spoke with Mrs. Genot about these Jews once, but I am certain that the Jews had already been taken away by that time."

The police did not consider Lena van Bladeren Hartog a suspect, probably because they ignored her obvious obfuscations, which could have been motivated by fear or by her worry that her gossip about the hidden Jews had done real harm. On June 10, 1963, a few months before the police reopened the case, Lena van Bladeren Hartog died in Veenendaal.

After fleeing Germany in February 1937, **IRENE HOLLÄNDER** settled in Lima. Six months later, Edith Frank's favorite cousin remarried, primarily, it seems, to ensure that her daughters, Ursula and Dorothée, would be well provided for. Her second husband, Siegfried Holzer, was a doctor, a native of Berlin, and, like Irene, a refugee.

Otto Frank reestablished contact with Irene after a long period of silence. "I remain interested in everyone we knew in the past and everyone who, like you, was so close to Edith," he wrote to her on June 13, 1958. "I am especially happy to know that you are all well and have been so successful in building new lives for yourselves."

In the 1960s, Irene and her family moved to the United States. She survived her elder daughter, Ursula, by three years and died on March 19, 1974, in Boston. Her younger daughter, Dorothée Fraifeld Jenkins-Kronheim, lives in the United States and has two sons.

JULIUS AND WALTER HOLLÄNDER became U.S. citizens on November 13, 1944. Even after the war, they barely managed to scrape by as factory workers and lived in very modest circumstances in Leominster, Massachusetts. In late June 1945, an airmail letter from Alice Stern Frank and a telegram from Herbert Frank informed them of Edith Frank's death. For a few weeks after that, they continued to cling to the idea that Anne and Margot might have survived. "My last hope is that you will find the children. Walter and I will do everything for you. In case you will come to the U.S.A. we have the money saved for you three," Julius wrote to Otto on June 29, 1945.

But in August they learned that their nieces were dead. "We loved Margot and Anne as if they were our own children," the grieving Julius wrote. "Our life is empty now. Edith and the girls was all we had." Julius had been engaged briefly in the late 1920s but neither he nor his brother had ever married. Like many other refugees, Julius and Walter wrote in English and avoided using the German language.

Later, friends and relatives agreed that Julius never recovered from all he had suffered. "The older of the two is only the shell of his former self," Otto wrote in a letter of October 1, 1952, during a visit to the United States. "He is very depressed and nervous, and it pained me greatly to see him in this condition. His younger brother is much better."

In 1954, encouraged by Heinz Jacobowitz, the former administrative chief of their firm in Aachen, the brothers decided to apply for reparations under the Federal Republic of Germany's statute providing for compensation for losses suffered during the Nazi period. As often happened, the Holländer brothers' case dragged on in a long, painful, and degrading process. They had to compile minutely detailed lists of their economic and personal losses; the burden of proof was placed on the injured parties.

In mid-1955 Walter Holländer received his first rebuff from the Aachen district attorney's office: he was advised to drop his claim for compensation for "deprivation of freedom" because his detention in Sachsenhausen immediately after the November 1938 pogrom had been too brief to qualify him. Also, his internment in the Zeeburg refugee camp in Holland could not be regarded as a "National Socialist measure."

Losses sustained through "displacement from professional activity" had to be documented with detailed records of the family firm's income and expenses before expropriation. To establish "losses to property and assets sustained by abandonment of household goods," those losses, too, had to be documented in detail. What that meant was that the applicant had to specify the individual pieces of furniture abandoned, the kind of wood they were made of, and the resale value of each piece.

In June 1956, the German government came up with the cynical idea of reminding Germany's forced emigrants that they might have left some tax debts behind when they fled the country. "RE: The charging of outstanding tax debts or other public debts against reparation payments," read the notice Walter Holländer received. "According to section 21, paragraph 4, of the amendment to federal law of September 18, 1953, outstanding taxes and other debts owed the government can be subtracted from reparations payments even if these debts are already nullified under the statute of limitations. You are therefore requested to provide information as to whether and in what amounts any outstanding taxes or other debts exist in the name of Walter Hollander (formerly Holländer)." The Holländer brothers were unable to provide any detailed figures in their application. Along with their business and their real estate, they had also lost their firm's books.

In December 1956, Heinz Jacobowitz sent a letter to the Cologne attorney who was representing the Holländer brothers: "I was with Julius and Walter Holländer when they received the news after the war that their closest relatives had been exterminated. The experience was deeply distressing. I think it is safe to say that the Holländer brothers have never quite recovered from the blow. . . . Ever since this dreadful event, they have retired from life, as it were, and led a sad and pitiable existence. The injury done to their souls can never be 'made good.' But I am writing to you so that at least on a material level they receive some prompt reparation. I do not know if you were aware of these facts, but my assumption is that the Holländer brothers are too modest and retiring to have apprised you of them."

After two and a half years of exhausting legal arguments that met only with counterarguments, this letter may have finally helped secure for the brothers, at the end of December 1956, monthly pensions of 600 marks each for the duration of their lives. But in the meantime the health of both men had declined considerably. Julius suffered from rheumatism and had undergone a serious intestinal operation and a cataract operation on his right eye. Walter had emphysema. Neither of them could work anymore, but they would not retire, fearing they might sink into poverty or be unable to afford necessary medical treatment. They had, however, managed to lay away considerable savings. "They have a very good income," Heinz Jacobowitz wrote, "from their employment, their investments, their savings accounts, and their German pensions." Jacobowitz estimated their assets at $100,000 to $200,000.

"They reproach themselves for not having accomplished more," Otto Frank wrote in June 1958 to Edith's cousin Irene. "I have advised them to come to Europe for a while, really relax, and enjoy life a bit, but they no longer have the confidence. They have withered away in this backwater." The brothers warded off suggestions of this kind by saying they were no longer in the habit of spending money.

In 1963, they moved to New York, living in the rundown Sherman Square residential hotel at the corner of Broadway and Seventieth Street. On October 4, 1967, Julius died there when he fell into an elevator shaft. Walter inherited his brother's savings. "Walter's desperate loneliness is a source of great pain to me. The two brothers turned their backs on everybody and everything and became recluses," Otto wrote to Irene Holländer in January 1968.

"Now Walter is more alone than ever." Walter died in New York on September 19, 1968. Along with bequests of stock to some relatives, he left $25,000 to the Anne Frank Fonds and $5,000 to Selfhelp, an organization dedicated to assisting European Jewish refugees. The considerable remainder went to the United Jewish Appeal for the support of Jews in Europe and Israel and of Jewish emigrants to the United States.

KUNO LODEWIJK VAN DER HORST was still living with Jan and Miep Gies when the residents of the secret annex were arrested. Jan and Miep immediately urged him to find another hiding place. Their apartment in the Hunzestraat had become too dangerous for him. From then on, Kuno stayed in hiding—undisturbed—in Hilversum.

After the liberation of Holland, he moved to the United States, married his young love Henny, and joined his father's business. In 1935, Hendrik van der Horst had developed a chrome plating process that radically increased the durability of motors and other machinery. He was on a business trip in America when the United States entered the war. Returning to Hilversum was no longer an option for him, and he founded the business that still exists today under the name of United van der Horst, Ltd.

After the war, Kuno van der Horst maintained some contact with Miep Gies and Otto Frank. He died in Dallas, Texas, on May 17, 1968, at the age of forty-eight.

On the day the Franks, the van Pelses, and Fritz Pfeffer were arrested, **JOB JANSEN** seems to have been living in Winterswijk, near the German border. His job was to guard the properties of the German theater there. That month he was arrested for theft and jailed in Münster. After his release in February 1945, he was arrested again, this time by the Canadians, who had taken that area.

In 1946 Jansen was tried and convicted of "assisting the enemy in wartime." One of the charges against him, among others, was "the denunciation of the Jew O. H. Frank." Jansen was sentenced to four years and six months in prison, of which he probably served barely two and a half.

Otto Frank had been among those testifying against him. "He is the one who does the real dirty work," he told the political division of the criminal police on August 21, 1945, using much stronger language than was his custom. "I hope Mr. Jansen is already behind bars or . . . will be arrested." Jansen tried to exonerate himself: "If I were to stand before Mr. Frank, look him in the eye, and deny that I wrote that letter, he would surely believe me. I am no anti-Semite, and I have always respected Mr. Frank and considered him a person of high standing."

From at least June of 1941 Jansen had lived apart from his Jewish wife, the former Opekta employee Jetje Bremer, but it was most likely her marriage to this man she described as a "mysterious figure" that saved her life. Seven of her ten siblings were murdered in 1943 in Auschwitz or Sobibor.

Along with them, she also had to mourn the death of one of her six children. On August 18, 1942, her barely twenty-three-year-old son, Robert, was executed in the Neuengamme concentration camp. His father had allegedly denounced him and his brother Josephus, who was two and a half years older, for making anti-German statements. Josephus survived the concentration camp.

On May 17, 1950, Jetje and Job Jansen were divorced. The "theater administrator and actor" spent his last years in The Hague. When his death seemed imminent, the couple remarried, presumably to assure Jetje of support for her old age. Four months later, on September 20, 1952, Job Jansen died at age sixty-five.

After his return from Auschwitz, Otto Frank saw **MARTHA CHARLOTTE KALETTA** almost every day. "I would do anything to help her. She is worth every effort," Otto wrote on September

20, 1945, to Fritz Pfeffer's son. At that point Charlotte had not yet given up hope that Fritz might return. Two months later, she held his death certificate in her hand. Now, with practically no means of support, she went to work sewing gloves for about 35 guilders a week and relied, as she had during the war, on help from friends and acquaintances. In the early postwar years, Otto stood by her. "If you can get women's clothes and stockings," he wrote to his brothers-in-law in the United States, "please send them."

On March 3, 1953, the Berlin marriage bureau finally responded to Kaletta's repeated petitions by recognizing her posthumous marriage to Fritz Pfeffer, retroactive to May 31, 1937. As his widow, she was entitled to compensation, and the German state granted her a modest monthly pension. The German authorities disputed, however, her claim that she had "lived illegally in Amsterdam" and "suffered injuries to body or health."

She was never able to learn how and where her son died. The only thing the Jewish community in Berlin told her in response to her query was that he had been "deported to an unknown destina-

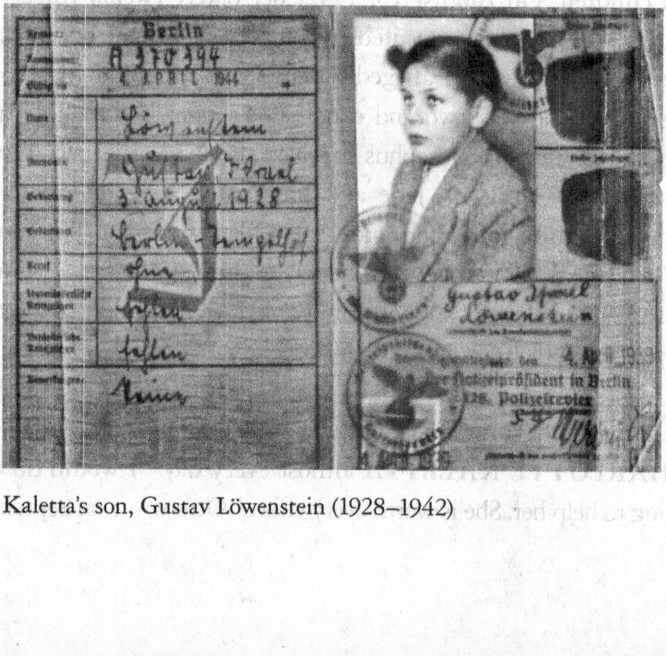

Kaletta's son, Gustav Löwenstein (1928–1942)

tion with the twentieth eastbound transport on October 3, 1942." Today we know that in the last week of September 1942 Gustav and Ludwig Löwenstein were taken from the Levetzow Street synagogue in Berlin, which the Nazis were using as a collection point, and loaded onto a railroad car. On September 26, the car was coupled onto a deportation train from Frankfurt am Main. Because the Theresienstadt concentration camp was becoming overcrowded, the train was sent to Riga.

Riga was full, too, and the train continued to Raasiku, near Tallinn, in Estonia. Barely 10 percent of the prisoners survived the harsh selection there. All the others, according to one account, "were driven over a kind of ramp into pits already dug into the dunes. But before that, they had to strip and put their valuables, eyeglasses, watches, etc., into small suitcases. Everything was done with such rapidity and under a barrage of shouting from the guards that the victims had no chance to collect their thoughts. Six or eight Estonian policemen were detailed to shoot the prisoners, and the bodies were covered with sand." Of the 812 Berlin Jews on the train, perhaps only nineteen survived.

In the 1950s, Charlotte broke off her connections with Otto Frank and the Gies family, perhaps because of the unflattering picture Anne's diary and the dramatizations based on it had painted of her husband and shown to all the world, perhaps because Otto had chosen another woman to marry. She lived a quiet life in Amsterdam until her death on June 13, 1985.

In the fall of 1987, Joke Kniesmeijer, then a senior staff member of the Anne Frank Foundation, was strolling through the Amsterdam flea market when she happened on some books, letters, and photos from Charlotte Kaletta's estate, items that created a portrait of "Dr. Dussel" quite different from the one in Anne's diary.

One morning in the fall of 1942, when **SOL KIMMEL** was in school, his mother was taken away in a roundup. She was later deported to Auschwitz and murdered. Sol, whom Anne had decided she would marry when she was in the Montessori school, was taken in by the family of his mother's sister. When they thought he was no longer safe with them, they arranged for him to go into hiding with a farmer who was hiding several other Jews as well. Everything went well for more than a year. Then in February 1945 the Nazis raided the farm and shot the farmer and one of the Jews. On February 8, 1945, Sol was interned in Westerbork, and he remained there as one of 876 prisoners until the camp was liberated on April 12, 1945.

After the war, Sol studied chemistry in Amsterdam, then completed graduate studies at Princeton University. But after all he had been through, he wanted to live in Israel. Sol Kimmel became a highly regarded professor of chemistry and worked in cancer research until his retirement. He is married, has two children, and lives in Haifa.

After his arrest, **JOHANNES KLEIMAN** was held in jail on Amstelveenseweg along with Victor Kugler. "When I sat next to Kleiman in a room at prison before we were separated," Otto Frank wrote to his brother shortly after the war, "I told him how I felt his imprisonment on account of helping us, but his only answer was 'I don't regret it.'"

After more than a month and several interrogations, the two helpers were transferred to the Weteringschans prison on September 7. From there, they were taken four days later to the Amersfoort concentration camp. "Mr. Kleiman was luckier than I," Kugler said later, "because he could capitalize on his earlier stomach surgery." Indeed, the International Red Cross had interceded on his behalf, and he was allowed to go home on September 18.

A few days later, Kleiman again took charge of Opekta's operations. When Otto moved to Basel in 1952, Kleiman assumed complete control of the firm. Then, too, after the Franks' move to

Switzerland, he served not only as Otto's private secretary with power of attorney but also—at ever-increasing cost of his own time—as head receptionist and tour guide at the Anne Frank House and as go-between and adviser to Otto Frank in his dealings with the publishers of Anne's diary. Kleiman was, as Ernst Schnabel said of him, "in a sense the Franks' pater familias." Otto's benevolent guardian spirit is an equally appropriate description of this selfless man who never recovered from his stomach ailment but nonetheless continued to work tirelessly.

Kleiman died of a stroke while at work in his office on January 30, 1959. He was sixty-three. "It isn't every day you come across such an honest, decent human being," Victor Kugler said of him.

A circumstance that had previously been guarded as an embarrassing family secret saved **HANNELORE "HANSI" KLEIN**'s life in 1943. Hannelore's maternal grandmother was Christian. When Hannelore's older sister was summoned to labor service on July 5, 1942, the very day Margot Frank was called, the girls' grandmother, who lived in Amsterdam, went to the German authorities and was able to make them believe that her dead husband, who had in fact been a Jew, had been an "Aryan." This "fact" made her three granddaughters only "half Jews" because their mother was a pure "Aryan." Consequently, after months of living in fear, Hannelore and her family came under the protection of Hans Georg Calmeyer and his "interior administration" in the Reich Commissariat for the Occupied Dutch Territories. Classified as "doubtful cases," they were removed from the deportation lists. Hannelore switched from the Jewish lyceum to the regular girls' lyceum and lived out the final years of the war in Amsterdam. Her Jewish father's chronic tuberculosis saved him from deportation.

In 1947, Hannelore married Rudi Nussbaum, a young student of physics of German-Jewish extraction whom she had first met when she was thirteen. He had survived the war in hiding with a

Dutch farm family. Otto Frank was a witness at their wedding. The Nussbaums had three children. In 1956, they moved to Geneva, where Rudi worked for the European Center for Nuclear Research (CERN). A year later, they emigrated to the United States and settled in Portland, Oregon. Hannelore, who changed her name to Laureen, became a professor of literature at Portland State University. Rudi enjoyed great success in his field, but on a trip to Amsterdam in the summer of 2011, he died after a fall. Since then, Laureen has lived in Seattle.

After his arrest on August 4, 1944, **VICTOR GUSTAV KUGLER** was held at the Amstelveenseweg jail at first, then transferred along with Johannes Kleiman to the Weteringschans prison. On September 11, they were both put on a train to Amersfoort, and Kugler began an odyssey through several of Holland's work camps.

"We were to be taken to Germany several days later, but it was our great good fortune that the Americans bombed the railroad station. . . . But since the camp was overcrowded and had to be evacuated quickly, . . . our transport was ordered to a work project in Zwolle," Kugler recalled. "That was toward the end of September 1944. I stayed in Zwolle until Christmas. From there, we were sent to labor service in Wagenlingen, where we stayed until the end of March 1945. Finally, we were supposed to go to Germany. We marched from Wageningen by way of Arnheim to Zevenaar and stayed there overnight. Zevenaar is the last station before Emmerich am Rhein. Just before we reached the village, an English fighter plane dove on our column—made up of about four hundred men, four horses, and a wagon—and strafed us. Several men were killed. . . . Bullets striking the roadway raised clouds of dust. A companion . . . and I . . . took shelter behind one of the trees along the roadside. When the shooting stopped, . . . we slipped through a narrow alley between two houses and crawled into a chicken coop. After about an hour, we came out and told people our story. They advised us to follow the paths through the fields and knock at the first farmhouse we came to. All the people in this region were 'good,' they told us. We followed their advice and asked a farmer to put us up, which he did, even though it was dangerous for him to do so. . . . By taking further and often necessary detours . . . we arrived after two days at my hometown of Hilversum." Kugler remained hidden there until the arrival of Canadian forces in Holland and the capitulation of the Germans on May 7.

His wife, Maria, was unable to cope with these events. "When she heard of them," Otto Frank learned, "she had to go into a sanitarium," and even later she was unable to regain her equilibrium. She died on December 6, 1952, only a few weeks before her twenty-fifth wedding anniversary.

On June 7, 1955, Kugler married Lucie "Loes" van Langen, a woman twenty-seven years younger than he, and the couple emigrated to Toronto. Kugler's attempts to establish himself in his previous field failed. "I've been unable to achieve anything in the past year, no matter how hard I have tried," Kugler reported in early March 1959. Scraping by first as an electrician and later as a bookkeeper, Kugler lived in modest circumstances.

For his work in helping the Franks, in 1973 the Yad Vashem memorial in Jerusalem honored him—like the other helpers—with the Medal of the Righteous and planted a tree in his name on the Boulevard of the Righteous Among the Nations. In 1977, the Canadian Anti-Defamation League honored him with a $10,000 award. "I'm delighted for any and all recognition he receives, and he is surely in need of financial help," Otto Frank said. On December 16, 1981, after a long illness, Victor Kugler died in Toronto at age eighty-one.

MAARTEN KUIPER was sentenced to death for the murder of seventeen resistance fighters and Jews and for his part in the deportation of several hundred Jews. He was executed on August

Maarten Kuiper

30, 1948. Although Otto Frank, Johannes Kleiman, and Victor Kugler testified that he was present at 263 Prinsengracht during the arrest of the Jews in the secret annex on August 4, 1944, his presence cannot be proved. Perhaps they were misled by the appearance in the Dutch press of his picture among those of the most dangerous bounty hunters in Holland. Kuiper had also belonged to the so-called Silver Fir death squad that on orders from higher up, perhaps even from Hanns Albin Rauter, the highest-ranking SS officer in the Netherlands, "planted silver firs," code for assassinating resistance fighters. Kuiper left three children.

SANNE, ILSE, AND FRANZ LEDERMANN spent four months in the Westerbork transit camp. Their "Palestine papers" afforded them protection for those four months, but on November 15, 1943, they learned that they would be deported the next day. On the morning of November 16, Ilse Ledermann wrote a few hasty lines to her daughter Barbara, and a fellow prisoner mailed the letter for her: "My darling, we are about to depart on our first long journey in a long time. My little Barbara, we will see each other again." This was Ilse Ledermann's last journey. All three of the Ledermanns were sent to the gas chambers immediately upon arrival in Auschwitz on November 19, 1943.

With the help of a friend named Manfred, **BARBARA LEDERMANN** was able to acquire a false ID card in the spring of 1943 and go underground in Amsterdam. Using the assumed name of Barbara Waarts and rendered "Aryan" by her blond hair and blue eyes, she became an important courier in the resistance movement. As long as her parents and her sister, Sanne, were in Westerbork, she maintained a regular correspondence with them and even sent them packages.

Twenty years old at the end of the war and beginning a career as a dancer and actress, she found herself in love and wanted to remain in Holland. In the mid-1930s her father had applied for Dutch citizenship and had been placed on the waiting list. Then the Germans occupied Holland. Barbara applied to the Dutch authorities again in 1945, but instead of Dutch citizenship, all she got back was the 200-guilder fee her father had paid with his application. "This whole business is so utterly senseless," she wrote to Otto Frank in September 1947.

In 1947, Barbara emigrated to New York, where she had relatives. She managed to find work as an actress and dancer and was eventually hired by the Ringling Brothers circus. A year later, she took a job as a saleswoman for a cosmetics firm in Baltimore. In her free time, she continued to act in amateur theater. In 1950, she married Martin Rodbell; the couple had four children. Rodbell, a biochemist, went on to win the Nobel Prize in Physiology or Medicine in 1994 for the "discovery of G-proteins and the role of these proteins in signal transduction in cells." He died on December 7, 1998.

Only in her later years has Barbara Ledermann begun to speak about her personal history. In the mid-1950s, it seemed unlikely to her that accounts of German war crimes and persecution of the Jews would find a receptive audience. On the occasion of the world premiere of *The Diary of Anne Frank*, she wrote to Otto Frank: "Since America is trying so very hard to be friendly with Germany I have an idea that the play will have to be mostly a love story and the persecution, inhumanity and suffering will have to be very subdued to not upset the general political trend."

Barbara Ledermann Rodbell lives in North Carolina.

ARTHUR SIEGFRIED LEWINSOHN was prepared to obey his summons to the Westerbork collection camp on May 21, 1943, because he "could not believe that anything bad would happen to people with my kind of background." His life partner, Sighilde Albinger, a native of Innsbruck in the Tyrol who went by the name Jutta, saved him from that step. Albinger, an ardent anti-Fascist with no religious affiliation, had been picked up and jailed in an SA roundup in Berlin in October 1933. On her release, she fled Germany and joined friends in Holland. The former actress managed to scrape by in Amsterdam as a housemaid. She met Arthur Lewinsohn in late 1938. Because his experience as an *onderduiker*, or person in hiding, was more typical than that of the Franks, I recount it here in some detail.

"[She] arranged for me to go into hiding in a friend's cellar. Once a bed was set up and a jerry-rigged toilet tied into a sewer pipe running through the cellar, I moved in," Lewinsohn recalled. "Helpers working illegally supplied me with food coupons and sometimes warned me of police raids. Then I would stay for a short time with other people, whose names I rarely ever knew. . . . But finally my situation became so dangerous . . . that I had to leave the cellar."

Lewinsohn spent the remaining occupation period in Albinger's apartment, where a hiding place he could barely squeeze into had been built between a wall and a sliding door. This hideaway was so small that the idea never occurred to unbidden visitors that someone could fit into it.

In September 1946, he did what the Nuremberg racial laws, effective in occupied Holland, had prevented him from doing: he married the woman who had saved him and he remained in Holland. That was not his original plan. Like many others, he had tried unsuccessfully in 1938 to emigrate to South America.

After the war, he worked for a chemical company in Amsterdam. In 1959, he returned to Germany with his wife and moved into a retirement home in Bad Münstereifel. He died there on December 5, 1971, just a few weeks before his eighty-seventh birthday.

WILLEM GERARD VAN MAAREN was regarded for many years as the main suspect in the police investigations of the betrayal. Johannes Kleiman and Victor Kugler in particular suspected him, citing his suspiciousness and his constant snooping. Also, the fact that he continued to steal from his employers even after the arrest did nothing to improve his credibility. Acquaintances and neighbors agreed that he was an unpleasant person, but there was no evidence of contact with the Nazis.

Shortly after the war, Kleiman expressed his suspicions about van Maaren in a letter to the investigative branch of the police but did not make a formal accusation. Van Maaren remained in his job as warehouseman, for regardless of people's feelings toward him, he was, as Miep Gies said, a "good worker." She did not like him either; however, she did not think him guilty of the betrayal. Toward the end of 1945, Kleiman and Otto Frank, who before his arrest had known van Maaren only through what his employees told him, suggested to van Maaren that he seek a job elsewhere.

It was probably Otto Frank who set the investigation of van Maaren in motion in 1947 with a visit to the police department's investigative branch, and starting in January 1948 the police interrogated one witness after another in the Frank case. In late March, van Maaren himself was the last to appear. In early February he had written a detailed letter to the investigating authorities in which his main concern seemed to be to divert attention from his thievery. He had had nothing to do with the betrayal, he said. The investigation was "provisionally" terminated for lack of evidence, but several conditions were imposed, among them the withdrawal for ten years of van Maaren's right both to vote and to run as a candidate for political office. Van Maaren appealed this judgment, and in the appeal proceeding on August 13, 1949, it was overturned on all counts. In 1963, after Simon Wiesenthal had tracked down Karl Silberbauer, the investigation was reopened but then closed again on November 4, 1964, for lack of any decisive new evidence.

Van Maaren died in Amsterdam on November 28, 1971, at the age of seventy-six.

JACQUELINE VAN MAARSEN was one of the first people Otto Frank showed Anne's original diaries to after the war. She didn't read them, and even after he gave her a copy of the first printed edition in 1947, she read it only reluctantly and then never looked at it again for several years. This reminder of her friend was too painful for her. In 1948 she completed her secondary schooling. She spent the year of 1952 in London as an au pair. Two years after her return, she married Ruud Sanders, whom she had known by sight since childhood. He had survived the war by going into hiding.

Jacqueline has received numerous awards for her work as a bookbinder, and since 1990 she has published three books—all translated into several languages—that offer a candid view of her friendship with Anne Frank. Jacqueline and her husband live in Amsterdam. They have three children and seven grandchildren.

LUDWIG JACOB MEHLER, the rabbi of the liberal Jewish congregation in Amsterdam, helped many German immigrants integrate into Dutch society. Together with his wife and two children, he was deported to Bergen-Belsen in 1943 and died there. The date of his death is given as April 10, 1945. He was thirty-eight years old.

His wife and children emigrated to the United States after the war. In 1999, his daughter, Suzanne, published her recollections of the Nazi period, *Appel Is Forever: A Child's Memoir.*

GERTRUD NAUMANN was one of the first of his German friends whom Otto Frank contacted after the war. They met and corresponded regularly, and Otto remained a father figure for Gertrud, providing her with good advice and counsel.

Until her marriage, Gertrud worked in the accounting division of I. G. Farben. On November 24, 1949, she married Karl Trenz. Before the war, he had worked at the German embassy in Ankara. He was drafted at the beginning of the war and not released from a British prisoner of war camp until 1948. Karl and Gertrud, who had three children, made their home only a five-minute walk from Marbachweg in Frankfurt. Almost every year until Otto's death, usually in the fall, they visited Otto and Fritzi Frank at their house in Birsfelden, near Basel. Gertrud Naumann died in Frankfurt on December 1, 2002.

OPEKTA in Amsterdam came through the war intact. On April 1, 1944, the Bureau of Economic Investigation informed the company that under current regulations Opekta was "no longer required to register" with the office. The agency was apparently basing its decision on the fact that Opekta was a branch of the "Aryanized" German Pomosin-Werke.

Otto Frank saw things differently after the war. Although ownership issues between the Pomosin-Werke and Opekta Cologne remained unresolved for several years, Otto and his employees remained in complete control of Opekta Amsterdam AG, although its profitability from year to year left much to be desired. Having survived the war and a concentration camp, Robert Feix, the founder of Opekta, reopened the legal battle with his cousins. Only in September 1952 did the parties reach an agreement: The Pomosin-Werke would remain with the Scheinberger brothers; Opekta Cologne and Rovag in Switzerland would go to Feix. In the meantime, however, Otto Frank had had Opekta's expired right to use of the international Opekta trademark transferred to Opekta Amsterdam, much to Feix's displeasure.

For nearly five years, Feix on the one side and Otto Frank and Johannes Kleiman on the other fought over who should own Opekta Amsterdam. Feix proposed giving them "a reward for their loyalty" because they had "kept the company going through the whole difficult period" of the war years. Otto declined and provoked Feix by suggesting that he himself would grant Feix right of first refusal to buy the company. Feix nonetheless decided not to initiate legal proceedings. "I am, of course, convinced," he noted, "that we would prevail in court, but I also believe that Mr. Frank does not want to see things come to this and probably cannot afford to, given the exposure that publication of his deceased daughter's diary has brought him."

Negotiations dragged on because Otto Frank was giving most of his attention to the diary and its dramatization. Only in mid-January 1959 were matters finally settled: Robert Feix (1893–1973) bought up the shares of the Netherlands Opekta Company (including international trademark rights) for 100,000 guilders. Johannes Kleiman was to remain as director of the joint-stock company and share in its profits until 1962. He died, however, on January 30, 1959, just a few days after the closing of the deal. In early March, Jan Dikker was named interim director, and in October, Kleiman's secretary, Adriana Kwakernaak, and Ernst Wilhelm Hennig took over the directorship. Opekta was sold in 1982 and dissolved in the midnineties for lack of profitability.

(HANS) WERNER PFEFFER lost all his closest relatives in the war. His uncle in England, who had seen to his needs during the war, died suddenly. His mother, Vera Henriette Bythiner, fled from Berlin, as her ex-husband had, and made her way in Amsterdam as a housemaid. On September 32, 1942, at age thirty-eight, she was murdered in Auschwitz.

It seemed at first that his father, Fritz Pfeffer, had disappeared without a trace. "We still wait for your father, we may still hope," Otto Frank wrote to him on September 30, 1945. Otto was acting as a mediator, replying to a letter from Werner to Charlotte Kaletta that was apparently anything but friendly. Toward the end of the year, Werner learned of his father's death in the Neuengamme concentration camp.

Needing to earn his living, Werner had left school in 1944 at age sixteen. He worked days as a freelance photographer and attended a technical school in the evenings. In October 1946, he emigrated to New York. A friend of his father's arranged his first job for him, and he eventually found a teaching job at a factory that made rubber tires. Going now under the name Peter Pepper, he married, became a father, and in March 1951 moved with his family to California, where he continued to work in the tire industry.

In late 1994, when Jon Blair was making his Academy Award–winning film, *Anne Frank Remembered*, Werner had his only—and very emotional—meeting with his father's helper, Miep Gies. Two months later, on February 15, 1995, he died of cancer.

LUTZ PETER SCHIFF was Anne's heartthrob in her lyceum days, and she often thought of him when she was in hiding. His name and the names of his mother, Erika Levin Kosterlitz, and his stepfather, Rudolf Kosterlitz, appear on the registration list of the Westerbork transit camp for September 23, 1943. Because he had not obeyed the summons to labor service, he was regarded as a criminal case and placed in penal barrack 67. His mother and stepfather were sent to Theresienstadt on January 18, 1945. As Peter's biological father, Richard Schiff, had emigrated to the United States via Amsterdam in May 1937, Peter was registered on a list of "persons whose immediate family members are located in enemy countries" and who could therefore serve as exchange prisoners. But on February 1, 1944, he was deported to Bergen-Belsen. From there, he was sent to Theresienstadt on July 11, 1944, and then—together with his mother and stepfather—on to Auschwitz on September 28. He boarded still another transport train on October 8, this time for Dachau. On October 10, 1944, he was registered there as prisoner 116255 and transferred to the Kaufering satellite camp. According to his registry records, he was freed from Dachau-Kaufering by the U. S. Army in early May 1945. But the records are wrong. Peter probably died on an evacuation march through Upper Bavaria between April 26 and May 4. His mother and stepfather died in Auschwitz no later than February 28, 1945.

As a baptized Jew, **ANNELIESE SCHÜTZ** was deported to Theresienstadt. After the war, Anne's former tutor reestablished contact with Otto Frank and offered to translate Anne's diary into German, originally intending it for the use of Otto's family in Basel only. She is "a lady over fifty, nearly blind, and very much alone. That's why she wants to reconnect with me," Otto Frank wrote to his mother of the former journalist and champion of women's rights, who was in fact not fifty but about seventy.

Schütz's translation did not remain restricted to family use. In

1950, the Lambert Schneider Verlag in Heidelberg published 4,500 copies of the first German edition under the title *Das Tagebuch der Anne Frank.* Despite the book's success, Otto Frank was not very happy with the translation. On the whole it was accurate and true to the original, Otto Frank confided to a friend in 1958, but Anneliese Schütz had been too old to convey Anne's tone; several turns of phrase were schoolmarmish, and Schütz had misunderstood a number of Dutch idioms. A 1959 article in *Der Spiegel* pulled no punches: "Schütz made a literary grown-up's German out of Anne Frank's sharp, witty teenager Dutch. . . . There are also gross errors of translation in *Das Tagebuch der Anne Frank.*"

For her part, the translator was disappointed that Otto Frank did not share with her the income from the German edition, and she also publicly criticized the so-called Anne Frank myth, which "not only Otto Frank but also the German writer Ernst Schnabel helped fabricate."

A few days after August 4, the Abraham Puls moving firm stripped the **SECRET ANNEX** of its contents, and from then on the annex stood empty.

In June 1953, Maurits Alexander Wessels sold the building to Opekta in the person of Johannes Kleiman, who had right of first refusal on it. Kleiman paid 22,000 guilders—the equivalent of about 97,000 dollars today. Kleiman seems to have been a shrewd negotiator: ten years earlier, Wessels had paid the equivalent of almost 10,000 euros more.

But Opekta was not able to hold on to the dilapidated building. The textile firm Berghaus bought it in 1954, intending to build a new factory in the Prinsengracht/Westermark neighborhood. Opekta moved into new quarters at 8–10 Van Singelandtstraat. In January 1956, word got around that 263 Prinsengracht—and with it the Franks' hiding place—was scheduled for demolition. On

May 3, 1957, a group of interested Dutch citizens, Otto Frank among them, established the Anne Frank Foundation in Amsterdam to preserve the building and make it accessible to the public. But Otto did not want to establish a shrine: he would invest money only if the foundation also established an international youth center that would, in Anne's spirit, stand against intolerance and discrimination and encourage "cooperation among young people from around the world . . . so they will learn, despite differences of nationality, race, and religion, to work together toward true and lasting peace and a better future for all."

In October 1957, Berghaus, which had received from the city of Amsterdam a site on the outskirts of town for its factory, gave 263 Prinsengracht to the Anne Frank Foundation. Otto Frank found several donors willing to finance restoration of the building. "We have acquired the building," Kleiman wrote to Otto, "on the condition that it will never be used for commercial purposes." Otto doubtless understood how difficult it would be to prevent the annex from becoming a sentimental tourist attraction. He wanted it to be a place that would stimulate people to develop a sense of personal responsibility to act for the common good. But despite his reservations, he finally decided to trust in its symbolic power. He wished the original condition of the secret annex to be restored as closely as possible so that, as the foundation's mission statement put it, the documentary material, photographs, and models would provide visitors with a true picture of what the annex residents' life in hiding was like. (Reconstruction of the annex furnishings for filming was undertaken only many years later, after Otto's death.)

On May 3, 1960, exactly three years after the foundation was formed, the Anne Frank House opened as a museum. At the same time, the International Youth Center of the Anne Frank Foundation officially came into being, with Otto Frank as its first chairman. In 1964, these two organizations were united under the temporary leadership of Otto's friend and adviser the teacher Henri van Praag. Otto Frank, however, withdrew more and more from Amsterdam. His views and those of the foundation staff differed too much. He did not want his daughter's name used for political or commercial purposes. He feared for his—and all the more for her—ideals.

The Anne Frank House has long since been modernized, with more exhibit rooms and a museum shop added to it. Today, the foundation has a staff of about 150. The secret annex exerts a powerful draw on the public. Every year more than a million people from all over the world are guided through its cramped rooms. In Amsterdam only the Van Gogh Museum and the Rijksmuseum attract more visitors.

On October 1, 1946, the International Military Tribunal at Nuremberg convicted **ARTHUR SEYSS-INQUART,** Reich commissioner for the occupied Netherlands, of major war crimes and sentenced him to death. He was executed on October 16.

In 1987, the financial director of the Anne Frank Foundation in Amsterdam contacted Seyss-Inquart's thirty-year-old grandson, Helmut, asking if he was interested in cooperating with the foundation. Helmut Seyss-Inquart's father and aunts had continued to espouse Nazi ideas even after the war, but Helmut, a teacher in Austria, held views diametrically opposed to those of his family and wanted to support the Anne Frank Foundation in its work against racism and discrimination. Helmut saw his mission as one of introducing its perspective into Austrian schools.

His good intentions precipitated a major battle. Dick Houwaart, a board member of the Anne Frank Foundation, declared that the grandson of a Nazi criminal would never be permitted to set foot in the foundation. The story occupied the press for months, and editorial writers were united in criticizing the foundation's rebuff of Helmut Seyss-Inquart. Holland's leading historian of the Holocaust, Louis de Jong, said Dick Houwaart had made a serious error. Simon Wiesenthal praised Seyss-Inquart's intention to work against fascism, anti-Semitism, and racism.

Helmut's response? He could well understand, he said, that the name Seyss-Inquart called up such powerful feelings in some people that they could not sit down at the same table with a member of his family. The personal animosity of members of the Anne Frank Foundation, however, pained and discouraged him.

Helmut Seyss-Inquart lives with his wife and two children in Bürmoos, Austria. He works as a teacher for children with special needs.

KARL JOSEF SILBERBAUER, who arrested the eight residents of the annex, was injured in a motorcycle accident on October 9, 1944, and not discharged from the Amsterdam military hospital until February 1945, at which time he immediately returned to his home in Vienna. According to a report of the Viennese chief prosecutor dated February 27, 1964, Silberbauer was arrested and imprisoned after the war because of his service in the Gestapo. He was "released after six weeks, however, because no punishable behavior could be proved against him."

On July 13, 1946, he was sentenced to a year's imprisonment for mistreating Communists during his Gestapo tenure in Vienna. He was consequently discharged from public service. On November 7, 1952, however, his petition for a retrial was granted, and on January 22, 1954, he was acquitted and permitted to return to the police force. Although Otto Frank was aware of the former SS man's identity, he harbored no desire for vengeance against "Silberthaler," as he referred to him in order to protect him from exposure.

In October 1963, more than nineteen years after the arrest at 263 Prinsengracht, Simon Wiesenthal tracked Silberbauer down after two years of research—led astray at first in a search for the fictitious Silbernagel or Silberthaler and never with any assistance from Otto Frank. When Wiesenthal finally came up with the right

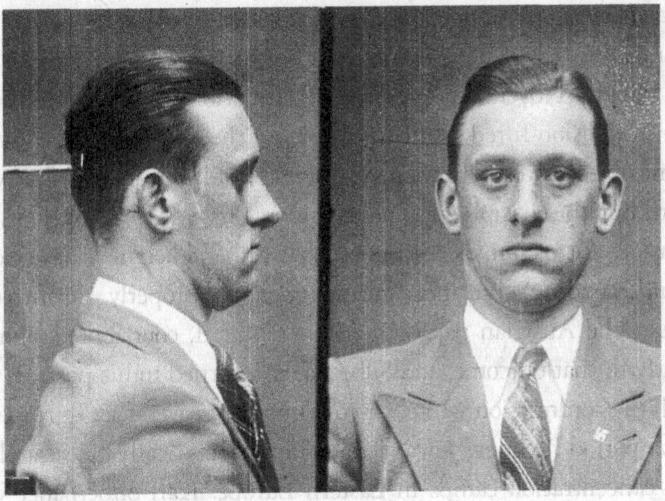

Karl Josef Silberbauer

name, the Austrian Ministry of the Interior was alerted, did some investigating of its own, and found Silberbauer's name on the roster of the Viennese police force, although it did not inform Wiesenthal. Silberbauer was immediately suspended and an investigation of him initiated. Overnight he was in the public eye. "The Silberbauer affair has caused a dreadful hullabaloo here," the Amsterdam police chief, Ynze Taconis, wrote to his Viennese counterpart in November 1963. "We hear that Wiesenthal is coming to Amsterdam tomorrow to meddle in the betrayal of the Frank family. He will certainly not be welcome here. I do not need Mr. Wiesenthal to help me conduct a Dutch investigation!"

"He is very fond of children, animals, and flowers. People like that can't do the kinds of things he is being accused of," Silberbauer's mother-in-law wrote to Otto Frank. The Silberbauer family was lacking a sense not only of guilt but of responsibility. "What would you have done, Mr. Frank, if one of your soldiers had not obeyed your commands? He too had to do what he was told to do."

Silberbauer offered nothing to help clarify who betrayed the Franks.

In early November 1964 the investigation was broken off and the suspension lifted. When the chief of the Vienna police department objected to this action, a further round of interrogations was held, but the disciplinary commission again voted to lift the suspension. Otto Frank's testimony that Silberbauer may have been "condescending" but had otherwise acted properly during the arrest, the Austrian paper *Volksblatt* reported, contributed significantly to that outcome, and Silberbauer returned to his post. In the end, the commission wrote, "it could not be proved that during the Nazi period he knew Jews were being systematically eradicated in the concentration camps in Eastern Europe. Karl Silberbauer was merely a low-ranking police officer to whom one of the greatest secrets kept by the highest levels of leadership in the German Reich was not entrusted." Furthermore, there was no evidence that "Silberbauer could possibly have profited financially from Jewish assets."

From 1965 until his retirement, he was given office duties and worked primarily sorting fingerprints and photographs of criminals. A journalist reported in 2011 that Silberbauer had acted as a "special liaison" for the Gehlen intelligence organization in the mid-1950s and then for the intelligence service of the Federal Republic of Germany, but those claims cannot be substantiated. It is also scarcely credible that none other than Wilhelm Harster hired him. They can hardly have known each other. The former commander of the security service in Holland was transferred to Italy in August 1943, months before Silberbauer arrived in Amsterdam.

Karl Silberbauer died on September 2, 1972.

All **EDWARD "HELLO" SILBERBERG** wanted after liberation was "just to live a normal life, like everybody else." Because his family had spent all their money while they were in hiding, Hello worked for a time in a furniture factory in Brussels. When

Holland was finally liberated—more than eight months after Belgium—his first thought was to see his grandparents in Amsterdam. Lacking a valid passport, though, he was classified as stateless, and his application for a visa to Holland was rejected. He traveled there illegally and found his grandparents, who had survived the war hiding in an attic near Amsterdam.

Hello did not want to stay in Europe permanently. Like so many others, the Silberbergs had wanted to emigrate to the United States before the war, and though an uncle had provided an affidavit, they could not get an emigration permit. In December 1947, Hello boarded a ship for New York; his parents followed a few months later.

In 1950, during the Korean War, he was drafted and lost another two years of his life. On his return, he married his great love, Marlyse, whom he had first met in Brussels but then repeatedly lost contact with. The Silberbergs had a son and a daughter, and Ed, as he calls himself now, became a partner in a company that markets laboratory apparatus.

Hello read his friend Anne's diary immediately after its publication and responded to it in a touching letter to Otto Frank. "Even if Anne had not mentioned me in her diary and even if I had not known all of you, I would have been deeply moved by it," Hello wrote, "for we, too, who lived in a 'secret annex' for more than two years, can understand, and identify with, every one of Anne's thoughts. I am convinced that I will never encounter another person who can formulate those thoughts as clearly and powerfully and with such a sharp admonition for the future. I am honored to be able to help in spreading the word about Anne's work." Ed and Marlyse Silberberg live in Sag Harbor, New York. Ed often gives talks to schoolchildren.

MARTINUS SLEGERS, whom Jan Gies had asked to keep a careful watch on 263 Prinsengracht after the robbery on April 9,

1944, continued to work as a night watchman until his retirement in 1953. A father of three, he died at age eighty on September 20, 1965. Although he always lived within reach, he was never questioned about anything that happened at 263 Prinsengracht.

OLGA SPITZER, in whose Villa Larêt Anne Frank stayed at least twice in the 1930s, spent practically every summer in Sils Maria until 1969. This active woman—whose social program for juvenile delinquents remains a model of its kind—died on January 9, 1971. She left her house to the University of Geneva, which used it as a conference center. To the great displeasure of her family, it was sold a few years ago, and today it is in private hands.

MILLY STANFIELD, who was ten years younger than her cousin Otto Frank, studied cello at the Royal Academy of Music. Throughout the 1930s, she was a master student of Pablo Casals and a correspondent for the *Strad*, a magazine for string players and teachers. During the war she performed in charity concerts for the Red Cross. Because there was no postal service between enemy countries, she remained ignorant of the fate of the Franks, whom she had last visited in 1938. Immediately after the war, she received word from Otto: "Now I am a beggar, having lost everything except my life."

Even though Milly and Otto saw each other only rarely, they felt a close bond from their early years on. "Any liberal ideas and freer thoughts I had later started to form in conversation with the Franks," she wrote to Otto in 1956.

In June 1945, she became Pablo Casals's personal secretary in England and the British representative for his international music festivals. Later, she served as administrator of the International Cello Centre in London, founded by her friend and colleague Maurice Eisenberg, taught cello at various English schools, and earned a reputation as a music critic. In 1967, she moved to the United States. In 1989, at the age of ninety, she stopped teaching. Until her death on February 14, 2001, she lived in a retirement home in West Orange, New Jersey.

MAX STOPPELMAN was forced to leave Auschwitz on a death march on January 18, 1945. "Our first destination was the concentration camp Gleiwitz I," Stoppelman's brief journal notes say, "where we were hounded from one barrack to another. Many prisoners were killed because a group of guards used them as targets in a so-called shooting contest. Then we walked again, this time to Gleiwitz II, where many more prisoners died in a shooting contest." From Gleiwitz the prisoners were taken in open railroad cars to Mauthausen. "At the way stations, those who had been trampled to death were thrown out of the cars, piled up, and burned. When we finally reached Mauthausen, four or five loaves of bread were tossed into each car. Those still alive practically tore each other to pieces fighting for the bread. There was still nothing to drink. We ate snow." Because there was no room in Mauthausen, the death train rolled on to Sachsenhausen and from there south to Flossenbürg. When he was caught on the food line twice in one day, he was transferred to the satellite camp Plattling as punishment. There, as one of the few survivors, he was liberated by the Americans.

From the hospital in Plattling, Max wrote to Miep and Jan Gies on May 19, 1945: "Dear Jan, Miep, and, I hope, my dear mother, I am in the hospital and being very well cared for." Max was particularly grateful to Jan, who had found him and his wife, Stella, their hiding place in Laren in the fall of 1943.

Max returned to Amsterdam in July 1945 and gradually reestablished himself there, this time in the textile business. In 1947, he met Lotte, the woman who would become his second wife in 1951, when the Red Cross was finally able to confirm that his first wife, Esther "Stella" Delden Stoppelman, had died at age twenty-four in Bergen-Belsen on December 5, 1944. Lotte and Max Stoppelman lived in Bussum, Holland. Max died in 2005. His mother, Hendrina Saartje Stoppelman, lived until 1979.

Despite his wealth and position of influence in New York, **NATHAN "CHARLEY" STRAUS JR.**, the friend of Otto's youth and and his close contemporary, was unable to rescue the Franks by arranging their emigration to the United States. But he was of great help to Otto after the war.

In the 1920s, Nathan Straus had made a name for himself as a journalist and local politician. He later became chairman of the board of the radio stations WMCA in New York and WBNY in Buffalo and worked for the U.S. Housing Authority, where he championed the cause of low-income housing. He died on September 13, 1961. Until his death, he remained a loyal friend and adviser to Otto.

IET "IETJE" SWILLENS completed the preparatory course at the Amsterdam girls' lyceum in 1947 and began studying psychology at the University of Amsterdam. She left to marry in 1954 but resumed her studies in the 1970s. On completing them, she worked as a teacher in a vocational school. Until her death on September 1, 2001, she lived in the Amsterdam suburb of Amstelveen.

ELISABETH "BEP" VOSKUIJL did not want to continue living at home after the arrest of the Franks, for fear of endangering her family. She found a rental room with the van Wijk family on Joos Banckersweg in Amsterdam West, about fifteen minutes from the city center by bicycle. The van Wijks' son, Cor, was in labor service in Germany, so his room was empty.

He was freed by the Russians in 1945 and returned home shortly thereafter. He took to the girl in his room straight off, as she did to him. They broke off their existing engagements and married on May 15, 1946.

Bep's father, Johannes Hendrik Voskuijl, did not live to see the birth of his grandchildren. Opekta's former warehouse foreman died of cancer in late November 1945. Otto Frank attended his funeral on December 1.

Bep and Cor van Wijk had four children: Ton, Cor, Joop, and Anne-Marie. The family maintained contact with Otto Frank until his death. In the postwar years, they saw one another about once a month, later about three times a year. For the children, the visits of "Uncle Otto" were a special treat.

Miep Gies considered it "a grave oversight on the part of the police" that Bep van Wijk was not questioned in the 1948 investigation of the betrayal at 263 Prinsengracht. The life her sister Hendrika Petronella had led may well have made Bep shy of making public appearances. "Nellie" was arrested on October 26, 1945, spent several years in custody in Groningen, and was finally charged with collaborating with the Germans. She was not able to pick up her life again until 1953.

Bep could certainly have helped clear up various inconsistencies, especially in the statement of Lena van Bladeren Hartog, the cleaning woman. When the investigation was reopened in 1963, Bep was interviewed, but only in regard to Willem van Maaren's role.

Bep died on May 6, 1983, in Amsterdam. The war years had transformed this once cheerful young woman into an anxious person constantly struggling to maintain her equilibrium. She was never able to get over the deaths of the annex residents and of her friends Anne and Margot in particular.

Right after the war, **BETTY AND JUANITA WAGNER** tried to contact their pen pals Margot and Anne Frank by sending a letter to Merwedeplein. It reached Otto Frank in September 1945. He replied with a detailed report of what had happened to his family. In 1956, Betty heard a radio report about the Broadway success of Anne's diary. She read the book and kept it from then on with the letters, photos, and postcards the Franks had sent her. Thirty years later, a friend convinced her that her packet of documents, which contained the only known letters written in English by the Frank girls, should be made public. On October 25, 1988, Swann Galleries in New York auctioned the collection off. It went to an anonymous bidder who then gave it to the Simon Wiesenthal Center in Los Angeles, where it is a prized item in the center's permanent exhibit.

Juanita Jane Wagner spent her last years in Redlands, California, where she died of a heart attack on Christmas Eve of 2001. Betty Ann was a teacher and founded an international aid organization for missionaries and students in Burbank, California. The proceeds from the auction sale were of great help to her.

ILSE WAGNER was taken from Amsterdam to the Westerbork transit camp in January 1943. Several weeks later, together with her mother and grandmother, she was deported to the Sobibor death camp. All three died in the gas chamber on the day of their arrival, April 2, 1943.

KAREL OSCAR MARIE WOLTERS, the attorney in charge of liquidating Pectacon, was promoted in 1942 to the position of assistant to Meinoud M. Rost van Tonningen, president of the Nederlandsche Bank, financial adviser to Arthur Seyss-Inquart, and chief of the Bureau of Economic Investigation. In February 1943, to van Tonningen's displeasure, Wolters volunteered for duty with the Waffen-SS; his next assignment was as an SS judge in the reserves. Finally, at the end of September 1944, he was sent to the eastern front. Shortly before, on September 5, his brother Oscar, his junior by three years and a medical student and resistance fighter, was summarily shot at the Vught concentration camp. Wolters's sister Aline also fought in the resistance and was arrested.

Toward the end of the war, Wolters was wounded in the shoulder. After the liberation of Holland, he was arrested in Scheveningen, sentenced in June 1948 to eight years in prison, and

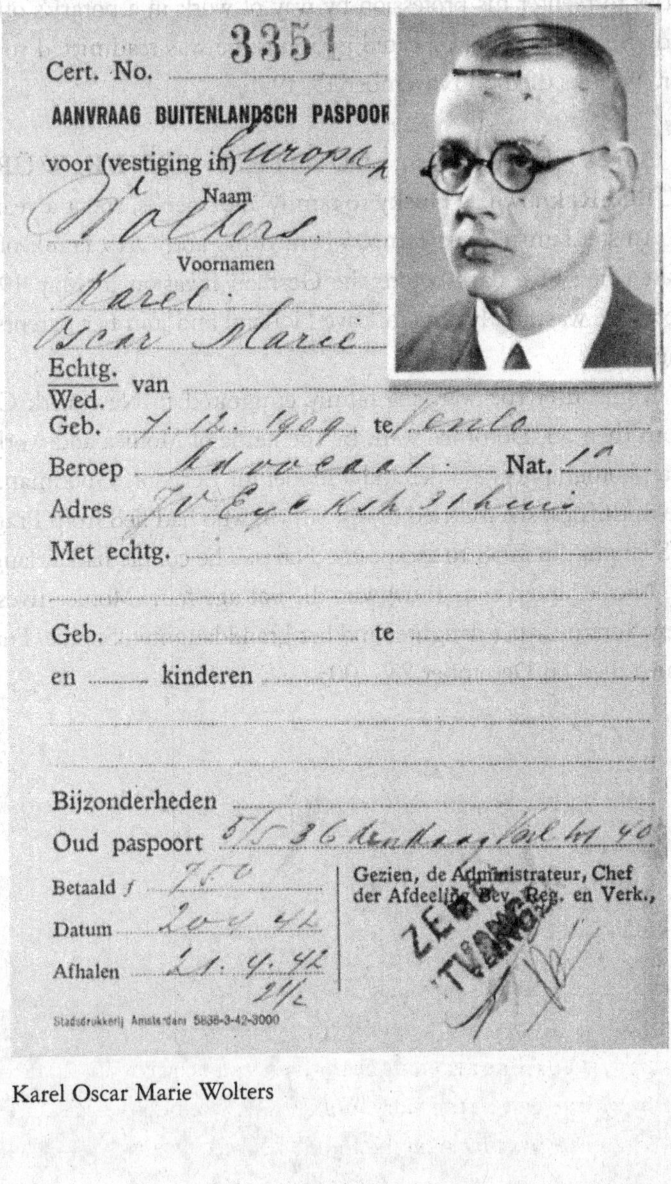

Cert. No. 3351

AANVRAAG BUITENLANDSCH PASPOORT

voor (vestiging in) Europa

Naam Wolters

Voornamen Karel Oscar Marie

Echtg./Wed. van

Geb. 7. 12. 1909 te Venlo

Beroep Advocaat Nat. N

Adres

Met echtg.

Geb. te

en kinderen

Bijzonderheden

Oud paspoort

Betaald *f* 7.50

Datum 20 4 42

Afhalen 21. 4. 42

Gezien, de Administrateur, Chef der Afdeeling Bev. Reg. en Verk.,

Stadsdrukkerij Amsterdam 5838-3-42-3000

Karel Oscar Marie Wolters

disbarred. He served several years at forced labor in a coal mine near Limburg. His sentence shortened, he managed in the early fifties to reenter his profession by way of work in a notary's office, and after submitting repeated petitions, he was readmitted to the bar. Wolters died on November 15, 1996.

Anne's second cousin **DOROTHEE SOPHIE WÜRZBURGER,** known as Hucky to family and friends, spent a year in an Amsterdam refugee camp, where Anne and Otto Frank often visited her. Five days before the German invasion in May 1940, Dorothee was finally able to leave Holland and join her parents in England.

Right after the war, the family emigrated to New York City. From then on, Dorothee went by the name of Monica and worked as a photographers' model and a model for Bergdorf Goodman. In the midfifties, she married Frank Smith, who had fled from Prague to Shanghai in 1938 to escape the Nazis. The couple had a daughter, Nicole, and a son, Tony, who died at age four. Monica lives in New York near her daughter and her granddaughter, Sophie. Frank Smith died on December 23, 2003.

A NOTE BY MIEP GIES

Over the past fifty years, ever since the publication of Anne Frank's diary, I have been asked again and again how I found the courage to help the Franks. This question, posed sometimes with admiration and sometimes with disbelief, has always made me uncomfortable. Yes, of course it takes courage to do one's duty as a human being, of course one has to be prepared to make certain sacrifices. But that's true in many of life's situations.

Why then, I keep asking myself, do people ask such a question? Why do so many hesitate when the time comes to help their fellow human beings?

It took me a long time to understand. Most children are told by their parents from an early age on: "If you are good and well-behaved, everything will work out for you later in life." The logical reverse of this philosophy is: Anyone who gets into trouble must—*must*—have behaved badly and made some serious mistakes. It's that simple. Everyone gets the life he or she deserves; it's that simple. If we really believe this, it's easy to go on minding our own business and to decide against helping people in need. But is it that simple?

Miep and Jan Gies, ca. 1970s

My life taught me better. I learned early that people could find themselves in trouble without necessarily having done anything wrong. I was born in Vienna and was five years old at the beginning of World War I. My mother kept telling me that I was a good little girl, that she loved me, and that she was pleased with how I was doing at home and at school.

When I was nine, we did not have enough to eat. I still remember the hunger pangs distinctly, the piercing pains in my stomach and the unpleasant fits of dizziness I had to try to overcome. And I shall never forget the shock when my mother sent me to Holland. A relief action to help starving children had been organized. On a bright and bitter-cold December day in 1920 my mother took me to the train, hung a big sign with a strange name on it around my neck, said good-bye, and left me. She had no other choice, of course, but I did not understand that until much later. I was extremely underweight and suffering from tuberculosis, and I felt terribly lonely. What had I done to deserve being so sick and alone? Hadn't my mother always assured me that I had done nothing wrong? So I experienced as an eleven-year-old how quickly people can find themselves in difficulty—and through no fault of their own. That, I knew from personal experience, was exactly what was happening to the Jews in World War II. And therefore it was only natural for me to help as much as I could.

When we are shocked to think that six million children, women, and men were driven to their deaths and we ask ourselves, "How could such a thing happen?" we should keep in mind the indifference of normal human beings the world over, good, hard-working, and often God-fearing individuals. Of course, it was the Nazi regime that was responsible for the mass murder, but if not for the apathy of people not just in Germany and Austria but everywhere—basically decent people, no doubt—the horrible slaughter could never have assumed the proportions it did.

When, as actually happens even today, young people come up

to me saying they cannot believe that Hitler could have murdered the Jews for no reason at all, I fear that this remark reflects precisely the view that no such thing could befall truly innocent, blameless people. Then I tell them about Anne Frank and ask them if this child, this young girl, could conceivably have done anything that would justify the cruel fate she suffered.

"No, of course not," they answer, usually quite mortified. "Anne Frank was innocent."

"Just as innocent as the other six million victims," I then add.

Thus, Anne's life and death have special meaning for all those who are subject to prejudice, discrimination, and persecution today. Anne stands for the absolute innocence of all victims.

I should like to use the publication of this biography of Anne Frank as an opportunity to clear up another common misunderstanding. It is often said that Anne symbolizes the six million victims of the Holocaust. I consider this statement wrong. Anne's life and death were her own individual fate, an individual fate that happened six million times over. Anne cannot, and should not, stand for the many individuals whom the Nazis robbed of their lives. Each victim had his or her own ideals and outlook on life; each victim occupied a unique, personal place in the world and in the hearts of his or her relatives and friends.

In their racial madness, Hitler and his accomplices tried to claim just the opposite: they portrayed the Jews as a faceless enemy even as they annihilated six million individuals, extinguished six million individual lives. Most of humanity did not even want to know what was happening.

Anne Frank was only one of the Nazis' victims. But her fate helps us grasp the immense loss the world suffered because of the Holocaust. Anne has touched the hearts and minds of millions; she has enriched all of our lives. Let us hope she has also enlarged our horizons. It is important for all of us to realize how much Anne and all the other victims, each in his or her own way, would have contributed to our society had they been allowed to live.

To my great and abiding sorrow, I was not able to save Anne's life. But I was able to help her live two years longer. In those two years she wrote the diary that gives hope to people all over the world and calls for understanding and tolerance. It confirms my conviction that any attempt at action is better than inaction. An attempt can go wrong, but inaction inevitably results in failure.

I was able to save Anne's diary and thus make her greatest wish come true. "I want to be useful or give pleasure to the people around me yet who don't really know me," she wrote in her diary on March 25, 1944, about one year before her death. "I want to go on living, even after my death!" And on May 11, she noted: "You've known for a long time that my greatest wish is to become a journalist someday and later on a famous writer."

Through her diary Anne really does live on. She stands for the triumph of the spirit over evil and death.

Amsterdam, January 1998

NOTES

Partial List of Archives and Institutions Consulted

HOLLAND:

Anne Frank Stiftung, Amsterdam (Anne Frank Foundation)

NIOD—Nederlands Instituut voor Oorlogsdocumentatie (The Netherlands Institute for War Documentation merged in 2010 with the Centrum voor Holocaust- en Genocidesstudies, Amsterdam, to form the NIOD Instituut voor Oorlogs-, Holocaust- en Genocidesstudies, Amsterdam)

Stadsarchief, Amsterdam (Amsterdam City Archives)

Joods Historisch Museum, Amsterdam (Jewish Historical Museum)

Kamer van Koophandel en Fabrieken, Amsterdam (Chamber of Commerce and Industry)

Nationaal Archief, The Hague (National Archives)

Het Nederlandse Rode Kruis, The Hague (Netherlands Red Cross)

Het Utrechts Archief, Utrecht

Archief Herinneringscentrum Kamp Westerbork (Camp Westerbork Memorial Center Archives)

Archief Eemland (Kamp Amersfoort)

Archief Nationaal Monument Kamp Vught

Personal papers of Miep and Paul Gies, Hoorn

Personal papers of Gerlof Langerjis, Amsterdam

Personal papers of Rian Verhoeven, Amsterdam

Personal papers of Ben Wegman, Meppel

SWITZERLAND:

Anne Frank Fonds, Basel (Anne Frank Fund)

Personal papers of Buddy and Gerti Elias, Basel

GERMANY:

Landesamt für Bürger- und Ordnungsangelegenheiten, Entschädigungsbehörde, Berlin (State Office for Civil and Administrative Affairs, Reparations Division, Berlin)

Brandenburgisches Landeshauptarchiv, Potsdam (Central State Archives of Brandenburg)

Hessisches Hauptstaatsarchiv, Wiesbaden (Central State Archives of Hessen)

Landesarchiv Berlin (State Archives of Berlin)

Stadtarchiv Aachen (Aachen Municipal Archives)

Historisches Museum Frankfurt

Wirtschaftsarchiv IHK Köln und Frankfurt (Economic Archives of the Cologne and Frankfurt Chambers of Industry and Commerce)

Institut für Zeitgeschichte, Munich (Institute of Contemporary History)

Deutsches Literaturarchiv (DLA), Marbach am Neckar

Archiv des Internationalen Suchdienstes (ITS), Bad Arolsen (Archives of the International Tracing Service)

Deutsche Dienststelle (WASt), Berlin (German Agency—Wehrmacht Information Office)

KZ-Gedenkstätte Dachau (Dachau Concentration Camp Memorial)

Erich Maria Remarque Archiv, Universität Osnabrück

Archiv *Der Spiegel*, Hamburg

Deutscher Wetterdienst, Offenbach (German Weather Service)

Personal papers of Gertrud Trenz, Frankfurt

Personal papers of Cor Suijk, Aachen

CZECHOSLOVAKIA:

Gedenkstätte Theresienstadt (Theresienstadt Memorial)

AUSTRIA:

Österreichisches Staatsarchiv, Vienna (Austrian State Archives)
Simon Wiesenthal Archiv, Vienna
Archiv der KZ-Gedenkstätte Mauthausen, Vienna (Archives of the Mauthausen Memorial)
Personal papers of Ulrich Feix, Innsbruck
Personal papers of Jules Huf, Vienna

ENGLAND:

Personal papers of Ernst Michaelis, Bushey

ISRAEL:

Yad Vashem, Jerusalem
Beit Theresienstadt, Givat Haim-Ihud (Theresienstadt Martyrs Remembrance Association)
Personal papers of Hannah Goslar Pick, Jerusalem

UNITED STATES:

National Archives II, College Park, Maryland
YIVO Institute for Jewish Research, New York
Surrogate's Court, New York County
United States Holocaust Memorial Museum, Washington, D.C.
Straus Historical Society, Smithtown, New York
New York Public Library, New York
Massachusetts Archives, Boston
New York City Department of Health
Personal papers of Ed Silverberg, New Jersey
Personal papers of Barbara Ledermann Rodbell, North Carolina
Personal papers of Eduardo M. Fraifeld, Virginia
Personal papers of Monica Smith, New York

Personal papers of the van der Horst family, North Carolina

Personal papers of Suzanne Morine, Colorado

Unless otherwise indicated, quotations of the diary are from *The Diary of Anne Frank: The Revised Critical Edition*, ed. David Barnouw and Gerrold van der Stroom, trans. Arnold J. Pomerans, B. M. Mooyaart-Doubleday, and Susan Massotty, New York: Doubleday, 2003. This edition contains three versions of the diary: Anne's original text (version A), her revision (version B), and the combined version of the two (version C) that Otto Frank revised and first published in 1947.

1. THE ARREST

The reconstruction of events before and after the arrest on the morning of Aug. 4, 1944, is based on the following sources:

Interviews with Miep Gies conducted between March 20, 1997, and March 16, 1998.

Police interrogation of Karl Josef Silberbauer, March 4, 1964, State Criminal Investigation Department, Amsterdam, Doc. 1, K. J. Silberbauer.

Police interrogation of Johannes Kleiman, Jan. 12, 1948, Ministry of Justice, Amsterdam, W. G. van Maaren file.

Police interrogation of W. G. van Maaren, March 31, 1948, Ministry of Justice, Amsterdam, W. G. van Maaren file; Oct. 6, 1964, State Criminal Investigation Department, Amsterdam, Doc. 1, K. J. Silberbauer.

Police interrogation of Lammert Hartog, March 20, 1948, Ministry of Justice, Amsterdam, W. G. van Maaren file.

Police interrogation of Otto Heinrich Frank, Dec. 2, 1963, State Criminal Investigation Department, Amsterdam, Doc. 1, K. J. Silberbauer. These records and those cited above are stored in the archives of the Netherlands State Institute for War Documentation in Amsterdam.

Harry Paape, "The Arrest," *The Diary of Anne Frank: The Revised Critical Edition*, ed. David Barnouw and Gerrold van der Stroom, trans. Arnold J. Pomerans, B. M. Mooyaart-Doubleday, and Susan Massotty, New York: Doubleday, 2003, pp. 21–27.

Rick Kardonne and Eda Shapiro, *Victor Kugler: The Man Who Hid Anne Frank*, Gefen Publishing House: Jerusalem, 2008.

Miep Gies and Alison Leslie Gold, *Anne Frank Remembered*, New York: Simon and Schuster, 1987.

Assets at 263 Prinsengracht, Cadastre Office Amsterdam, no. 3305/4.

Victor Kugler to Ernst Schnabel, letter of Sept. 17, 1957, AFS.

Interview with Jan Gies, *Televizier* magazine, May 7, 1977.

"Blik in de afgrond, Maarten Kuiper, misdadiger van de Euterpeststraat," *Elseviers Weekblad*, Nov. 29, 1947.

Interview with Joop van Wijk (son of Bep Voskuijl), May 16, 2007.

Interview with Paul Gies (son of Miep Gies), e-mail, May 18, 2007.

Otto Frank, Johannes Kleiman, and Victor Kugler all stated that on the day of the arrest they saw four agents of the security service. Whether there were other men present at some point can no longer be determined.

It also remains unclear how many warehouse employees apart from the foreman, Willem van Maaren, and his assistant, Lammert Hartog, were at work on Aug. 4, 1944. Miep Gies notes in her book that after the arrest two other employees were present who had not known about the hiding place in the annex. If Miep's recollection is correct, there must have been four employees present, including Willem van Maaren and Lammert Hartog.

What is certain is that Bep Voskuijl left the building after the arrival of the Security Service to attend to an errand assigned her by Johannes Kleiman. It remains unclear when she returned. Although she stated under oath in June 1974 that she returned the same day at about 5:00 p.m., she told her children that she didn't dare return to work until the next morning. Miep Gies, on the other hand, repeatedly stated that she went into the annex on Aug. 4, and she always maintained that she and Bep together found Anne's diary. This lack of clarity does not change the fact that Bep and Miep jointly decided to store in Miep's desk drawer the diary and the loose pages they had found.

2. ANNE IN FRANKFURT

13 "Anne Frank was born": For both her daughters, Edith Frank kept baby books, now in the archives of the Anne Frank Foundation (AFS), Amsterdam. Also helpful in reconstructing details of Anne's early years were interviews with Iet Swillens, Gertrud Naumann Trenz, and Hilde Stab. Jürgen Steen of the History Museum, Frankfurt, provided information on the social, political, and family background.

17 " 'At many points in my life' ": Kati Stilgenbauer to Otto Frank, letter of Feb. 24, 1952, AFS.

17 "Although Edith had grown up": Otto Frank, unpublished interview by Arthur Unger, Feb. 1977.

19 "Anne's strong will": Otto Frank to Jean Grossman Schick, in Jean Grossman Schick, *The Story Within Her Story*, ca. 1950, AFS.

19 " 'In these times . . .' ": Letter of July 21, 1917, AFS.

20 " 'I used to be teased' ": Archives of the Lessing Gymnasium, Frankfurt.

20 "After a dull semester": Otto Frank's curriculum vitae, Hessisches Hauptstaatsarchiv, Wiesbaden.

21 " 'The Jews are our scourge' ": Quoted from Heinrich von Treitschke, "Unsere Aussichten," *Preussische Jahrbücher*, Nov. 1879.

22 "Pim": Otto Frank, interview by Arthur Unger, Feb. 1977, in *Anne Frank's Family*, by Mirjam Pressler, New York, 2011.

22 "Good Paula": Buddy Elias told me about "the two Paulas" and about the abbreviation of the word *Omi* (see p. 23).

23 "Oma Holländer was known": Otto Frank to Jean Grossman Schick, *The Story Within Her Story*.

27 " 'Did you know' ": Letter of Jan. 27, 1935. Gertrud Naumann Trenz's estate is administered by her daughter and son-in-law. It includes all other letters to Gertrud Naumann from Edith as well as those from Otto Frank and Alice Stern Frank.

3. EXODUS

29 " 'I was very surprised' ": Otto Frank's letters to his mother and sister, Anne Frank Fonds.

29 "Jean Frank": J. M. Frank, *Mémoire du Style*, Paris, 1998.

30 "On April 12, 1922": Carol Ann Lee, *The Hidden Life of Otto Frank*, New York: Morrow, 2003.

37 " 'for the protection' ": "Regulation for the Protection of the German People," *Reich Law Gazette*, Feb. 4, 1933.

38 " 'Those who will not change' ": Handwritten notes of Lieutenant General Liebmann on remarks of Reich Chancellor Hitler to the commanding officers of the army and navy on Feb. 3, 1933; Thilo Vogelsang, ed., *Vierteljahrsheft für Zeitgeschichte* 2, 1954.

39 " 'You, more than the others' ": Letter of May 1917, Anne Frank Fonds.

42 " 'Jewish firms are henceforth' ": Order of the Municipal Government of Cologne, quoted in Hazel Rosenstrauch, ed., *Aus Nachbarn werden Juden*, Berlin, 1988.

42 "'It is a matter of honor'": Quoted in Rosenstrauch, *Aus Nachbarn wurden Juden.*

42 "'Nothing can rob us'": *Frankfurter Israelitisches Gemeindeblatt*, vol. 11, no. 8, Frankfurt am Main, April 1933.

44 "'Wherever they burn books'": Heinrich Heine, "Almansor," *Historisch-Kritische Gesamtausgabe der Werke*, in cooperation with the Heinrich-Heine-Institut, ed. Manfred Windfuhr, Hamburg, 1994, vol. 5, p. 16.

44 "Otto's fresh start in business": Information about the Pomosin-Werke in Frankfurt and Opekta in Cologne was provided by Ulrich Feix in several interviews in June 2007; correspondence with Jürgen Weise, Stiftung Rheinisch-Westfälische Wirtschaftsarchiv zu Köln (April 23–25, 2007); petition to the District Court Frankfurt am Main, Robert Feix vs. Konservenfabrik und Trocknungswerke Hessenland GmbH, Dec. 31, 1937, private files of Ulrich Feix.

44 "sent to Amsterdam as a trustee": Notes written by Robert Feix after a conference with Otto Frank and Johannes Kleiman, May 10, 1955, private archives of Ulrich Feix.

45 "'Pomosin Import Utrecht'": Frans Hofhuis, interview by author, Hilversum, May 15, 2007.

45 "'After it became clear'": Otto Frank to Erich Elias, letter of Aug. 5, 1933, quoted by Hans-Rudolf Nelken, attorney, in letter to Robert Feix, Nov. 2, 1954, private archives of Ulrich Feix.

45 "at odds with customs officials": Note from Feix archives.

45 "'a purely Dutch enterprise'": Note from a conference between attorney Joachim Rieke and Mr. Sauerbrey, both of the Pomosin-Werke; Otto Frank; and Johannes Kleiman, Dec. 1941, OFA 18, AFS.

45 "no longer regarded himself as their trustee": Note from Feix archives.

46 "For permission to use the trademark": Otto Frank to Erich Elias, letter of Aug. 5, 1933.

46 "'Because Mr. Frank cannot'": Hans-Rudolf Nelken to Robert Feix, Nov. 2, 1954.

46 "an attorney had arranged": According to statements in Otto Frank's curriculum vitae, attested to under oath.

47 "moved into a sublet apartment": The landlady was Marianne van Buren.

47 "a small two-room office": Miep Gies in various interviews with the author.

48 "'I often feel'": Letter of Feb. 28, 1916, Anne Frank Fonds.

48 "'Robert has sold'": Letter of July 21, 1916, Anne Frank Fonds.

50 "Edith's relatives": Personal collections of Eduardo M. Fraifeld, Danville, Virginia, and Monica Smith, New York, archives of the Victoria School, Aachen.

55 "'Won't someone offer'": Otto Frank to Jean Grossman Schick, *The Story Within Her Story.*

4. A NEW HOME

56 "Among the guests": Juliane Duke, *New York Times*, June 11, 1989; Barbara Ledermann Rodbell, interview by author, March 5, 1997.

57 "She had come": Elfriede Markovits Frank, interview by author, March 14, 1997.

58 "'Anne has made the adjustment'": Letter of July 23, 1934.

58 "Montessori school on Niersstraat": The first Montessori school in Amsterdam was founded in 1917 through private initiative. Between 1926 and 1940 a total of ten public Montessori elementary schools (numbered 1–10) were founded.

58 "On her first day": Hannah Goslar Pick, interviews by author, July 26–28, 1997. Barbara Ledermann Rodbell provided recollections of this period as well.

62 "German dominated": Anna Harting, interview by author, July 5, 1997.

63 "As director of the press office": Trude Maurer, *Auch ein Weg als Deutscher und Jude: Hans Goslar (1889–1945)*, Berlin, 1990.

66 "'I see what a firm foundation'": Letter from Otto Frank to Helene Elias, Nov. 26, 1945, Anne Frank Fonds.

67 "incapable of mastering": According to information from Erika Prins, AFS.

67 "Whether Edith Frank": Edith Frank's difficulties with Dutch were recollected by Jacqueline van Maarsen Sanders. Laureen Nussbaum was a source of information about the experience of German children in Holland.

67 "A note she wrote": Undated letter (June 30, 1935), private papers of Frans Hofhuis, Hilversum.

69 "They themselves had been educated": Archives of the Lessing Gymnasium, Frankfurt; archives of the Victoria School, Aachen.

71 "The school made considerable allowances": Kitty Egyedi, in various interviews with the author between July 7, 1997, and March 27, 1998. Kitty asked me at that time to protect her identity and not use her last name. I complied with her wishes. In the meantime, her name has appeared frequently in print, for example, in *Inside Anne Frank's House: An Illustrated Journey through Anne's World*, New York: Overlook, 2004.

73 "But Otto Frank, at almost six feet": According to a passport dated 1969, Otto Heinrich Frank was 1.74 meters tall. OFA, AFS.

73 "urgently needed support": Harry Paape, ". . . Originally from Frankfurt-am-Main," *The Diary of Anne Frank: The Revised Critical Edition*, p. 8.

74 " '80,000 Gulden in the form of advertising' ": Note for the files, Ulrich Feix archives.

74 "This trained electrician": Victor Kugler collection, AFS.

74 "A young Austrian woman": Miep Gies, interviews by author.

75 " 'She is a very unselfish person' ": Letter to Alice Stern Frank, Sept. 1, 1945, Anne Frank Fonds.

77 "Anne especially was prone": Recollections of Hannah Goslar Pick and Iet Swillens in interviews with the author.

78 " 'Anne is awake by six' ": Stephan Elias to his family in Basel, undated, OFA 17/71, AFS.

79 " 'Do you sometimes' ": Anne Frank Fonds.

79 "Edith Frank heard": Irma Holländer to Ilse Holländer, personal collection of Eduardo M. Fraifeld, Danville, Virginia.

80 "In October 1937": Reconstruction of the events based on the archival material in the private papers of Eduardo M. Fraifeld.

82 " 'This morning' ": Postcard of Dec. 23, 1935, Anne Frank Fonds.

83 "Olga Wolfsohn Spitzer": Buddy Elias, conversations with author; Gerard Spitzer, correspondence with author, Oct. 1997.

84 " 'How are things' ": Anne Frank to Alice Stern Frank, July 30, 1941, Anne Frank Fonds.

85 " 'Perhaps we could' ": Letter of Jan. 13, 1941, Anne Frank Fonds.

85 " 'Last week' ": Edith Frank to Gertrud Naumann, Dec. 22, [1937], personal papers of Gertrud Naumann, Trenz, Frankfurt am Main.

5. GROWING DANGER

91 "Walter Holländer recalled": Application for reparations to the city of Aachen, Aug. 1, 1954, Archives of the Düsseldorf District Government, Office of Reparations, Central Archives of the Federal Republic of Germany. Julius Holländer's application is here as well.

92 " 'about 300,000 applications' ": See Richard Breitman and Alan M. Kraut, *American Refugee Policy and European Jewry, 1933–45,* Bloomington: Indiana University Press, 1987.

93 " 'General Counsel' ": Departement van Justitie aan Procureur-General, Directeur van Politie te Amsterdam, letter of Nov. 17, 1938. Archief van de Procureur-General aan het Gerechtshof te Amsterdam, 1930–38, archive no. 307, inventory no. 102, in Noordhollands Archief, Haarlem.

94 "C. M. J. F. Goseling": See Louis de Jong, *Het Koninkrijk der Nederlanden in de Tweede Wereldoorlog, deel I, Voorspel,* The Hague, 1969, pp. 485–86.

94 " 'the Jew Walter Holländer' ": Holländer's discharge papers are in his reparations file. The Sachsenhausen discharge list of Nov. 28, 1938, is in the Special Archives for Nazi Crimes Documentation, Moscow.

94 "The message": *Jewish Prisoners in the Sachsenhausen Concentration Camp, 1936–1945,* exhibition at the Sachsenhausen Memorial and Museum, 1995.

95 "anti-Semitic 'terror groups' ": *De IJzeren Garde,* copy, Amsterdam, 1942, NIOD, Doc. II, 1060, Amsterdam (on Tonny Ahlers, see also Lee, *Hidden Life of Otto Frank*).

96 "When Otto's cousin": Cal Fussman, "A Date with History: Milly Stanfield, the Woman Who Would Have Saved Anne Frank," *Newsday,* March 16, 1995.

97 " 'to march in' ": Quoted from Hitler's order to invade Austria, March 11, 1938, *Internationaler Militärgerichtshof,* vol. 34, p. 336.

97 " 'We were cut off' ": Holländer's reparations file.

98 "Huize Oosteinde": A pass issued by the camp commander on Dec. 14, 1939, is in the reparations file.

99 "The firm of B. Holländer": Real estate files of the Royal District Court, Aachen, vol. 169, p. 6724, Archives of the Aachen District Court.

99 "His cousin Ernst": Notes of Eduardo M. Fraifeld, Danville, Virginia.

99 "On February 24, 1939": Information taken from the passenger list of March 25, 1939, New York Passenger and Crew Lists, 1897–1957, in Records of the Immigration and Naturalization Service, National Archives, Washington, D.C., microfilm T715–6307.

99 "he later said": Julius Holländer's reparations file.

99 "On February 27, 1939": Julius Holländer's reparations file. This file also contains a certificate from the Deutsche Golddiskontbank to the chief administrator of the city of Aachen, Oct. 28, 1955.

100 "sold their house on Liebfrauenstrasse": Real estate files of the Royal District Court, Aachen, vol. 202, p. 8042.

100 " 'As security against all claims' ": Notarized copy, p. 43, of the registry of deeds, vol. 169, p. 6724.

102 " 'What can one say' ": Letter of Dec. 1938, Anne Frank Fonds.

102 "She was among the exceptions": A stamp in her passport shows that Rosa Holländer traveled to Amsterdam on March 24, 1939.

102 "Before Julius Holländer": On Mach 20, 1939, Julius Holländer was registered with the Police Department's aliens' bureau as residing at 37 Merwedeplein. Files of the aliens' bureau 1930–71, GAA 5225, Archief van de Politie, nos. 3859–4140. Copy in AFS.

103 " 'I think every German Jew' ": Letter of Dec. 24, 1937, personal collection of Elfriede Markovits Frank. Hedda Eisenstaedt to Otto Frank, letter of June 16, 1963, AFS.

103 " 'I always tried to get away' ": Otto Frank to Nathan Straus, April 30, 1941, Otto Frank Files, VIVO Institute for Jewish Research, New York, © Anne Frank Fonds, Basel.

103 "presumably on behalf of the Pomosin-Werke": Note in Robert Feix's files, May 10, 1955.

103 " 'Papi is going' ": Letter of Dec. 2, 1937, Anne Frank Fonds.

104 " 'Shortly before the outbreak' ": Otto Frank to Nathan Straus, April 30, 1941.

104 " 'I am worried about my family' ": Edith Holländer Frank to Hedda Eisenstaedt, letter of Dec. 24, 1937.

104 " 'My husband is very tired' ": Edith Frank to Gertrud Naumann, Dec. 22, [1937], personal papers of Gertrud Naumann Trenz, Frankfurt am Main.

105 "moving on as quickly as possible": In reply to his application for entry into the United States, van Pels received a letter from the American consulate in Rotterdam that read in part: "Your names

have been added to the waiting list of immigrants under the German quota on Feb. 10, 1939. . . . Do not write to us. We will contact you as soon as it is your turn. Based on the present demand it is probable that this will be about indefinite." Van Pels collection, AFS.

105 " 'had emigrated . . . with 3,000 Reichmarks' ": Otto Frank to Trude Heymann, letter of Nov. 29, 1963, AFS.

108 "Ludwig Jacob Mehler": Erika Prins, AFS, interview with the author, May 15, 2007.

108 "how he could know": Dorothea Zucker-Franklin in a conversation with Erika Prins, AFS.

109 " 'My dear little Anne' ": Otto Frank to Anne, letter of May 12, 1938, in *The Diary of Anne Frank: The Critical Edition*, June 19, 1942, version A.

110 " 'The nervous little thing' ": Edith Frank to Willi and Hedda Eisenstaedt, Dec. 24, 1937, Anne Frank Fonds.

112 " 'We often listen' ": Margot's letter of April 27, 1940, to Betty Ann Wagner and Anne's letter of April 29, 1940, to Juanita Wagner are in the Simon Wiesenthal Center, Museum of Tolerance, Los Angeles, CA. Copies of these letters are in the archives of the AFS, Amsterdam.

6. TRAPPED

116 "Only a few weeks earlier": Fussman, "A Date with History."

119 "probably the application of the Frank family": "All the papers have been destroyed there," Otto Frank to Nathan Straus, letter of April 30, 1941.

121 " 'We Germans have not come' ": Quoted in Louis de Jong and Joseph W. F. Stoppelman, *The Lion Rampant: The Story of Holland's Resistance to the Nazis*, Querido: New York, 1943.

122 "Naturally, she was affected": Otto Frank, lecture, 1968, Anne Frank Fonds.

122 " 'Sleeping with Daddy' ": Anne Frank to Alice Stern Frank, letter of Nov. 1940, Anne Frank Fonds.

123 "benefited from the general economic upswing": Hein A. M. Klemann, *Nederland 1938–1946: Economie en samenleving in jaren van oorlog en bezetting*, Amsterdam, 2002.

123 "Pectacon sales representatives": Gies and Gold, *Anne Frank Remembered.*

124 "A statement by": On the matter of Pectacon's deliveries to the German forces, see also David Barnouw and Gerrold van der Stroom, *Wer verriet Anne Frank?*, Münster, 2005, pp. 23ff.

124 " 'During the occupation period' ": NIOD, Doc. I, W. G. van Maaren, quoted in Barnouw and van der Stroom, *Wer varriet Anne Frank?*, p. 26.

124 "Opekta was merely one": In *The Hidden Life of Otto Frank*,. Carol Ann Lee speaks of conclusive proof that Opekta Amsterdam supplied goods to the German forces. She does not provide specifics, however.

124 " 'half-Jewish' owners": Ulrich Feix as well as Walther Scheinberger stated this in interviews with the author in June 2007.

125 " '[Our] pectin . . . made jam jell' ": Miep and Jan Gies in conversation with Harry Paape, NIOD, Feb. 27, 1985, copy in AFS.

125 " 'a profiteer and trader' ": A. C. Ahlers to the Austrian Ministry of the Interior, Jan. 15, 1964, Austrian State Archives (ADR), file Karl Silberbauer.

125 "in Amsterdam alone": The lists of the Zentralauftragsstelle (central office for placing orders) that have been preserved confirm this.

125 "which had formerly housed": According to the Amsterdam street address book, cited in Barnouw and van der Stroom, *Wer verriet Anne Frank?*, pp. 84–85, 111.

126 "This pharmacist, chemist, and inventor": File of Arthur Lewinsohn, Reg. No. 160 768, Reparations Division, Berlin.

126 "On a Saturday morning": Johannes Kleiman, ca. 1954, personal papers of Miep and Paul Gies.

127 " 'Anne and I love to go visit' ": Letter of December 1940, Anne Frank Fonds.

130 "La Synthèse N.V.": Paape, ". . . Originally from Frankfurt-am-Main."

131 " 'Strike! Strike! Strike!' ": Translated from the Dutch original, a facsimile of which is in B. A. Sijes, *De Februari-Staking*, The Hague, 1954.

132 " 'The individual registering' ": "Order for the Occupied Territories of the Netherlands," order 6 (on the requirement to register for persons of full or partial Jewish blood), Jan. 10, 1941.

133 "With the help of Dutch officials": Jacob Presser, *The Destruction of the Dutch Jews*, New York: Dutton, 1969.

135 " 'I haven't gotten as many gifts' ": Margot Frank to Alice Stern Frank, Feb. 22, 1941, Anne Frank Fonds.

137 "SS commander Rauter reported": B. A. Sijes, *De Februari-Staking*, The Hague, 1954.

138 "On Friday, April 18": On Tonny Ahlers, see also Lee, *Hidden Life of Otto Frank*, and Barnouw and van der Stroom, *Wer verriet Anne Frank?*

138 " 'He [Tonny Ahlers] said straight out' ": Quoted in Ernst Schnabel, *Anne Frank: A Portrait in Courage*, trans. Richard and Clara Winston, New York: Harcourt, 1958.

138 " 'I didn't like him' ": Ibid.

138 " 'In matters of business' ": Otto Frank to the Office for National Security, Aug. 21, 1945, file A. C. Ahlers, Nationaal Archief, The Hague.

138 "Joseph Jansen was also a member": I am indebted to Hans van der Veen, Theater Instituut Nederland, and Gerlof Langerija, Amsterdam, for this information about De Voortrekkers.

139 "radio plays for Radio Hilversum": Otto Frank's friend Abraham Cauvern was working in the radio-play department of Radio Hilversum at the time, and that is where Frank met Jansen. Cauvern called himself Albert and was able, with the aid of a counterfeit identity card, to hide the fact that he was Jewish. He and his wife, Isa, later went into hiding separately.

139 " 'if I still received shipments from Germany' ": Otto Frank to the Office for National Security, Aug 21, 1945.

139 "A 'difficult young man' ": Quoted from Tonny Ahlers's social welfare file, as reported in Eric Slot and Paul Arnoldussen, "Verrader Ahlers een lastpak en avonturier," *Het Parool*, March 28, 2002.

140 "by drowning himself": On March 20, 1938, at about 12:15 p.m., the military police turned Tonny Ahlers, then still a minor, over to the Amsterdam police. Ahlers had been picked up in Zutphen, where he had tried to commit suicide because of "disappointment in love." His father picked him up from the police station at 1:45 p.m. Police log of the Amsterdam Police in Gemeentearchief Amsterdam, 3213. I am grateful to Gertjan Broek, Amsterdam, for this information.

140 "During the February strike": Lee, *Hidden Life of Otto Frank*, cites Tonny Ahlers's file, National Archief, The Hague.

140 "a permanent employee of the security service": Slot and Arnoldussen, "Verrader Ahlers."

140 "But Ahlers claimed he visited Otto often": Ahlers made this

claim in letters of Dec. 27, 1963, Jan. 15, 1964, and Dec. 20, 1966. See Barnouw and van der Stroom, *Wer verriet Anne Frank?*, pp. 45ff., and Lee, *Hidden Life of Otto Frank*.

140 "Ahlers registered a small business": On Dec. 15, 1942, and effective Feb. 4, 1943, A. C. Ahlers registered himself with the Amsterdam chamber of commerce as the sole owner of "Petoma." He described his business as trade in surrogate products "that are not subject to any particular sales regulations"—that could, in other words, be bought and sold without coupons. (This meant, de facto, that he could deal on the black market.) On Aug. 14, 1944, the business went bankrupt, but it was registered again on Nov. 21, 1946 (Archiv der Kamer van Koophandel, Amsterdam, 33059114). Ahlers's wife, Martha, reportedly referred to business dealings between Petoma and Opekta or Gies and Company. However, in an interview with Gerlof Langerijs and the author on Nov. 3, 2006, she expressed herself more cautiously, saying that Petoma was "only a fantasy" of her husband's, "nothing serious," and that there had been no contact with Opekta.

141 "much more depressed than he was": Otto Frank to Nathan Straus, letter of April 30, 1941.

141 " 'How long will it be' ": Otto Frank to Nathan Straus, letter of April 30, 1941.

143 "The two bachelors": Reparations files of Julius and Walter Holländer.

143 "Julius had arrived": "Incoming Passenger and Mail Ships," *New York Times*, April 5, 1939.

143 " 'Walter Holländer is' ": A copy of the discharge document is in Walter Holländer's reparations file.

143 " 'He will depart' ": Walter Holländer's name is on the *Volendam*'s passenger list of December 17. New York Passenger and Crew Lists, 1897–1957, Records of the Immigration and Naturalization Service, National Archives, Washington, D.C., microfilm T715–6430. According to the *New York Times* ("Incoming Passenger and Mail Ships") Walter arrived in New York on December 30, 1939.

143 "Julius worked night shifts": Boston Committee for Refugees to Susan Kramer, National Refugee Service, letter of June 16, 1941, Otto Frank file, YIVO Institute.

143 "for about twenty dollars a week": Equivalent to about $250 in present-day currency.

144 "the affidavit for Anne Frank": Boston Committee for Refugees to Susan Kramer.

144 "He immigrated to the United States": Obituary of J. Hiatt, www.clarku.edu/alumni/clarknews/spring 01/memoriam.cfm.

144 " 'I will never forget' ": Otto Frank to Julius and Walter Holländer, letter of Aug 20, 1945, Anne Frank Fonds.

144 "a 'serious, sardonic, rather shy' person": *Time*, April 4, 1932.

145 "In July 1928": The vacation in Sils Maria is documented by a postcard of July 23, 1928, from Nathan Straus to Erich Elias: "We are very happy here with Otto and Edith." Archives of the Straus Historical Society, Smithtown, New York.

145 "As early as the summer of 1910": Interviews by the author with Joseph Nathan Straus, New York, April 16–May 1, 2007, and with Joan Adler, Straus Historical Society, April 4–25, 2007.

145 " 'liberal, almost Socialistic Democrat' ": *Time*, April 4, 1932.

145 " 'You are the only person' ": Otto Frank to Nathan Straus, letter of April 30, 1941.

146 " 'discussions were pending with the "joint" ' ": Otto Frank is referring to the American Jewish Joint Distribution Committee, an organization founded in 1914 by American Jews to aid Jews in other countries, primarily in Europe.

146 "his net worth": According to the "finances list" of the Central Office for Jewish Emigration, undated but about Jan. 1942, in Archiv der Höheren SS- und Polizeiführers, 77 no. 239h, NIOD, Amsterdam.

146 " 'We do want to help' ": Helen Sachs Straus to Augusta Mayerson, letter of May 28, 1941, Otto Frank file, YIVO Institute.

146 " 'That you are preparing affidavits' ": Augusta Mayerson to Nathan Straus, letter of June 3, 1941, Otto Frank file, YIVO Institute.

147 " 'Many people have been waiting for months' ": Otto Frank to Julius Holländer, letter of Nov. 24, 1941, private papers of Miep Gies © Anne Frank Fonds.

147 " 'We can delay' ": Breckinridge Long to his colleagues in the State Department, memorandum of June 26, 1940, www.pbs.org/wgbh/amex/holocaust/filmmore/reference/primary/barmemo.html.

147 " 'I found that he' ": Fred L. Israel, ed., *The War Diary of Breckinridge Long*, Lincoln: University of Nebraska Press, 1966.

147 " 'I was successful this past year' ": Otto Frank to Nathan Straus, letter of April 30, 1941.

147 "Sales in spices": Reparations file, Otto Heinrich Frank, W 22054, Central State Archives of Hessen.

149 "'We're not likely'": Letters from Anne to her relatives in Basel, Anne Frank Fonds.

150 "Eva Kämpfer": Tape recording, personal collection of Barbara Ledermann Rodbell, Chapel Hill, North Carolina.

152 "'I am afraid, however, the news is not good news'": Nathan Straus to Otto Frank, letter of July 1, 1941, Otto Frank file, YIVO Institute.

153 "'The only way'": Otto Frank to Nathan Straus, letter of Sept. 8, 1941, Otto Frank file, YIVO Institute.

153 "'I know it is impossible'": Ibid.

154 "'I am afraid that'": Augusta Mayerson to Helen Straus, letter of Nov. 12, 1941, Otto Frank file, YIVO Institute.

154 "'I was informed'": Otto Frank to Nathan Straus, letter of Sept. 8, 1941.

154 "'Your mother . . . appears to feel well'": Otto Frank to Julius Holländer, letter of Nov. 24, 1941, private papers of Miep Gies © Anne Frank Fonds.

154 "'Dearest Mother'": Otto Frank to Alice Stern Frank, postcard of Sept. 14, 1941, Anne Frank Fonds.

154 "'I wanted to have some peace again'": Ibid.

155 "'I have been tentatively accepted'": *The Diary of Anne Frank: The Revised Critical Edition*, July 5, 1942, version B.

155 "'Jewish institutions'": Quoted in Presser, *Destruction of the Dutch Jews.*

156 "'You're scared to do anything'": *Diary*, June 20, 1942, version A.

156 "'Situations are changing'": Otto Frank to Nathan Straus, letter of Sept. 8, 1941.

157 "among them, Gerard Oeverhaus": Lee, *Hidden Life of Otto Frank.*

157 "'But as Margot is going to be 16'": Otto Frank to Nathan Straus, letter of Oct. 12, 1941, Otto Frank file, YIVO Institute.

157 "no longer permitted to leave": Augusta Mayerson to Nathan Straus, letter of Oct. 2, 1941, Otto Frank file, YIVO Institute: "We had confirmation of the fact that Germany is issuing no exit permits to persons between the ages of eighteen and forty-five, who are at present residing in Germany or German-occupied areas."

157 "'You can imagine'": Otto Frank to Nathan Straus, letter of Oct. 12, 1941.

157 " 'My brother and I' ": Julius Holländer to Nathan Straus, letter of Oct. 6, 1941, Otto Frank file, YIVO Institute.

157 " 'Mr. and Mrs. Straus' ": Augusta Mayerson to Maurice Krinsky, Boston Committee for Refugees, letter of Oct. 17, 1941, Otto Frank file, YIVO Institute.

158 " 'You are able' ": Otto Frank to Julius Holländer, letter of Nov. 24, 1941, private papers of Miep Gies.

158 "Karel Wolters": I have drawn on Paape, ". . . Originally from Frankfurt-am-Main"; David Barnouw, ed., *Correspondentie van Mr. M. M. Rost van Tonningen, deel II, mei 1942–mei 1945*, Amsterdam, 1993; Lee, *Hidden Life of Otto Frank*; and research conducted by Gerlof Langerijs, reparations file, Otto Heinrich Frank.

160 " '[Otto Frank's] letter is urgent' ": Helen Straus to Augusta Mayerson, handwritten letter of Nov. 12, 1941, Otto Frank file, YIVO Institute.

160 " '$2,000 bank deposits' ": Augusta Mayerson to Julius Holländer, letter of Nov. 12, 1941, Otto Frank file, YIVO Institute.

161 "After the premature death": Interviews with Wolfgang Scheinberger and Ulrich Feix; Report of the Claims Resolution Tribunal of Oct. 24, 2002.

162 "repeatedly arrested and detained": Although Feix was officially listed as a concentration camp prisoner, he was nonetheless able to convince the relevant authorities that his experiments with pectin were "crucial to the war effort." He was consequently able to secure his release from Dachau and officially conduct his research for the benefit of the Nazis. After the war, the Americans therefore temporarily held him on suspicion of collaboration.

162 "two representatives from the Pomosin-Werke": Undated protocol of this meeting, copy in AFS. The two representatives were Heinrich Siegfried Sauerbrey and the firm's attorney, Joachim Rieke.

162 " 'shrewdly not complied' ": Note for the files, May 10, 1955, private papers of Ulrich Feix.

163 "canceled that same day": Note of Dec. 11, 1941, in the files of the National Refugee Service, Otto Frank file, YIVO Institute: "Application for Cuban visas for Otto Frank has been cancelled. . . . Let Mrs. Straus know to take no action in view of present international situation."

163 "She was in the midst of a school year": Information about daily life and Anne's life at school in 1941–42 was provided by Jetteke Frijda (in several interviews with the author, starting on April 28,

1997), Iet Swillens, Hannah Goslar Pick, and Jacqueline van Maarsen Sanders.

163 "a story Anne would write": "My First Day at the Lyceum," *Anne Frank's Tales from the Secret Annex*, trans. Ralph Manheim and Michel Mok, New York: Doubleday, 1983.

165 " 'There are only four girls' ": Margot Frank to Alice Stern Frank, letter of April 11, 1942, Anne Frank Fonds.

165 " 'Margot has plenty of company' ": Otto Frank to Julius Holländer, letter of Nov. 24, 1941, private papers of Miep Gies.

166 " '[Anne] is experiencing a growth spurt' ": Ibid.

167 "Another friend": Lucia van Dijk Hendriks, conversations with author from Dec. 12, 1997, to April 1998.

167 "Otto employed two NSB members": One of them was named Daatselaar.

168 "Private concerts": The Ledermann family's guest book is in the Holocaust Memorial Museum, Washington, D.C.

168 "Anne was too young": However, Anne Frank did read *Egmont* in hiding. See Anne Frank, *Mooie-zinnenboek*, ed. Gerrold van der Stroom, Amsterdam, 2004, pp. 79–81.

169 "*The Princess with the Long Nose*": Laureen Nussbaum in conversation with the author.

169 " 'We take this opportunity' ": Joodse Raad voor Amsterdam (Jewish Council) to Otto Frank, Dec. 22, 1941, and Dec. 25, 1941, AFS.

171 "Oma Holländer": *Het Joodse Weekblad*, Feb. 27, 1942, AFS.

171 "Within the next three days": This and all other anti-Jewish orders are cited from the relevant "Verordnungsblatt für die besetzten niederländischen Gebiete" in Presser, *Destruction of the Dutch Jews.*

7. INTO HIDING

174 " 'On Friday, June 12th' ": *Diary*, June 14, 1942, ver. A.

175 "strange and utterly new experience": Unpublished text by Anne Frank, undated, NIOP, Amsterdam.

175 " 'Every kind of sport' ": *Het Joodse Weekblad*, June 12, 1942.

176 " 'Stolen . . . from in front of the residence' ": The historian J. Vis found the police log entry in the Gemeentearchief, Amsterdam, in May 1999.

177 " 'I'm not permitted' ": Margot Frank to Alice Stern Frank, April 11, 1942, Anne Frank Fonds.

177 "Hello Silberberg": Edward Silberberg, interview by author, March 6, 1997, and correspondence thereafter.

179 "her childhood friend Kitty": Recollections of Kitty Egyedi.

180 " 'There'll be no more' ": Otto Frank to Julius Holländer, letter of Nov. 24, 1941, private papers of Miep Gies.

182 " 'My dear loved ones' ": Otto Frank to the Elias family, letter of July 4, 1942, Anne Frank Fonds.

188 "Lutz Peter Schiff": Archives of the Dutch Red Cross (Het Nederlands Rode Kruis), The Hague; NIOD, Amsterdam.

188 "He went by Peter": Reparations file of Lutz Peter Schiff, Reg. No. 270762, State Office for Civil and Administrative Affairs, Reparations Division, Berlin. Further information from his closest childhood friend, Ernst Michaelis, and from Anne's diary.

192 "Their tenant, Werner Goldschmidt": Reparations file of Werner Goldschmidt; Anne's diary.

192 "Otto and Edith Frank had spread the notion": Victor Kugler to Ernst Schnabel, letter of Sept. 17, 1957, Deutsches Literaturarchiv (DLA), Marbach; copy in archives of the AFS.

193 " 'Mr. Frank . . . had often said' ": Ibid.

194 " 'Since electricity, water, and gas' ": Ibid.

194 "some of the family's silver": Franz Hofhuis, interview by author, Hilversum, May 15, 2007.

195 " 'Dearest Lunni' ": Otto Frank to Helene Elias, postcard of July 5, 1942, Anne Frank Fonds. The reconstruction of the events preceding the Franks' going into hiding draws on the recollections of Hannah Goslar Pick, Jacqueline van Maarsen Sanders, Jetteke Frijda, Barbara Ledermann Rodbell, Edward Silberberg, and Miep Gies.

199 " 'About 700 Jews' ": Special edition of *Het Joodse Weekblad*, July 14, 1942, facsimile in Presser, *Destruction of the Dutch Jews*.

200 " 'Re: Deportation' ": Quoted in Gerhard Schoenberner, *Der gelbe Stern: Die Judenverfolgung in Europa 1933–1945*, Hamburg, 1960.

8. THE SECRET ANNEX

207 "Later, she pasted": "A Room Full of Dreams," in *Anne's World*, Anne Frank House.

210 "every fifteen minutes": Boudewijn Zwart, the keeper of the Amsterdam carillons, interview by author, Jan. 26, 1998, and followup correspondence.

210 " 'Twelve forty-five' ": "Lunch Break," Aug. 5, 1943, *Anne Frank's Tales from the Secret Annex.*

212 " 'nightly freedom' ": "Freedom in the Annex," Aug. 6, 1943, *Tales from the Secret Annex.*

216 "Jan was a member": Paul Gies and Gerlof Langerijs, interviews by author, 2007–11.

218 " 'With the help of our business connections' ": Victor Kugler to Ernst Schnabel, Sept. 17, 1957, DLA, Marbach.

223 " 'a sign of friendship' ": Jacqueline van Maarsen Sanders, interview by author.

223 "Some months later": Ibid.

224 " 'a fateful, unforgettable pounding' ": Nanette Blitz Konig, presentation to the Argentinian Senate, June 2011.

228 " '1½ years on' ": This is Anne's comment on her entry of Nov. 10, 1942.

229 "She would take care": Unpublished text, undated; the original is located in the NIOD.

230 "they had known Pfeffer": Undated statement of Otto Frank, AFS.

231 "Born in the Hessian city": The information that follows on Fritz Pfeffer, Charlotte Kaletta, Werner Pfeffer, and Gustav and Ludwig Löwenstein comes from the reparations files of Friedrich Fritz Pfeffer, Peter Pepper (Werner Pfeffer), Martha Charlotte Kaletta, and Gustav Löwenstein, all in the State Office for Civil and Administrative Affairs, Berlin, Section 1, Reparations Division; from the correspondence of Kaletta and the Löwenstein family, 1939–41, AFS; and from the exhibition *We Too Might Move On*, Anne Frank House, Amsterdam, 2012.

233 " 'Anne could imitate' ": Victor Kugler to Ernst Schnabel, Sept. 17, 1957, DLA, Marbach.

233 "the farewell letter": Fritz Pfeffer to Charlotte Kaletta, Nov. 15, 1942, AFS.

234 "his only son, Werner": After his emigration and until his death, Werner Pfeffer went by the name of Peter Werner Pepper.

235 " 'I pray to God' ": Charlotte Kaletta to Leah Löwenstein, July 10, 1939, AFS.

235 "to Raasiku in Estonia": Details of the transport on Sept. 26, 1942, are in Monica Kingreen and Wolfgang Scheffler, "Die Deportationen nach Raasiku bei Reval," *Buch der Erinnerung: Die*

aus Baltikum deportierten deutschen, österreichen und tschechoslovakischen Juden, ed. W. Scheffler and D. Schulle, Munich, 2003.

237 "It was thanks": Otto Frank to Jean Grossman Schick, *Story Within Her Story*.

238 "While Margot": Jetteke Frijda, interviews by author.

239 " 'Well, let's see' ": Otto Frank to Jean Grossman Schick, *Story Within Her Story*.

240 "Kugler, however, enjoyed": Victor Kugler to Ernst Schnabel, Sept. 17, 1957.

240 "devouring books": These notes on Anne's reading material are taken from a letter by Otto Frank dated 1945, Anne Frank Fonds.

242 " 'You have to be reasonable' ": Otto Frank to Helene Frank Elias, Aug. 31, 1917, Anne Frank Fonds.

244 "Edith Frank's state of mind": Written statement from Miep Gies, Dec. 3, 1997.

246 "it was invariably Edith": Otto Frank, lecture, 1968, AFF.

246 " 'On the one hand' ": Otto Frank, lecture, 1968.

246 " 'like an adult' ": Otto Frank, 1968 talk.

247 " 'At a crucial moment' ": Ernst Schnabel to Tutti Fischer Bermann, Dec. 1957, A. S. Fischer, Deutsches Literaturarchiv (DLA), Marbach.

248 "so Otto Frank later recalled": Otto Frank to Jean Grossman Schick, *Story Within Her Story*.

249 "The prime mover": Otto Frank to Jean Grossman Schick.

250 " 'I got on better' ": Otto Frank, lecture, 1968.

253 " 'You know how' ": Otto Frank's letters of Aug. 31, 1917, June 16, 1918, and June 27, 1918, to Helene Frank Elias, Anne Frank Fonds.

254 "They celebrated their engagement": The notices of engagement and marriage are in the private collection of Eduardo M. Fraifeld, Danville, Virginia.

254 "After the war": Cor Suijk, in numerous conversations with the author from Jan. 10, 1997, to April 1998.

254 "Ernst Schnabel's judgment": Ernst Schnabel to Rudolf Hirsch, Feb. 27, 1958, A. S. Fischer, DLA, Marbach.

254 "analysis seventy-four lines long": Loose sheets, dated Feb. 8, 1944, in NIOD, Amsterdam. In 2001 the Anne Frank Fonds published this text in an "emended edition." The passages from Anne's text quoted here are taken from p. 181 of that edition.

257 "Otto's brother": Herbert Frank told this story to Cor Suijk in the mid-1970s.

258 "When he told": Written statement from Miep Gies, Dec. 3, 1997.

261 "'I have a kind'": Letter, summer 1942, Anne Frank Fonds.

9. LIVING IN FEAR

266 "'Anne didn't write'": Otto Frank to his family in Basel, undated, AFS.

268 "7.50 guilders": Ad van Liempt, *Kopfgeld: Bezahlte Denunziationen von Juden in den besetzten Niederlande*, Munich, 2005.

268 "about the equivalent": According to calculations of the Internationaal Instituut voor Sociale Geschiedenis (IISG), www.iisg.nl.

268 "raised the amount to 25 guilders": Police interrogation of Karl Josef Silberbauer, March 1964, State Criminal Investigation Department, Amsterdam. Doc. 1, K. J. Silberbauer, NIOD.

270 "A little less than four months": On March 17, 1942, at 10:50 a.m. a fire broke out at 263 Prinsengracht. A half hour later, Victor Kugler reported it to the police station on Marnixstraat. Police files, Amsterdam Municipal Archives. Thanks to Gerlof Langerijs for this reference.

272 "'When we started running low'": Otto Frank, letter of June 10, 1971, to Yad Vashem, Anne Frank Fonds.

273 "sound of the vacuum cleaner": Aug. 5, 1943, ver. B. On the use of the vacuum cleaner, see also Nov. 3, 1943, ver. B.

274 "'With the help of'": Statements of Arthur Lewinsohn, in the Arthur Lewinsohn file, Reg. No. 160 768, Reparations Division, Berlin, and in the file of Sighilde Flora Franziska Lewinsohn, née Albinger, Reg. No. 302 016.

275 "What did they know": The information on M. A. Wessels was provided by Gerlof Langerijs and based on his interviews with Betty Wessels Polak, René Wessels, and Sonja Wessels Mouw in 2009. Archives consulted include Stadsarchief Amsterdam, IISG, Nationaal Archief, in The Hague, Beeldbank Kadaster Amsterdam, Kamer van Koophandel en Fabrieken Amsterdam. The name M. A. Wessels does not appear in the extant Calmeyer lists (Erich Maria Remarque–Archiv, Osnabrück). Because these lists are incomplete, it is altogether possible that Wessels received help from Calmeyer.

277 "One of these young thieves": See Dineke Stam, "Ik was de inbreker," *Anne Frank Magazine.*

277 "the night watchman, Martinus Slegers": Several incorrect spellings of Sleger's name are in circulation: Sleegers, Schlegers, Slagers, etc.

278 "why he called on Cornelis": Police report of April 9–10, 1944, AFS. Information on Cornelis den Boef is taken from the Amsterdam Municipal Archives and from Sytze van der Zee, *Vogelvrij: De jacht op de Joodse onderduiker*, Amsterdam, 2010.

278 "And what did Gezinus Gringhuis want": In *The Hidden Life of Otto Frank*, Carol Ann Lee indicates that there may have been contact between Martinus Slegers and Gringhuis. Sleger's name and address appear in a notebook of Gringhuis's that was confiscated after the war as evidence against him.

280 " 'Kugler never told his wife' ": Letter from Otto Frank to Alice Stern Frank, Sept. 1, 1945, AFS.

281 "he had acquired a fake identity card": Victor Kugler's false ID card, issued on Jan. 19, 1944, is in the archives of the AFS.

281 " 'a fanatic' ": Interview with the Canadian journalist Evelyn Wolfe, 1972. A copy is in the archives of the AFS.

281 " 'to the German home' ": Postcard of Nov. 11, 1943, to Victor Kugler, AFS.

282 " 'in the realm of feeling' ": Ernst Schnabel's judgment, in Ernst Schnabel, DLA, Marbach.

282 "Jopie, who was Anne's age": Until now, Kleiman's daughter, Jopie, has been called Corry in the Anne Frank literature. She was given that name—to her displeasure—to avoid confusion with Jacqueline "Jopie" van Maarsen.

284 " 'Being tight-lipped didn't help' ": Mrs. van Hoeve to Ernst Schnabel, ca 1957. Ernst Schnabel, DLA, Marbach.

285 "Like so many other Dutchmen": Information on Hendrina Saartje Stoppelman and Kuno van der Horst was provided by Kuno's sister Rozemarijn van der Horst in interviews with Gerlof Langerijs (2007–12).

286 "Only after the war": Wil Voskuijl van der Vennen, interview with Teresien da Silva and Erika Prins, March 9, 2006.

286 "The Voskuijls probably guarded": David Barnouw revealed in his book *Het Fenomeen Anne Frank*, Amsterdam, 2012, that in her diary entry of May 11, 1944, ver. A, Anne was referring to Bep's sister Hendrika Petronella Voskuijl.

286 "As early as November 1941": Personal record for Hendrika Petronella Voskuijl, Stadsarchief, Amsterdam.

288 " 'When I caught him' ": Victor Kugler to Otto Frank, Dec. 1963, AFF.

289 "One of the warehouse workers": Police interrogation of J. J. de Kok, Nov. 26, 1963, State Criminal Investigation Division, Amsterdam, Doc. 1, K. J. Silberbauer, NIOD.

289 "theft and fencing stolen goods": Police archives, Amsterdam.

291 " 'During the German occupation' ": Confidential report of the Rijksrecherche, Feb. 5, 1964, in the Austrian State Archives (ADR), file Karl Silberbauer, 55936-18/66.

292 " 'From April 18, 1941, on' ": A. C. Ahlers to the Austrian Ministry of the Interior re Karl Silberbauer, Jan. 15, 1964, Austrian State Archives, file Karl Silberbauer.

293 "large amounts of bread and milk": Police interrogation of L. Hartog, March 20, 1948, Ministry of Justice, criminal file van Maaren, NIOD, Amsterdam.

293 "Lena van Bladeren Hartog worked for the cleaning firm": Confirmed in writing by Miep Gies, Dec. 18, 1997.

293 "Sometime in July 1944": Police interrogation of Anna van Wijk Genot, Ministry of Justice, criminal file van Maaren, NIOD, Amsterdam.

293 "Bep went to Victor Kugler": Written statement of Miep Gies, Dec. 3, 1997.

294 " 'About a week before' ": Victor Kugler to Otto Frank, letter of Feb. 4, 1944, AFS.

295 " 'If Silberbauer's report is correct' ": Record of the interrogation of Willy Paul Franz Lages on Dec. 6, 1963, the Austrian State Archives, file Karl Silberbauer. At the time of this interrogation, Lages, who had been given a life sentence, was still in prison.

10. THE LAST TRAIN

296 "The Nazis had other things": Police interrogation of Karl Josef Silberbauer, March 4, 1964, State Criminal Investigation Department, Amsterdam. Doc. 1, K. J. Silberbauer, NIOD.

299 " 'That is some comfort' ": Franz Ledermann to Barbara Ledermann, July 7, 1943, personal collection of Barbara Ledermann Rodbell, Chapel Hill, North Carolina.

300 "Anne was far from unhappy": Otto Frank, lecture, 1968.

300 "The workday": Based in part on recollections of Kitty Egyedi in conversation with the author. Also recollections of Rachel Frankfoorder van Amerongen and Janny Brilleslijper Brandes in conversation with Willy Lindwer, in *Anne Frank: The Last Seven Months*, a documentary film.

301 " 'warm, loving human being' ": Lin Jaldati and Eberhard Rebling, *Sag nie, du gehst den letzten Weg: Erinnerungen*, Berlin, 1986, p. 395.

302 "Anne is reported": Elfriede Markovits Frank gave this account to the author, based on conversations between Rosa de Winter and Otto Frank.

305 " 'All that must' ": Otto Frank to Leni Elias, Sept. 14, 1945, Anne Frank Fonds.

306 "Since mid-July 1942": Records of the Westerbork camp are in the archives of the Netherlands State Institute for War Documentation, Amsterdam.

306 "498 men": Auschwitz archives, in Danuta Czech, *Kalendarium der Ereignisse im Konzentrationslager Auschwitz-Birkenau, 1939–1945*, Reinbek, 1989.

307 "Edith Frank supposedly smuggled": Lenie van Naarden de Jong, conversation with Willy Lindwer, *Anne Frank*.

307 "one of the women guards": Eline Hoekstra, Portland, Oregon, conversation with Cor Suijk, Jan. 1998.

309 "her former admirer": Edward Silberberg, interview by author, March 6, 1997.

312 " 'Compared with this' ": From the diary of SS Hauptsturmführer Kremer, entry of Sept. 2, 1942, in Gerhard Schoenberner, *Der gelbe Stern*, Hamburg, 1960.

314 "Others were shaved": Max Stoppelman, conversations and correspondence with author, April 1997–April 1998.

317 "a particularly dreadful block": Rosa de Winter-Levy, *Aan de Gaskamer Ontsnapt: Het Satanswerk van de SS*, Doetinchem, 1945.

318 "More selections": Archives of the concentration camp Auschwitz, in Danuta Czech, *Kalendarium der Ereignisse Auschwitz-Birkenau 1939–1945*.

318 "an SS man": Written statement by Lin Jaldati, April 5, 1951, copies in the Jaldati-Rebling literary estate, Academy of Arts, Berlin, and AFS.

319 " 'The four of us' ": Jaldati statement.

321 "through a barbed-wire fence": Numerous conversations with Nanette Blitz Konig, and her presentation to the Argentinian Senate, June 2011.

322 "Rosa de Winter had become": De Winter-Levy, *Aan de Gaskamer Ontsnapt.*

322 " 'Prisoner 64971' ": Information from the International Red Cross, Bad Arolsen, March 5, 1964, in Austrian State Archives, file Karl Silberbauer.

323 "But another girl, from Holland": Information based on a letter from Nanette Blitz Konig to Otto Frank, Oct. 31, 1945, AFF.

323 "she no longer had a mother": Hannah Goslar Pick, interview by author, 1997.

325 "Her father was dead": Iet Swillens, in conversation with author, based on a conversation between Hannah Goslar Pick and Iet Swillens in the summer of 1945.

325 "Peter van Pels, too": Max Stoppelman, in conversation with author, op cit.

326 "through the intercession": Otto Frank to Alice Stern Frank, July 8, 1945, Anne Frank Fonds.

327 "After several detours": Details according to the Committee of the International Red Cross, Bad Arolsen, Sept. 9, 1958, in Austrian State Archives, file Karl Silberbauer.

327 " 'On the 26th, the SS' ": Otto Frank to Alice Stern Frank, July 8, 1945.

327 "On Friday evenings": Hannah Goslar Pick, interview by author.

328 " 'I have no news of Edith' ": Otto Frank to Alice Stern Frank, March 15, 1945, Anne Frank Fonds.

328 "Andrew Pares": *The Story of Belsen* (pamphlet), Hannover, 1945; http://www.durhamrecordoffice.org.uk/pages/TheStoryofBelsen.aspk.

329 "Against the advice": Jaldati and Rebling, *Sag nie.*

11. LONGING

332 "Otto Frank had to confess": Otto Frank mentioned this on several occasions, e.g., in his 1968 talk and in a letter of April 28, 1974, to Milly Stanfield, AFS.

332 " 'Her outstanding traits' ": Otto Frank to Milly Stanfield.

334 "Otto Frank often told": 1968 talk, AFF.

EPILOGUE

Unless noted otherwise, all interviews referred to in these notes were conducted by the author.

Tonny Ahlers: David Barnouw and Gerrold van der Stroom, *Who Betrayed Anne Frank?*, NIOD, 2003; Lee, *Hidden Life of Otto Frank*; Austrian State Archives, File Karl Silberbauer; Amsterdam Municipal Archives; Amsterdam Chamber of Commerce; NIOD; Internationaal Instituut voor Sociale Geschiedenis; Interviews by Gerlof Langerijs and Melissa Müller with Martha Ahlers, Nov. 3, 2006, Dec. 4, 2006.

Nanette Blitz: Interviews; Nanette Blitz König to Otto Frank, Oct. 31, 1945; presentation to the Argentinian Senate, June 2011.

Isa and Ab Cauvern: Otto Frank to Alice Stern Frank, Dec. 12, 1945, Anne Frank Fonds; "Was schrieb das Kind?," *Der Spiegel*, April 1, 1959; Koosjevan der Geest-Kurpershoek, interview with Gerlof Langerijs; Nico Wijnberg, interview with Gerlof Langerijs; Dick Verkijk, *Radio Hilversum, 1940–1945: De omroep in de oorlog*, Amsterdam, 1974.

Julius Dettmann: Police interrogation of Karl Josef Silberbauer, March 1964; research by the AFS; research by Gerlof Langerijs.

The Diaries: Otto Frank to Milly Stanfield, Aug. 26, 1946, AFS; Otto Frank to Alice Stern Frank, Sept. 30, 1945, AFS; Nathan Straus Jr. to Otto Frank, Jan. 15, 1953, AFS; "Was schrieb das Kind?," *Der Spiegel*, April 1, 1959; Laureen Nussbaum, "Die Schriftstellerin Anne Frank" in Barbara Bauer and Waltraud Strickhausen, *Für ein Kind war das anders*, Berlin, 1999; David Barnouw, *Het Fenomeen Anne Frank*, Amsterdam, 2012.

Lucia van Dijk: Interviews, Dec. 12, 1997, to April 1998.

Albert Anton Dreher: www.joodsmonument.nl.

Bernd "Buddy" Elias: Interviews; family archives; various media reports.

Kitty Egyedi Gokkel: Interviews, July 7, 1997, to March 27, 1998.

Alice Stern Frank: Interviews with Buddy Elias; Johannes Kleiman to Alice Stern Frank, May 20, 1945; Otto Frank to family in Basel, May 27, 1945; Alice Stern Frank to Otto Frank, June 19, 1945; Alice Stern Frank to Otto Frank, Aug. 4, 1945, Anne Frank Fonds.

Jean-Michel Frank: Pierre-Emmanuel Martin-Vivier, *Jean-Michel Frank*, New York, 2008; Mirjam Pressler, *Grüsse und Küsse an alle*, Frankfurt, 2009 (*Anne Frank's Family*, New York, 2011); J. M. Frank, *Mémoire du style*, Paris, 1998.

Otto Heinrich Frank: Otto Frank to Adam and Zofia Kukulski, Aug. 27, 1962; Otto Frank to Alice Stern Frank, March 31, 1945; Anne Frank Fonds; Otto Frank to Leni and Erich Elias, June 21, 1945; Robert Frank to

Otto Frank, Aug. 1, 1945; Otto Frank to Milly Stanfield, Aug. 26, 1945; Otto Frank, March 16, 1946; Otto Frank to Rudolf Ripa, Jan. 9, 1947; Otto Frank to Robert and Lotti Frank, July 26, 1945; Julius Holländer to Otto Frank, July 25, 1945; Nathan Straus Jr. to Otto Frank, Oct. 25, 1945; Otto Frank to Julius and Walter Holländer, Aug. 20, 1945; Otto Frank to Robert and Leni Elias, July 7, 1945; Otto Frank to Joseph Süttendorf, July 13, 1947; interviews with Miep Gies; Gerrold van der Stroom, "The Diaries, 'Het Achterhuis' and the Translations," *The Diary of Anne Frank: The Revised Critical Edition*; Anna G. Steenmeijer, April 1998; interviews with Elfriede Geiringer and Eva Schloss; Otto Frank to Milly Stanfield, Dec. 6, 1978; interviews with Buddy Elias; interviews with Vincent Frank-Steiner, 1997–98; notarized will of Otto Frank, Dec. 15, 1978, Anne Frank Fonds; Federal Department of the Interior, Bern; Gerrold van der Stroom, "Anne Frank and Her Diaries," lecture presented at the conference *The History and Culture of the Jews in the Low Countries*, London, June 17–19, 1997.

Jetteke Frijda: Interviews; www.joodsmonument.de; Otto Frank to Alice Stern Frank, Dec. 12, 1945, AFS.

Jan and Miep Gies: Interviews with Miep Gies, 1997–98; interviews and correspondence with Paul Gies, 2007–08; personal papers of Paul and Miep Gies; Miep Gies and Alison Leslie Gold, *Anne Frank Remembered: The Story of the Woman Who Helped to Hide the Frank Family*, New York: Simon and Schuster 1987; Otto Frank to Robert and Lotti Frank, July 26, 1945; police interrogations of W. G. van Maaren, March 31, 1948, and Oct. 1964; Otto Frank to the Elias family, undated draft of a letter written to accompany a copy of the diary, AFS; written statement from Miep Gies, Dec. 3, 1997; notarized will of Otto Frank, Dec. 15, 1978; invitation from the German ambassador to the presentation of the Order of Merit of the Federal Republic of Germany to Miep Gies, Nov. 1989; personal papers of Gerlof Langerijs; Chancellery of Netherlands Orders to Gerlof Langerijs, Aug. 14, 2007.

Werner Goldschmidt: Reparations file, State Office for Civil and Administrative Affairs, Berlin; Amsterdam Municipal Archives; Ellen Schwarzschild, *Tagebuch: Niet lessen Als 't U blieft. Nicht lesen bitte*, Amstelveen, 1999; Beit Theresienstadt.

Hanneli Goslar: Interviews, July 26–28, 1997; Hannah Goslar to Iet Swillens, Aug. 4, 1946, personal papers of Iet Swillens; "Anne Frank, Die beste Freundin," *Frankfurter Allgemeine Zeitung,* June 13, 2004; Hans Joachim Pohl, "Der verlorene Transport," *Verkehrsgeschichtliche Blätter*, vol. 25 (1998); www.wikipedia.de/wiki/Verlorener_Zug.

Gezinus Gringhuis: Centraal Archief Bijzondere Rechtspleging, NIOD; research of the AFS.

Willem Grootendorst: NIOD; research by Gerlof Langerijs, April 2006–March 2007.

Lammert Hartog: NIOD; recollections of Miep Gies; Barnouw and van der Stroom, *Who Betrayed Anne Frank?*

Lena van Bladeren Hartog: Statements of Lena Hartog, NIOD; written statement of Miep Gies, Dec. 3, 1997; Barnouw and van der Stroom, *Who Betrayed Anne Frank?*

Irene Holländer: Interviews with Eduardo M. Fraifeld, 1997–98; Otto Frank to Irene Holländer, June 13, 1958, personal papers of Eduardo M. Fraifeld.

Julius and Walter Holländer: Julius Holländer to Otto Frank, June 29, 1945; Julius Holländer to Otto Frank, Aug. 27, 1945; Otto Frank to Julius and Walter Holländer, Oct. 1, 1952, Anne Frank Fonds; reparations files of Walter and Julius Holländer, Archives of the Düsseldorf District Government; Otto Frank to Irene Holländer, June 13, 1958; Otto Frank to Irene Holländer, Jan. 16, 1968, personal papers of Eduardo M. Fraifeld; Heinz Jacobowitz to Otto Frank, July 9, 1961, AFS; death certificates of Walter and Julius Holländer, Office of Vital Records, New York City Department of Health; estate of Julius Holländer, Surrogate's Court, New York County.

Kuno van der Horst: Kuno van der Horst to Otto Frank, Nov. 7, 1952, personal papers of Paul and Miep Gies; interviews and correspondence with the van der Horst family (USA) by Gerlof Langerijs, 2008; interviews and correspondence with Rozemarijn van der Horst (Hawaii) and Marjon Kok (Holland) by Gerlof Langerijs, 2008–12.

Job Jansen: Austrian State Archives; Amsterdam Municipal Archives; www.bremermisjpoge.net; Carol Ann Lee, *The Hidden Life of Otto Frank*, New York: Morrow, 2003; Sytze van der Zee, *Vogelvrij: De jacht op de Joodse onderduiker* Amsterdam, 2010.

Martha Charlotte Kaletta: Otto Frank to Peter Werner Pepper, Sept. 20, 1945, Anne Frank Fonds; reparations files of Gustav Löwenstein and Fritz Pfeffer, State Office for Civil and Administrative Affairs, Berlin; M. Kingreen and W. Scheffler, "Die Deportationen nach Raasiku bei Reval," *Buch der Erinnerung: Die ins Baltikum deportierten deutschen, österreichischen und tschechoslowakischen Juden*, Munich, 2003; interviews with Miep Gies; interviews with Joke Kniesmeijer, 1997; Nanda van der Zee, *The Roommate of Anne Frank*, Soesterberg, 2003.

Sol Kimmel: Rochelle Fürstenberg, "Heart to Heart," *Hadassah Magazine*, April 1995.

Johannes Kleiman: Otto Frank to Robert and Lotti Frank, July 7,

1945, AFS; interviews with Miep Gies; correspondence between Otto Frank and Johannes Kleiman, 1950s, personal papers of Paul and Miep Gies; Victor Kugler to Ernst Schnabel, 1958, papers of Ernst Schnabel, Deutsches Literaturarchiv, Marbach; Victor Kugler to Otto Frank, March 3, 1959, AFS.

Hannelore Klein: Interviews with Laureen and Rudi Nussbaum, 1997–2011.

Victor Kugler: Rick Kardonne and Eda Shapiro, *Victor Kugler: The Man Who Hid Anne Frank*, Jerusalem, 2008. Otto Frank to Alice Stern Frank, Sept. 1, 1945, AFS; Victor Kugler to Ernst Schnabel, papers of Ernst Schnabel, Deutsches Literaturarchiv, Marbach; Victor Kugler to Otto Frank, March 3, 1959, AFS; Otto Frank to Milly Stanfield, June 13, 1978, AFS; interviews with Miep Gies.

Maarten Kuiper: National Archives, II, College Park, Md.; Sytze van der Zee, *Vogelvrij*; Inger Schaap, *Sluipmoordenaars: De Silbertanne-Moorden in Nederland, 1943–45*, Hilversum, 2010; interviews with Gertjan Broek by Gerlof Langerijs, 2007–11; research of Gerlof Langerijs; research of the AFS.

Sanne, Ilse, and Franz Ledermann: Interviews with Barbara Ledermann Rodbell; Ilse Ledermann to Barbara Ledermann, Nov. 15, 1943, personal papers of Barbara Ledermann Rodbell.

Barbara Ledermann: Interviews with Barbara Ledermann Rodbell and Martin Rodbell; Barbara Ledermann to Otto Frank, Sept. 10, 1947, and June 13, 1955, AFS.

Arthur Siegfried Lewinsohn: Reparations file, State Office for Civil and Administrative Affairs, Berlin; Amsterdam Municipal Archives; interviews and correspondence with Hansmartin Unger, St. Gallen, 2011.

Willem Gerhard van Maaren: NIOD; interviews with Miep Gies; Harry Paape, "The Betrayal," *The Diary of Anne Frank: The Revised Critical Edition.*

Jacqueline van Maarsen: Interviews with Jacqueline van Maarsen Sanders.

Ludwig Jacob Mehler: AFS; www.joodsmonument.nl.

Gertrud Naumann: Interviews with Gertrud and Karl Trenz.

Opekta: Harry Paape, ". . . Originally from Frankfurt am Main," *The Diary of Anne Frank: The Revised Critical Edition*; correspondence between Otto Frank and Johannes Kleiman, 1950s, personal papers of Paul and Miep Gies; company files of Opekta Cologne and Opekta Amsterdam, personal papers of Ulrich Feix.

Werner Pfeffer: Otto Frank to Peter W. Pepper, Sept. 2, 1945, copy, Anne Frank Fonds; reparations file, State Office for Civil and Administrative Affairs, Berlin; interviews with Miep Gies; interviews with Joke Kniesmeijer; *Anne Frank Remembered,* directed by Jon Blair.

Lutz Peter Schiff: NIOD; letter from the Netherlands Red Cross, The Hague, Aug. 1, 2000; letter from the Dachau Concentration Camp Memorial, Jan. 21, 2009; reparations file, Office for Civil and Administrative Affairs, Berlin.

Anneliese Schütz: Laureen Nussbaum, in conversation with the author; Gerrold van der Stroom, "The Diaries, *Het Achterhuis* and the Translations," *The Diary of Anne Frank: The Revised Critical Edition*; Otto Frank to Alice Stern Frank, Sept 1, 1945, AFS; Otto Frank to Anneliese Schütz, May 8, 1960, AFS; "Was schrieb das Kind," *Der Spiegel*, April 1, 1959.

Arthur Seyss-Inquart: Interview with Helmut Seyss-Inquart, 1997; various media reports; personal papers of Helmut Seyss-Inquart; personal papers of Cor Suijk.

The Secret Annex: Jos van der Land and Herman Vuijsje, *Het Anne Frank Huis: Een biografie*, Amsterdam, 2010; Miep Gies and Alison Leslie Gold, *Anne Frank Remembered*; personal papers of Miep and Paul Gies; personal papers of Ulrich Feix.

Karl Josef Silberbauer: NIOD; *Volksblatt* (Vienna), Oct. 16, 1964; Austrian State Archives; Simon Wiesenthal Archive, Vienna; Resi Hauser to Otto Frank, Dec. 4, 1963, AFS; interviews with Jules Huf, 1997; http://www.wien.gv.at/kultur/archiv/geschichte/gestapo/biografien.html; Political Archives of the Foreign Office, Berlin; National Archives II, College Park, Md.; Christian Ritz, *Schreibtischtäter vor Gericht: Das Verfahren vor dem Münchener Landgericht wegen der Deportation der niederländischen Juden (1959–1967)*, Paderborn, 2012; Peter-Ferdinand Koch, *Enttarnt. Doppelagenten: Namen, Fakten, Beweise*, Salzburg, 2011. Contrary to the promise of this last book's title, Koch does not present any proof of Silberbauer's alleged activity for the West German intelligence service. My own research in the National Archives and in the Simon Wiesenthal archives in Vienna, as well as consultations with Christian Ritz and Wolfgang Krieger, both extremely knowledgeable about Wilhelm Harster, suggests that Koch is mistaken.

Edward "Hello" Silberberg: Interviews and correspondence; Hello Silberberg to Otto Frank, July 7, 1947, AFS.

Martin Slegers: Centraal Bureau voor Genealogie, The Hague; research by Gerlof Langerijs.

Olga Spitzer: Correspondence with her grandson Gerard Spitzer; interview with Buddy Elias.

Milly Stanfield: Otto Frank to Milly Stanfield, undated letter, ca. mid-1945, AFS; Milly Stanfield to Otto Frank, Nov. 29, 1956, AFS; Cal Fussman, "A Date with History: Milly Stanfield, the Woman Who Would Have Saved Anne Frank," *Newsday*, March 16, 1995; Bruce Chadwick, "Grieving

Cousin's Death," *New York Daily News*, Dec. 8, 1977; obituary, *New York Times,* March 4, 2001.

Max Stoppelman: Interviews with Max and Lotte Stoppelman, 1997–2003; Max Stoppelman's diary notes, personal papers of Max Stoppelman; www.joodsmonument.nl.

Nathan Straus Jr.: Interviews with Joseph N. Straus, 2007; interview with Joan Adler, Straus Historical Society, Smithtown, New York; New York Public Library, New York; correspondence between Otto Frank and Nathan Straus, AFS; YIVO Institute for Jewish Research, New York.

Iet "Ietje" Swillens: Interviews with Iet Swillens.

Elisabeth "Bep" Voskuijl: Interviews with Ton van Wijk, 2007; interviews with Joop van Wijk, 2007; Otto Frank to Alice Stern Frank, Dec. 1, 1945, Anne Frank Fonds; written statement from Miep Gies, Dec. 3, 1997; information from Yt Stoker, Amsterdam; information from Erika Prins, AFS; notarized will of Otto Frank, Dec. 15, 1978, Anne Frank Fonds; Amsterdam Municipal Archives.

Betty and Juanita Wagner: Susan Goldman Rubin, *Searching for Anne Frank: Letters from Amsterdam to Iowa*, New York: Abrams, 2003.

Ilse Wagner: Jacqueline van Maarsen, in conversation with the author; archives of the Netherlands Red Cross, The Hague.

Karel Oscar Marie Wolters: David Barnouw, ed., *Correspondentie van Mr. M. M. Rost van Tonningen*, Amsterdam, 1993; NIOD; National Archives, The Hague; personal papers of Ben Wegman; Amsterdam Municipal Archives; Gerlof Langerijs, in conversation with Chantel van Dam.

Dorothee Sophie Würzburger: Interviews with Monica Smith, 1997–2012; interviews with Nicole Smith-Brody, 2010–12.

ACKNOWLEDGMENTS

Many generous people have given me their time and their trust. They made themselves available time and again for interviews that lasted for hours, sometimes for days. Patiently and willingly, they answered questions about the most minute details. They directed me to important new sources and gave me access to many documents that had never been open to researchers before. They did their best to keep me from jumping to false conclusions. They read my drafts and made suggestions for improvements. I could not have written this book without their help. To them all, I am grateful indeed.

In Holland: Jacqueline van Maarsen Sanders and her husband, Ruud; Kitty Egyedi Gokkel, Lucia van Dijk Hendriks (deceased), Iet Swillens (deceased), Jetteke Frijda, and Annat Harting; Miep Gies (deceased), Paul Gies, and Gerlof Langerijs; Bep Voskuijl's sons Ton and Joop and her sister Will van der Vennen-Voskuijl; Max and Lotte Stoppelman (deceased); Martha van Kuik (deceased); Frans Hofhuis; Nicolaas Wijnberg (deceased); Alfred Siegfried Cohen; Gerrold van der Stroom; David Barnouw and Hubert Berkhout of NIOD; the former and current staff of the Anne Frank

Foundation, Amsterdam; Rian Verhoeven, Joke Kniesmeijer (deceased), Yt Stoker, Dineke Stam, Hans Westra, Erika Prins, Teresien da Silva, Gertjan Broek, Karolien Stocking, Ronald Leopold, Jan Eric Dubbelman, Menno Metselaar, Inger Schaap, Bert van Rijn, and many others; Ben Wegman; Sytze van der Zee; H. C. Giersthove and the Dutch Red Cross; Dick van der Horst and the Office for the Protection of Historic Monuments; Boudewijn Zwart, keeper of the Amsterdam carillons; Hans van der Veen and the Theater Institute of the Netherlands; Job Lisman and his team at Bert Bakker; and my translator, then and now, Gerda Meijerink.

In the United States, South America, and Canada: Laureen Nussbaum (née Klein), Seattle, and her husband, Rudi (deceased); Nanette Blitz Konig, her husband, John, São Paulo, and her daughter, Elizabeth Kahn, Miami; Barbara Ledermann Rodbell, North Carolina, and her husband, Martin (deceased); Ed "Hello" Silberberg and his wife, Marlyse, New Jersey; Monica Smith, née Dorothee Sophie Würzburger, and her daughter, Nicole Smith, New York; Gerard Spitzer, New York; Eduardo M. Fraifeld and his family, Danville, Virginia; Betty Wallerstein, San Francisco; Irving Straus, Joseph N. Straus, Joan Adler, and the Straus Historical Society; Rozemarijn van der Horst, Hawaii; Margaret Shannon, Washington Historical Research, Arlington, Virginia; Janice E. Akerhielm, New York; Bob Wolfe and the National Archives, Washington, D. C.; Carl Rheins and the YIVO Institute for Jewish Research, New York; the staff of the Anne Frank Center, New York; Arthur Unger, New York; Alison Gold, Santa Monica; Suzanne Morine, Denver; Egon Andre-Münzenberg, Vancouver; Sara Bershtel, Roslyn Schloss, and the team at Metropolitan Books; and my patient translators, Robert and Rita Kimber, for their—once again—magnificent work.

In Israel: Hannah Goslar Pick and her family, Jerusalem; the staff of the Yad Vashem Holocaust Memorial, Jerusalem; the staff of Beit Theresienstadt, Givat Haim-Ihud; the staff of the Central

Archive for the History of the Jewish People at the Hebrew University, Jerusalem.

In England: Eva Schloss, London; Ernst Michaelis, Bushey.

In Switzerland: Bernd "Buddy" Elias and his wife, Gerti, Basel; Elfriede "Fritzi" Frank (deceased); Vincent Frank-Steiner and his wife, Martina, Basel; Yves Kugelmann, Barbara Eldridge, Christoph Knoch, and the Anne Frank Fonds, Basel; Kathy Zarnegin, Basel; and Hansmartin Unger, St. Gallen.

In Austria: Simon Wiesenthal (deceased) and the staff of the Simon Wiesenthal Archives, Vienna; Jules Huf (deceased); Helmut Seyss-Inquart, Bürmoos; Gabriele Mayr and Ulrich Feix, Innsbruck; Christian Brandstätter, Vienna.

In Germany: Gertrud Naumann Trenz (deceased), her husband, Karl, and Hilde Stab Mag, Frankfurt; Cor Suijk, Aachen; Wolfgang Scheinberger, Radolfzell; Jalda Rebling, Berlin; Monika Tatzkow, Berlin; Jürgen Bogdahn of the Berlin Reparations Office; Jürgen Steen and the Frankfurt Historical Museum; Winfried Meyer and the Sachsenhausen Memorial and Museum; Albert Knoll and the Dachau Memorial; Ingrid Kussmaul and Angelika Lochmann of the German Literary Archives, Marbach; Manfred Capellmann and the Frankfurt Lessing Gymnasium; Gisela Hauff and the Aachen Victoria School; Herbert Lepper and the Municipal Archives of Aachen; the staffs of the State Court, Aachen; the Registry of Deeds, Aachen; the Jewish Congregation of Aachen and the Aachen and Munich Real Estate Associations; Uwe Wesp and the German Meteorological Service; Mirjam Pressler; Johannes Thiele, Doris Janhsen, Ilka Heinemann, and Lianne Kolf; my editor, Bernhard Suchy, Peter Sillem, and their colleagues at the Fischer Verlag.

Above all, I want to thank my husband, Rüdiger, and our children, Sophie and Max. They have accompanied me with understanding, patience, and love on the long road to completion of this new edition.

PHOTOGRAPHIC CREDITS

p. 26. © AFF/AFS
p. 35. © AFF/AFS
p. 49. Courtesy of Eduardo M. Fraifeld
p. 51. Courtesy of Eduardo M. Fraifeld
p. 52. Courtesy of Eduardo M. Fraifeld
p. 54. Courtesy of Gertrud Naumann Trenz
p. 57. Courtesy of Barbara Ledermann Rodbell
p. 59. Courtesy of Barbara Ledermann Rodbell
p. 61. © Gemeentearchief Amsterdam
p. 65. © United States Holocaust Memorial Museum, Washington
p. 68. Courtesy of the Lessing Gymnasium, Frankfurt am Main
p. 69. Courtesy of the Victoria School, Aachen
p. 83. © AFF/AFS
p. 87. Courtesy of Iet Swillens
p. 101. Aachener Adressbuch 1914, p. 117
p. 133. © AFF/AFS
p. 142. © Straus Historical Society
p. 149. © AFF/AFS
p. 150. © AFF/AFS
p. 170. © AFF/AFS
p. 185. © Photo Associated Press
p. 204. © Doubleday
p. 208. © dpa, Deutsche Presse Agentur

p. 222. Courtesy of Jacqueline van Maarsen Sanders
p. 225. Courtesy of Nanette Blitz Konig
p. 232. © AFF/AFS/Getty Images
p. 243. Courtesy of Eduardo M. Fraifeld
p. 251. Courtesy of Eduardo M. Fraifeld
p. 262. Courtesy of Ernst Michaelis
p. 263. © Ullstein Bilderdienst, Berlin
p. 276. Courtesy of Gerlof Langerijs
p. 310. Courtesy of Ed Silverberg
p. 314. © IMAGNO/Austrian Archives
p. 320. © National Archives, Washington
p. 352. © AFF/AFS/Getty Images
p. 360. © www.beeldbankwo2.nl
p. 362. © www.beeldbankwo2.nl
p. 370. © Yad Vashem
p. 376. © www.beeldbankwo2.nl
p. 389. © Österreichisches Staatsarchiv, Vienna
p. 397. Courtesy of Gerlof Langerijs
p. 400. © Joe Vitty/Los Angeles Times

INDEX

Page numbers in *italics* refer to illustrations.